TECHNOLOGY APPLICATIONS IN EDUCATION

A Learning View

TECHNOLOGY APPLICATIONS IN EDUCATION

A Learning View

Edited by

Harold F. O'Neil, Jr.
University of Southern California/CRESST

Ray S. Perez
Office of Naval Research

LEA LAWRENCE ERLBAUM ASSOCIATES, PUBLISHERS
2003 Mahwah, New Jersey   London

Lawrence Erlbaum Associates, Inc., Publishers
10 Industrial Avenue
Mahwah, NJ 07430

Cover design by Kathryn Houghtaling Lacey

Library of Congress Cataloging-in-Publication Data

Technology applications in education : a learning view / edited
by Harold F. O'Neil, Jr., Ray S. Perez.
    p. cm.
    Includes bibliographical references and index.
    ISBN 0-8058-3649-7 (cloth : alk. paper)
    1. Educational technology—Congresses. 2. Information tech-
nology—Congresses. I. O'Neil, Harold F., 1943– . II. Perez, Ray S.
    LB1028.3 .T39665   2002
    371.33—dc21   2002070661
                                                       CIP

Books published by Lawrence Erlbaum Associates are printed on acid-
free paper, and their bindings are chosen for strength and durability.

Printed in the United States of America
10 9 8 7 6 5 4 3 2 1

Contents

IV POLICY IMPLEMENTATION ISSUES

Preface

Technology Applications in Education: A Learning View[1] is designed for professionals and graduate students in the educational technology, training, assessment/evaluation, school administration, military psychology, and educational psychology communities. This edited book explores the state of the art of technology in K–16 education from a learning perspective rather than a hardware/software view. Learning, teaching, and assessment strategies are explored.

Chapter authors represent a variety of perspectives and disciplines, from computer science, cognitive and educational psychology, and educational administration. Authors represent government, business, and university communities from both within and outside the United States. These multiple perspectives contribute to our overall understanding of current technology use in education and help in identifying future research needs. Of interest in this book is the high level of agreement on the state of the art of

[1]The work reported herein was supported in part under the Educational Research and Development Centers Program, PR/Award Number R305B60002, as administered by the Office of Educational Research and Improvement, U.S. Department of Education, and in part by the Department of Defense Education Activity (DODEA). The opinions expressed herein are the opinions of the authors and do not reflect the positions or policies of the National Institute on Student Achievement, Curriculum, and Assessment, the Office of Educational Research and Improvement, or the U.S. Department of Education. Nor do they necessarily represent the official policy or position of the Office of the Secretary of Defense, the Department of Defense Education Activity or the Office of Naval Research.

technology, learning, and assessment and what needs to be done—that is, a range of research/evaluation studies on learning from technological environments. The major issue is learning, not hardware/software per se.

For example, in the area of assessment, technology itself is almost never the major issue when evaluating technology. Instead, primary attention should be paid to how technology is used by students and teachers to affect the quality and degree of learning and what learning outcomes result from these uses. Typical foci in evaluation of technology applications—such as the details of the technical arrangements, e.g., bandwidth, networks, or the distribution of technology and training—are necessary components but not sufficient conditions for educational improvement. The sufficient condition, rather, is student learning.

The authors also are in agreement that there is a paucity of research or theory on how students and adults learn when using computers and relevant technology and that technology must be integrated in instruction, as it will increasingly become a regular part of all sectors of ordinary life. For example, there are remarkably few large-scale evaluations of the impact of various computer-based instructional interventions on student learning (e.g., national samples like those of the National Assessment of Educational Progress [NAEP] or the Third International Mathematics and Science Study [TIMSS]).

The book focuses on the link of technology and clear instructional goals, technology and subject matter achievement, and the requirement for a variety of studies (using a range of methods) to determine and document the conditions that may be most useful to improve learning for particular groups of students, subject areas, and goals.

This book is divided into four main sections: (a) educational context (e.g., organizational and structural factors that contribute to the effective use of technology in school settings); (b) learning foundations (e.g., promising learning and teaching strategies); (c) assessment issues (e.g., promising technology-based assessment procedures and methods); and (d) policy implementation issues.

In summary, this book is characterized in the following montage of factors: (a) the primacy of learning as a focus for technology implementation; (b) a focus on technology uses in K–16 education; (c) a focus on the assessment of both individuals and teams; (d) a broad variety of methodological approaches from qualitative to instructional design to quantitative (e.g., structural equation modeling); (e) a need to support the development of technology-based curriculum and tools; and (f) a need for theory-driven and evaluation studies to increase our knowledge. The data that are reported were collected in various settings, for instance, schools, laboratories, and industrial settings. The authors are the researchers that, in many cases, have defined by their work the state of the art in both this country and overseas.

This book could not have come into existence without the help and encouragement of many people. Our thanks to our editor, Lane Akers of LEA, for his support and guidance in the publication process. We thank Ms. Joanne Michiuye and Ms. Katharine Fry for their excellent assistance in preparing the manuscript.

—*Harold F. O'Neil, Jr.*
Los Angeles

—*Ray S. Perez*
Arlington, Virginia

Foreword

Ray S. Perez
Office of Naval Research

Harold F. O'Neil, Jr.
University of Southern California/CRESST

INTRODUCTION AND OVERVIEW

This volume represents an update, revision, and expansion of a set of papers presented at a conference titled "Technology Applications in Education: A Learning View," held at the Institute for Defense Analyses in Alexandria, VA. The goal of the conference was to identify promising learning, teaching, and assessment strategies for the use and assessment of technology in educational settings. More specifically, papers were presented on the following topics: (a) educational context (e.g., organizational and structural factors that contribute to the effective use of technology in school settings); (b) promising learning and teaching strategies; (c) promising technology-based assessment procedures and methods; (d) policy implementation issues; and (e) a summary of current research on the effective use of technology in education.

In addition, conference speakers were asked to forecast research needs for the purpose of formulating a research agenda to support the classroom of the 21st century. Presenters represented a variety of perspectives and disciplines, including computer science, cognitive and educational psychology, and educational administration. Speakers represented government, business, and university communities from within and outside the United States. These multiple perspectives contributed to our overall understanding of current technology use in education and helped in identifying future research needs.

In recent years, interest in the use of technology in education has come into prominence as a national goal. Currently, more than 95% of public schools have computers (National Center for Education Statistics, 2000). However, knowledge about how to best apply this technology to educate and train has been an unresolved issue for researchers for more than 50 years (see Atkinson, 1968; Bitzer, Braunfeld, & Lichtenberger, 1962; Suppes & Morningstar, 1968). The continued interest in technology is attributed to the recognition that technology has pervasive effects on our daily lives and our economy, thus its expected impact on education. The term *technology* generally brings to mind the notion of hardware, silicon, and plastic computer platforms. Our topic is much broader. More specifically, technology is defined as a *systematic treatment* or an *applied science* (O'Neil & Baker, 1994). For example, Lumsdaine (1963) characterized technology as any process that can be repeated with the same consequences; it must be replicable. This broad definition of technology can be applied at multiple levels, from empirically validated procedures for teaching strategies (which may not involve any hardware), to a computer software tool designed to expand the problem-solving skills of students (e.g., spread sheets or graphing calculators), to a software program that presents information to students on a given topic and teaches them higher order thinking skills like problem solving.

David Thornburg (2000), an educational technologist and futurist, argued that the power of technology—and more specifically computer and telecommunication technologies—comes not just from the ability to perform old jobs in new ways, but also from the ability of these technology tools to enable us to do things in education that we were previously unable to do. For example, we are able to allow students to explore a 3-dimensional representation of a plant or animal cell in ways never experienced before (e.g., using virtual environment technology). These 3-D simulations provide levels of detail that students normally are not able to see. Thornburg believed that we are entering an age where we have the knowledge base and "we have the opportunity to use technologies [computers and telecommunication] in ways that support modern pedagogical thought devoted to the premise that all [students] are capable of learning, even if the pathways for each learner are different" (p. 1).

The vision of the classroom of the 21st century outlined by Thornburg (1999) provides a useful context for discussing a research agenda. His vision of the future of education and the role that technology will play was guided by two central ideas. First, how technology is used in education (e.g., the classroom) by educators is more important than the technology itself. Second, because technology has the potential to transform education, our thinking about education should be transformed as well, if our investment in technology is to be realized. He argued that "learning does not take place better or faster simply by replacing one instructional medium with another" (p. 1). The effective use of technology requires thought, professional development, experimentation, research, and a willingness to spend time and effort to develop effective strategies to integrate technology within the school curriculum.

Other factors that will drive the transformation of the education system are increased access to information and the half-life of the information. Not only is there exponential increase in the amount of information that teachers will have to teach and students will have to learn, but the half-life of information is shrinking. Furthermore, although skills such as literacy and numeracy endure throughout the lifetime of a student, new skills will be required of students.

In addition to the skills mentioned here, central to education will be a focus on teaching and fostering communication skills (writing and speaking) and higher order thinking skills (e.g., problem solving). These notions will lead to a paradigmatic shift in education from a major focus on teaching and learning content to a focus on how to use content. This is not to say that content will be ignored in the classroom of the future, but it should be taught within a framework that provides meaning and context.

The classroom of the 21st century will be based on a system in which learning is a constant and time is a variable. The central idea is that all students are capable of mastery. All that differentiates students is rate of learning—some are "fast" learners and others "slow" learners (Bloom, 1974). Perhaps that is an oversimplification, but with tailored instruction (as is offered with third-generation intelligent tutors) and other advanced technologies (e.g., cognitive task analysis) we can accelerate learning by one third and improve student performance by one third. These increased efficiencies may be accomplished in many complex subject areas. The classroom will also experience a dramatic shift from a place (the past) to an activity where the availability of inexpensive technologies can promote learning on demand, anywhere, any time (the future). The confluence of various technologies, telecommunications, battery operated hand held computers, and wireless access to the World Wide Web can provide access to knowledge wherever the learner is located—a classroom, on the school bus, at home, on the job, at a museum, or on a playground.

Technology enables teachers and students to have access to world knowledge resources (e.g., the Library of Congress) and virtual museums (e.g., the Guggenheim), or have an online chat with the world's foremost authority on genetics, or share material with other students interested in the same topic. The use of this technology connects isolated classrooms to the rest of the world. Yes, classrooms will be technology rich but technology is not the point—learning is. To support this learning vision of the classroom of the 21st century, not only do we need to build the infrastructure to scale up to support the use of technology on a districtwide basis, but we have to effectively design a learning technology.

The volume is divided into four main sections: the context of the use of technology in education, learning foundations, assessment issues, and policy implementation issues. The summaries of the chapters that follow provide an appraisal of the current knowledge base of what we know about what works in the use of technology and an attempt to identify the research needed to support the classroom of the 21st century. Readers are asked to engage in their own evaluations in answering the question "Do we know enough of the use of technology in education to support Thornburg's vision of the classroom of the 21st century?"

The section on the context of the use of technology is divided into five chapters. The first chapter, by Smith and Broom, explores the question of how teachers in the future will use information technology in their teaching and presents varying views of the future. The first view, offered by J. S. Brown (2000), suggests that technology has a pervasive effect or "transformative" effect on the nature of the curriculum and pedagogy. This view of the effect of technology is captured by Thornburg's vision of the classroom of the 21st century described previously. An alternative view, minimal change, is that teachers' use of technology can continue to reinforce and supplement their curriculum and instructional practices. This kind of use will not substantially alter the content of the curriculum, the nature of the pedagogy, or represent a revolutionary innovation in education. Smith and Broom propose that the future holds elements of both visions. Rather than a radical change in teaching caused by technology, they foresee a slow accretion in technology use by teachers as technology changes society and as innovative teaching tools and applications evolve. Smith and Broom state that a key factor influencing how teachers use computers is the socioeconomic level of the school. Schools in high-poverty areas tend to use computers primarily for "remediation of skills, mastering skills just taught, and learning to work independently" more than do low-poverty schools, which use computers for more sophisticated learning activities such as the analysis of information and problem solving. The authors identify four technology applications they feel form the basis for changing the way teachers teach in the future and in the short term. These applications are (a) Web-delivered Advanced Placement (AP) courses; (b) accessible databases on the Web of scientific, social, historical, and literacy information; (c) communications systems among students and teachers; and (d) Web-based resources for teachers.

Susan Chipman (chap. 2) characterizes three futures for the impact of computers on education. "Some believe that the availability of computerized instruction would result in the withering away of schools as we know them. Others believe that computers which were being so enthusiastically purchased would end up locked in closets and that schools would go on as before, as little changed by computers as they had been by prior waves of 'technology'. Still others saw in computers an opportunity for revitalization, an impetus to change, and a potential solution to the problems of limited attention, limited productivity and shortages of technically qualified teachers that beset education" (this volume, p. 31). According to Chipman, the determination of which future will come to pass depends on two kinds of factors, external and internal. External factors are changes in the use of computers in the general society that may have a direct impact on the use of computers in the schools. Internal factors are the ways in which the technology is used. Chipman concludes that technology will have a minimal impact on the schools, and that "classrooms will continue to look strikingly similar to the way they look now" (p. 46).

Thomas Hill (chap. 3) characterizes the use of technology by young people across several environments—public schools, a nonprofit training organization, and a Web-based company. Hill studied four 10-to-19-year-olds who demonstrated exemplar skill or expertise using the Internet, multimedia authoring tools, and collaborative systems. Chapter 3 provides indications of the skills, knowledges, and abilities that information technology workers and students will need to succeed in the technology-rich environment of the future. These skills include cognitive and social abilities and self-efficacy. The students learned how to use software programs not by reading documentation, but rather, by starting to interact with the software by "playing" with it, to initially develop a mental map or model of the structure of the technology (a software program). The students then updated and refined this mental map as they applied it to a variety of applications, all the time monitoring their own progress, mental effort, and success (i.e., self-regulation). Hill suggests that the development of these cognitive and social abilities and skills results in an individual capable of managing a continuous personal development program for a lifetime.

Dexter Fletcher (chap. 4) provides a comprehensive review of the literature on the effectiveness of technology in education and training. Fletcher reminds us that the answers to questions such as "What evidence is there that learning occurs better—more effectively and efficiently—with technology? and, perhaps more importantly at what cost!" are timely and important. Research efforts on the use of technology can be traced back to initial attempts in the mid-1950s with the work of Chalmers Sherwin (Bitzer, Braunfeld, & Lichtenberger, 1962). Fletcher cites more recent studies by several researchers (Burns & Bozeman, 1981; Hartley & Davies, 1978; Kulik, 1994; Niemiec & Walberg, 1985; Roblyer, 1988) using meta-analysis. Meta-analysis allows researchers to aggregate the results of many studies that are directed at addressing a common question such as "What is the effect of the use of technology-based instruction?" The magnitude of this effect can be reported in units of standard deviations using a common measure of merit called "effect size." For example, evaluating the effect of intelligent tutors, Gott, Kane, and Lesgold (1995) and Anderson, Corbett, Koedinger, and Pelletier (1995) reported effect sizes ranging from 1.05 to 1.50, which suggest roughly for an effect size of 1.5, an improvement from the 50th percentile to the 94th percentile. Based on his review, Fletcher suggested that the impressive effect for technology-based instruction has been its ability to tailor highly interactive instruction for all students by simulating one-on-one tutoring (one highly trained instructor with one student).

Chapter 5, by Ray Perez and Gary Bridgewater, describes an innovative technology project funded by the White House and the U.S. Department of Defense. The primary goal of this 4-year project was to develop and implement curriculum-based educational courseware and software management tools in the Department of Defense school system (DoDEA). The authors present lessons learned, conclusions, and policy recommendations that fall in several areas—infrastructure, professional development, and educational software development. For example, hardware and software stability must be in place before educational courseware and management tools are introduced. Perhaps more important, the message of the chapters in this section is that we know technology works and we have identified to a certain degree under what conditions it works and what external and internal factors influence it.

The next section, Learning Foundations, has three chapters. Richard Mayer (chap. 6) begins with an introduction to constructivist theories of learning and compares and contrasts these theories with past theories of learning by discussing the salient differences and emphases each offers. Within this context, Mayer discusses four basic issues in the psychology of academic learning: How do students learn? How should teachers teach? How should learning be assessed? And how should technology be used in education? Mayer then presents a cognitive constructivist model of technology-based learning with examples of the application of this theory to technology-based instruction. The primary tenet of constructivist theory, germane to the use of technology, is that of learning as knowledge construction. This view of learning prescribes quite different roles for students, teachers, and the use and design of technology. The role of the teacher is as a cognitive guide who works with students on "authentic" academic tasks. Rather than focusing on rote learning, the teacher promotes sense making by the student. The role of the student is to make sense of the information provided by reorganizing it and connecting it to prior knowledge. The role of technology and its design is to help guide learners in their efforts at making sense of new material and experiences.

John Bruer (chap. 7) reviews the contributions that cognitive science has made to our understanding of human cognition and its importance to technology-based learning. Bruer feels that these contributions will influence our theories of learning and the design of technology-based learning. According to Bruer, the fundamental tenet of cognitive science is that humans process information. He begins by providing a short history of the field of cognitive science, starting with F. C. Bartlett's (1932) work on long-term memory and schema theory. But perhaps the most important contributions to the design of technology-based instruction come from the application of cognitive science in the careful analysis of problem solving and learning in domains such as arithmetic, algebra, physics, science, and writing. This research is particularly important in the design of what Bruer calls *representational tools* to support students' thinking and problem solving. Examples of these representational tools are data mining, visual presentation of complex data sets, and hypertext. Bruer suggests that the next phase in research to be conducted is to investigate how these tools help students to learn.

The last chapter in this section (chap. 8), collectively authored by the Cognition and Technology Group at Vanderbilt University, continues the theme of theory driven technology-based instruction. The authors propose that the kind of learning required for the 21st century is for all students to develop the ability to think, solve problems, and become independent learners. Learning is no longer viewed as the accretion of new information, but rather, as a transformational process wherein conceptual representations and understanding evolve over time. The authors contend that this view encompasses the design of curriculum, instruction, and assessment. The teaching process includes being aware of preconceptions that students bring to learning situations, teaching in ways that make a student's thinking "visible" to other students, and helping students to reflect on their conceptions or mental models and reconcile them with those of other learners in learning environments.

The authors believe four critical design features must be included in these learning environments: (a) To establish knowledge-centered elements of a learning environment, instruction is organized around meaningful problems with appropriate goals; (b) to support a learner focus, instruction must provide scaffolds for solving meaningful problems and supporting learning with understanding; (c) to support assessment-centered activities, instruction must provide opportunities for practice with feedback, revision, and reflection; and (d) to create a community-centered learning environment, social arrangements of instruction must promote collaboration and distributed expertise, as well as independent learning.

The next section, Assessment Issues, has five chapters. Lawrence Frase (chap. 9) and his colleagues provide a description of the opportunities and challenges facing test developers that a technology-rich environment presents. Among those challenges, they describe users wanting tests to resemble complex naturalistic settings and still maintain the same psychometric properties, ease of administration, and scoring procedures as multiple-choice tests. Other emerging technologies described are the development of technology tools for test construction, understanding cognitive skill requirements, automatic test item generation, and automated essay scoring, to name a few. For example, a new tool for test construction is the use of tree-based regression techniques to develop detailed descriptions of the observable item stimulus features that signal particular required cognitive skills.

Baker and O'Neil (chap. 10) introduce a provocative notion of technological fluency. It is their contention that in order to create a more productive link between technology and learning we may need to change our conceptions of the cognitive skills, knowledge, and abilities that students in the 21st century will need to use technology effectively. They define technological fluency as an "individual's well-developed skills, propensities, and knowledges that are required to use, design and develop electronic and bionic hardware and software to enhance various aspects of life" (p. 246). This construct consists of three major components: performance in families of cognitive demands, core propensities reflecting affective and social components, and focused technology skills. Performance on these three components is seen within the context of a content domain and is specific to that domain. They illustrate the relation between technological fluency and content domain with several examples. The assessment of technological fluency, the authors conclude, presents many challenges to test developers.

The theme of new challenges for test developers is a recurrent one in Bennett's chapter (chap. 11). Perhaps a more daunting challenge described by Bennett is that afforded by the emerging technology in the development, management, and delivery of high-quality assessment instruments. For example, the use of Web-based technologies for online test administration offers a considerable advantage to test takers, such as being able to take a test any time and anywhere, with almost instant test feedback to the user, and a readily available test item bank for re-tests. Although these technologies hold the promise of making tests more precise and accessible, the issue remains of what infrastructure is needed to make online testing possible. The author describes the requirements for a supporting infrastructure. According to Bennett, significant portions of the infrastructure exist, although in a fragmented and often experimental state. We must integrate these various components into a coherent, efficient system.

The two remaining chapters in this section, by O'Neil and his colleagues (chap. 12) and by Klein and her colleagues at UCLA/CRESST (chap. 13), document specific assessment tools useful in 21st century classrooms. O'Neil et al. describe the need to measure teamwork skills in a practical way. Currently, few instruments exist to assess the performance of groups and collaborative teams. More important is to assess the effectiveness of the learning approaches given the increasing use of groups and collaborative approaches in Grades K-12 content domains. Reliable assessment instruments are needed not only in school settings but also in work environments. O'Neil et al. have successfully developed a reliable and valid short questionnaire that can be administered in a brief period of time to measure individual teamwork skills. Klein and her colleagues at the Center for Research on Evaluation, Standards, and Student Testing (CRESST) describe their research in assessment of an important technical skill, Web fluency. The authors point out that in 1997, 57 million people had access to the Internet from home, work, or school (U.S. Census Bureau, 1999). It was also estimated that, at the time, there were more than 1.5 billion Web pages on the World Wide Web, and that number was growing by 1.9 million per day. Searching the Web to gather the right content is quite a challenge, and the ability to search the Web is an important skill and should be measured. Klein et al. succeeded in presenting a coherent set of indices to measure and characterize students' Web expertise. In summary, and more important, to teach Web fluency you must have some way of measuring to what extent students have this skill and their progress in acquiring it.

The final section, Policy Implementation Issues, has two chapters. Seidel and Cox (chap. 14) focus on management issues. They suggest that there is a continuing controversy surrounding the failure of widespread technology use by the education and training establishments. Technologists feel if they push these establishments harder with each new innovation, widespread use will occur. When it doesn't, blame is cast on one or another of the traditional stakeholders—teachers, school administrators, parents, and so on. Rather than casting blame, the authors contend that the needs of all of the stakeholders who influence the implementation, experimentation, or innovation taking place are not addressed, and need to be. Their attitudes and perceptions reflect unique cultures, define the real domain of influence, and therefore hold the keys to the opportunities for cultural change, which is necessary for programmatic success.

Finally, Bentley and Hargreaves (chap. 15) investigate learning futures from an English perspective. The authors are among the most influential thinkers in England on this topic. In England, information and communication technologies (ICT) play a key role in education policy. The country has invested in creating an infrastructure in schools that is based on these technologies. The authors report the progress thus far on a national grid for learning (including access and content), a vision to transform Grade K-12 education, and the role of the workplace and university communities, and conclude with challenges for policy and practice. What is most interesting about chapter 15 are the many lessons learned that can be applied to U.S. education.

AUTHOR NOTE

Address correspondence to: Harold F. O'Neil, Jr., University of Southern California/ National Center for Research on Evaluation, Standards, and Student Testing (CRESST) Rossier School of Education, 600 Waite Phillips Hall, University Park, L.A., CA, 90089. Ray S. Perez, Office of Naval Research, 2431 Inglewood Ct., Falls Church, VA 22043.

The work reported herein was supported in part under the Educational Research and Development Centers Program, PR/Award Number R305B60002, as administered by the Office of Educational Research and Improvement, U.S. Department of Education, and in part by the Department of Defense Education Activity (DODEA). The opinions expressed herein are the opinions of the authors and do not reflect the positions or policies of the National Institute on Student Achievement, Curriculum, and Assessment, the Office of Educational Research and Improvement, or the U.S. Department of Education. Nor do they necessarily represent the official policies or positions of the Office of the Secretary of Defense, the U.S. Department of Defense Education Activity, or the Office of Naval Research.

REFERENCES

Anderson, J. R., Corbett, A. T., Koedinger, K. R., & Pelletier, R. (1995). Cognitive tutors: lessons learned. *The Journal of the Learning Sciences, 4*, 167–207.

Atkinson, R. (1968). Computerized instruction and the learning process. *American Psychologist, 23*, 225–239.

Bartlett, F. C. (1932). *Remembering: A study in experimental and social psychology.* New York: Macmillan.

Bitzer, D. L., Braunfeld, P. G., & Lichtenberger, W. W. (1962). Plato II: A multiple-student, computer-controlled, automatic teaching device. In J. E. Coulson (Ed.), *Programmed learning and computer-based instruction* (pp. 205–216). New York: John Wiley.

Bloom, B. (1974). Time and learning. *American Psychologist, 29*, 682–688.

Brown, J. S. (2000 March/April). Growing up digital: How the web changes work, education, and the ways people learn. *Change, 32*(2), 11–20.

Burns, P. K., & Bozeman, W. (1981). Computer-assisted instruction and mathematics achievement. *Educational Technology, 21*(10), 29–32.

Gott, S. P., Kane, R. S., & Lesgold, A. (1995). *Tutoring for transfer of technical competence* (AL/HR-TP-1995-0002). Brooks AFB, TX: Armstrong Laboratory, Human Resources Directorate.

Hartley, J., & Davies, I. K. (1978). Notetaking: A critical review. *Programmed Learning and Educational Technology, 15*, 207–224.

Kulik, J. A. (1994). Meta-analytic studies of findings on computer-based instruction. In E. L. Baker & H. F. O'Neil, Jr. (Eds.), *Technology assessment in education and training* (pp. 9–33). Hillsdale, NJ: Lawrence Erlbaum Associates.

Lumsdaine, A. (1963). Instruments and media of instruction. In N. L. Gage (Ed.), *Handbook of research on teaching* (pp. 583–682). Chicago, IL: Rand McNally.

National Center for Education Statistics. (2000). *The condition of education 2000* (NCES 2000-062). Washington, DC: U.S. Department of Education, National Center for Education Statistics.

Niemiec, R., & Walberg, H. (1985). Computers and achievement in the elementary schools. *Journal of Educational Computing Research, 14,* 435–439.

O'Neil, H. F., Jr., & Baker, E. L. (Eds.). (1994). *Technology assessment in software applications.* Hillsdale, NJ: Lawrence Erlbaum Associates.

Roblyer, M. D. (1998). The other half of knowledge. *Learning and Leading with Technology, 25*(6), 54–55.

Suppes, P., & Morningstar, M. (1968). Computer-assisted instruction. *Science, 166,* 343–350.

Thornburg, D. D. (1999, December). *Technology in K-12 education: Envisioning a new future.* Paper presented at the conference "Forum on Technology in Education: Envisioning the Future" sponsored by the U.S. Department of Education, Office of Educational Technology, Washington, DC. Available 23 January 2002 from www.air.org/forum/wpapers.htm

Thornburg, D. D. (2000). *Renaissance 2000.* Unpublished paper available at the Thornburg Center. Available 23 January 2002 from www.tcpd.org.

U.S. Census Bureau. (1999). *Computer use in the United States: Population characteristics.* Washington, DC: U.S. Department of Commerce.

THE CONTEXT

Chapter 1

The Landscape and Future of the Use of Technology in K–12 Education

Marshall S. Smith
Michael Broom
Stanford University

This chapter explores the question of how teachers in 2007 will use information technology (IT) in their teaching. This chapter grew from a talk given in 1998. Eighteen months later, while writing a final draft, the notes from that presentation seem archaic. The average new desktop computer is double in power and capacity to what it was in 1998 and costs the same or less now than it did in 1998. Cellular phones with Internet access were rare then, but are now commonplace. Furthermore, dozens of energetic entrepreneurs have started web-based companies aimed at providing services to K–12 schools and educators.

By the time this book is published, personal computers will again have doubled in capacity, access to the Internet will be much less expensive, and the market will have separated the strong from the weak web-based companies. The incredible rate of change of technology contrasts sharply with the stately pace of change in K–12 education, a contrast that creates challenges and opportunities.

The political and educational context for the chapter is the vigorous standards-based reform effort in the United States, which contains as a central theme a focus on improving the quality of the curriculum and pedagogical practice. The serendipitous overlap in time of the standards based reforms and the information technology revolution may be viewed as providing a special opportunity for achieving the goals of the school reforms.

This chapter is divided into three main parts. The first establishes a baseline for exploration. It makes the point that, during the 1990s, the nation established the foundation for extensive use of technology in schools and classrooms. Access in schools and libraries to computers and the Web is now widespread, on its way to becoming universal. Use of technology in the classroom, however, is more sporadic; few teachers use technology to offer educational experiences previously unavailable. In addition, "digital gaps" exist between rich and poor students for both access to and use of technology. Although the access gap is closing, the gap in use remains substantial. As well, although the knowledge base is growing in size and quality, little is known about the effectiveness of technology for increasing student achievement, motivation, socialization, and creativity.

The second part of the chapter looks into the future. In particular, it considers whether information technology will simply support and amplify conventional classroom practice or whether it will have, in Brown's (2000) terminology, a "transformative" effect on the nature of the curriculum and pedagogy. It begins to explore how teachers will use technology in 2007 by imagining what the technology environment surrounding them will look like. The quality and power of technology will continue to increase to the point where it will be able to deliver practically anything that can now be imagined. Moreover, technological advances will make powerful computing tools available to almost everyone at affordable prices. Outside of schools, it can be expected that educational and training uses of information technology will be commonplace.

Widespread access to technology, including the Internet, is also expected inside schools, but there is less certainty about its use in instruction. Our hypothesis is that technology can stimulate and support teachers to transform teaching and learning in the schools, to make available to all children rich experiences and activities typically not available in U.S. institutions or any other nation's schools. However, a number of barriers and challenges must be overcome. The chapter concludes by suggesting policies and strategies that might be put into place to help the nation achieve that goal.

THE CURRENT TECHNOLOGY AND LEARNING ENVIRONMENT IN K–12 EDUCATION

To better understand where the future of technology in education is headed, it is important to establish a baseline for changes by examining the advances over the last decade. This section focuses on three such advances: student access to and use of technology in school, student access to and use of technology in the home, and the effects of technology use on student outcomes.

Student Access to and Use of Technology in U.S. Schools

Over the past decade, technology grants and donations from businesses, parents, and the government have led to the increasing presence of computers and the Internet in U.S. schools. Currently, over 95% of public schools have computers (National Center for Education Statistics [NCES], 2000). This figure is, at best, a crude measure of student access, however, because it includes schools that use computers solely for administrative purposes. A more useful indicator is the percent of U.S. classrooms that have a computer designated for instructional use: In 1998, more than 75% of U.S. schools met this criterion (*Education Week* & the Milken Exchange, 1998).

Another common measure of access to technology is the number of students for each instructional computer in a classroom. Table 1.1, based on studies by the NCES (2000), shows steady and significant gains along this dimension over a 10-year period.

These findings show progress; nonetheless, student access still falls short of the four to five students per computer that the President's Committee of Advisors on Science and Technology (1997) set as a "reasonable level for the effective use of computers within the schools" (p. 21). The NCES reported, however, that there is no difference in access to computers between low and high poverty schools.

The last decade has also seen a significant increase in student access to the Internet in school. In 1998, 95% of schools had at least one computer connected to the Internet (NCES, 2000). Once again, this measure is crude; thus, it is important also to examine the percent of instructional rooms within which there is access to the Internet. Table 1.2 indicates that steady and significant gains also have been made on this measure, reaching almost two thirds of all classrooms in 1999.

Furthermore, students in an additional 25% to 30% of instructional rooms also have access to the Internet in a school computer lab (Anderson

TABLE 1.1
Students/Computer within Schools Ratio Over Time

Year	1989	1992	1995	1998	1999
Student/Computer Ratio	19	14	9	6	6

Note: Data from "The Presence of Computers in American Schools" by R. E. Anderson & A. Ronnkvist, 1999, [Online], Center for Research on Information Technology and Organizations. Available: http://www.crito.uci/edu/tlc/findings/computers_in_american_schools/ and *Internet Access in U.S. Public Schools and Classrooms: 1994–1999* (NCES No. 2000086), by National Center for Education Statistics, 2000, Washington, DC: U.S. Department of Education.

TABLE 1.2
Percent of Instructional Classrooms with Access
to the Internet Over Time, Disaggregated by Poverty

Year	1994	1996	1997	1998	1999
Classrooms in Low-Poverty Schools	4	18	36	62	74
Classrooms in High-Poverty Schools	2	5	14	39	39
All Classrooms	3	14	27	51	63

Note: Data from *Internet Access in U.S. Public Schools and Classrooms: 1994–1999* (NCES No. 2000086), by National Center for Education Statistics, 2000, Washington, DC: U.S. Department of Education.

& Ronnkvist, 1999). This increases the figure in Table 1.2 for 1999 for "All Classrooms" from 63% to approximately 90%.

Still, these findings must be examined with caution. The increased presence of the Internet in classrooms has not led to equal distribution among classrooms. Table 1.2 shows the percent of classrooms in very low and very high poverty schools that had access to the Internet over the last few years. Although significant progress has been made for both low and high poverty schools, a clear disparity in access continues to exist. In fact, as Table 1.2 shows, the Internet access gap between classrooms in very high and very low poverty schools has actually been growing. Additionally, in very low poverty schools, there were, in 1999 7 students per instructional computer with Internet access as compared to, on average, 16 students in very high poverty schools.[1]

These data suggest that student access to technology has progressed significantly over the past decade. This progress is partly due to the federal government strongly backing the development of technical infrastructure in schools through financial assistance programs like the e-rate and the technology literacy challenge grants (NCES, 2000; President's Committee, 1997). In addition, many states, districts, businesses, and parents have provided support (NCES, 2000). Despite this progress, however, inequities in Internet access remain based on the socioeconomic composition of the schools.

In contrast to the considerable documentation on student access to technology, less is known about how students use that technology. Recent survey evidence, reported in 2000, indicates that close to 50% of the U.S. student population uses computers and the Internet at school in some way several times per week (Becker, 2000). Surprisingly, students in low and high poverty schools use the technology with about equal frequency (Becker, 2000). Although these findings indicate that a large proportion of the

---

[1]See NCES (2000). In low poverty schools, less than 11% of the students are eligible for free or reduced price lunch, whereas in high poverty schools, 71% or greater of students are elibigle.

U.S. student population is using technology in school, they do not necessarily indicate that technology is being used to broaden student educational experiences.

A common concern among policymakers, researchers, and educators is that only a few schools or teachers employ technology to really enhance or extend learning activities. Cuban, for example, argued that classroom computers are primarily used in ways that reflect traditional instruction. That is, students use computers to practice skills (word processing applications, drills, and games), to replace an encyclopedia or dictionary, or to gain computer literacy (Anderson & Ronnkvist, 1999; Cuban, 1998). Cuban's claims are somewhat supported by a 1998 study of U.S. classroom teachers. Table 1.3 displays several relevant findings of that study.

The uses with the highest frequency in Table 1.3, although allowing students to gain important skills, are less likely to expand or modify the nature of their learning. Moreover, how students use technology appears to be related to their school's socioeconomic level. Students in high poverty schools are more likely to use computers primarily for "remediation of skills, mastering skills just taught, and learning to work independently" than are students in low poverty schools, who make more frequent use of computers for more sophisticated learning activities (e.g., to present information to an audience or analyze information) (Becker, 2000; Becker & Sterling, 1987).

Overall, despite continued inequities, these findings indicate that within the next few years access to instructional computers and possibly to the Internet could be universal in U. S. schools. Such a result, however, will require continued attention from the federal and state governments to ensure that students in high poverty schools have the same level of access as students in low poverty schools.

The nature of the use to which the new information technology is now put is less encouraging. Far fewer than a majority of U.S. teachers use technology as a core instrument for enhancing their curriculum or their pedagogy, and those that do are much more likely to teach in advantaged neighborhoods.

TABLE 1.3
Percent of Teachers Having Their Students
Use Different Types of Software

Word Processing	CD-ROM Reference	WWW	Games/ Drills	Simulations	Graphics	Spreadsheet/ Database	Multimedia Authoring	E-mail
50	36	29	28	23	21	16	9	7

Note: Data from "The Presence of Computers in American Schools" by R. E. Anderson & A. Ronnkvist, 1999, [Online], Center for Research on Information Technology and Organizations. Available: http://www.crito.uci.edu/tlc/findings/computers_in_american_schools/

Student Access to and Use of Technology at Home

In general, student access to technology at home has lagged behind student access in school. Approximately 57% of all students have a computer present in their homes, and 33% of all students have access to the Internet (Becker, 2000). The relation of social class to access is much greater at home than at school (Anderson & Ronnkvist, 1999). For example, Table 1.4 draws from a study by Becker (2000) that uses U. S. census data from current population surveys (CPS) carried out in 1997 and 1998. The CPS data show that only 22% of households in the $0–20,000 income range had a computer and only 6% had an Internet connection, whereas in the $75,000 households the corresponding percentages were 91% and 69%, respectively. These are huge differences.

The Becker study also showed that even though almost all students with a computer in their home will use it, only about half turn it on at least 3 days per week. Students tend to use the computer to play recreational games, although an increasing percentage use it for word processing. A much smaller percentage of students, just 25% use the Internet from home. Disparities in home use are also related to family socioeconomic level. Students from high income families are twice as likely to use word processing applications and four times as likely to use e-mail as students from low income families.

The Educational Effectiveness of Technology Use

As the use of technology has increased, so has the amount and quality of research examining the effects of technology on students. Nonetheless, there is not enough evidence concerning whether and under what circumstances the use of information technology can have a powerful independent effect on student outcomes. This section first summarizes the research literature on the effects of specific applications of technology (computer-based instruction, hypermedia, and distance education) on student academic

TABLE 1.4
Percent of Households in 1998 with a Computer
or a Computer with Internet Access, Disaggregated by Poverty

Household Income	$0– 20,000	$20,000– 40,000	$40,000– 60,000	$60,000– 75,000	$75,000+
Computer	22	45	70	82	91
Computer with Internet	6	20	40	55	69

Note: Data from "Who's Wired and Who's Not" by H. J. Becker, 2000, [Online], University of California, Irvine. Available: http://www.gse.uci.edu/doehome/DeptInfo/Faculty/Becker/packard/text.html

achievement, providing examples of well-respected and innovative software.[2] It then considers how technology affects student motivation, socialization, and creativity.

Computers have been used in educational settings for computer-based instruction (CBI) for 35 years. The most common form of CBI is computer-aided instruction (CAI), which typically presents individual students with short units of instructional material and then asks questions designed to test each student's comprehension of the material. Usually, the answers are simple multiple choice or true–false statements, so the computer can easily analyze the answers and, based on the student's performance, provide an appropriate level of instruction in the future.

Over the past two decades, a number of studies (meta-analyses) have summarized in statistical form the results of many of the evaluations and studies of CBI interventions. J. Kulik (1994) summarized 97 controlled quantitative studies carried out in elementary and secondary schools. Each study compared achievement outcomes in classes taught with CBI with outcomes in classes taught without CBI. He found that students who received CBI scored higher and progressed faster over the school year (roughly 3 months on a grade equivalent scale) than students receiving traditional instruction. Kulik also looked at differences among size effects when studies were categorized by kind of CBI intervention. "Tutoring" programs, including "drill-and-practice" and other CAI applications, show the second largest average effect size (0.38 SD).[3] Earlier, C. Kulik and J. A. Kulik (1991) found that students from low income families benefited more than students from higher income families from CAI-like interventions.[4]

J. Kulik (1994) also examined one specific CAI intervention, the Stanford-Computer Curriculum Corporation (CCC) materials, which were evaluated in over 20 controlled experiments from the late 1950s through the early 1980s. The CCC program, which probably best fits in the "tutoring" category, showed reasonably consistent results that averaged 0.40 SD.

As a benchmark to judge the overall effectiveness of the computer interventions, J. Kulik (1994) examined meta-analyses of other "innovations." He found that computer tutoring with an effect size of 0.40 SD was clus-

---

[2]It is important to point out that these categories are not discrete—a hypermedia environment can use some characteristics of computer-assisted instruction—but the categories reflect how technology is commonly referred to.

[3]The largest effect size was for Logo. Kulik, however reported some problems with the Logo studies and concluded that "the case for strong benefits from Logo therefore seems unproven . . ." (p. 20).

[4]The Kuliks' carried out a meta-analysis that included 254 studies comparing CAI to traditional instruction. All the studies had to take place in an actual classroom, provide quantitative results measured for both CAI and conventionally instructed groups, and not have serious methodological flaws. On average, students receiving CAI scored slightly higher (about 0.30 SD) on posttest achievement measures than students receiving traditional instruction.

tered with "peer and cross-age tutoring," "mastery learning," and "classes for gifted" with effect sizes around 0.40 *SD*. Only one intervention examined, "accelerated learning," which had a substantially larger effect size and a number of others appeared much less effective. When considering the results for computer tutoring, keep in mind the improvements that recent technological changes make possible in its potential effectiveness—the other interventions studied by J. Kulik (1994) may not reap the same benefits from technology. Thus, the comparative advantage of CAI may be expected to increase in coming years.

More ambitious computer environments are also becoming increasingly available. Hypermedia software, for example, provide students the chance for interactive learning activities using videodiscs, computer simulations, and multimedia. One popular hypermedia video series is called "The Adventures of Jasper Woodbury." The videos, each of which is about 20 minutes in length, end with Jasper asking the students to help him solve a realistic, open-ended problem based on the information given in the video. For example, one video ends with the main character having just purchased a boat with malfunctioning lights and a small, temporary gas tank. From information given in the video, students evaluate whether or not they can safely navigate their new boat home, given both the limitations of time and fuel as constraints. To solve this problem, students must use higher order math skills that involve mathematical reasoning, probability and statistics, and geometry. Studies have consistently shown that students taking the Jasper series outperform students receiving traditional math instruction. Jasper students not only develop a stronger sense of mathematical problem-solving and reasoning skills, but are also able to transfer their knowledge to new problems (Cognition and Technology Group, 1994). A 1998 meta-analysis of studies of hypermedia instruction showed small, positive effects on student academic achievement as compared to students receiving traditional instruction (Liao, 1998).

Schacter and Fagnano (1999) argued that much of the CAI species of computer applications are based on a behaviorist theory of learning. To examine alternative approaches, the authors set out a structure based on three other learning theories—Piaget and Vygotsky's sociocultural learning theory, constructivist theory, and cognitive science—and provided examples of computer applications that exemplify each theory. To demonstrate sociocultural learning theory, Schacter and Fagnano used a class of applications they labeled "computer supported collaborative learning." These applications create opportunities for students to collaborate with each other and to manipulate digital text and other objects with the purpose of building knowledge and understanding of their own work. Perhaps the best known of this category is Scardamalia and Bereiter's computer-supported intentional learning environments (CISL). Overall, Schacter and Fagnano claimed that "software that is based on socio-cultural theories of learning improves student learning" (p. 335).

Each of the two other theoretical categories developed by Schacter and Fagnano (1999) has a variety of applications. Within the constructivist theory category, the authors included both the use of the computer as a "tool for design" and to support "project-based learning." Their primary example of a design tool is Papert's Logo, which gives students the power to design and build their own games and solutions. An application that fits the project-based learning label is the Global Learning and Observations to Benefit the Environment (GLOBE) project. This project involves students from over 8,000 schools in 85 countries, in a worldwide network of students, teachers, and scientists working together to study and understand the global environment (GLOBE Program, 2000). Students make environmental observations using structured protocols at or near their schools, and report the data on the Internet. Students use the data to explore their own community's environmental science issues. At the same time, scientists use the data in their research and to provide feedback to the students to enrich their science education. Comprehensive and well-designed studies of GLOBE indicate that participating students scored significantly higher on assessments of measurement taking, sound sampling and measuring principles, and data interpretation when compared to students in non-GLOBE classrooms (Means et al., 1997). In addition, the GLOBE students have a greater understanding of the environment, increased knowledge of what it means to act like a scientist, and an appreciation of the power and utility of the Web (Means et al., 1997).

Schacter and Fagnano's (1999) third theoretical category, cognitive science, includes a class of applications called intelligent tutoring systems (ITS). These applications are based on a model that has the computer continually assessing the progress of learners and "intelligently" adjusting instruction to bring students to the point where they can approximate the behavior of an expert as they solve the problem. Intelligent tutoring systems for geometry, scientific inquiry, and statistics show considerable promise. Schacter and Fagnano (p. 335) reported that treatment groups surpass control groups significantly in amount, depth, and speed of learning.

In addition to traditional CAI and these more ambitious applications, there has been a recent, marked growth in the use of IT for distance education. Most of the broader research literature on distance education has been carried out at the postsecondary level rather than the K–12 level. Again, the literature is disappointing in its quality and scope. The studies contain little careful work, for example, on different strategies of distance learning, including whether students learn better alone or in groups, or what kinds of instructor feedback are particularly helpful. Nevertheless, three separate and recent syntheses of studies carried out in the postsecondary and the K–12 sectors, each across hundreds of studies, show that distance education has either small, positive effects or "no effect" at all when compared to traditional instruction (Cavanaugh, 1999; Moore & Thompson, 1990; Russel, 2000). No effect means that students who receive distance education do as well as students who receive the live instruction. Moreover, many studies used primitive forms of technology, such as simple videos or auditory transmissions of people lecturing. It is now a simple matter to augment lectures with supporting data and displays that help enrich the educational experience for distance learners. The implications for providing new and essentially equal opportunities to people in poor and/or rural areas of the world are staggering.

Besides academic achievement, technology also seems to affect other aspects of student performance. Some evidence has accumulated that innovative technology use in the classroom can have positive effects on student motivation, as well as student self-esteem and classroom behavior (e.g., attendance and time-on-task; Means & Olson, 1995; Schofield, 1997). A number of studies have also shown that classroom social dynamics change dramatically when technology is used in the classroom (Becker, 1998; Schofield, 1997). In a review of the literature, Schofield (1997) indicated that teachers tend to move away from a traditional lecture-style format. Their classes involve a greater amount of teacher interaction with small groups and individual students, student collaboration and cooperation, students teaching the teacher and one another, and students better regulating their own learning. Fewer studies have examined the effect of technology on student creativity. One study found that a computer's media-rich environment encourages students to be more creative when designing multimedia presentations, even though students sometimes become more involved in the creative aspects of presentation design than gathering content for their reports (Means & Olson, 1995).

In summary, the body of evidence for the effectiveness of technology to improve student educational experiences is growing and, on balance, the results are positive. Computer-assisted instruction has shown consistent and substantial effects for improving basic skills, especially for students from low income families. There appear to be clear and positive effects for a variety of other classes of computer-based learning, including collaborative activities, applications that provide the chance for students to actively design and/or construct projects, and intelligent tutoring systems. Moreover, students receiving education at a distance appear to learn as well or better when contrasted with students who are present at the place and time where the education or training is being delivered. Some uses of hypermedia and constructivist learning also show promise for students to develop higher order thinking skills and to increase their motivation, socialization, and creativity. Yet even with these encouraging results, there is only a shallow understanding of the way technology might be most effectively used in many classrooms. As information technology becomes more powerful, what is needed is a far more aggressive research, development, and evaluation agenda.

WHAT DOES THE FUTURE HOLD
IN STORE FOR K–12 EDUCATION?

With this sense of the current place of technology in classrooms, the discussion may progress to the changes that might occur over the next 5 to 7 years. It focuses on the question of whether information technology will continue to be used by most teachers to reinforce and supplement their typical curriculum and instructional practices or lead to "transformative" changes in the practices of teachers.[5]

Imagine the characteristics of the technology environment surrounding classrooms in 2007. Of particular interest are the hardware and software applications that provide expanded opportunities for teaching and learning and the use of IT for training and education purposes by profit and not-for-profit institutions outside of K–12 schooling. The chapter then examines the uses within schools and the kinds of impediments and supports that exist to help determine the nature of that use. The final section considers policies and strategies that might be used to stimulate and support a "transformative" use of technology in K–12 teaching and learning.

---

[5]What specifically might be seen as transformative of teaching and learning in K–12 schools? To answer that question, consider the ways in which IT has changed the nature of business processes in the private sector. The following five stand out:

1. The development of written, audio, and visual networks that allow practically instant communication among all employees, customers, and management, individually and in groups.
2. A concept of quality service to the customer that includes constant and timely customer feedback and improvement based on the feedback.
3. The elimination of time and place as constraints on everyday transactions and providing and obtaining information.
4. The construction of data systems that allow gathering, organization, and dissemination of information far more quickly and adequately than in the past.
5. The integration of video, sound, and real-time interactive systems to support production and learning.

None of these activities could have existed in the same form 20 years ago. It is not difficult to imagine teaching and learning analogues to these new business processes. Just as intranets facilitate continuous interaction among private sector employees of the same company, *networks* that link together teachers, parents, and students within the same schools and districts

What Will the Technology Environment Surrounding Typical K–12 Classrooms and Teachers Look Like in 2007?

Moore's "law" predicts that the speed and power of computers will double every 18 months, and the cost of computing power will be reduced by half.[6] There is every reason to believe that that this law will hold or be exceeded over the next 6 years (Kurzweil, 1999). Simultaneously, the World Wide Web will advance into adolescence, growing bigger, faster, and more able to support complex, useful activities. The potential implications for education and training are staggering. This section suggests a few of the hardware and software changes that are likely to come about over the next 5 years and that could have a powerful influence on K–12 teaching. It also looks at how institutions outside of K–12 schools, such as businesses and colleges, will make use of technology in their efforts to educate and train their employees and students.

Technology hardware will become substantially more powerful and more affordable. Over the next 5 years, bandwidth will grow at a rapid pace and schools and homes will be connected through cable modems, DSL, Internet 2 and wireless technologies that offer huge increases in capacity. The Web will have the potential to deliver great amounts of information at the fidelity and density of high quality television, for example, while simultaneously providing an interactive environment supported by complex background programs to store and analyze human responses. By 2007, almost every school, classroom, library, community center, and home in the United States and throughout the rest of the developed world will be able to have full access at an affordable cost to high speed connections to the Web and tremendous computing power. It is plausible to argue that the "ac-

---

and even across the world are growing in frequency, enabling more sustained professional conversation. Technology enabled diagnostic information that facilitates substantial individualization of student instruction will be focused and important forms *of customer feedback* and service while distance learning and tutorial services available through the Web 24 hours a day, every day (24/7) provide powerful examples of the elimination of the *constraints of time and place.* School and school systems already are using technology to develop better *technology driven data* systems to support resource allocation decisions and the Web supports worldwide networks of students, teachers, and scientists who gather and analyze data about the global environment. Existing examples have been supplied of using the computer and the Web to extend teaching and learning through providing students with *interactive, hypermedia applications* and computer-based collaborative learning environments. These are only a few of the possible analogues.

[6]In 1965, Gordon Moore, co-founder of Intel, observed that the number of transistors per square inch on integrated circuits had doubled every year since the integrated circuit was invented. Moore predicted that this trend would continue for the foreseeable future. In subsequent years, the pace slowed down a bit, but data density has doubled approximately every 18 months. Most experts expect Moore's Law to hold for at least another 2 decades (ZDWEBOPIEDIA, 2000).

cess" digital divide will not exist in the developed world; however, the "use" digital divide will most likely remain.

The power of desktop and handheld personal computers/communications equipment will continue to increase, and the cost per unit power will drop even more rapidly. By Christmas 2000, powerful computers were packaged as game machines with the capacity to access the Web and to be hooked up to television sets at less than $300 (Sony PlayStation, 2000). Moreover, computing capacity will no longer be fixed in place while students and teachers move around. As miniaturization of technology increases, people will routinely carry their computing machinery with them to support them wherever they are. Within 3 years, the number of handheld devices with significant computing capacity will exceed the total number of other computing devices, and within 10 years it is expected that the aggregate power of handheld devices will exceed the aggregate power of all other computing devices (Horn, 2000).

The increase by 2007 in computing power and speed will spawn powerful, new applications, as well. One area that is expected to stand out will be the use of greatly improved machine-based language translation and voice recognition capacity. In a different area, new tools will bring the mass of information on the Web more under control. Search engines and agents supported by artificial intelligence and content analysis routines, and expert and user evaluations in consumer guides for online applications will enable sophisticated and customized exploration of the Web. Powerful programs will be available for students and others to explore and analyze massive new quantitative and qualitative databases already being developed on the Web. Communication by e-mail, voice, image, and streaming video will be available to almost everyone. The increase in capacity to link together people with a common purpose will be extraordinary.

Specialized tools and applications for supporting teaching and learning in many different settings will also be commonplace. Many are already established and operating. They include platforms designed to guide trainers, professors, and others to create web-based lessons and courses. The purpose of the platforms is to make it as easy as possible to put instructional content on the Web. The platforms will incorporate sophisticated communication systems as well as diagnostic tools, such as intelligent tutors that operate to guide instruction and assessment components (AT&T Learning Network, 2000; Blackboard.com, 2000; eCollege.com, 2000).

Both public and private sector organizations will use these and other advances in hardware and applications to educate and train people throughout the society. Indeed, many already have done so. Private sector companies, large and small, are investing huge amounts of money and effort into using web- and other computer-based technology to train their employees. Numbering just 400 in 1988, now more than 1,600 corporate "universities" serve over 54 million students per year (Meister, 1998). Public sector agencies, including the federal government, are not far behind.

Colleges and universities across the world also are moving toward greatly expanded use of information technology to educate students. A large number of announcements concerning such efforts were expected in fall 2000. By 2007, we expect thousands of postsecondary institutions will sponsor courses on the Web available to residential and nonresidential students.[7] Among the traditional institutions, entrepreneurial graduate schools and nimble community colleges are leading the way (Block & Dobell, 1999; Moe, Bailey, & Lau, 1999). For example, Harvard, Columbia, and Chicago Business Schools are already marketing their courses outside of their campuses; and Stanford's School of Engineering has placed a master's program online for international distribution (Stanford Center for Professional Development, 2000; Unext.com, 2000). Community colleges in many communities around the nation will offer courses on the Web that are often indistinguishable from upper level courses in many secondary schools (About: Distance Learning, 2000).

Moreover, growing numbers of new private profit and not-for-profit institutions dedicated to distance learning and operating as direct competitors of the established higher education institutions are expected. Within the next 7 years, there could be a dozen new virtual universities, each with over 10,000 full-time equivalent students, as well as hundreds of other schools within and outside the United States, all battling for a share of the market.

Advancements in the technology also will spur improvements in the quality of instructional delivery on the Web. The courses will gradually evolve from "talking heads" into more elaborate and interesting mixtures of lectures, graphics, photos, demonstrations, video, and interactive problem solving. Simulations, immersion techniques, and the use of online databases are expected to be popular as bandwidth and competition increase. There is also expected to be an emphasis on the development of networks of learners supporting and tutoring each other, and of students controlling more of the pace and focus of courses. For many courses, online sites will make trained tutors available to students on a 24-hour-a-day, 7-days-a-week schedule (24/7). These changes could alter the role of professors and trainers from providers of knowledge to coaches and facilitators of learning.

The picture of 2007 presented here locates 2.7 million teachers in U.S. K–12 classrooms surrounded by a society whose members use powerful technology in their homes and workplaces, in varied ways to improve and

---

[7]This is already happening in hundreds of schools throughout the developed world (Moe, Bailey, & Lau, 1999).

extend the nature of their basic work processes. An important use of IT will be to educate and train adults. The question to consider now concerns how those teachers will use the same technology in their workplaces to educate children and youth.

What Will Happen to K–12 Instruction: Competing Visions

Imagine two opposing answers to this question stemming from different assumptions about the malleability of current educational institutions and the potential power of information technology in the society as a whole.

The first of these answers, the *minimal change* argument, draws its logic and data from the history of innovations intended to change teaching and learning in K–12 education. Over the years, dozens of innovations such as "new math" and "project learning" have been introduced into the schools, but few have lasted. Innovations designed to influence the core of teaching and learning rarely extend beyond 25% of teachers or schools (Cuban, 1998; Elmore, 1996). Adherents to the minimal change prediction argue that the "grammar of schooling"—its rules, structure, incentives, traditions, and multiple demands—militate against widespread adoption of any significant innovation. Mandatory attendance, strong unions, professional norms and public expectations, decentralized and "loosely coupled" authority structures all operate to maintain the basic structure and practice in schools. The "grammar of schooling" slows change to a crawl.[8]

Beyond the culture and the stability of practice, those predicting minimal change would also point to a variety of specific impediments to using technology in ways that could alter conventional approaches to teaching and learning. Three barriers to the short-term spread of technology stand out.

Lack of Data on Educational Technology Effectiveness. According to one hypothesis, technology has not had a greater impact on teaching and learning in schools because teachers do not yet see special advantages of using computers and the Internet. The small number of valid studies on the effectiveness of using technology other than CAI to improve student achievement and the even smaller literature on effective uses of technology to promote significant changes in instruction are not convincing to many teachers and other researchers (Center for Research on Information Technology and Organizations [CRITO], 1999). Without knowing what the ben-

---

[8]This characteristic of American schools has positive as well as negative consequences. It preserves the good aspects of the schools and it protects the schools from many ill-conceived changes pressed on them from frantic policymakers.

efits would be in their own classrooms, teachers are unwilling to invest in efforts to use technology that change their pedagogical practices.

Lack of Support. Teachers do not receive the support they need to use technology in innovative and sometimes complicated ways. A recent report indicated that most teachers receive professional development to learn about "computer technology and software mechanics" rather than how to integrate computers into their instruction (CRITO, 1999). Many teachers also have little or no on-the-job technical and instructional support (CRITO, 1999).

Difficulty in Finding Digital Content. Teachers find it extremely difficult to find digital content (e.g., both software and Internet Web sites) that is relevant to and easily integrated into their curriculum. Many who search for digital content find it somewhat or very difficult to find instructional software (59%) and Web sites (48%) to meet their specific classroom needs (*Education Week* & the Milken Exchange, 1998). This may be due to few adequate evaluations of software that help teachers differentiate the good from the bad, and also because digital content is still not well aligned with state and district standards (*Education Week* & the Milken Exchange, 1998).

In sum, this argument makes a powerful case for believing that there will be only modest change due to technology. In this scenario, the majority of teachers will not move much beyond the use of technology in their classroom as a communication and management tool and to support student work in conventional areas such as writing, computer-aided instruction of basic skills, and searching for information. These uses will not substantially alter the content of the curriculum or the nature of the pedagogy. For most teachers, computers and the Web will provide a somewhat better way to do some of the traditional things that are done in most classrooms, not a revolutionary innovation.

There is an opposing view, however. This view holds that the transformation of teaching and learning is not only likely, but will be an inevitable byproduct of the technology revolution. Proponents of this *transformative change* argument would draw a distinction between information technology and prior innovations in education. Unlike other education innovations that serve as the primary examples for much of the literature on innovation, the use of information technology is not limited to schools. Expanded use of computers and the Web is not like moving to a phonics-based curriculum in reading, or to instituting multi-aged classrooms. Information technology has become an integral part of society. In 2007, teachers, principals, parents, school board members, and other policymakers in schools and school systems will be surrounded by a society that will expect technology to change what and how the nation does its work. Many people will use computers and the Web to learn new material at work and at home through distance learning, simulations, and problem-based training. Surely they will expect the schools to use the same techniques.

Advocates of this view could argue that a powerful new force for change will also operate within the schools. Many of the 750,000 new teachers who will enter K–12 schools between now and 2007 will have been exposed to active and imaginative use of information technology throughout their lifetimes and most recently in their own collegiate academic experience. These new teachers will make up over 25% of the total teaching force. When they enter the teaching profession, many will bring experience, vision, and skill in the use of technology to help motivate and change the learning experiences of their students.

Furthermore, private entrepreneurs will avidly seek ways to influence teachers and policymakers to use computers and the Web in classroom instruction. The energy and imagination of the entrepreneurs is new to public education. The private sector has always had a play in the K–12 market, but until recently this has occurred mainly through the textbook and other national companies that have dominated the content side of the education market. The lack of nimbleness of these large corporations has matched the glacial speed of change of the schools. Information technology and especially the Web are changing the marketing dynamic, however. Small, fast moving companies focused on using the Web will find potentially profitable niches in the education market.

In effect, the schools will be surrounded by examples of the power of technology to transform the way that the nation does business. This will create a powerful set of expectations that should help drive significant change in classrooms.

The two visions of the future—minimal change or transformative—reflect two powerful forces pulling schools in opposite directions. One force would produce the caution and slow change people have come to expect from public education. This force would push schools to stay with the traditional curriculum and pedagogy while increasing the supportive use of technology. The other force would pull schools to operate in concert with a society whose institutions are substantially changing their basic work processes and would support change toward more extensive and innovative application of information technology in the core areas of curriculum and instruction.

What Do We Think Will Happen?

Which of these forces will win out? As with most complex social matters, it is foolish to predict but even more foolish to predict an extreme position. Our guess is that the future holds elements of both visions. One way to think about technology and teaching is that rather than pulling reluctant educational institutions whole hog into a new arena of operation, technology's ultimate influence may be more subtle—like the tendrils of a plant reaching into new territory, attaching themselves to existing structures, seeping into crevices, gaining a secure hold. Before long, the plant tendrils take up so much space, they literally subsume or replace whatever originally occupied that space. Similarly, even in the absence of deliberate policy initiatives, we expect that uses of technology will move naturally into traditional practice thereby creating the potential in the long run to transform the way people behave and think about teaching and learning.

Looking over the landscape, there are at least four new applications of technology that are likely to occur naturally in the schools over the next 7 years. Taken together, these applications introduce new content, pedagogy, and communication strategies into schools. The seeds of these innovations are already planted and they are being watered by the energy and enthusiasm of profit and not-for-profit organizations, which are often in partnership with school districts, universities, and teacher unions. It is expected that these applications will happen, perhaps not in the way described here, but somehow. These applications have the potential to influence the way that teachers and students conceive and go about their work and to have a substantial positive effect on student achievement.

Web-Delivered Advanced Placement (AP) Courses. In 2000, over 40% of U.S. high schools did not have AP courses. Most of these schools are in poor and/or rural areas. The lack of access to AP courses creates a low ceiling in many of the subject matter areas and, therefore, puts students desiring to go to competitive colleges at a serious disadvantage. Almost all of these schools are expected to be able to provide AP courses to their students within the next 3 to 5 years. The method of delivery initially will be a mixture of Web and computer discs, and within 5 years, it will be entirely on the Web.[9] The federal government has set aside money to provide an incentive to states for all schools to provide students with an opportunity to take AP courses. That incentive, and the fact that AP courses have structured syllabi and assessments that are widely accepted and valued, make AP offerings an attractive investment for public and private entrepreneurs. Similar courses, such as the Regents' curricula in New York, also offer attractive targets for energetic entrepreneurs.

The power of the technology-based AP courses to change school instruction does not rest in the challenging nature of the subject matter. Imagine,

---

[9]Currently, a small number of vendors sell Advanced Placement coursework to schools, organizations, and individuals. Examples include Apex Learning (2000), Archipelago Distributed Learning (2000), and Academic Systems (1999).

for a moment, a small school in rural America that decides to use a web-based AP course for beginning (AB) calculus. Five students in the 12th grade are "ready" for the course. Their teacher, however, knows almost no calculus because he has been teaching algebra, trigonometry, and solid geometry. The school contracts with a private firm that makes the web-based course available to the five students and the teacher on a 24-hour-a-day, 7-day-a-week (24/7) basis. They also make available an online tutoring service on a 24/7 basis—a minimum number of hours of tutoring are packaged with the course fee.

The course is designed so that students will work on the course when they choose, but they will meet 3 days a week to go over their progress, take scheduled interim tests under their teacher's supervision, and discuss difficult concepts and problems. During the meetings, some students who find the material less difficult than others will act as tutors for the others; the teacher, who is aware of the literature on the positive effects of student study groups, may urge groups to form outside of the class. The teacher, in effect, will operate like a coach—motivating, directly helping when he can, finding assistance when assistance is needed.

If the literature on distance learning is at all valid, the students in this web-based AP course will do as well as or better than they would have done in a regular class taught in the traditional manner. Now consider what happens to the teacher. Over the first few years, the teacher will learn first-year calculus, so that the course becomes a powerful professional development experience. Beyond that, the teacher has also learned another way of teaching that places greater control in the hands of the student and yet provides important and satisfying results for the teacher. This would be a significant step toward transformational change.

Easily Accessible Databases on the Web of Scientific, Social, Historical, and Literary Information.   One of the more extraordinary characteristics of the Web is its ability to motivate people and organizations to make available to the world large important databases. Records and diaries of the fallen soldiers in a critical civil war battle, collections of 17th-century English jokes, and much of the data gathered by the U.S. census are merely a few examples of the kinds of data that are now or could be on the Web. Over the next few years, the capacity and speed of computers and web networks will substantially increase. These improvements, along with the development of easily used analysis tools, will make the process of interrogating web databases increasingly easier, reaching the point where third and fourth graders will have no problems in obtaining the data necessary to answer many questions. These resources, available in every classroom, will make problem- and project-based approaches to curriculum far easier to develop and monitor.

Communication Systems Among Students and Teachers.   A straightforward and important change in schools will be the linking of students, teachers, parents, and principals together in a common network. Individuals will have their own e-mail address and web page, and there will be frequent work-based communication among all members. Student study groups, student tutorials, teacher subject- and curriculum-based groups, and other informal networks will be simple to establish on the web-based system. Group projects will be easier for teachers to assign and monitor. Regular communication between parents and teachers will be commonplace and will be supported, when necessary by instantaneous language translation (albeit not perfect). Before 2007, voice and video over the Web will seamlessly support written communication. Increases in the quality and variety of ways to use the communication systems could also have a positive effect on school community by generating a greater interconnectedness among students and teachers leading to a strengthening of the school's social fabric.

Web-Based Resources for Teachers.   The Web will help make teaching a less lonely job by connecting teachers with each other and by becoming a warehouse of resources. By 2007, many teachers will receive web-based professional development, often set in a problem- or case-centered format. The content of the professional development will be aligned with state standards and be able to be tailored to the individual needs of the teacher or school faculty. In addition, portals for teachers established by their local district or state (or from some other source) will contain lesson, project, and unit plans aligned with their standards that have been evaluated by experts and teachers for their content validity and by other teachers as useful in practice. Some states already make available versions of these materials on the Web. The more useful portals will encourage feedback from teachers who use the materials posted on their pages and will treat the plans like "open source" computer code, open to continuous and thoughtful modification and improvement. Many lesson and unit plans will contain specific instructions for using data for lessons that are available on the Web. Teachers will be able to easily interrogate the portals to locate plans that fit their needs and also to contact directly teachers who have earlier used or developed the plans. Use of portals like this will emphasize the importance of professional communication about teaching practice, which in the long run will lead to an improvement in instruction. These ideas are only the beginning of the kinds of services and materials that will be available to teachers to reduce their isolation, increase their sense of professionalism, and make innovation easier as the tasks of creating and trying out new ideas becomes a shared responsibility.

    These four sets of technology applications will alter the practice of many teachers in the short run. Each is related to the nature of the curriculum and instruction, and makes life simultaneously more challenging and more manageable for teachers. Each fits well and can easily be adapted to support instruction aligned to state and local standards, and each could provide for user feedback and continuous improvement through web-based communication. Finally, each activity potentially contains a deep aspect of professionalism for teachers—the challenge to learn and use new approaches, the development of networks based on the substance of work, and an openness to the use of new tools to extend effectiveness.[10]

Embedded in these four applications are elements that address some aspects of the three impediments to the expanded use of technology in classrooms that were highlighted earlier. With respect to the need for information about effectiveness, the AP course results, based on nationally accepted examinations, will provide powerful and practical information about the effectiveness of web-based course delivery. Moreover, the mix of expert and user information in the teacher portals on the Web about the effectiveness and ease of use of curriculum projects and plans will provide further information about how and whether to use technology to meet certain curricular goals. And powerful diagnostic and assessment routines embedded in CAI or in stand-alone capacity will provide practical and powerful evaluative information to teachers about their students.

The central concern of teachers about their need for technology support may be ameliorated by the new applications. The private sector often turns to technology to teach how to integrate technology applications into the work processes. Professional development on the Web will help. Similarly, expert and user reviews posted on the Web will provide powerful feedback to application and software developers who should, in turn, use the feedback to guide their own efforts to continuously improve their products. But the day-to-day support and the need for insuring the reliability of the hardware will not be a job for teachers; schools and districts will need to make these a priority.

Finally, the problems of finding digital content are also amenable to technology solutions. The combination of intelligent agents and content analysis techniques will be a technical solution to reduce some of the problems of searching the Web. The existence of teacher portals on the Web with evaluative data and recommendations by experts and users will go even further.

---

[10]Other applications that will probably be prevalent in 2007 could have been highlighted. For example, the next years will show substantial progress toward the integration of diagnosis, instruction, and assessment in web applications, a path that could easily lead to more powerful individualization of teaching. Language instruction particularly for nonnative speakers could be changed dramatically by the use of voice and video and language translation routines. Novice teachers will join web-based support groups to help them through their early years of teaching.

Policy Implications

This chapter has argued that the inevitable growth in technology will spawn some substantial (although perhaps not transformative) changes in teaching and learning. Given this, one policy position could be that the forces of the market and societal expectations should be left unrestrained and allowed to run free. From this perspective, technological changes are self-reinforcing, that is, they have qualities to resolve potential impediments to classroom change. However, the quality and fairness of access to these technological changes are not guaranteed. It may be possible to do better.

To begin, what is effective and powerful about schools right now must be protected. This will take constant vigilance as the technology reforms take hold because the urge to reform indiscriminately can be overwhelming. On the positive side, more might be done to improve the quality of support for the thoughtful and fair spread of effective uses of information technology. Three areas stand out as requiring deliberate and sustained reform strategies and action by practitioners, researchers, and policymakers. Each of these areas could act as a deterrent or an accelerator to implementing substantially improved curriculum and instruction.

Research and Evaluation.   Teachers need solid reasons to make substantial and sometimes controversial changes. Clear and strong evidence that the use of technology would improve the quality of their work and of student learning would be a powerful incentive for teachers to use technology in new and interesting ways. There is evidence that CAI works better than conventional teaching, especially for the basics with initially low achieving students; and it is expected that improvements in the motivating and diagnostic aspects of this application will show even better results, although that research remains to be done. Also, research on distance learning suggests that it is as effective as, or even more effective than, conventional teaching, but more information is needed about the conditions under which distance learning is most effective, especially for K–12 students. The data that will naturally come from AP examinations will not be enough.

Beyond these areas, understanding of the effectiveness of information technology applications in K–12 schooling is sadly lacking. Focused and thoughtful research and development and evaluation is needed in all areas of the use of IT discussed—CAI and distance learning, professional networks, web-based tutoring, the professional development of teachers, collaborative learning and problem-centered activities (Office of Educational Technology, 1999; President's Committee of Advisors on Science and Technology, Panel on Education Technology, 1997). This means knowing the negatives as well as the positives, and how technology might impede and enhance learning. Work must be done on topics directly linked to technology itself. For example, some critics argue that the use of computer technology and the Web will isolate students such that they will not learn important social skills.

Results of the research will be useful both for improving the quality of the curriculum and instruction and for convincing policymakers and the public, as well as teachers, that information technology is a useful tool for improving the quality of schools. Such results are especially important for technology-enabled curriculum projects and pedagogical strategies based on constructivist and other theories that differ in approach and rhetoric from conventional teaching. The public must view these approaches as providing value beyond what is possible using traditional instruction.

The research must address both the basic issue of how students learn effectively in these settings and the engineering issue of how best to configure the interventions to maximize their effectiveness. Results of this research would operate as intrinsic incentives for teachers by meeting their professional sense of responsibility while also helping them to meet the powerful extrinsic demands for increased test scores.

Finally, research should be carried out to figure out more useful ways of evaluating different approaches to using technology to enhance teaching and learning. It should not shy away from randomized field trials when they can be appropriately employed. The technology must be harnessed to carry out the evaluations; the new technology will provide powerful tools for collecting and analyzing data and feeding it back to the users to improve the quality of their work.

Assessment. The current standards-based reforms have much momentum. Until recently, there has been little reason to believe that support for these reforms will abate. However, now the often ill-considered strategies taken by states and districts in their choice of assessment and accountability strategies pose a substantial threat to the original goals of the reforms.

For one thing, states often purchase and use generic, norm-based tests to be the primary assessment instrument to be used in their accountability strategies. These tests can lead to a narrowing of instruction by teachers as they attempt to match their teaching to the test characteristics. Moreover, the psychometric makeup of norm-referenced tests puts a premium on detecting differences in scores among students rather than on assessing performance based on a standard of achievement in the subject matter area, such as whether or not a student can read independently with understanding. Consequently, the assessments offer less information to teachers about the performance of students than is needed. Finally, tests designed to be used in many states are not explicitly aligned with the standards of any one state (except after the fact in a superficial fashion). This condition reduces the sensitivity and validity of the assessments to curricula and instruction that are specifically aligned to the state standards.

The use of shallow, norm-referenced assessments that are unaligned with state standards is one of the important problems that prompted the standards-based reform movement in the early 1990s—now it seems that many states are reinstituting the very practice that helped make education mediocre. The bottom line is that states that do not invest in high quality, challenging assessments that are deliberately and thoughtfully aligned with their state standards will fail in their overall standards-based reform efforts and simultaneously will hinder their progress toward effective use of technology.

Information technology may someday provide a remedy to this deepening problem. Many online instructional applications of the future will contain diagnostic and assessment components—assessment will become part of the ongoing process of instruction. In addition, many applications will have online portfolios to store student work. The Educational Testing Service (ETS) and other organizations have made substantial advances toward the capacity to rapidly score online performance assessments. Finally, a number of reports on reading have suggested that now there is a much better working knowledge of the components and the developmental characteristics of the process of learning to read. Putting these four components together, the result could be online assessment systems that would provide a vast improvement in the capacity to assess student work and progress.

Continuous diagnostic information would keep teachers aware of the needs of each student. Online portfolios would offer another window on student progress and could be used as one of the multiple measures required when students are administered high stakes assessments. Online assessments should be able to use conventional short answer and performance items and over time be enhanced by some of the simulation opportunities available by use of the Web. Scoring such assessments and feeding the results back to teachers and students and parents is a task that can be accomplished using web-based technology within days, rather than the months now taken by traditional test publishers. (Imagine, a company (or a school system) that would allow a wait of 5 months for an evaluation of its performance to be scored—would you buy from that company?)

The nation is faced with both a crisis and an opportunity for assessment. The technology and the know-how exists to meet both challenges. How leaders respond will have a substantial effect on the quality of the nation's schools. An investment of $10 a student/year in such an effort would have a dramatic payoff for American education.

The Digital Divide.   The nation must not lose sight of the potential that technology applied to education could create inequality rather than reduce it. The focus must remain on incentives, policies, and practices that provide opportunities to the least advantaged in the society.

A critical step is to continue to ensure that all schools are fully equipped with computers that are ready for the new instructional software and have broadband access to the Internet. The e-rate is a powerful policy instrument here because it targets resources to the neediest schools.

Supporting equality of use is more difficult and will require creativity and leadership. Instructional software must have demonstrated effectiveness and be easy to use for teachers. The market may be able to stimulate that condition. But the government will need to create incentives for the private sector to enter into markets that appear unprofitable and difficult to penetrate. One example is to stimulate development of high quality software focused on providing support for students that speak limited English, are disabled, or have trouble learning to read or to calculate. Similarly, school communication systems should be designed with the diversity of the society squarely in mind; teachers must be able to communicate with parents in the language of the parents. Governments must also consider ways of making available to rural and inner-city youngsters the same opportunities to take advanced instruction (e.g., Advanced Placement courses) that are available to suburban students.

The problems are even more difficult outside of schools. Powerful technology will be available and affordable to almost all families. There is worry, however, about the *Sesame Street* effect. An early study of *Sesame Street* found that a low income child that watched *Sesame Street* learned more from it than did a middle income child that watched it (Ball & Bogatz, 1970; Bogatz & Ball, 1971; Cook et al., 1975). But, because a greater percentage of middle income students watched it, the result of the program was to expand the average learning gap between low and middle income students. Unless researchers are very thoughtful about how to design and promote educational software for the home, technology could produce an expansion, rather than a reduction, of the learning gap.

CONCLUSIONS

This chapter has argued that a variety of important changes attributable to the use of information technology will occur by 2007. Local networks will enhance the capacity of parents to communicate with teachers about their children, children to work together on projects and to help each other with homework, and teachers to engage in professional conversations among themselves. Distance learning will make AP courses on the Web available to hundreds of thousands of students who now do not have access to them. Web-based applications will stimulate project-based and independent student learning. Diagnostic tools will enable CAI to be individualized to the particular needs of students. These are just a few of the many potential technology applications that will exist by 2007.

These modest predictions should be met even though there are traditional constraints on change. Powerful expectations on the schools will stem from the widespread use of IT in society and especially from examples in closely related sectors such as adult training and higher education. The combination of these expectations with new technologies, tools, and applications, new teachers who are comfortable with technology, and energetic and fast-moving entrepreneurs will pave the way. Many applications will be supported by Web businesses that have a strong belief in customer service and will work hard to make their product as useful as possible.

A number of these applications are transformative in the sense that they will lead to significant changes in teacher work—with students, parents, and other teachers. Although these changes are expected to affect tens of thousands of schools, as are others that are not yet imagined, they will not happen on a universal basis in a day, a year, or even 7 years. Just as the transformative changes of electricity took 25 years, so may this transformation. It will happen by evolution, not revolution. It is expected, however, that there will be strong evidence of these changes during the coming years.

To a substantial extent, these changes are inevitable. Yet, a few thoughtful and focused policies should be continued or initiated by public and private sectors to help ensure that the changes are of the highest quality and shared by all students. In particular, the federal government and private foundations should support a comprehensive research, development, and evaluation effort to assure teachers that the new uses of technology improve the effectiveness of their instruction. This information would also be comforting to parents and policymakers.

Student assessments are another area of policy concern. The current use in many states of shallow, norm-referenced assessments that are not aligned with state standards will endanger the chances of any effective reform be sustained. This includes information technology reforms—the use of these tests represents the strongest impediment in the entire education system to productive change. At the same time, the power of the new technology may provide a way to develop and deliver far better and cost-effective assessments.

Finally, the nation must insure that all students have the opportunity to benefit from the potential that information technology provides.

ACKNOWLEDGMENTS

We thank the Spencer Foundation and the Carnegie Foundation for the Improvement of Teaching for their support. We also thank Jennifer Test, Jennifer O'Day, Diane Rogers, and Harry O'Neil for their comments and insights on earlier drafts of this chapter.

REFERENCES

About: Distance Learning. (2000). Distance learning college degree directory. [Online]. About.com, Inc. Available: http://distancelearn.about.com/education/distancelearn/library/blpages/blcollegedegrees.htm [2000, July 6].

Academic Systems. (1999). [Online]. Academic Systems Corporation. Available: http://www.academic.com [2000, July 6].

Anderson, R. E., & Ronnkvist, A. (1999). *The presence of computers in American schools.* [Online]. Center for Research on Information Technology and Organizations. Available: http://www.crito.uci.edu/tlc/findings/computers_in_american_schools/ [2000, July 5].

Apex Learning. (2000). Advanced Placement courses via the Internet. [Online]. Available: http://www.apex.netu.com [2000, June 6].

Archipelago.com Distributed Learning. (2000). Archipelago—Multimedia distance learning and education. [Online]. Available: http://www.archipelago.com [2000, July 6].

AT&T Learning Network®Virtual Academy. (1999). *Virtual Academy.* [Online]. AT&T. Available: http://www.att.com/learningnetwork/virtualacademy/index2.html [2000, July 6].

Ball, S., & Bogatz, G. A. (1970). *The first year of Sesame Street: An evaluation.* Princeton, NJ: Educational Testing Service.

Becker, H. J. (1998, April). *The influence of computer and Internet use on teachers' pedagogical practices and perceptions.* Paper presented at the meeting of the American Educational Research Association, San Francisco, CA.

Becker, H. J. (2000). *Who's wired and who's not.* [Online]. University of California, Irvine. Available: http://www.gse.uci.edu/doehome/DeptInfo/Faculty/Becker/packard/text.html [2000, July 5].

Becker, H. J., & Sterling C. W. (1987). Equity in school computer use: National data and neglected considerations. *Journal of Educational Computing Research, 3,* 289–311.

Blackboard.com. (2000). [Online]. Blackboard Inc. Available: http://blackboard.com [2000, July 6].

Block, H., & Dobell, B. (1999). *The e-Bang theory.* San Francisco, CA: Banc of America Securities, Equity Division.

Bogatz, G. A., & Ball, S. (1971). *The second year of Sesame Street, A continuing evaluation.* Princeton, NJ: Educational Testing Service.

Brown, J. S. (2000, March/April). Growing up digital: How the web changes work, education, and the ways people learn. *Change, 32*(2), 11–20.

Cavanaugh, C. S. (1999). *The effectiveness of interactive distance education technologies in K–12 learning: A meta-analysis.* (ERIC Document Reproduction Service No. Ed430547)

Center for Research on Information Technology and Organizations. (1999). Teaching, learning and computing 1998. [Online]. University of California, Irvine. Available: http://www.crito.uci.edu/tlc/html/tlc_home.html [2000, July 6].

Cognition and Technology Group at Vanderbilt. (1994). From visual word problems to learning communities: changing conceptions of cognitive research. In K. McGilly (Ed.), *Classroom lessons: Integrating cognitive theory and classroom practice* (pp. 157–200). Cambridge, MA: MIT Press.

Cook, T. D., Appleton, H., Conner, R. F., Shaffer, A., Tamkin, G., & Weber, S. J. (1975). *"Sesame Street" revisited.* New York: Russell Sage.

Cuban, L. (1998). High–tech schools and low-tech teaching. *Journal of Computing in Teacher Education, 14*(2), 6–7.

eCollege.com. (2000). [Online]. Available: http://www.ecollege.com [2000, July 6].

Education Week and the Milken Exchange. (1998). Technology counts '98: Putting technology to the test. *Education Week on the Web.* [Online]. Available: http://www.edweek.com/sreports/tc98/ [2000, July 5].

Elmore, R. F. (1996). Getting to scale with successful educational practices. In S. Fuhrman & J. O'Day (Eds.), *Rewards and reform* (pp. 294–329). San Francisco: Jossey-Bass.

GLOBE Program (2000). Global learning to benefit the environment. (2000). [Online]. Available: http://www.globe.gov [2000, July 5].

Horn, P. (2000, May 5). *Impact of IT on the future of the research university: Briefing for the National Research Council.* New York: Sloan Foundation.

Kulik, C., & Kulik, J. A. (1991). Effectiveness of computer-based instruction: An updated analysis. *Computers and Human Behavior, 7,* 75–94.

Kulik, J. (1994). Meta-analytic studies of findings on computer-based instruction. In E. L. Baker & H. F. O'Neil, Jr. (Eds.), *Technology assessment in education and training* (pp. 9–33). Hillsdale, NJ: Lawrence Erlbaum Associates.

Kurzweil, R. (1999). *The age of spiritual machines: When computers exceed human intelligence.* New York: Viking.

Liao, Y. C. (1998). Effects of hypermedia versus traditional instruction on students' achievement: A meta-analysis. *Journal of Research on Computing in Education, 30*(4), 341–359.

Means, B., Coleman, E., Lewis, A., Quellmalz, E., Marder, C., & Valdex, K. (1997). *GLOBE Year 2 evaluation: Implementation and progress.* [Online]. Menlo park, CA: SRI International. Available: http://www.globe.gov/sda-bin/wt/gh/GRR+L(en)+Dg(gmx/el)Gn(GLOBE~20Program~20Evaluation) [2000, July 5].

Means, B., & Olson, K. (1995). Technology and education reform: Technical research report. [Online]. U.S. Department of Education. Available: http://www.ed.gov/pubs/SER/Technology/ [2000, July 6].

Meister, J. (1998). *Corporate universities: Lessons in building a world-class workforce.* New York: McGraw-Hill.

Moe, M., Bailey, K., & Lau, R. (1999). *The book of knowledge.* San Francisco, CA: Merrill Lynch.

Moore, M. G., & Thompson, M. M. (1990). *The effects of distance learning: A summary of literature. Research monograph number 2.* Southeastern Ohio Telecommunications Consortium. (ERIC Document Reproduction Service No. ED330321)

National Center for Education Statistics. (2000). *Internet access in U.S. public schools and classrooms: 1994–1999* (NCES No. 2000086). Washington, DC: U.S. Department of Education.

Office of Educational Technology. (1999, December). *Forum on technology in education: Envisioning the future.* A working meeting sponsored by the U.S. Department of Education, Washington, DC.

President's Committee of Advisors on Science and Technology, Panel on Education Technology. (1997). *Report to the President on the use of technology to strengthen K–12 education in the United States.* [Online]. Available: http://www.whitehouse.gov/WH/EOP/OSTP/NSTC/PCAST/k-12ed.html [2000, July 5].

Russel, T. L. (2000). *The "No significant difference phenomenon."* [Online]. TeleEducation New Brunswick. Available: http://cuda.teleeducation.nb.ca/nosignificantdifference/ [2000, July 6].

Schacter, J., & Fagnano, C. (1999). Does computer technology improve student learning and achievement? How, when, and under what conditions? *Journal of Educational Computing Research, 90,* 329–343.

Schofield, J. W. (1997). Computers and classroom social process—A review of the literature. *Social Science Computer Review, 15*(1), 27–39.

Sony PlayStation. (2000). *PlayStation2.* [Online]. Sony Computer Entertainment America Inc. Available: http://www.playstation.com/news/ps2.asp [2000, July 6].

Stanford Center for Professional Development. (2000). Online MSEE degree with an emphasis on telecommunications. [Online]. Available: http:/scpd.stanford.edu/ce/telecom/onlinedegree.html [2000, July 6].

Unext.com. (2000). [Online]. Available: http://www.unext.com [2000, July 6].

ZDWEBOPEDIA. (2000). *Moore's law.* [Online]. ZDNet & internet.com Corporation. Available: www.zdwebopedia.com/Microprocessors/Moores_Law.html [2000, July 6].

Chapter 2

Gazing Yet Again Into the Silicon Chip: The Future of Computers in Education

Susan F. Chipman
Office of Naval Research

In the early 1980s, I gazed into the silicon chip (Chipman & Butler, 1983, 1985), seeking to give a U.S. perspective on the way that microcomputers would affect the future of education. I revisited the topic in late 1991 (Chipman, 1993). Now two decades into that future, it is time to reflect and to gaze into the future once again. In the early 1980s, some believed that the availability of computerized instruction would result in the withering away of schools as we have known them. Others believed the computers that were being so enthusiastically purchased would end up locked in closets and that the schools would go on as before, as little changed by computers as they had been by prior waves of educational "technology" (Needle, 1982). Still others saw in computers an opportunity for revitalization, an impetus to change, and a potential solution to the problems of limited individual attention, limited productivity, and shortages of technically qualified teachers that beset education (Melmed, 1984). Each of these alternative futures had not only its believers but also its active promoters. For each person who saw in technology the promise of making outstanding instruction available everywhere—in the home, in the remote rural location, in the urban classroom—there seemed to be another who considered technology as an unwelcome distraction of attention and financial resources that would be better spent attaining the traditional goals of a liberal education (Boyer, 1983).

As was true in 1991, today it seems that the preceding paragraph could be converted right back into the present tense without serious loss of accuracy: In 1991, a then recent report touted computer technology as a tool for bringing about radical restructuring of the schools (Sheingold & Tucker, 1990), whereas another (Alexander, 1991) considered technology irrelevant and unnecessary for educational reform. A recent report (Coley, Cradler, & Engel, 1997) commented that this range of views continues to exist. Except we now know that radical change certainly did not happen quickly.

Gazing into the silicon chip yet again, what basis is there for deciding which alternative future will come to pass? If we decide that computer technology probably will have major effects on education, how can we predict the detailed form of that impact? There seem to be at least two major aspects to the potential impact of technology on education. One is *external*. Computer technology is changing the social environment that surrounds schooling; it is changing the nature of the work for which students are preparing in the schools. Some change in schooling can be expected, and is already occurring, as an echo of this change in the larger society. The last few years have brought a major new dimension to these external influences: the enormous growth of the Internet/World Wide Web. The other aspect of change is *internal*. As computers become available, or potentially available, for schooling, they may be applied to perform a wide variety of functions. Depending on what those functions may be, there is a possibility of very profound change. The greatest uncertainty in predicting the impact of new technology lies in the difficulty of predicting the functions, especially the completely novel functions, to which it is applied (Nickerson, 1982). The growth of the World Wide Web and its still emerging but clearly major impact on commerce and intellectual exchange are a striking example of the unanticipated.

EXTERNAL INFLUENCES

Nearly as soon as the digital electronic computer was invented (circa 1945–1950), there was interest in applying computers to education. At that time, computers were exotic and expensive research devices, and little came of the efforts to apply computers in education (although some programs in educational use today date from that era). By 1980, the role of computers in the larger society had changed. Computers were becoming pervasive in the workplace and it was evident that there were and would continue to be many attractive job opportunities in computer-related work. This created a much more favorable climate for introducing computers into schools. There was widespread demand that they be introduced. Experiencing the impact of computers in the workplace, middle-class and professional parents wanted to make computer-related job opportunities available to their children through appropriate education and certainly wished that their children be prepared to meet emerging expectancies for at least minimal computer literacy (cf. R. E. Anderson, 1982). Those concerned for the welfare of less advantaged children did not wish to see them left behind either, despite those who raised doubts about the educational implications of the new technology (H. Levin & Romberg, 1983). A survey of teachers by the National Education Association showed that teachers also had favorable attitudes toward the introduction of computers into the schools (Norman, 1983).

In the 1980s, TV and print advertising campaigns by computer companies reinforced the idea that familiarity with computers is vital to one's child's future. It was not uncommon for PTAs to raise money to provide computers for their schools. The general climate of opinion was well represented by the U.S. National Commission on Excellence in Education (1983), which recommended that a semester of computer science become part of the core curriculum required of all secondary students. An Advanced Placement course in computer science was codified by the College Entrance Examination Board. Local school systems moved to integrate computers and computer applications throughout the curriculum (Wierzbicki, 1983), and the states began to mandate educational computing courses (Barbour & Editors of Electronic Learning, 1984). Laws were proposed to reward with tax benefits computer companies that donate computers to schools (Mace, 1983a, 1983b). Some colleges began to mandate that every student have a computer (Wierzbicki, 1984).

The initial wave of excitement over computers has passed, but providing computers for the schools is still popular. For example, grocery stores in many areas of the United States have conducted regular promotions for well over a decade in which vast quantities of grocery store receipts can be collected by schools and turned in for computer equipment. As of 1997, on the average, there was one computer for every 10 students in U.S. schools, with a range varying from 1–6 to 1–16 in various states (Coley et al., 1997); more are to be found in relatively affluent than in economically poorer schools. Under the Clinton administration, there were initiatives aimed at connecting every school to the Internet, subsidies for those connections via telephone service taxes, and other efforts to reduce the "digital divide" between rich and poor children.

However, the real significance of this phenomenon is unclear. Even though computers of reasonable power are becoming rather cheap by the standards of the workplace, they and their software remain expensive by the standards of financially impoverished schools. My experience circa 1990 with the "community advisory committee" concerned with computers for the Arlington County, Virginia, public schools is instructive, especially considering that Arlington is one of the most affluent communities in the country. It took 2 or 3 years to achieve the top priority goal of purchasing one classroom's supply of Macintosh computers for one (not each) of the three high schools in order to make it possible to teach the AP Computer Science with a Pascal compiler of reasonable speed. Merely replacing the antique and failing computers used to teach computer literacy classes and the like was an equally prolonged and gradual process because so little money was allocated for the purpose. Obviously, the ratio of computers to students remains low. It seems likely that most school systems will manage to provide the computers necessary to provide computer literacy and simple programing instruction. Very low cost computers are adequate for that purpose. Educational computing applications in which one or a few computers per classroom can be used meaningfully are also likely to be practical. In contrast, sophisticated applications of computers, including sophisticated instructional applications, tend to demand much more expensive machines. Although relatively cheap web computers are now being made, the demands of web browsers have also made many still-working computers obsolete.

The prevalence of computers in the larger society is bringing about redefinitions of traditional skills that have consequences for the curriculum. Obviously it is word processing, rather than simple typing, that has become the useful vocational skill, and the schools are attempting to provide appropriate experience. (At the same time, "keyboarding" has become a computer literacy skill now seen as appropriate for every student, making some degree of typing skill attractive to many who would not have acquired it before.) However, the time may be near when speech recognition technology will be good enough to displace keyboarding with dictation. Computer database search skills seem to be the obvious successor to more traditional instruction in the use of book indices and library card catalogs (which are, of course, vanishing as libraries become computerized). The growing use of the World Wide Web as an information resource places quite a premium on sophisticated information search and retrieval skills, such as the use of Boolean expressions.

As early as 1983, there was serious discussion of more profound changes in the college preparatory curriculum to reflect the impact of computer technology (Conference Board of the Mathematical Sciences, 1983). At all age levels, there is a concern for increased emphasis on learning what computations need to be performed and also on skill in approximating answers in order to verify the reasonableness of computational results—the skills emphasized by the ready availability of electronic aids to perform the computations themselves. Many such changes in the curriculum will be occurring without conscious awareness that they are attributable to computer technology: Commonsense feelings about what should be in the curriculum will be shifting as computer technology pervades the environment surrounding the schools. Such changes will be slow and conservative, with good reason. Because the older generations who use sophisticated computer tools for mathematics were educated originally to do those computations manually, nobody knows whether it is possible to learn to effectively use the computer tools without mastering the computations first, and there are no good ideas about how to teach direct use of the tools. It could be that comprehension of what sophisticated tools are doing requires prior personal experience with the detailed execution of those manipulations.

Already in the early 1980s, the potential implications of computers for the mathematics curriculum and the related issues and concerns were quite evident. The worry that use of calculators in schools might "rot the mind" emerged very early and led to numerous research studies on the subject. In the Derry and LaJoie volume (1993), the concept of using computational power to carry out low level aspects of tasks so that students can focus on developing higher level aspects and metacognitive skills was generalized widely beyond mathematics. The difference when one goes beyond mathematics is that the tools to execute the lower level aspects of other tasks, such as scientific reasoning, may not yet exist outside the toy worlds provided by the experimental educational programs.

Noneducational software developments are a major influence on the educational applications, and this is true not merely because of associated changes in the working world for which students must prepare. The very large investments associated with widespread, popular workplace applications of computers ultimately result in good, sophisticated user-friendly programs. Consequently, these applications, or slight modifications of them, will be the ones most readily available to schools.

Word processing has been an excellent example of this phenomenon. An enormous commercial investment went into the development of useful word processing facilities. The background provided by that investment made it possible to develop good word processing programs for microcomputers quite rapidly. Although such word processing programs were somewhat complex for instructional use with young children, subsequent modification into a useful educational tool, the *Bank Street Writer* (Kurland, 1983a, 1983b), for example, was quite rapid and relatively inexpensive. At one time, the *Bank Street Writer* had very high penetration of the school marketplace, but in 2000, it was no longer being sold. Most likely, it was replaced by the word processors that come bundled with most computers. Word processing is an attractive personal computer function for almost everyone. It rapidly emerged as the dominant use of personal computers (*Consumer Reports*, 1983). As of 1998 (Becker, 1999), word processing was the most frequent use of computers in classrooms as well, especially at the elementary school level. For young children, in particular, word processing offers the possibility of circumventing the very fine motor control demands of the physical writing process, a major barrier to both initial composition and later revision. More sophisticated extensions of word processing facilities that have also been successful as commercial products—spelling and grammatical checkers—are certainly attractive to teachers of writing as tools that can help to reduce the burden of paper correction. Although aids to the higher level aspects of writing—outlining and brainstorming programs—have been produced, none seems to have enjoyed a great level of success and popularity. This may have implications for educator's efforts to produce such tools (e.g., Salomon, 1993).

Database programs, equation solvers, and graphic generators are other examples of sophisticated software tools that have been developed for the commercial market but may be adaptable to various educational uses. By the early 1980s, exploration of the potential educational applications of such tools was an emerging trend (Barbour & Editors of Electronic Learning, 1984). The commercialization of the World Wide Web has put powerful market forces behind the development of search engines that are easier to use, so we can expect great improvements there that will be educationally useful.

Although there have been many benefits to the sophisticated tools that have been borrowed for educational use, there may be both a gloomy message and a somewhat arbitrary bias in what has happened. The long and expensive evolution of commercial tool software for the workplace (i.e., computer programs that can be used over and over again, day after day, by a very large number of users) does seem to carry a negative message about the prospects for the development of software for specifically instructional purposes. Presumably, each student user would use a given lesson only once, not over and over again, and the total population of potential courseware users is both smaller and less rich in financial resources than the population of tool users. Specifically educational software tools lie somewhere in between these two extremes. It is likely, for economic reasons, that the quality of specifically educational software will be significantly inferior to the quality of generic computer tools. In the early 1980s, this reality had a rapid impact on the uses to which school put the computers they were purchasing. The limitations of the computers and of the instructional software available for them tended to shift usage away from intended uses in subject matter instruction and toward computer literacy instruction and instruction in the use of computer-based tools (Barbour & Editors of Electronic Learning, 1984; Center for the Social Organization of Schools, 1983a, 1983b; Sherman, 1983; Wright, 1982; Wujcik, 1984). This was still true in the year 2000.

INTERNAL CHANGES

The nature of the internal changes to schooling that computers will create depends greatly on the uses to which they are put. What is the range of possible or likely uses? Consider each of several major uses and their potential impact: computers as a new subject of instruction, computers as instructional devices, computers as tools naturally integrated into such activities as writing or science laboratories, and computers as tools in support of the teacher's teaching activities.

Computers as a New Subject of Instruction

For several reasons, in the early 1980s, many believed that the introduction of computers into the schools would, in and of itself, bring about significant change. There was a transitory period in which one heard speculation about radical changes to student and teacher roles because it often seemed that some of the students knew more about computers than did the teachers, so that teachers might have to defer to their students' expertise. One does not hear such speculations so often today. It did not take long for specialist teachers for computer-related subjects to emerge. By now, some of those early expert children have had time to become teachers themselves. Besides, the fabled phenomenon of the child computer whiz proved to be rare. A project at Bank Street in New York City, long a favorable environment for the emergence of child prodigies of all kinds, failed to find any truly expert children (Kurland, Mawbry, & Cahir, 1984). Studies of computer learning showed that many students learn as distressingly little about programing as they do about other subjects (Linn, 1985; Mayer, 1982; Pea, 1983, 1987; Pea & Kurland 1984, 1987; Pea, Kurland, & Hawkins, 1987; Soloway, Ehrlich, Bonar, & Greenspan, 1982). Computer programing is quite a demanding subject (Kurland, Clement, Mawby, & Pea, 1987).

Still, whether because it is a useful way to accommodate to expert children or simply because computers were scarce, computers became known for promoting independent group work in an "activity center" while the teacher might provide instruction to another group of students. An early study showed that many teachers liked the fact that computers seemed to be conducive to cooperative group problem solving and learning; many seemed to be more interested in this social effect than they were in computing itself (Sheingold, 1981).

However, group learning activities should not be regarded as an inevitable consequence of the educational use of computers, even though continuing scarcity is likely to exert a force in that direction. The use of such group instructional strategies is a cultural matter. Group work is a fairly common instructional strategy, but attitudes regarding its desirability vary considerably. If one highly values individual performance, as many in this country do, then the orderly classroom scene of each student working separately is preferred. Some would certainly like to see each student equipped with a computer: In 1985, Apple so equipped some experimental classrooms, going so far as to provide each student with an additional home computer. Perhaps this vision is financially unrealistic. Alternatively, one computer could be used to instruct an entire class as a single group, in a rather traditional way. As of 2000, this was being done in some military "electronic classrooms." In brief, no massive impact of computers on the social structure of schooling should be expected. Computer instruction will be modified to suit the demands of the school and classroom culture into which it is being introduced. At most, it may serve as a catalyst for change in unstable situations, where many already want to make a change in the style of instruction.

In the early 1980s, there was great interest in programing as a subject of instruction, and many had high expectations for widespread cognitive benefits of programing experience (Nickerson, 1983; Papert, 1980, 1987). That enthusiasm has faded. One problem was that there had been little time to evolve effective ways of teaching programing (Mayer, 1982). It turned out that many students, and many of their teachers, did not master key concepts of programing (e.g., recursion) that were thought to be potentially important for general cognition (J. R. Anderson, Farrell & Sauers, 1984; Bayman & Mayer, 1983; Kurland & Pea, 1985; Linn, 1985; Pea, 1983, 1987). It began to seem that instruction must systematically identify and develop key ideas, and that students may need help in making the connections between representations of reality on the computer screen and reality itself. These issues remain open and lively.

The broad claims for the cognitive value of learning programing seemed to have faded by 1991. But perhaps their echoes were evident in the high hopes, expressed by many chapters in Derry and LaJoie (1993), that computers will help students to make explicit and to reflect on their own thought processes, in other words, that computers will help to develop metacognitive skills. To the extent that the computer does make thought processes explicit, students' thinking about their own thinking likely will be captured by the computer metaphor, as scientific cognitive psychology has been. This may provide a foundation for educating students to be more cognitively effective, but it will also require some education in the limits of the metaphor.

Computers as Instructional Devices

This is a complex topic because it has so many different aspects. There is a continuum of possibilities that can be ordered roughly according to the complexity of the programing effort required to produce them.

Drill and Practice. This was the first major instructional use of computers, and it may well remain the dominant use. Computers are widely used for remedial drill and practice, despite considerable criticism of this use.

One important reason for the early dominance is the fact that the programing of such activities is relatively easy and undemanding of creativity. The first application of any technology is likely to be to perform functions that one was already performing in other ways. It may be that teachers find computerized drill and practice to be an attractive aid in their work, relieving them of some dreary and demanding efforts such as the checking of papers, the maintaining and verifying of many students' attention during practice sessions, and so on.

For students who seem to need extra practice, or special practice, the computer alternative may be particularly attractive and cost-effective. This use of computers in schools has been subsidized by federal Title I (compensatory education) funds. Although there were early expressions of the belief that computers are intrinsically motivating, it was soon appreciated that there may be important individual differences in reactions to computers and variations in the motivational value of different forms of interaction with computers (Malone, 1980, 1981). It is not obvious that interaction with a computer will be as motivationally effective as the concern and attention of a human teacher. Most experimental evaluations of computer instruction profit from the novelty of the computer and the brevity of interactions with it. To consider one extreme, it is very clear that adults who spend long hours at repetitive tasks do not enjoy the experience; children are no more likely to do so.

Traditional Computer-Assisted Instruction. This category corresponds to somewhat more advanced instructional programing than is required for drill and practice and includes the much maligned electronic page turner. Such software presents concepts and content in a relatively straightforward manner. The computer offers management of the student's study efforts through pacing and interspersed questions. In the more sophisticated variants, the computer may respond differentially to student responses with preprogramed responses of its own. This mode ranges from mere computerization of a book to more substantial investment in the empirical investigation of probable student responses and appropriate instructional responses to them. This can be an effective way to present instruction; when the curriculum remains constant, it is typically faster but no more effective than traditional instruction (Orlansky & String, 1979). However, Kulick (1994) estimated the average effect size of such computer tutoring to be about one half standard deviation improvement. The development of CBT often involves a reanalysis and improvement of the curriculum, and the time savings may result in more instructional coverage. Except in situations where it is important to be able to provide instruction or training to small numbers of individuals at arbitrary times or in situations in which student or trainee time is highly valuable, it is not obvious that the production of such instruction is worthwhile. Prolonged, isolated interaction with a computer is likely to be less attractive than the more social atmosphere of the classroom. And young children require supervision from someone to ensure their safety. If only for this reason, the notion that computerized instruction of this kind could lead to greatly enhanced educational productivity and/or the withering away of traditional schools and classrooms is unrealistic, especially in a society in which it is normal for both parents to leave the home for work. In fact, recent survey results show very little use of such CBT in the classroom (Becker, 1999). The current rush to web-based instruction for older students—college students, military trainees, corporate employees—is a major new development that may bring the use of standard CBI to levels never before seen.

Simulations.   From the outset, simulations became a popular form of educational software. They make environments safe and accessible to students that would otherwise be inaccessible. They make it possible to experience an approximation of phenomena that otherwise might merely be talked about. They represent a unique contribution of computers to the educational process, or at least a contribution that would be difficult to duplicate by other means. They open up new possibilities in teaching, and a great deal of creativity has gone into the creation of simulations. Often simulations are a central component of more elaborate and sophisticated instructional systems to be discussed later.

To be effective, simulations must be integrated with a larger curricular context, whether it is also computerized or realized by the teacher in the classroom. Sheingold, Kane, and Endreweit (1983) found that successful curricular integration was rare: Often simulation software was simply played with in the guise of "computer literacy." At present, this situation continues. Unless someone makes a major investment in revising standard texts to include and refer to such adjunct facilities, it is unlikely that they will be widely used. Most teachers (admittedly not the outstanding few) need supporting suggestions from teacher manuals that point out the existence of these additional facilities and describe how to use them effectively. Even with such revisions, the logistical problems of bringing in equipment, having the right software available at the right time, and so on, can present formidable barriers to use. It seems likely that the computer would have to be a permanent feature of the classroom to make such uses likely and frequent. Additional capabilities (e.g., the possibility for a teacher to key in the topic of a planned lesson, to ascertain that there is available software relevant to that topic, and to have instant access to the software) would seem to be necessary in order to support these applications. Nearly 20 years after I first pointed this out (Chipman & Butler, 1983), we still do not see such facilities available to teachers, although today there is no question of their technical feasibility. Stronger evidence of educational value than exists now will be required to convince anyone to make these investments. Consequently, it seems most likely that such applications will be effectively realized in specialized courses in mathematics or science, where a sufficient density of computer applications may be developed to make the use of the computer a regular part of the classroom routine and to justify the constant presence of computer facilities.

Intelligent Computer-Assisted Instruction

In the early 1980s, the brightest promise of computers in education seemed to be offered by programs that employ artificial intelligence techniques (J. R. Anderson, Boyle, & Reiser, 1985; Sleeman & Brown, 1982; Wenger, 1987). The earliest artificially intelligent tutoring systems with the possibility of practical educational use were then being developed (J. R. Anderson, 1984): the LISP Tutor (J. R. Anderson & Reiser, 1985), which began to be used in courses at Carnegie-Mellon University, and the Geometry Tutor (J. R. Anderson, Boyle, & Yost, 1985), which was soon to see a practical trial in a Pittsburgh high school (Schofield, 1995; Schofield, Evans-Rhodes, & Huber, 1990). The attraction of such systems has been the prospect of providing each student with individualized tutorial interaction, approximating what an individual human tutor might provide. In addition to academic tutors of mathematics and programing and scientific reasoning, tutors of maintenance diagnosis skills—a practical application of interest to military research sponsors—have received considerable development effort (Gott, 1989). In one of the most thorough and careful evaluations of an artificially intelligent tutor yet done, the SHERLOCK troubleshooting tutor was found to be impressively effective (Gott, 1989; Gott & Lesgold, 2000). The promise of intelligent tutoring systems may be coming to fruition, but it is happening very slowly. As of 1991, with the exception of the programing tutors used by Anderson in courses for which he personally had instructional responsibility at Carnegie-Mellon University (CMU), intelligent tutors remained research and development experiments and demonstrations; none was in widespread use for instruction or training. By the year 2000, Anderson and his associates had built several tutors for high school mathematics. The first year algebra word problem tutor has been used by thousands of students, with very positive evaluation results (Koedinger, Anderson, Hadley, & Mark, 1995). A company, CarnegieLearning, has been hatched by CMU to market these tutors, but they are not yet in truly wide use. A few intelligent tutors have been built for practical training use in the military (e.g., McCarthy, Pacheco, Banta, Wayne, & Coleman, 1994) and industry (Lesgold & Nahemow, 2001) and research and development demonstrations of complex military training applications are becoming more numerous. A physics homework problem tutor is being built in a collaboration between Kurt VanLehn of the University of Pittsburgh and physics professors at the Naval Academy. Still, the practical implementation of this instructional technology has been very slow.

In its complete form, an artificially intelligent tutoring system is a very complex program incorporating many features of less complex forms of instructional computing. At its core, there is likely to be a simulation if the tutor is teaching about the operation of some dynamic system—be it the economy or the circulatory system or Newtonian physics or the operation of a ship's steam power plant. Typically, a tutor incorporates an expert system so that it has the capability to solve problems in the domain of the tutor in a flexible variety of ways, to match the many correct solutions that a student might have. Like a human tutor, an artificial tutor must know the subject matter. A tutor must have pedagogical knowledge and strategies to guide interaction with the tutee. A central concept of the intelligent tutoring approach is that instructional interaction should be sensitively adapted to the needs of the individual student, determined by detailed estimates of the state of student knowledge at the moment of the instructional interaction. This last feature, modeling the student's state of knowledge, is probably the most challenging task that faces the builder of an intelligent tutoring system, and it is likely to require the greatest online computational power.

Each intelligent tutor incorporates what is likely to be the first attempt at a detailed and complete cognitive theory of the knowledge in the domain of the tutor. Intelligent tutoring entails a serious and continuing investment in cognitive research on the nature of the skill being taught (cf. Schraagen, Chipman, & Shalin, 2000). Today there is confidence that the quality of the knowledge or skill representation underlying intelligent tutoring is critical. It is less certain whether there is a significant effect of a detailed student model and the associated tailoring of instructional moves. This is an issue for current research. It is an issue complicated by the lack of direct implications from the student model to instructional acts: There are many options that must be considered and empirically evaluated.

Intelligent tutoring systems offer boundless opportunities for instructional research that could never have been done before. The instructional actions of an automated tutor can be programed and controlled in the way that the actions of human tutors never can be. The actions of the student can be tracked and recorded in a detail that would not otherwise be possible, although sophisticated analysis techniques are needed to assimilate and make sense of such unprecedented masses of data. Today there are many design decisions involved in building any artificially intelligent tutor; in most cases, there is no research basis for the decisions. Exploration of the consequences of different pedagogical decisions is a wide open area for research.

In addition to the multidisciplinary technical complexity of building true artificially intelligent tutoring systems, and the associated costs, intelligent tutoring systems have proven to be controversial in several ways. Some people are resistant to the idea that their cognitive skills—whether in mathematics or in tactical decision making—can be analyzed. The didactic style of the Anderson style tutor is out of educational fashion, especially in the education research community. Discovery environments and experiences are in, despite little evidence for their effectiveness. Researchers such as Lepper (Lepper, Woolverton, Mumme, & Gurtner, 1993) have questioned the extent to which human tutors can actually be emulated by artificial systems, especially the affective aspects of human tutoring. They rightly pointed out that computers would have difficulty interpreting such data as the tutee's facial expression, but grant the possibility that a computer might use alternative indicators. (Furthermore, it is highly probable that neural net technology could enable computers to interpret students' facial expressions.) Still, they wondered whether an effective affective response to the student could be generated by the computer. The point is well-taken, but researchers already know that intelligent tutors can be well-received by students (Schofield et al, 1990) and can be highly effective instructionally (J. R. Anderson, Boyle, Corbett, & Lewis, 1990; J. R. Anderson, Conrad, & Corbett, 1989; Gott, 1989, 1995). Perhaps greater attention to the affective dimension of instructional interaction will improve the effectiveness of artificially intelligent tutors. On the other hand, students may not expect or require affective sensitivity from a computer tutor.

At present, Anderson is talking about intelligent tutors that do "high-density" sensing: tracking visual attention, recognizing faces and facial expressions. This is all in the range of technical feasibility, although expensive and demanding of computational resources. The work of researchers who are studying the linguistic details of human tutorial interaction for the purpose of emulating it (Di Eugenio, Moore, & Paolucci, 1997; Fox, 1993; Freedman, 1996; Graesser, Person, & Magliano, 1995; Hume, Michael, Rovick, & Evens, 1996; Littman, 1990; Merrill, Reiser, Ranney, & Trafton, 1992; Moore, Lemaire, & Rosenblum, 1996; Rosé, 1997; Rosé, Di Eugenio, & Moore, 1999) has also led to considerable advances in understanding the principles of tutorial interaction, as contrasted to the ad hoc character of earlier systems that Lepper et. al. (1993) criticized.

Computers as Tools for Learners

In the early 1980s, it seemed evident that computerized changes in the way writing, laboratory experimentation, and drafting were being done outside the school would gradually transfer, without much drama, into the way that these skills are taught within schools. The possibility of using word processing computers for writing instruction coincided with rising concern over the neglect of writing instruction in U.S. schools (Edwards, 1982; Frederiksen & Dominic, 1981). Little writing instruction existed, but there was widespread public support for a major reform of writing instruction. It seemed possible that a computerized approach to writing instruction might emerge as the primary mode of that reform. Computerized prompting of the writing process, word processing support, and correction facilities of varying sophistication were already available as likely elements of an instructional package. Innovative computer-based approaches to writing instruction were being developed for the elementary school classroom, notably Bolt, Beranek, and Newman's project Quill (Bruce & Rubin, 1993; Collins, Bruce, & Rubin, 1982; Rubin & Bruce, 1985). These involved the use of the computer in such classroom projects as the production of a newspaper, the recording of scientific data, or sharing of movie reviews written by individual students. Levin's experimental project emphasized the development of writing as out-of-context communication by putting students in San Diego into network communication with students in Alaska (J. A. Levin, Boruta, & Vasconcellos, 1982). Such innovations are compatible with some styles of classroom organization and not with others; it seemed likely that they would be adopted in places where the style of classroom organization was favorable to them and that they would be ignored elsewhere.

Many experiments have been undertaken, but as of 1990, Becker (1990) was still reporting that programing and computer literacy dominated secondary school use of computers, whereas drill and practice in basic skills dominated elementary school use. Significant use of applications—word processors, databases, spreadsheets, graphics programs—was still being reported as a recent phenomenon. In contrast, the picture had changed substantially by 1998 (Becker, 1999). Table 2.1 shows the computer use reported by a nationally representative sample of teachers.

Although drill and practice and similar learning games are still common uses at the elementary school level, word processing and associated "library research" analogues, such as the use of CD-ROM reference materials and the World Wide Web (WWW), have become prominent. As of 1998 (Becker, Ravitz, & Wong, 1999), frequent use of computers was most common in English classes at both the middle school level (28%) and high school level (19%). Business (18%) and vocational (13%) classes also accounted for a large percentage of the classes in which computers were frequently used. *Other than drills and learning games, computer-based instructional programs are not even mentioned.* The use of various kinds of tool software is quite common. *"Programing" has disappeared from the recent reports;* "computer skills" now seems to mean the use of tool software. On the other hand, 24% of SAT-takers from the high school class of 1996 did report some computer programing experience (Coley, Cradler, & Engel, 1997). Earlier I had ex-

TABLE 2.1
Percent of Teachers Having Their Students Use Different Types of Software by Grade Level

	Word Processing	CD-ROM Reference	WWW	Games/ Drills	Simulations	Graphics	Spreadsheet/ Database	Multimedia Authoring	E-mail
Elementary	65%	54%	26%	63%	33%	26%	10%	14%	7%
Middle	44%	32%	26%	21%	18%	19%	16%	8%	6%
High	45%	29%	34%	11%	21%	20%	20%	8%	8%
All teachers	50%	36%	29%	28%	23%	21%	16%	9%	7%

pected that computer use in math and science classes would be more prominent than it is, largely because of the investments being made in educational software for these subjects. Frequent computer use is common in math classes at the middle school level but not at the high school level, and math teachers are particularly unlikely to use the Internet (Becker, 1999). Some high school math teachers use skill drill software, and a single successful program with more challenging goals, the Geometry Sketchpad, accounts for much of their computer use (Becker et al., 1999). An interesting development, circa 1991, was educators' great interest in using and teaching a new form of composition called hypermedia. This trend was not yet evident in the early 1980s, although both the general concept of hypermedia and some specific implementations have a rather long history. As of 1998, it remained a relatively uncommon use. Perhaps burgeoning job opportunies in Web site authoring will change that.

Computers as Tools to Support Teaching Activities

Reviewing all the possible ways in which computer technology might have an impact on education in the early 1980s, we (Chipman & Butler, 1983, 1985) realized there was a major, neglected possibility. Computers might be tools for teachers, rather than tools for or teachers of students. There was little discussion then of such uses. We suspected that this reflected the low value society places on teachers: Just as their pay is relatively low, little thought is given to providing teachers with tools to facilitate their work. The computers purchased for schools were and are thought of as being for the children, not for the teachers. This seemed strategically unfortunate. Teachers with access to computers as tools to facilitate their daily work—in preparing worksheets or keeping records—are more likely to appreciate the potential value of computers for their students and to think of ways in which the computer can be incorporated in their classroom teaching. Early on, personal computers were somewhat expensive for teachers to purchase, but by 1998, 80% of teachers had a home computer (Becker et al., 1999). Not surprisingly, as of 1998 (Becker, 1999), teachers who had desktop computers at school with access to the Internet or Internet access at home were much more likely to use the Internet as a teaching resource.

SUMMARY PREDICTIONS

It seems likely that classrooms will continue to look strikingly similar to the way they look now. Instruction in computer skills has been added to the curriculum without significant changes in the organization or appearance of the school. Of course, there are computers in the schools to support such teaching, mostly in specially designated classrooms or labora-tory facilities. As the years pass, replacing and maintaining the necessary equipment becomes an increasing problem, even for relatively affluent districts. Instruction in or with computers does not automatically bring about radical change; it has been and can continue to be assimilated to the dominant model of teaching, whatever that happens to be in a particu-lar school and community. Today, for example, there is a strong associa-tion between a teacher's use of the Internet and belief in a constructivist philosophy of education (Becker, 1999). Teachers are just beginning to publish papers about how the Internet can be used; little real research on its educational impact is yet to be found. But certainly, wiring the schools and making it possible for students to touch the Internet is not going to turn many student frogs into princes, any more than mere exposure to LOGO led to deep mathematical understanding: Effective use of the Internet as an information resource is quite demanding of cognitive and meta-cognitive skills.

In the early 1980s, it seemed likely that the juxtaposition of the desire for curriculum reform in high priority areas such as mathematics, science, and writing with the advent of relatively affordable computer technology would result in investments in curriculum developments that integrate the use of the computer. This has happened at the research and development level. NSF Science Education Directorate and other sources of support have fi-nanced, for example, the development of intelligent tutors that relate to most of the high school mathematics and programing curriculum, as well as to some important topics in science. In addition, Department of Defense investments in tools for building tutors of equipment maintenance skills could be applied to vocational education (cf. Behavioral Technology Lab-oratory, 1988; Munro, 1994; Munro et al., 1997; Towne, 1987). Yet, it is questionable whether the potential of these technological advances will be realized in widespread school use. Expense remains a major barrier, partic-ularly for intelligent tutoring technology. The required computers are much less expensive than they once were, at less than one quarter the cost of comparable computing power in the early 1980s, but their cost is still, it seems, too much in relation to what society is willing to invest in education.

Because the application of technology to education is lagging its pene-tration elsewhere in society (not leading as it was in the first attempts at computer instruction in the 1960s), the prognosis is more favorable than it was the first time around. But the slow pace of change since the early 1980s must make us more pessimistic than we were then. As predicted in the ear-lier versions of this chapter, school use of computers has come to be domi-nated by the use of general purpose computer tools designed for business and other adult use. As such tools have become easier to use, there seems to be less felt need for special child-oriented versions.

Expense is not the only problem to be overcome. Thorough revision of the curriculum is needed to integrate technology effectively. Even the most substantial examples of technological innovations, such as Anderson's LISP Tutor or algebra word problem tutor, do not teach the entire course. Isolated simulations or other special activities, however attractive when examined in isolation, are even more problematic. Without curriculum revision that integrates them and points to them in the teacher guides, the logistical difficulties of integrating such activities into the curriculum will discourage most teachers. As the novelty value declines, the use of these activities in the belief that they provide a valuable "computer literacy" experience will decline.

It seems possible, although not quite as likely as it did in the early 1980s, that inexpensive computer facilities will be used increasingly for drill and practice, eventually becoming an unnoticed change in the nature of the "seatwork" that now occupies so much of student time. Built-in correction and monitoring features may make this time somewhat more instructionally effective. In contrast, I cannot foresee that computers will take over a great deal of instructional delivery. Because human beings are very social beings, and because young children in particular require human attention and human supervision, there will be great resistance to the idea of children spending large portions of their time in isolated interaction with a computer. Lepper et al. (1993) may have exaggerated the extent to which the unique qualities of human interaction are essential for every instructional interaction, but at a more global level, they are certainly correct.

For essentially social and emotional reasons, it seems unlikely that large increases in the "productivity" of teachers (cf. Melmed, 1984) are either desirable or possible. Therefore, the prospects of reduced human labor costs are not there to justify large expenditures on computer equipment and correspondingly large research and development investments to produce high quality instructional software. The promise of technology lies primarily in the prospects of improved student achievement, either through its direct effects or through a shift in the allocation of teacher resources to students most in need of individual help (Schofield, 1995; Schofield et al., 1990). Does society care enough about the quality of education to make big investments? Unfortunately, the evidence suggests that it does not. For this reason, it seems likely now, as it seemed likely in the early '80's, that the primary impact of computer technology on education will come through the adaptation to educational uses of sophisticated computer tools developed in the commercial marketplace for adult users. As mass production brings the price of these tools downward, they will become more common in the schools.

This prediction could be wrong. The view through the silicon chip is clouded. But the challenge to would-be revolutionaries is clear. The challenge is to develop innovative instruction that is actually used in the nation's schools and has a significant positive effect on the learning of a significant number of students. This is a challenge, however, that cannot be met without substantial subsidies from the federal government, subsidies both for the work of researchers and developers and for the schools that implement the technology (as drill and practice software has been subsidized by Title I).

ACKNOWLEDGMENTS

This chapter draws heavily on two prior works entitled, "Gazing into the Silicon Chip: The Impact of Microcomputers on Teaching and Learning." Chipman and Butler (1983) was prepared in October 1983 at the request of OECD-CERI to give a U.S. perspective on educational computing. At that time, Chipman was Assistant Director for Learning and Development of the National Institute of Education, and Butler worked with her as the primary person responsible for research on educational technology. In 1985, an updated version was made available as Learning Technology Center Report No. 85.2.3 of Peabody College of Vanderbilt University. A third, significantly updated version appeared in a discussion chapter in Derry and LaJoie (1993) called "Gazing Once More into the Silicon Chip: Who's Revoluntionary Now?" Chipman now manages basic research in cognitive science, as well as projects in applied training technology, at the Office of Naval Research. The opinions expressed herein are the personal opinions of the author and do not necessarily represent the official policy or position of the Office of Naval Research.

REFERENCES

Alexander, L. (1991). *America 2000: An education strategy.* Washington, DC: U.S. Department of Education.

Anderson, J. R. (1984, January). *Proposal for the Development of Intelligent Computer-based Tutors for High-School Mathematics.* Carnegie-Mellon University.

Anderson, J. R., Boyle, C. F., Corbett, A., & Lewis, M. (1990). Cognitive modeling and intelligent tutoring. *Artificial Intelligence, 42,* 7–49.

Anderson, J. R., Boyle, C. F., & Reiser, B. J. (1985). Intelligent tutoring systems. *Science, 228,* 456–462.

Anderson, J. R., Boyle, C. F., & Yost, G. (1985). The geometry tutor. In *Proceedings of the International Joint Conference on Artificial Intelligence—85* (pp. 1–7). Menlo Park, CA: American Association for Artificial Intelligence.

Anderson, J. R., Conrad, F. G., & Corbett, A. T. (1989). Skill acquisition and the LISP Tutor. *Cognitive Science, 13,* 467–505.

Anderson, J. R., Farrell, R., & Sauers, R. (1984). Learning to program in LISP. *Cognitive Science, 8*, 87–129.

Anderson, J. R., & Reiser, B. J. (1985). The LISP tutor. *Byte, 10*, 159–178.

Anderson, R. E. (1982). National computer literacy, 1980. In R. J. Seidel, R. E. Anderson, & B. Hunter (Eds.), *Computer literacy: Issues and directions for 1985* (pp.). New York: Academic Press.

Barbour, A., & Editors of Electronic Learning. (1984, October). Computing in America's classrooms 1984—EL's fourth annual survey of the states. *Electronic Learning*, pp. 39–44.

Bayman, P., & Mayer, R. E. (1983). Diagnosis of beginning programmer's misconceptions of BASIC computer programming statements. *Communications of the Association for Computing Machinery, 26*, 667–670.

Becker, H. J. (1990, April). *Computer use in United States schools: 1989 An initial report of U.S. participation in the I.E.A.* Paper presented at the annual meeting of the American Educational Research Association, Boston, MA.

Becker, H. J. (1999, February). *Internet use by teachers: Conditions of professional use and teacher-directed student use. Teaching, learning and computing: 1998 national survey* (Rep. No. 1). Center for Research on Information Technology and Organizations, University of California, Irvine.

Becker, H. J., Ravitz, J. L., & Wong, Y. T. (1999, November). *Teacher and teacher-directed student use of computers and software. 1998 national survey* (Rep. No. 3). Center for Research on Information Technology and Organizations, University of California, Irvine.

Behavioral Technology Laboratories. (1988). *The intelligent maintenance training system.* Redondo Beach, CA: Behavioral Technology Laboratories, University of Southern California.

Boyer, E. L. (1983). *High school: A Carnegie foundation report on secondary education.* New York: Harper & Row.

Bruce, B. C., & Rubin, A. D. (1993). *Electronic Quills: A situated evaluation of using computers for writing in classrooms.* Hillsdale, NJ: Lawrence Erlbaum.

Center for Social Organization of Schools. (1983a). *School uses of microcomputers: Report from a national survey* (Issue No. 1). Baltimore, MD: Center for Social Organization of Schools, Johns Hopkins University.

Center for Social Organization of Schools. (1983b). *School uses of microcomputers: Report from a national survey* (Issue No. 2). Baltimore, MD: Center for Social Organization of Schools, Johns Hopkins University.

Chipman, S. F. (1993). Gazing once more into the silicon chip: Who's revolutionary now? In S. Derry & S. Lajoie (Eds.), *Computers as cognitive tools* (pp. 341–367). Hillsdale, NJ: Lawrence Erlbaum Associates.

Chipman, S. F., & Butler, P. A. (1983). *Gazing into the silicon chip: The impact of microcomputers on teaching and learning* (Unpublished paper, October 1983, written at the request of OECD-CERI). Washington, DC: National Institute of Education.

Chipman, S. F., & Butler, P. A. (1985). *Gazing into the silicon chip: The impact of microcomputers on teaching and learning* (Learning Technology Center Tech. Rep. No. 85.2.3). Nashville, TN: Peabody College of Vanderbilt University.

Coley, R. J., Cradler, J., & Engel, P. K. (1997). *Computers and classrooms: The status of technology in U.S. Schools.* Policy Information Report. Princeton, NJ: Educational Testing Service.

Collins, A., Bruce, B. C., & Rubin, A. D. (1982). Microcomputer-based writing activities for the upper elementary grades. In C. R. Vest, F. W. Scanland, F. B. Withrow, H. J. Clark, E. L. Shriver, N. Voke, & M. S. Brown (Ed.), *Proceedings of the Fourth International Learning Technology Congress and Exposition* (pp. 134–140). Warrenton, VA: Society for Applied Learning Technology.

Conference Board of the Mathematical Sciences. (1983). *The mathematical sciences curriculum K–12: What is still fundamental and what is not.* Report to the National Science Board Commission on Pre-college Education in Mathematics, Science and Technology. Washington, DC: Conference Board of the Mathematical Sciences.

Derry, S., & Lajoie, S. (Eds.). (1993). *Computers as cognitive tools.* Hillsdale, NJ: Lawrence Erlbaum Associates.

Di Eugenio, B., Moore, J. D., & Paolucci, M. (1997). Learning features that predict cue usage, ACL-EACL97. In *Proceedings of the 35th Annual Meeting of the Association for Computational Linguistics, 1997,* pp. 80–87. Madrid, Spain. New Brunswick, NJ: Association for Computational Linguistics.

Edwards, K. (1982). Problems related to the teaching of writing in the public schools. In B. Cronnell & J. Michael (Eds.), *Writing: Policies, problems, and possibilities.* Los Alamitos, CA: SWRL Educational Research and Development Center.

Fox, B. A. (1993). *The Human Tutorial Dialogue Project: Issues in the design of instructional systems.* Hillsdale, NJ: Lawrence Erlbaum Associates.

Frederiksen, C. H., & Dominic, J. F. (Eds.). (1981). *Writing: The nature, development, and teaching of written communication. Volume 2: Writing, Process, Development and Communication.* Hillsdale, NJ: Lawrence Erlbaum Associates.

Freedman, R. (1996). *Interaction of discourse planning, instructional planning, and dialogue management in an interactive tutoring system.* Unpublished doctoral dissertation, Northwestern University.

Gott, S. P. (1989). Apprenticeship instruction for real-world tasks: The coordination of procedures, mental models and strategies. In E. Z. Rothkopf (Ed.), *Review of research in education* (Vol. 15, pp. 97–169). Washington, DC: American Educational Research Association.

Gott, S. P. (1995). *Tutoring for transfer of competence.* Brooks AFB,TX: Air Force Armstrong Lab, Human Resources Directorate. (ERIC Document Reproduction Service No. ED382817)

Gott, S. P., & Lesgold, A. M. (2000). Competence in the workplace: How cognitive performance models and situation instruction can accelerate skill acquisition. In R. Glaser (Ed.), *Advances in instructional psychology* (pp. 239–327). Hillsdale, NJ: Lawrence Erlbaum Associates.

Graesser, A. C., Person, N. K., & Magliano, J. P. (1995). Collaborative dialogue patterns in naturalistic one-to-one tutoring. *Applied Cognitive Psychology, 9*(6), 495–522.

How our readers are using computers. (1983, September). *Consumer Reports, 48*(9), 470–471.

Hume, G., Michael, J., Rovick, A., & Evens, M. (1996). Hinting as a tactic in one-on-one tutoring. *Journal of the Learning Sciences, 5*(1), 23–47.

Koedinger, K. R., Anderson, J. R., Hadley, W. H., & Mark, M. (1995). Intelligent tutoring goes to school in the big city. In J. Greer (Ed.), *Artificial intelligence in education, 1995* (pp. 421–428). Charlottesville, VA: Association for the Advancement of Computing in Education.

Kulick, J. A. (1994). Meta-analytic studies of findings on computer-based instruction. In E. L. Baker & H. F. O'Neil (Eds.), *Technology assessment in education and training* (pp. 9–33). Hillsdale, NJ: Lawrence Erlbaum Associates.

Kurland, D. M. (1983a, January). *Educational software tools: The rationale behind the development of the* Bank Street Writer. The Conference on Writing Through Technology, Stonebridge, MA.

Kurland, D. M. (1983b, April). *Software for the classroom* (Tech. Rep. No. 15). New York: Center for Children and Technology, Bank Street College.

Kurland, D. M., Clement, C. A., Mawby, R., & Pea, R. D. (1987). Mapping the cognitive demands of learning to program. In R. D. Pea & K. Sheingold (Eds.), *Mirrors of minds: Patterns of experience in educational computing* (pp. 103–127). Norwood, NJ: Ablex.

Kurland, D. M., Mawbry, R., & Cahir, N. (1984, April). *The development of programming expertise in adults and children.* Paper presented at the annual meeting of the American Educational Research Association, New Orleans.

Kurland, D. M., & Pea, R. (1985). Children's mental models of recursive LOGO programs. *Journal of Educational Computing Research, 1,* 235–243.

Lepper, M. R., Woolverton, M., Mumme, D. L., & Gurtner, J.-L. (1993). Motivational techniques of expert human tutors: Lessons for the design of computer-based tutors. In S. P. Lajoie & S. J. Derry, (Eds.), *Computers as cognitive tools* (pp. 75–106). Hillsdale, NJ: Lawrence Erlbaum Associates.

Lesgold, A., & Nahemow, M. (2001). Tools to assist learning by doing: Achieving and assessing efficient technology for learning. In D. Klahr & S. Carver, *Cognition and instruction: 25 years of progress* (pp. 307–346). Hillsdale, NJ: Lawrence Erlbaum Associates.

Levin, H., & Romberg, R. W. (1983, February). *The educational implications of high technology*. Institute for Research on Educational Finance and Governance, Stanford University.

Levin, J. A., Boruta, M., & Vasconcellos, M. T. (1982). Microcomputer-based environments for writing: A writer's assistant. In A. C. Wilkinson (Ed.), *Classroom computers and cognitive science* (pp. 219–232). New York: Academic Press.

Linn, M. C. (1985). The cognitive consequences of programming instruction in classrooms. *Educational Researcher, 14,* 14–29.

Littman, D. C. (1990). *Strategies for tutoring multiple bugs.* Unpublished doctoral dissertation, Yale University.

Mace, S. (1983a). Firms continue computer giveaway. *Infoworld, 5*(38).

Mace, S. (1983b). Road to U.S. computers in schools paved with bills. *Infoworld, 5*(39).

Malone, T. W. (1980). *What makes things fun to learn? A study of intrinsically motivating computer games.* Palo Alto, CA: Xerox Palo Alto Research Center.

Malone, T. W. (1981). Toward a theory of intrinsically motivating instruction. *Cognitive Science, 4,* 333–369.

Mayer, R. E. (1982, October). *Diagnosis and remediation of computer programming skill for creative problem solving.* Final Report to the National Institute of Education. University of California at Santa Barbara.

McCarthy, J. E., Pacheco, S., Banta, H. G., Wayne, J. L., & Coleman, D. S. (1994, November). *The Radar System Controller Intelligent Training Aid.* Paper presented at the 16th Interservice/Industry Training Systems and Education Conference, Orlando, FL.

Melmed, A. S. (1984). Educational productivity: The teacher and technology. *T.H.E. (Technological Horizons in Education) Journal, 11,* 78–82.

Merrill, D. C., Reiser, B. J., Ranney, M., & Trafton, J. G. (1992). Effective tutoring techniques: Comparison of human tutors and intelligent tutoring systems. *Journal of the Learning Sciences, 2*(3), 277–305.

Moore, J. D., Lemaire, B., & Rosenblum, J. A. (1995). Discourse generation for instructional applications: Identifying and exploiting relevant prior explanations. *Journal of the Learning Sciences, 5*(1), 49–94.

Munro, A. (1994). Authoring interactive graphical models. In T. de Jong, D. M. Towne, & H. Spada (Eds.), *The use of computer models for explication, analysis and experiential learning.* Berlin, Heidelberg, & New York: Springer Verlag.

Munro, A., Johnson, M. C., Pizzini, Q. A., Surmon, D. S., Towne, D. M., & Wogulis, J. L. (1997). Authoring simulation-centered tutors with RIDES. *International Journal of Artificial Intelligence in Education, 8,* 284–316.

National Commission on Excellence in Education. (1983). *A nation at risk: The imperative for educational reform.* Washington, DC: U.S. Government Printing Office.

Needle, D. (1982). Group fights growing use of micros in schools. *Infoworld* (May 10).

Nickerson, R. S. (1982). Information technology and psychology—A retrospective look at some views of the future. In R. A. Kasschau, R. Lachman, & K. R. Laughery (Eds.), *Information technology and psychology: Prospects for the future* (pp. 203–237). New York: Praeger.

Nickerson, R. S. (1983). Computer programming as a vehicle for teaching thinking skills. *Journal of Philosophy for Children, 4*(3–4), 43–48.

Norman, C. (1983). *Computers in the classroom: National Educational Association Survey Report.* Washington, DC: National Educational Association.

Orlansky, J., & String, J. (1979). *Cost-effectiveness of computer-based instruction in military training* (P-1375). Alexandria, VA: Institute for Defense Analysis.

Papert, S. (1980). *Mindstorms: Children, computers and powerful ideas.* New York: Basic Books.

Papert, S. (1987). Computer criticism vs. technocentric thinking. *Educational Researcher, 16*(1), 22–30.

Pea, R. (1983). *Programming and problem solving: Children's experience with LOGO. Paper presented at a symposium entitled "Chameleon in the classroom: Developing roles for computers"* (Tech. Rep. No. 12). New York: Center for Children and Technology, Bank Street College.

Pea, R. (1987, June–July). The aims of software criticism: Reply to Professor Papert. *Educational Researcher, 16*(5), 4–8.

Pea, R. D., & Kurland, D. M. (1984). On the cognitive and educational benefits of teaching children programming: A critical look. *New Ideas in Psychology, 2,* 137–168.

Pea, R. D., & Kurland, D. M. (1987). On the cognitive effects of learning computer programming. In R. D. Pea & K. Sheingold (Eds.), *Mirrors of minds: Patterns of experience in educational computing* (pp. 147–177). Norwood, NJ: Ablex.

Pea, R. D., Kurland, M. D., & Hawkins, J. (1987). LOGO and the development of thinking skills. In R. D. Pea & K. Sheingold (Eds.), *Mirrors of minds: Patterns of experience in educational computing* (pp. 178–197). Norwood, NJ: Ablex.

Rosé, C. P. (1997). *Robust interactive dialogue interpretation.* Unpublished doctoral dissertation, School of Computer Science, Carnegie Mellon University.

Rosé, C. P., Di Eugenio, B., & Moore, J. D. (1999). A dialog based tutoring system for basic electricity and electronics. In S. P. Lajoie & M. Vinet (Eds.), *Proceedings 9th International Conference on Artificial Intelligence in Education, AI-ED 99* (pp. 759–761). Amsterdam: IOS Press.

Rubin, A., & Bruce, B. (1985). QUILL: Reading and writing with a microcomputer. In B. A. Hutson (Ed.), *Advances in reading/language research* (Vol. 3, pp. 97–117). Greenwich, CT: JAI Press.

Salomon, G. (1993). On the nature of pedagogic computer tools: The case of the writing partner. In S. P. Lajoie & S. J. Derry (Eds.), *Computers as cognitive tools* (pp. 179–196). Hillsdale, NJ: Lawrence Erlbaum Associates.

Schofield, J. W. (1995). *Computers and classroom culture.* Cambridge, England: Cambridge University Press.

Schofield, J. W., Evans-Rhodes, D., & Huber, B. (1990). Artificial intelligence in the classroom: The impact of a computer-based tutor on teachers and students. *Social Science Computer Review, 8,* 24–41.

Schraagen, J. M., Chipman, S. F., & Shalin, V. L. (Eds.). (2000). *Cognitive task analysis.* Hillsdale, NJ: Lawrence Erlbaum Associates.

Sheingold, K. (1981). *Issues related to the implementation of computer technology in schools: A cross-sectional study* (Memo No. 1). New York: Center for Children and Technology, Bank Street College.

Sheingold, K., Kane, J. H., & Endreweit, M. E. (1983). Microcomputer use in schools: Developing a research agenda. *Harvard Educational Review, 53*(4).

Sheingold, K., & Tucker, M. S. (Eds.). (1990). *Restructuring for learning with technology.* New York: Center for Technology in Education, Bank Street College.

Sherman, M. (1983). *Computers in education: A report, recommendations, resources.* Concord, MA: Bates.

Sleeman, D., & Brown, J. S. (Eds.). (1982). *Intelligent tutoring systems.* New York: Academic Press.

Soloway, E., Ehrlich, K., Bonar, J., & Greenspan, J. (1982). What do novices know about programming? In B. Schneiderman & A. Badre (Eds.), *Directions in human–computer interactions* (pp. 27–54). Hillsdale, NJ: Ablex.

Towne, D. M. (1987). The generalized maintenance trainer: Evolution and revolution. In W. B. Rouse (Ed.), *Advances in man–machine systems research* (Vol. 3, pp. 1–63). Greenwich, CT: JAI Press.

Wenger, E. (1987). *Artificial intelligence and tutoring systems: Computational and cognitive approaches to the communication of knowledge.* Los Altos, CA: Morgan Kaufman.

Wierzbicki, B. (1983). Boston revolutionizes its public-school system. *Infoworld, 5*(37).

Wierzbicki, B. (1984). College students learn to live with computers. *Infoworld, 6*, 35–36.

Wright, D. (1982). *Instructional Use of Computers in Public Schools* (NCES Rep. No. 82-245). Washington, DC: National Center for Education Statistics.

Wujcik, A. (1984). *Report to the task force on the status of technology use in schools.* Washington, DC: National Institute of Education.

Chapter 3

Future Vision of Learning and Technology for Continuous Personal Development

Thomas P. Hill
Hewlett Packard Company

Research on technology innovations (Nass & Mason, 1990) indicates that it is necessary to look at two sets of dimensions in order to understand how technology innovations emerge: how technology supports the tasks people want to do and technology as a "box." Technology is viewed as a box when salient characteristics of technology functionality are identified. In a similar manner, this chapter focuses first on the cognitive and social dimensions of interactive learning for continuous personal development. Second, it discusses how technology designers need to respond to these user requirements in developing new technologies. Technology trends are explored and described in terms of product feature sets, infrastructures, and integrated systems. Finally, learning and technology dimensions are analyzed and discussed, indicating trends for research, standards, policy, and industry initiatives.

Based on the observations of youth, age 10–19 years, working at either a nonprofit organization that trains youth on Internet use, a web development company, or in high school project environments, there is a fundamental shift in youth perceptions and use of technology. To understand the characteristics of these new perceptions and uses, consider how four exemplary young people (shown in Table 3.1) are using the Internet, multimedia authoring tools, and collaboration systems. These youth were chosen based entirely on their exemplary skill sets to understand trends in use of learning and technology from a subject perspective. Future research observing women and multi-ethnic subjects would increase understanding of use of technology skills in the general population.

TABLE 3.1
Participants—Study of Young People's Use of Internet Technology

Subject	Background	Observations (1-year period)
Ron	10 years. Male. 5th grade. Public school.	Interactive Game Design of User Interface Screens
	Used computers in home, school, and Digital Clubhouse. Internet literate within 4 months of access during observation. Computer game time 15–25 hrs/wk.	Demonstrated understanding of programing defaults, profiles, options, algorithmic modeling. Used Photoshop to create and edit graphics.
Tim	15 years. Male. 10th grade. Public school.	Internet-Based Group Research Project
	Used computers in home, school, and Digital Clubhouse. Internet literate for over 3 years prior to observation. Internet access, 17 hrs/wk.	Displayed collaboration skills with 4 peers using the Internet for research, ability to map resources to problems, and developed multimedia slide presentation in PowerPoint.
Doug	18 years. Male. 12th grade. Public school.	Web Site Production—Professional
	Used computers in home, school, and Digital Clubhouse. Internet literate 4 years prior to observation. Internet access 10 hrs/wk. Multimedia tool use 5–7 hrs/wk.	Demonstrated abilities to perform graphic design work at professional level, work in team, create interactive Web site features, developed a guide to building a Web site. Used Photoshop and Dreamweaver web authoring tools.
Steve	19 years. Male. Freshman. Community college.	WWII Personal History Interview—Producer
	Used computers in home, school, and Digital Clubhouse. Internet literate 5 years prior to observation. Internet access 15 hrs/wk. Multimedia tool use 10 hrs/wk.	Produced a personal history of his grandfather's WWII experiences using the Internet for audio, graphic content, and created a multimedia video presentation using Premiere and Photoshop.

RON: USED ITERATIVE SKILLS

Ron demonstrated cognitive skills often observed in programers or computer systems designers. He used Adobe Photoshop to create screen images for users to set up team schedules, team color schemes, playing fields, default options, and profiles. The interactive game has over 35 screens of content with flow positions and page notations on each screen (with no flow diagram of processing between pages). He thinks in terms of computer processing flow models, defaults, triggers, profiles, options, contingent situations, iterative processing, and continuous results. His motivation to design, author, and publish indicates a high level of self-efficacy (a person's belief in their ability to achieve a particular result).

TIM: SHOWED COLLABORATIVE SKILLS

In his freshman high school class, Tim and four classmates developed a complete Internet-based presentation on ecosystems of steppe grasslands. The team sent e-mail messages to experts in the field at major U.S. universities. The research team used chat rooms and e-mail between themselves to create their presentation. They reviewed key findings from university research on the Internet. The presentation bar charts, graphs, and other visual aids were created using Microsoft PowerPoint and Excel. The final presentation document was placed up for review on a poster board similar to the poster board presentation approaches used in major academic conferences. Tim's group project demonstrates how young people work socially in a dynamic, engaging, and intimate way. They seek out mentors (without introductions) and assume answers are available from others in a virtual social network designed around the project.

DOUG: DEVELOPED SELF-EFFICACY

Doug developed web page development skills at the Digital Clubhouse, then during his senior year in high school he worked as an intern at a web design and development company. He was asked by the management team to coproduce a completely new site that needed to be completed within 3 months. He comanaged a team comprised of designers, content capture staff, Hyper Text Markup Language (HTML) page developers, and database (for product purchase) support. The site was innovative in its use of three-dimensional images, which could be viewed by special glasses. The site used image mapping (click on an area of the screen to launch a program) and mouse rollover (display a description of what a button did) features to increase viewer interest. The GumbyWorld site (GumbyWorld, 2000) was premiered in San Francisco at the FAO Schwartz store in August 1998 and within the first week it received a Top 5 Site award from Yahoo. Doug developed a guide to Web site development that is used in new site development today. He developed skills to such a high level of expertise that he was able to write a guide for others to develop Web sites quickly, essentially mentoring others and providing continuity in project management. His work illuminates how self-efficacy and metacognitive skills are strengthened by this interactive design and development activity.

STEVE: CREATED A MENTAL MAP

Steve worked on a multimedia project through the summer with his grandfather, interviewing him about his experiences during World War II and how he was wounded behind friendly forces during an air attack at the Battle of the Bulge. The interview helped Steve understand from a first-person perspective the real emotions surrounding the war experience and provided him with an opportunity to teach his grandfather how to use digital storytelling tools. They worked on a storyboard together for the 3½ minute digital video presentation. The script called for band music, so Steve went to the Internet and found the Air Force Band site. He downloaded the music he thought appropriate as an audio track. They both wrote a voice script. Steve digitally recorded a description of the air attack, how aircraft cannon wounded his grandfather, and his stateside recovery. Next, Steve used a digital video-authoring tool, Adobe Premiere, to create the final multimedia presentation. Premiere is a complex authoring tool used by professional digital video editors to develop broadcast quality digital video programs.

Steve was successful in using the software in just a few days, without a formal course. He described his learning process in the following way: "Oh, I looked at a sample program already completed, looked at the defaults, used the HELP function when I had a questions and then just started inserting digital audio tracks and graphics based on a timeline." He knew the iterative character of computer programs. In addition, he understood the interaction between the continuous processing of computer programs and the properties, options, defaults, and parameters to guide the multimedia content development process. The speed at which he was able to handle the learning task indicates that he was referring to a mental map on the use of any software program.

Today, young people demonstrate in a variety of tasks, projects, and programs that they have the cognitive and social abilities to use new multimedia and network centric technologies optimally and with self-efficacy (Bandura, 1997). Youth have developed mental models for using technology at school, home, and work by becoming totally immersed in computer-network environments. Young people seem to have the ability to define, create, and update their own mental model on the use of technology with minimal support from traditional event-oriented courseware. Their ability to self-organize (Barab et al., 1999) learning strategies integrated with technology seems to speed learning processing, and continuously flow through daily activities. Computing features and collaboration networks are a salient part of their everyday world. Their sense of self-efficacy, ability to self-monitor and adjust, and consciously design their own computing environments provides an indication of the future young people are creating by optimizing technology and networks. The following discussion outlines the dimensions of continuous personal development based on research and as exhibited by young people in cognitive and social domains.

DIMENSIONS OF CONTINUOUS PERSONAL DEVELOPMENT: UNDERSTANDING THE USE OF TECHNOLOGY MENTAL MAP

> The way we learn is by trying something, doing it, getting stuck . . . and when we are stuck we're ready for the critical piece of information. The same piece of information that made no impact at a lecture makes a dramatic impact when we are ready for it. We don't have to study it. It just hits. (Norman, 1994, p. 36)

Research focused on the cognitive characteristics of individuals using technology has identified scripts (Schank, 1990), or mental maps, as key components in the successful use of computing technologies. Schemas, or mental maps (Anderson, Howe, & Tolmie, 1996; Johnson-Laird, 1983), are preparatory plans (Singer, 1980) for later use by individuals to solve or know how to act in situations they confront. To better understand computer sessions by users, a specific type of schema, or preparatory plan, is of interest: the story schema. *Story schemas* (Meadowcraft & Reeves, 1989) are cognitive scripts that people develop to help them identify the key characters in a plot, understand plot structure, anticipate important content, guide attention, aid in the proper storing of information about the story, and make the ongoing processing of the incoming content more efficient.

Stories have a specific structure not dissimilar to the structure of a user session on a computer. First, users get oriented to the system. Second, they must overcome various task challenges in using the system. Finally, they achieve their session goal, thus ending their session after the goal/problem is resolved. Story schemas have three properties of interest in understanding a user session: *hierarchical organization, instantiation,* and *prediction* (Throndyke & Yekovich, 1979). Hierarchical organization implies that the most salient information about how to use the technology is stored in memory at the top immediately available for recall and the least or incidental at the bottom of the memory stack. Knowing what is important about the use of a new technology is critical to gaining continuing success. Instantiation is the process of matching incoming content with computer session mental map elements. In the use of technology, individuals with well-developed "use of technology" mental maps are effective in handling all the content input about what to do to make certain things happen on the screen and how to respond when a change occurs on the screen. Finally, as the use of technology mental map becomes mature, it can become predictive to help a user understand what is likely to happen next on the screen. The experience of Steve learning Adobe Premiere by using the technology is an excellent example of the predictive property of a well-developed use of technology script.

In the social arena, it is likely that social scripts about relationships, group work, messaging, and mentoring are overlaid onto the use of technology schema employed by young people. Their quick adoption of chat room environments, e-mail messaging, and cellular phone use anywhere indicates an ability to quickly update their scripts of social relationships. The following analysis outlines the key properties of a use of technology schema in cognitive and social domains.

PROPERTIES OF THE USE OF TECHNOLOGY MENTAL MAP: COGNITIVE DOMAIN

The following set of properties was selected based on observations of young people and early adopters using technology. Cognitive domain properties that reveal things about trends in characterizing how technology will be used in the future include *design, self-publishing, iteration, self-efficacy,* and *metacognitive skills.* These cognitive abilities are evident in an individual who is consciously competent in their use of technology.

Design

One property demonstrated by all four young people mentioned in the examples is their construction of knowledge, or development of skills that are relevant to them. Based on their point of view and experience, young people build on a personal knowledge and skill base in developing new skills or knowledge. Learning systems researchers (Barrett, 1992; Duffy & Cunningham, 1996; Edlson, Pea, & Gomez, 1996; Hannafin, 1995; Krajcik et al., 1998; Mayer, 1996, 1999) have identified active learning with construction of knowledge by the individual. Schon (1990) observed that education and design environments are similar in that both occur under complex and uncertain environments and knowledge is generated, reflected on, and evaluated. Bridge civil engineering design students using a personalized design environment were more successful at submitting prototypes that worked and gained a deeper understanding of their designs than students who did not use a personalized design environment (Gal, 1992). During the design process, students seem to be generating learning aids (Edlson, Gordin, & Pea, 1999) that jumpstart their learning process. For a math student, learning aids may include a page of formulas with comment shortcuts to estimations, visualization models, or venn diagrams. Research in social learning theory supports design as an important dimension of learning. Bandura (1977) found in his social learning research that individuals who generated their own learning aids retained and learned skills quicker and more effectively.

Self-Publishing

Self-publishing is the ability to structure personal information and knowledge distributed effectively without an intermediary. Many young people demonstrate an astonishing interest and motivation to self-publish their thinking, ideas, or personal interests with their friends, family, or anonymous visitors. They set up personal Web sites with their background, schools attended information, portfolio of completed work in school or job, and views on current topics or extra curriculum groups like band, drama, or sports. These personal Web sites employ basic HTML (hypertext web pages), hyperlinks (links to other web pages), animated GIFs (digital images), audio clips, graphics from reports, sophisticated tools (web page visit counters, visit reporting to see the domain names of people visiting their site and meta tags or keywords to direct visitors to the site from search engines). Some young people have registered their personal web pages with major search engine sites like Yahoo, Excite, and Infoseek. Their interest in structuring information, knowledge about themselves, and their interests shows a high level of trust in others, interest in gaining feedback (most sites have e-mail boxes direct to the page author), and adjusting their site accordingly. Young people are using their self-publishing skills to structure information about themselves and the world at large, thus establishing a framework for development of Internet social networks that share and build information.

Iteration

Iteration is the ability to navigate through content, gleaning only the salient points in a recursive way until all-important learning features are gathered. Ron's game design ability indicates an ability to think in an iterative mode. Young people's use of technology mental map includes the iteration dimension as a fundamental framework for understanding computers and their processing functionality. Preset system defaults (preferences for system performance), options, and user profiles (preferences for user specific functions) provide many of the parameters, behaviors, and boundaries for processing. Knowledge of how these preset features guide programing provides a user with an ability to control program functioning. Iterative thinking skill offers a young person a deep understanding of the basic architecture and processing characteristics of computers and communications systems that rely on computers.

More importantly, iterative thinking is a master, or expert, level of thinking that novices generally do not demonstrate when reviewing new material. Kintsch (1993) observed that learning is generally a strategic process. She further stated that many studies have indicated that qualitative differences in strategy use are important in differentiating individuals with little or no experience and those with knowledge in a particular domain. Kintsch's research (1993) indicated that novices process information in a linear, straightforward manner, whereas experts process material recursively. Experts make repeated passes when reviewing material, focusing selectively on certain types of content. In addition, novices make fewer inferences about the content than experts. Experts are able to elaborate the incoming information with extensions from their own knowledge base. Novices generally focus on superficial features (Jacobson & Archodidou, 2000) of a problem or situation, and experts attend to the underlying principles of a structure or problem. A way to speed their understanding of a domain faster than traditional linear-sequential methods would be to jumpstart their knowledge of domain fundamental principles, types, or concepts, and then suggest that they iterate through the domain content.

Self-Efficacy

Self-efficacy is people's belief in their ability to perform a particular behavior. Self-efficacy (Bandura, 1977) at enhanced levels provides the internal impetus for individuals to move ahead confident in their ability to perform a task or learn a new skill. Of interest is research indicating that self-efficacy moderates intelligence. Students of above average intelligence, but with limited sense of self-efficacy, continued to perform poorly in schoolwork (Bandura, 1997). Therefore, self-efficacy development is of paramount importance in any learning technology system. Young people today have a highly developed sense of self-efficacy in regard to technology use. They see a problem and immediately drive forward to find a solution with little or no sense of possible failure or unproductive result. Steve, in the previous example, expressed this sense of self-efficacy when attacking learning a new complex software program: "Oh, I looked at a sample program already completed, looked at the defaults . . ." He already had a mental model of how the software worked. He only needed to get this application's version of the model, apply it to his application model, and he was ready to start at a higher level of task flow.

Beliefs in personal efficacy have been shown (Bandura, 1997) to have a greater impact on academic performance than personal, social, and occupational outcomes expected for proficient performance. Bandura (1997) further observed that efficacy beliefs are important in support of creativity to override established ways of thinking and search for new knowledge.

Moreover, perceived efficacy is necessary to persist in innovative endeavors requiring prolonged investment in time and effort, those where the outcome is uncertain, those where progress is seemingly slow, and those devalued by others for thinking incongruent with present norms. In the future, systems will need to monitor self-efficacy development as individuals use interactive learning network technology to gain the ultimate benefit from continuous personal development systems.

Metacognitive Skills

Land and Greene (2000) identified three attributes of metacognitive knowledge and related skills: an awareness of one's own cognition and the degree to which cognitive efforts are successful, knowledge about different cognitive demands of different learning tasks, and procedural knowledge of strategies to employ when present strategies are not working. Learners demonstrate highly developed metacognitive knowledge related to the use of technology to solve learning problems when they employ metacognitive skills (Kintsch, 1993) while constantly seeking feedback on their learning performance. Young people seemed to make mental notes about their strategies and then proceed to modify their behavior. To constantly update a use of technology mental map, individuals must continuously monitor results of present approaches to technology, as well as evaluate their learning strategies for effectiveness and ease of application. Metacognitive abilities can be employed to select learning strategies when domain specific knowledge is inadequate (Land & Greene, 2000). Metacognitive skills can be used specifically to monitor ongoing comprehension or progress in solving a problem, to plan future learning processing activities, to redirect attention to problematic areas, and to deploy the appropriate remedial strategy. Successful learners and those with expertise in a given domain demonstrated advanced metacognitive skills. Some young people demonstrate an ability to assimilate and apply metacognitive skills (Bandura, 1997; Zimmerman, 1995), creating an opportunity to enhance learning productivity.

Metacognitive skills need constant reinforcement, updating, and monitoring. Bandura (1977), Zimmerman (1995), and Bouffard-Bouchard, Parent, and Larivee (1991) observed that learners are motivated to new levels of achievement based on self-monitoring using feedback. He argued that learners are active agents in monitoring their performance. Individuals set their own standards for achievement and performance. Learners keep notes, learning aids, and relationships with those who know to develop continuity of learning strategy results during the personal development process. The ability to self-monitor, make midcourse learning strategy corrections, and keep developing new strategy skills is essential to the success of a continuous personal learning program. Self-motivation increases as control and successful results from metacognitive skills become evident.

The result of the integration and deployment by the individual of these cognitive skills is enhanced levels of conscious competence. Many individuals from 10 to 19 years old demonstrate an ability to continuously learn as part of a flow (Csikszentmihalyi, 1990) experience. Learning in this mental state is an unconscious experience. The individuals' mental model enables their consciousness to be harmoniously ordered, resulting in great enjoyment and a sense of losing themself in the experience. Individuals working at this level of peak performance are in a continuous state of personal development. They know when to see new mentors, seek learning resources, and how to organize these resources for optimal personal development. When learning strategies are not proving successful, individuals who are proficient in these metacognitive skills know how to monitor results, make adjustments, and keep moving ahead in a continuous learning path to obtain a long-range development goal.

PROPERTIES OF THE USE OF TECHNOLOGY MENTAL MAP: SOCIAL DOMAIN

It is striking to researchers how completely young people and Internet early adopters have embraced the social characteristics or features of new technologies (Brown & Duguid, 2000; Scardamalia & Bereiter, 1996). Young people today are the creators of virtual social networks integrating their social life with technology. They are innovators in the creation, development, and growth of these virtual social networks. There is vibrancy, energy, and value creation power intrinsic to virtual social networks that attracts young people and is beginning to attract thousands of users from all stages in life. Today, most are users of content instead of builders, but over time this ratio will change as users understand the value of creating content that is personally relevant. The creation, development, and distribution of content will be critical to the successful evolution of knowledge repositories for continuous personal development.

One form of virtual social network observed in young people is the *personal technical support network*. A set of peers that have technical expertise are linked together to continuously update an individual's understanding of technology and support solving technical problems as they arise. The personal technical support network is employed often to solve major technical problems such as system crashes, network failures, or how to install new application software.

Social domain characteristics that assist in understanding how technology use will emerge in the future include *dynamism, mentoring, engagement, intimacy*, and *community knowledge building*. These social domain skills are evident in individuals who have successfully developed a virtual social network supporting their use of technology.

Dynamism

The dynamism property is the ability of a person to quickly assess a social situation, participate in an animated manner in social discourse, and respond to fast-moving topic threads of conversation. Salomon (1997) suggested that a dynamic reciprocal relationship exists between people in distributed discourse, and Barab et al. (1999) advised an intentional dynamic aspect. Young people demonstrate both the reciprocity and intentional aspects of social dynamics when using technology. They think first of going to a chat room, sending an e-mail message or setting up a personal Web site, and telling their friends about an update to their Web site. Often, even after seeing someone in school who is in the same neighborhood, the young person will log onto America Online Messenger and begin a dialog. When they are logged on doing research or homework, they can receive a notification that a "buddy" is online and available. So, that individual will stop doing whatever they are doing and begin an extended chat. In some respects, these dynamic interactions are replacing the social dialog reserved exclusively for the telephone. However, electronic network use seems to be additive in many households, as the telephone and the computer are used simultaneously by various family members, or it may be used when more privacy is required. The social dynamic of online interactive systems is indeed astonishing, and it indicates a virtual social network fabric that is energetic, powerful, and active.

Mentoring

For purposes of this chapter, the term *mentoring* means to accompany an individual during a period of learning while working toward a knowledge objective. For thousands of years, going back to Plato's dialogs with groups of students, accompaniment during the learning process has been viewed as essential. Aubrey and Cohen (1995) noted that, in both Asian and Western cultures, accompaniment has been a fundamental framework component of the learning process. In Asia, the learning of any skill involving self-improvement is called the "way." In Western culture, the derivation of the words "career" and "coach" come from the journey metaphor. Career comes from the French *carrier*, meaning a track for racing horses, and coach comes from the French *coche*, meaning a chariot or wagon. The meaning for coach is extended to include the driver who guides the vehicle (Aubrey & Cohen, 1995).

Although in daily usage the term *mentoring* is used for many accompanying types of people and activities, three specific types of accompanists have been defined—mentors, coaches, and tutors. *Mentors* are generally defined to be the farthest removed from the learner, and are focused more on career development because they have already made it to the pinnacle of their career. A *coach* is a person closer to the learner's experience, working on bringing the learner to a new level of skill or expertise. A *tutor* may be a peer or someone who has just recently completed the learning experience and thus has the most accurate and updated information on developing a task or skill. Young people demonstrate tutoring skills proficiently in their use of technology. Mature young people show coaching skills in assisting younger peers. Finally, young people who have reached a new stage in life and who develop long-term relationships display mentoring ability. An interesting characteristic of the mentoring dimension is that young people seem to understand that the only way they can be effective and keep their skills updated is to tutor each other often. One individual has skills related to networking, another on operating systems, and yet another on applications using multimedia authoring tools. They know that sharing their expertise moves all of them ahead, that the technology is too complex to master, and that approaching each other with "intelligent humility" will harvest learning benefits in the end. Mentors who have already been there can provide encouragement to individuals with a limited sense of self-efficacy to assist them in building a personal efficacy foundation supporting long-term continuous learning.

Engagement

Engagement is the ability of a person to actively focus, participate, and contribute salient ideas during group interaction. Individuals demonstrating high levels of self-efficacy show increased levels of engagement (Zimmerman, 1995). Young people often take an active role in performance of tasks involving their peers. Engaging their peers in chat rooms, e-mail, group projects, and other collaborative endeavors is a salient characteristic of their virtual social networking abilities. High levels of participation trigger and sustain a dynamic process of knowledge generation by peers, subject matter experts, and teachers. The "community of knowledge builders" (Bereiter & Scardamalia, 1993) as an informal working group places participation demands on its members. Members must remain engaged in the knowledge development process to continue their informal membership. Intense involvement focuses attention on the knowledge activity before the group, with individuals providing feedback on the productivity of a skill or accuracy of a knowledge point. The intention of young people to join with others to generate a new understanding related to a skill or topic is another aspect of engagement. The engagement dimension implies intent on the part of learners to actively join into dialog with peers, subject matter experts, and teachers. Because of engaging discussion and activity, an individual's attention can be focused on learning content of greatest value. Thus, engaging activity can heighten the learning experience for individuals and group engagement enhances opportunities for continuous development of enriching content relevant to the group.

Intimacy

Intimacy is the emotional closeness shown by young people in social networks. Intimacy is a salient characteristic of virtual social networks comprised of young people. Rapport, affiliation, and the bond between members are observed when connecting many virtual *personae* representing each member over the network. The popularity of *avatars* (graphic characters representing a person on the display screen) and multi-user games are indicative of the integration of virtual personae into their personal social networks. Yet, there is a downside to certain types of virtual social networks. The growth of anonymous chat rooms, multi-user games, and discussion groups has led to the formation of what Beniger (1987) called *pseudo-community*. The contrived intimacy of anonymous social networks should not distract from opportunities for sincere intimacy necessary for intellectual growth and knowledge generation. Many young people send e-mail, participate in special interest discussion groups, and chat with subject matter experts daily yielding productive learning results. An oftentimes "do it" attitude during group or one-to-one network sessions demonstrates a preference for directness and simplicity. Simplicity as seen in messages (sometimes misconstrued as lack of form) between members indicates sincerity while developing rapport and emotional closeness. As communities of learners are connected together in increasingly larger networks, the need for maintaining sincerity, intimacy, and simplicity will become more pronounced.

Community Knowledge Building

Construction of content by a group of young people brings together many social domain dimensions already described, but with an added element of knowledge building. As indicated by the example with Tim's group research project, young people working in groups can develop content quickly, engaging subject matter experts and accessing resources over the Internet. They work closely using e-mail and chat rooms to communicate with each other to get the job done. Collaboration during the construction of knowledge content is an effective way to enhance deep learning of a concept or skill (Kozma, Chin, Russell, & Marx, 2000). Collaborating groups over time can become "communities of practice" (Brown & Duguid, 1991; Cambridge, 1999), building value for their members. Learning communities of practice groups come into existence around a topic or concept (Arias, Eden, Fischer, Gorman, & Scharff, 1999) and they thrive on group development of content, resource access, and subject matter expert group discussions. Communities of practice networks develop in a four-stage process—attract members, promotion of participation, build loyalty, and capture value (Hagel & Armstrong, 1997). As a critical mass of members is developed, knowledge and intellectual capital are generated at a rate that sustains membership growth. The Educational Object Economy web community (Educational Object Economy, 2000) exemplifies how groups continuously build valuable content. The Educational Object Economy offers teachers, students, administrators, and schools resources, papers, discussion forums, a directory to over 1,200 Java learning objects, and server software for building other knowledge development communities.

TECHNOLOGY TRENDS

The Internet supports the development of the cognitive and social attributes of the use of technology mental map along several dimensions. For example, the World Wide Web enables a user to "push" (Brown, 2000) content by creating a personal web page, and then posting it onto a Web site for thousands of users to see. The push characteristic of the Web supports the self-publishing cognitive dimension. The "pull" capability of the Web allows the user to retrieve content based on selection controls established by the user, thus enabling an enhanced sense of self-efficacy. In addition, the hypertext linking aspect of the Internet supports nonlinear iterative learning (Jacobson & Archodidou, 2000). The Internet has numerous dimensions of interest in understanding the use of technology mental map. The most important dimensions for the discussion of future learning capabilities are granular content and intelligent objects, object repositories, network centric access, and mobile augmented reality.

Granular Content and Intelligent Objects

Most learning content today is in the form of very large blobs: massive binders of technical information, 40–100 slides of PowerPoint slides of new product training content, or hundreds of pages of Word documents for learning courseware. These large blobs do not lend themselves to short iterative cycles or passes to allow the learner to infer key meanings. As learners iterate through the material, they can recursively select salient content, make connections between concepts, and assimilate new content based on their own understanding of the expert script for that topic or skill. Using small "chunks," or objects, of material allows individuals to take content in small increments during each learning experience, make annotations or comments, add metadata or an index, and begin to create their own database of learning aids. The granular character of content supports continuous learning processing.

As objects become more sophisticated, they will become "smart" to other possible uses. For example, a calculator object may be responsive in a situation where the user shifts calculations from algebra to calculus and then automatically link to the tools site on the network and download the associated calculus formulas. Smart objects support users' needs for simplification of interfaces (the complexity is transparent to users) and allows them to concentrate on the learning task at hand rather than on how to obtain the tools to achieve learning goals. Researchers (Anderson, 2000; Roschelle & Kaput, 1996) have developed component-based systems that offer modular design, flexible component integration, and rapid prototyping.

Object Repositories

Learners are seeking ways to self-publish their content, develop content with others, and access the most current content. Object repositories of learning content provide the means of responding to these needs. Object repositories will store vast numbers of learning object content, with metadata (indexing information), and handle (access identification) information for quick retrieval over the Internet. Repositories will be established by existing content providers—publishers, universities, media vendors, and corporations—but a second evolution step is possible. After these first stage repositories are established, users will begin to create integrated learning modules and make them available to other users. Secondary markets for "edited" objects are likely to evolve first from the academic community and then consortiums of corporations seeking to reduce generic content development costs. Today there are public libraries and commercial bookstores, and in the future there will be public learning object repositories and commercial object repositories.

Network Centric Access

The network provides the framework for the linking of valuable learning resources with the individual located anywhere—classroom, business, or at home. Learners, by managing the access to these resources, can develop a higher level of self-efficacy and interact with mentors, coaches, or tutors. The network offers a dynamic, targeted, and powerful set of links to an individual's virtual social network, with no intermediaries. Individuals will be able to launch agents (programs that automatically retrieve information) to access local and remote networks in search of specific learning objects and make them available to learners at a time and place of their convenience. Templates for competency management, curriculums, learning modules, and progress tracking can be downloaded and used based on experts who develop these templates rather than local sources. High quality content, templates, tools, and support people (mentors, coaches, and tutors) will be accessed by the learner directly from a desktop, laptop, or outside using a personal digital assistant (e.g., the PalmPilot).

The Internet infrastructure to support learning object exchange and development will need to be based on existing Internet standards established by the World Wide Web Consortium (W3C), including Hyper Text Markup Language (HTML), Extended Markup Language (XML), and Resource Description Framework (RDF). Lagoze (1996) completed a fundamental analysis of many issues that emerge in the development of an infrastructure to support the exchange of network objects. The object repository infrastructure should be responsive to the continuous evolution of metadata, object use, and developer requirements. An outline of how a responsive framework can evolve and be developed to support the exchange of learning content on the Internet has been developed by Hill (1998). Hill proposed a Learning Object Metadata Framework supported by a set of dynamic repository servers that would support the continuous updating of learning object metadata, in a similar way Internet Domain Name Servers support users typing in the name of a site and immediately being linked to the site. Industry groups, standards organizations, federal agencies, and academic institutions are reviewing how to best implement a prototype of the architecture described in Learning Object Metadata Framework.

Mobile Augmented Reality

Mobile laptop, handheld, and satellite-based geographic positioning systems and augmented reality computing platforms hold promise as centers of learning activity and management. Applications are emerging using mobile handheld geographic positioning systems, like Magellan, with information relayed by sensors in the physical world, or "post-it notes" from others who have been to a geographic location previously. Spohrer (1999) proposed the implementation of a supporting infrastructure of intelligent sensors linked to databases of learning content, responsive wearable viewers (special glasses), or other media to create a "WorldBoard." Teachers could post information notes to students venturing out on a walk in a seal sanctuary, noting key points of learning along the way. Students could visit the area in a virtual way using Internet site information, and set up experiments in advance by sending information to sensors and instruments at the site. When students arrive on the site, they can see the results and the context of the environment and its impact on experiment parameters. Student profiles can be used by the teacher to guide individual students to key guideposts based on their experimental interests, previous skills, or learning already completed—a personalized learning event programed by the teacher for an individual student.

Students can participate in developing the guidepost knowledge database. They can post their observations at the seal sanctuary, results of their experiments or comments on what other students should look for, and rate information based on their perspective of its learning value. In this sense, the process is akin to presenting posters at a school science fair, but in the physical world. Learners are actually involved in the design of their learning experience and the design of learning experiences for others. As they complete these learning experiences, they develop a conscious level of competence about the process of learning they performed and use personal learning platforms, like personal digital assistants, to capture this understanding for later use. The personal digital assistant platform can be a foundation architecture for creation of a learning appliance offering simplified learning environment support to many users intimidated by today's complex technology.

The learning appliance can provide integrated access to learning object repositories, simplified authoring tools (requiring no special training, i.e., PowerPoint), Internet links to templates, tool repositories, and learning management software. Authoring multimedia, interactive, hyperlink courses of the future will be as easy to develop and maintain as word processing programs are today. Mobile computers supporting creation of learning aids, tools, content objects, and other learning resources out in the real environment where they are used will meet design requirements of users. Subject matter experts situated in locations around the world supporting guideposts in physical space with integrated Web sites can be available for mentoring or coaching over the network. These mentors will offer learners unique opportunities to gain immediate answers to questions. Learners can record answers in learning aid form guided by templates and add metadata for later retrieval. User customized profiles support automating learning processing and offer increasing levels of intimacy between users and subject matter experts by customizing interactions, agents, and collaborating environments. Virtual social networks will be established, maintained, and operated transparently by using a personalized learning environment; learners will set the options, defaults, and parameters of social communities of practice.

Learning management applications shift the locus of control to the learner to support continuous personal development during numerous lifelong learning challenges. A platform environment enabling individuals to take control of their learning resources, manage their career, and initiate new learning processing functions will likely emerge as a necessity over the next 10 years. The development of an individual learning database of ideas, concepts, templates, learning aids, and portfolio material provides a way for the user to review, monitor, and examine previous successful learning activities. The database and self-monitoring functions provide continuity in the management of diverse learning activities, including augmented reality observations, computer-based training modules, tests, exercises, labs, mentoring, and coach and tutor feedback.

SUMMARY

To understand the characteristics of emerging learning technology applications over the next 10 years, this chapter used a dimensional approach in the identification of trends in learning and interactive technologies as observed today in young people, ages 10–19 years old. Cognitive and social elements of a mental map observed in young people indicate the development of a specialized mental map for the use of technology. The use of technology mental map supports the quick adoption, learning, and control of new technologies and network applications at an astonishing pace. Cognitive dimensions defined include design, self-publishing, iteration, self-efficacy, and metacognitive skills. The result of the development of these cognitive abilities is an individual capable of managing a continuous personal development program for a lifetime.

Social dimensions identified include dynamism, mentoring, engagement, intimacy, and community knowledge building. Learners exercising skills along these social dimensions build sophisticated virtual social networks. These networks support both continuous personal development and act as a "personal technical support center" for assistance with technology issues.

Trends in technologies enabling the development of the use of technology mental map were discussed in four groups: content becoming granular and intelligent, object repositories supporting a content infrastructure, network centric frameworks for access, and mobile augmented reality bringing the learning experience to the world outside of the classroom. These four technology groupings were discussed based on their ability to respond to users' needs as described in cognitive and social dimensions.

DISCUSSION

Today, young people employ a highly developed use of technology mental map enabling them to use technology effectively and to solve immediate learning problems. The development of the use of technology mental map means they have a foundation set of skills, abilities, and knowledge to manage learning resources available on networks. The development of the use of technology mental map is triggered by the need to survive in an informational society (Castells, 1996). Castells proposed that, for informational societies, the source of productivity lies in the technology of knowledge generation, information processing, and symbol communication. He further argued that what is specific to development in informational societies is the action of knowledge on knowledge itself as the main source of productivity. Systems that enable personal knowledge development enhancing cognitive learning dimensions of design, self-publishing, iteration, self-efficacy, and metacognitive skills will result in increased competence. Conscious competence will propel learners into a mode where continuous personal development is possible. Conscious competence combined with virtual social networks and personal knowledge about individual learning skills can be called personal learning intelligence. It will be the interaction of individuals using personal learning intelligence with knowledge, information, and data resources that will create a powerful dynamic of continuous personal development driving demand for personal learning resources.

Ubiquitous networks linking individuals with other individuals of similar interests, personal learning profiles, and career objectives will enable people to establish and maintain a virtual social network crucial to support of continuous learning. Social frameworks offer support, encouragement, and trust necessary to overcome learning obstacles. When networking technologies are implemented supporting social dimensions of dynamism, mentoring, engagement, intimacy, and community knowledge building, significant contributions are made to the continuous personal learning support system. Many virtual social networks support the establishment of personal technical support centers, informally sharing information about how to use technology, how to overcome technical glitches, and what is "in" and "out" for technology use. In the future, waves of learning processing technology will sweep through various virtual social networks, one of the ways for these waves of adoption to build are the actions of technology champions. Technology champions will seek, find, and broadcast recommendations on learning templates, tools, objects, mentors and master faculty, test tools, and other learning productivity enhancements that can be downloaded. Waves of technology adoption can occur on a huge scale as exemplified by the adoption of the Navigator browser that was downloaded 30 million times in 12 months from mid-1994 to mid-1995. Learning technology champions can focus on 1.2 million computer and network programers, offering an outstanding opportunity for making significant learning productivity enhancements to a major group over a relatively short period of time.

For corporations, policymakers, higher education staff, and others concerned with trends in continuous personal development outlined, here are several important initiatives to consider for research, standards, policy, and industry programs:

>   *Research:* This means coordinated research into the characteristics, attributes, and variables related to learning, self-efficacy, productivity, personal learning intelligence, design, metacognitive skills, and virtual social networking to drive understanding of user initiated, controlled, and designed continuous learning.

>   *Standards:* Although many standards efforts are underway, coordinated initiatives working closely with World Wide Web Consortium and the International Standards Organization are a necessity. Learning technology groups are working on diverse projects, much of the work needed has been completed by the NSF sponsored Digital Libraries Initiative and the American Publishers Association funded Digital Object Identifier project. A joint project with these agencies would leverage work in the field to develop learning object Internet framework.

>   *Policy:* As network learning content is developed, visionary leadership needs to emerge in regard to enabling a learning object economy to evolve and prosper. Hill (2001) proposes that an economic infrastructure modeled after the regulations and institutions supporting the financial services industry be established as the foundation for growth of a learning object economy. Learning object exchange and repositories are a fundamental infrastructure component necessary for any learning network architecture supporting continuous personal development to thrive. Jurisdiction issues are already becoming evident where state higher education organizations are asking state legislatures to "de-certify" online learning curriculum certified in other states. Designing, forming, and enabling succeeding waves of learning technology adoption should be a goal of learning technology strategists.

>   *Industry:* Many startup companies are offering learning server technology, but the actual delivery implementations are web page delivery systems (i.e., electronic books lacking in interactivity). Industry leaders, joining with policy leaders, innovators, and visionaries, will need to place a renewed emphasis on engaging, interactive, and productive applications that raise the standard for electronic learning applications. Industry leaders and corporations need to be actively involved and support the development of prototype systems of the infrastructure necessary to support continuous personal development applications.

Key components are poised on the threshold of an opportunity to achieve levels of learning productivity technology adoption that were impossible as recently as a few years ago. The Internet and intranets available within corporations, higher education institutions, and government agencies offer unique opportunities for enhancing the quality of learning content being received by individuals; enabling people to initiate, control, and solve their learning problems; and amplifying the knowledge development process by people contributing to each others' success in learning strategy development via learning communities of practice. Focusing resources on intense learning situations can help to achieve results. For example, during key transition periods in people's lives (e.g., high school to college, during early college, and college to career), people seem to be more open to learning new skills, concepts, and learning strategies than at other times. During these transition phases, there seems to be a high level of "learning elasticity," or an ability to be open, strive, and work at developing new skills, concepts, or understanding. Targeting essential research, standards, policy, and research strategies and programs on one of these transition segments holds the promise of achieving significant results.

ACKNOWLEDGMENTS

Core concepts of this chapter were presented at the Department of Defense Education Activity Conference held at the Institute for Defense Analysis, Virginia, on December 9, 1998. This chapter was produced by the author in his capacity as a cofounder of the Educational Object Economy Foundation and a program manager of advanced learning technologies at Hewlett Packard Company. The study of young people using the Internet and multimedia technology was conducted at the Digital Clubhouse Foundation in Sunnyvale, California. The author appreciates the insights into social and cognitive domains offered by Jim Spohrer, founder of the Educational Object Economy Foundation. Paul Chatelier, White House—OSTP, offered ideas in forming the concepts of life transitions, technology adoption windows, and "learning elasticity." Thanks to Steve, Doug, Trent, and Ron for their stories of technology use at the Digital Clubhouse that move us closer to understanding how young people today, the adults of tomorrow, may use technology for personal development. Finally, a thank you to the author's master's degree advisors, Cliff Nass and Byron Reeves at Stanford University, who steadfastly taught dimensional analysis techniques in the Social Responses to Communication Technology research program focused on the psychological and sociological effects of media. Author contact: t.hill@hp.com.

REFERENCES

Anderson, T. (2000). *Knowledge components* [Online]. Available: http://www.learningcomponents.com/presentation/Index2.htm. May 5, 2000

Anderson, T., Howe, C., & Tolmie, A. (1996). Interaction and mental models of physics phenomena: Evidence from dialogues between learners. In J. Oakhill & A. Granham (Eds.), *Mental models in cognitive science: Essays in honour of Phil Johnson-Laird* (pp.). East Sussex, UK: Psychology Press.

Arias, E., Eden, H., Fischer, G., Gorman, A., & Scharff, E. (1999, December). Beyond access: Informed participation and empowerment. In C. Hoadley & J. Roschelle (Eds.), *Proceedings of Computer Support for Collaborative Learning 1999* (pp. 20–32). Stanford, CA.

Aubrey, A., & Cohen, P. M. (1995). *Working wisdom: Timeless skills and vanguard strategies for learning organizations.* San Francisco: Jossey-Bass.

Bandura, A. (1977). *Social learning theory.* Englewood Cliffs, NJ: Prentice-Hall.

Bandura, A. (1997). *Self-efficacy—The exercise of control.* New York: Freeman.

Barab, S. A., Julkowski-Cherkes, M., Swenson, R., Garrett, S., Shaw, R. E., & Young, M. (1999). Principles of self-organization: Learning as participation in autocatakinetic systems. *Journal of Learning Sciences, 8*(3–4), 349–390.

Barrett, E. (1992). Sociomedia: An introduction. In E. Barrett (Ed.), *Sociomedia: Multimedia, hypermedia and social construction of knowledge* (pp. 1–12). Cambridge, MA: MIT Press.

Beniger, J. R. (1987). Personalization of mass media and the growth of pseudo-community. *Communication Research, 14*(2), 352–371.

Bereiter, C., & Scardamalia, M. (1993). *Surpassing ourselves: An inquiry into the nature and implications of expertise.* Chicago, IL: Open Court.

Bouffard-Bouchard, T., Parent, S., & Larivee, S. (1991). Influence of self-efficacy on self-regulation and performance among junior and senior high school age students. *International Journal of Behavioral Development, 14*, 153–164.

Brown, J. S. (2000). Growing up digital: How the Web changes work, education, and the ways people learn. *Change, 32*(2), 11–20.

Brown, J. S., & Duguid, P. (1991). Organizational learning in communities-of-practice: Toward a unified view of working, learning and innovation. *Organizational Science, 2*(1), 40–57.

Brown, J. S., & Duguid, P. (2000). *The social life of information.* Boston: Harvard Business School Press.

Cambridge, D. (1999, December). Supporting the development of a national constellation of communities of practice in scholarship and teaching. In C. Hoadley & J. Roschelle (Eds.), *Proceedings of Computer Support for Collaborative Learning 1999* (pp. 81–84). Stanford, CA.

Castells, M. (1996). *The information age: Economy, society and culture: Vol. 1. Rise of the network society.* Malden, MA: Blackwell.

Csikszentimihayli, M. (1990). *Flow: The psychology of optimal experience.* New York: Harper & Row.

Duffy, T. M., & Cunningham, D. J. (1996). Constructivism: Implications for the design and delivery of instruction. In D. H. Jonassen (Ed.), *Handbook of research for Educational Communications and Technology* (pp. 170–198). New York: Macmillan.

Edlson, D. C., Gordin, D. N., & Pea, R. D. (1999). Addressing the challenges of inquiry-based learning through technology and curriculum design. *Journal of Learning Sciences, 8*(3–4), 391–450.

Edlson, D. C., Pea, R. D., & Gomez, L. (1996). Constructivism in the collaboratory. In B. Wilson (Ed.), *Constructivist learning environments: Case studies in instructional design* (pp. 151–162). Englewood Cliffs, NJ: Educational Technology Publications.

Educational Object Economy (2000). Educational Object Economy web site [Online]. Available: http://www.eoe.org. January 1, 2000

Gal, S. (1992). Computers and design activities: Their mediating roles in engineering education. In E. Barrett (Ed.), *Sociomedia: Multimedia, hypermedia and social construction of knowledge* (pp. 435–465). Cambridge, MA: MIT Press.

GumbyWorld (2000). Web site devoted to Gumby and other cartoon characters [Online]. Available: http://www.gumbyworld.com. December 15, 2000

Hannafin, M. J. (1995). Open ended learning environments: Foundations, assumptions, and implications for automated design. In R. D. Tennyson & A. E. Baron (Eds.), *Automated instructional design: Computer based development and delivery tools* (pp. 101–130). New York: Springer-Verlag, NATO Special Programme on Advanced Educational Technology.

Hagel, J., III, & Armstrong, A. G. (1997). *Net gain: Expanding markets through virtual communities.* Boston: Harvard Business School Press.

Hill, T. P. (1998). *The learning object metadata framework* [Online]. Available: http://www.learnalytics.com. November 8, 1998

Hill, T. P. (2001). *The Human Capital Reserve Board: A Parable.* Online available: http://linezine.com/6.2/articles/thhcrbap.htm. September 28, 2001

Jacobson, M. J., & Archodidou, A. (2000). The design of hypermedia tools for learning: Fostering conceptual change and transfer of complex scientific knowledge. *Journal of Learning Sciences, 9*(2), 145–199.

Johnson-Laird, P. N. (1983). *Mental models.* Cambridge, MA: Harvard University Press.

Kintsch, E. (1993). Principles of instruction from research in human cognition. In J. M. Spector, M. C. Polson, & D. J. Muriada (Eds.), *Automating instructional design: Concepts and issues* (pp. 23–42). Englewood Cliffs, NJ: Educational Technology Publications.

Kozma, R., Chin, E., Russell, J., & Marx, S. (2000). The roles of representations and tools in the chemistry laboratory and their implications for chemistry learning. *Journal of Learning Sciences, 9*(2), 105–143.

Krajcik, J., Blumenfeld, P. C., Marx, R. W., Bass, K. M., Bass, J., Fredricks, J., & Soloway, E. (1998). Inquiry in project based science classrooms: Initial attempts made by middle school students. *Journal of Learning Sciences, 7*(3–4), 313–350.

Land, S. M., & Greene, B. A. (2000). Project based learning with the World Wide Web: A qualitative study of resource integration. *Educational Technology Research & Development, 48*(1), 45–68.

Lagoze, C. J. (1996). The Warwick framework: A container architecture for diverse sets of metadata. In *D-Lib Magazine Online* (July/Aug.). Available: http://www.dlib.org/dlib/july96/lagoze/07lagoze.html. August 6, 1996

Mayer, R. E. (1996). Learning strategies for making sense of expository text: The SOI model for guiding three cognitive processes in knowledge construction. *Educational Psychology Review, 8,* 357–371.

Mayer, R. E. (1999). *The promise of educational psychology: Learning in the content areas.* Upper Saddle River, NJ: Prentice-Hall.

Meadowcraft, J. M., & Reeves, B. (1989). Influence of story schema development on children's attention to television. *Communication Research, 16*(3), 352–374.

Nass, C. I., & Mason, L. (1990). On the study of technology and task: A variable-based approach. In J. Fulk & C. Steinfeld (Eds.), *Organizations and communication technology* (pp. 46–67). Newbury Park, CA: Sage.

Norman, D. A. (1994). Comments made in a panel discussion: Transforming and preserving education traditional values in questions (J. Kernan, Moderator). *EDUCOM Review* (Nov./Dec.), pp. 36–40.

Norman, D. A. (1998). *The invisible computer—Why good products can fail, the personal computer is so complex, and the information appliances are the solution.* Cambridge, MA: MIT Press.

Roschelle, J., & Kaput, J. (1996). Educational software architecture and systemic impact: The promise of component software. *Journal of Educational Computing Research, 14*(3), 217–228.

Salomon, G. (1997). No distribution without individuals' cognition: A dynamic interactional view. In G. Salomon (Ed.), *Distributed cognitions, psychological and educational considerations* (pp. 111–135). New York: Cambridge University Press.

Scardamalia, M., & Bereiter, C. (1996). Computer support for knowledge building communities. In T. Koschmann (Ed.), *Theory and practice of an emerging paradigm* (pp. 249–266). Hillsdale, NJ: Lawrence Erlbaum Associates.

Schank, R. C. (1990). *Tell me a story: A new look at real and artificial memory.* New York: Scribner's.

Schon, D. (1990). *The theory of inquiry: Dewey's legacy to education.* Presented at the second annual meeting of the American Educational Research Association, Boston, MA.

Singer, J. L. (1980). The power and limitations of television: A cognitive affective analysis. In P. H. Tannenbaum & R. Abeles (Eds.), *The entertainment functions of television* (pp. 31–65). Hillsdale, NJ: Lawrence Erlbaum Associates.

Spohrer, J. (1999). Information in places. *IBM Systems Journal, 38*(4).

Thorndyke, P. W., & Yekovich, F. R. (1979). *A critique of schemata as a theory of human story memory* (P-6307). Santa Monica, CA: Rand.

Zimmerman, B. (1995). Self-efficacy and educational development. In A. Bandura (Ed.), *Self-efficacy in changing societies* (pp. 202–226). New York: Cambridge University Press.

Chapter 4

Evidence for Learning From Technology-Assisted Instruction

J. D. Fletcher
Institute for Defense Analyses

Should we use computer-based technology to teach? What evidence is there that doing so produces, assists, or promotes learning? What evidence is there that learning occurs better (i.e., more effectively or efficiently) with technology? Are the benefits of technology-assisted instruction worth whatever must be given up to get them?

These questions do not yield facile answers, but they seem timely and appropriate given the current state of the art. We have been applying technology in learning long enough to expect to find evidence suggesting that these efforts either are or are not worth pursuing. In fact much such evidence has been presented in the research literature. This chapter attempts to summarize this evidence and the case it makes for the use of technology (specifically, computer-based technology) in instruction.

Contrary to some casual understanding, research, development, use, and assessment of computer technology in the teaching–learning process did not begin with the introduction of personal computing in the late-1970s. Such work began much earlier.

For instance, the University of Illinois Coordinated Research Laboratory began developing what Chalmers Sherwin in the mid-1950s called "a workbook with feedback" (Bitzer, Braunfeld, & Lichtenberger, 1962). The development became the well-known Programed Logic for Automated Teaching Operations (PLATO) project, which was intended to unleash the creative instructional energies of professors and other instructional personnel who would proceed to produce and implement PLATO lessons for their classes. At about the same time, the IBM Research Center was support-ing research and development of programs to teach binary arithmetic, stenotypy, psychological statistics, and German reading (Uttal, 1962). Ef-forts to integrate computer-assisted instruction with higher education (Hol-land, 1959) and elementary school education (Porter, 1959) were begun at Harvard University. Similar efforts were initiated at Stanford University to apply and help verify research findings from mathematical psychology, cog-nitive psychology, and psycholinguistics by incorporating them in elemen-tary school mathematics, beginning reading, college-level Russian, and mathematical logic programs of instruction (Atkinson & Wilson, 1969; Fletcher, 1979; Suppes, 1964). Other early efforts, such as those at the Uni-versity of Texas, U.S. Naval Academy, University of Southern California, Bolt, Beranek, and Newman, Inc., Air Force Personnel and Training Re-search Center, and Pennsylvania State University, could also be listed.

In short, there have been more than 45 years of research, development, use, and assessment of computer applications in instruction. By now, we should have some idea of the promise offered by such applications. We should know whether investment is warranted for further research and de-velopment or even if these applications are ready for large-scale implemen-tation.

WHAT INSTRUCTIONAL TECHNOLOGY ARE WE TALKING ABOUT?

It may be a good idea to identify, roughly, what we are talking about. Ba-sically, the topic concerns interactive instruction that is tailored on demand to the needs of individual learners. Much of this instruction depends on computer technology for delivery and presentation and includes such ap-plications as computer-based instruction, interactive multimedia instruc-tion, "intelligent" tutoring systems, networked tutorial simulation, and web-based instruction.

Today's emphasis on distributed learning and instruction leads us to de-scribe these technologies as asynchronous because they can deliver instruc-tion and mentoring (problem solving, performance aiding, and support) anywhere and at anytime. These technologies are frequently used in resi-dential classroom settings, but they do not require learners to gather at spe-cific times and specific places in order to learn. There may be (and often is) a (human) instructor in the equation, but there is no requirement that the instructor and the students be actively engaged at the same time.

One technology for asynchronous instruction should not be forgotten. This technology is remarkable for its easy portability and ubiquity, its ran-dom access to text, graphics, and color, its modest environmental requirements, its minimal power requirements, and, especially, its low cost. It has been available and in use for over 500 years. It is, of course, the technology of books.

Gutenberg's development of movable, metallic type may be seen as the second of three major revolutions in instruction. First was the development of writing. Before writing, the content of high quality instruction was available only synchronously, face to face, as instructors engaged their students in learning. Writing made the content of instruction available anytime, anywhere. Gutenberg's press and the books it printed effected a second revolution in instruction by making the content of high quality instruction widely, asynchronously, and (eventually) inexpensively accessible.

A third revolution in instruction may now be occurring. It is founded on the rapid and continuing development of computer technology. The computer-based instructional technologies listed above make both the content and the interactions, the tutorial give and take, of high quality instruction widely, asynchronously, and inexpensively accessible. They are available anytime and anywhere, and they can initiate relevant and appropriate instructional interactions on their own. They can be designed to adapt and respond to the needs and intentions of individual learners. They may foment a third revolution in instruction that is at least as significant as the first two.

These new and emerging instructional technologies will affect what, how, where, when, and for whom instruction and learning take place. They can provide expert mentors, tutors, guides, and coaches tailored to every learner or groups of learners. They can provide decision aiding and problem-solving assistance as well as instruction. They can adjust the pace, content, difficulty, and sequencing of instructional material and its presentation to individuals or groups of individuals in accord with their needs and intentions. If we use them well, they can become the foundation for a society of lifelong learners who can contend with rapid changes in work, commerce, and daily living, in other words, learners who function and compete successfully in a rapidly changing, technology-driven world economy.

INDIVIDUALIZATION AND INTERACTIVITY IN INSTRUCTION

Many intuitively appealing arguments have been made for the use of computer technology in instruction. They include immediate reinforcement of student responses, privacy of responses, culture-free fairness, infinite patience, and sensory immersion. All these capabilities have been verified to some extent by empirical research. But where is the leverage? What matters most and makes the most difference? Individualization seems to be the key.

The principal payoff from application of computer technology in instruction may come from their capabilities to tailor highly interactive environments to the needs of each individual learner.

The value of these capabilities may be seen in comparisons of one-on-one tutoring (one instructor with one student) with one-on-many classroom instruction (one instructor with 20–30 students). Benjamin Bloom (1984) and his students at the University of Chicago completed three such comparisons. Such a difference in instructional presentation might be expected to favor one-on-one teaching. What is surprising is how much it matters. Across these studies, the difference in student achievement amounted to two standard deviations. This difference is roughly equivalent to raising the achievement of 50th percentile students to the 98th level of achievement.

Some reasons for this difference are suggested by other research comparing one-on-one tutoring with one-on-many classroom instruction. Consider, for instance, some findings on the time it takes for different students to reach the same instructional objectives:

- Ratio of time needed by individual kindergarten students to build words from letters: 13 to 1 (Suppes, 1964)
- Ratio of time needed by individual hearing-impaired and Native American students to reach mathematics objectives: 4 to 1 (Suppes, Fletcher, & Zanotti, 1975, 1976)
- Overall ratio of time needed by individual students to learn in grades K–8: 5 to 1 (Gettinger, 1984)

This classroom diversity presents a daunting challenge to teachers using current methods of instruction. How can they ensure that every student has enough time to reach given instructional objectives? At the same time, how can they allow students who are ready to do so surge ahead? How can they cope with this variability? The answer, of course and despite heroic efforts to the contrary, is that they cannot. Most classrooms contain many students who, at one end of the spectrum, are bored and, at the other end, are overwhelmed and lost. By contrast, one-on-one tutoring allows teachers to adjust pace and content to the needs and abilities of individual students. They can proceed as rapidly or as slowly as needed. They can skip what individual students have mastered and concentrate on what they haven't.

This difference in time to reach given objectives seems initially due to ability, but prior knowledge very quickly takes over (Tobias, 1982). Despite efforts to sustain common levels of knowledge in classrooms, current school practices appear to increase these differences by about 1 year for every year students spend in elementary school (Heuston, 1997). For instance, the average spread of academic achievement in grade three is about 3 years. By grade six, it increases to about 6 years.

Another factor that may explain the difference in outcomes between one-on-one tutorials and one-on-many classroom settings is the intensity of the instruction. The interactivity of one-on-one instruction compared to classroom interactivity has been studied by Graesser and Person (1994). They compared instruction using one-on-one tutoring with classroom practice in two curriculum areas: research methods for college undergraduates and algebra for seventh graders. They found the following:

- Average number of questions teachers ask a class in a classroom hour: 3.0
- Average number of questions asked by any one student during a classroom hour: 0.1
- Average number of questions asked by a student and answered by a tutor during a tutorial hour:
  Research methods: 21.1
  Algebra: 32.2
- Average number of questions asked by a tutor and answered by a student during a tutorial hour:
  Research methods: 117.2
  Algebra: 146.4

How could a classroom teacher answer 20–30 questions asked by each of 25–30 students each hour? How could a classroom teacher prepare and present during each hour of instruction, 115–145 questions adapted to the needs of each student and then provide feedback for every answer received? These considerations are obviously rhetorical. Classroom instructional practice cannot compete with tutorial instruction in the interactivity and adaptability of the instruction provided.

Why not provide one-on-one tutorial instruction to all students? The answer is obvious. We can't afford it. One-on-one instruction may be an instructional imperative, as Scriven (1975) suggested, but it is also an economic impossibility. The result is, as Bloom stated, a 2-Sigma problem. How can we, in real instructional practice, fill the two standard deviation (the 2-Sigma) gap between classroom and tutorial instruction?

Enter computer technology. Because computers can interact with learners and tailor instructional presentations to their needs, and because the computer capabilities needed to do this are less expensive than human tutors or expert consultants, some of the gap between one-on-one and one-on-many instruction can be filled, affordably, by computer technology. Computers allow us to substitute the capital of technology for the labor of human instructors. They may effect a third revolution in instruction by making individualized instructional interactions affordable.

SOME FINDINGS

Does this substitution of computers for human tutoring work? Can it fill Bloom's 2-Sigma gap? Can it create environments in which learning occurs more effectively and/or more efficiently? The following section summarizes results that have emerged from research on the effectiveness of technology applied to the problems and processes of instruction.

Technology Can Be Used to Teach

A number of studies have compared technology-based instruction to simply doing nothing. These studies did not seek to determine if these applications are a good way to teach or if they teach the right things, but simply to see if they teach anything at all.

Their findings suggest that they do. For instance, single studies by Crotty (1984) and Verano (1987) and two studies by Allan (1989) compared applications of interactive multimedia instruction with placebo treatments in which no instructional material was presented. The average effect size for these studies was 1.38 standard deviations, suggesting, roughly, an average improvement in student achievement from the 50th to 92nd percentile performance.

Significant evidence that avoids "horse race" (control group vs. experimental group) comparisons comes from early studies by Suppes, Fletcher, and Zanotti, who used computer-based instruction to provide mathematics instruction to 69 Native American (1975) and 297 hearing-impaired (1976) students. These studies developed a model for the progress, or "trajectory," of each student using CBI to learn mathematics as measured by scores on standard tests. The studies used no instructional input other than the amount of time (time on task) students spent in the CBI curriculum to predict their achievement.

The investigators found that from the 20th to 39th sessions (about 240 minutes) of computer-based instruction, they could predict to the nearest tenth of a grade placement, the score that each student would obtain on a standardized measure of total mathematics achievement based on total time in the instruction. Different students, of course, began at different levels and progressed at different rates. But different goals could be set for different students if instructional time was held constant, or different amounts of time could be assigned to different students to ensure that threshold levels of learning (as measured by the tests) were achieved. If time spent in the curriculum had no effect, no predictions would have been possible. In these studies, the precision of the predictions was as notable as the fact that they could be made and validated at all.

Technology Can Be Used to Increase Instructional Effectiveness

The more interesting question is, of course, whether technology-based instruction is an improvement: Does it allow us to create learning environments that are any better than those we already have? A typical study addressing this issue compares an approach using technology, such as computer-based instruction or interactive multimedia instruction, with what may be called "conventional instruction," using lecture, text-based materials (perhaps including programed text, and/or laboratory, hands-on experience with real equipment). There have been many such evaluative comparisons made. The findings from these studies provide a picture of what has been learned.

Early studies of effectiveness used a *box-score approach*. Investigators would determine the proportion of evaluations in which experimental group means exceeded control group means by some statistically significant extent and then report the experimental treatment as favorable or not depending on whether this proportion was large or small.

Vinsonhaler and Bass (1972) used a box-score approach to review over 30 published, empirical evaluations of computer-based instruction involving more than 10,000 students. For those who view technology-assisted instruction as a recent phenomenon, the early date of this review is worth noting. The authors found positive or equal results in 30 of the 34 studies they included for review. They found a median achievement gain among the CBI students of 40%.

Hedges and Olkin (1980) showed that the box-score approach has very low power (low ability to detect statistically significant differences) for the treatment effect sizes and sample sizes characteristic of instructional research. They also showed that the power of the box-score approach decreases as the number of studies included in the review increases.

Today, reviewers are likely to use an analysis of analyses, or *meta-analysis* (Glass, 1976). Meta-analysis allows reviewers to aggregate the results of many studies that attempt to answer a common question, such as the effect of using technology-based instruction, and report the magnitude of this effect in units of standard deviations using a common measure of merit called *effect size*.

The main drawback in using effect sizes is that they are, basically, a measure of standard deviations and not especially meaningful to individuals who are not statisticians. For this reason, the effect sizes reported here are accompanied by rough translations to percentiles. They show that an effect size of, say, 0.50 is roughly equivalent to raising the performance of 50th percentile students to that of 69th percentile students.

For instance, Kulik (1994) performed many such studies for technology-based instruction. From his own work and that of his colleagues, he reported an overall effect size of 0.35, which is roughly equivalent to raising the achievement of 50th percentile students to that of 64th percentile students by exposing them to technology-based instruction.

Examination of results from meta-analyses concerning the use of technology-based instruction, tracking improvements in both technology and instructional approaches, produces the results shown in Fig. 4.1, which suggest progress toward Bloom's targeted effect size of two standard deviations.

In Fig. 4.1, computer-based instruction summarizes results from 233 studies that involved straightforward use of computer presentations using text, graphics, and limited animation, as well as some degree of individualized interaction. The effect size of 0.39 standard deviations suggests, roughly, an improvement of 50th percentile students to the performance levels of 65th percentile students.

Interactive multimedia instruction involves more elaborate interactions adding more audio, more extensive animation, and (especially) video clips. The added cost of these capabilities may be compensated for by greater achievement—an average effect size of 0.50 standard deviations as compared with an effect size of 0.39 for garden-variety computer-based instruction. An effect size of 0.50 for interactive multimedia instruction suggests an improvement of 50th percentile students to the 69th percentile of performance.

Intelligent tutoring systems involve a capability that has been developing since the late 1960s (Carbonell, 1970), but has only recently been expand-

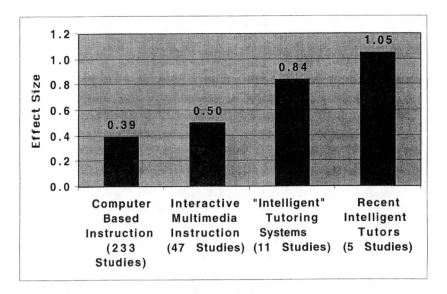

FIG. 4.1.   Some effect sizes for technology-based instruction.

ing into general use. In this approach, an attempt is made to directly mimic the one-on-one dialogue that occurs in tutorial interactions. The key component is that computer presentations and responses are generated in real time, on demand, and as needed or requested by learners. Mixed initiative dialogue is supported in which either the computer or learner can ask or answer open-ended questions. Notably, these interactions are generated as required. Instructional designers do not need to anticipate and prestore them. This approach is computationally more sophisticated and it is more expensive to produce than standard computer-based instruction. However, its costs may be justified by the increase in average effect size to 0.84 standard deviations, which suggests, roughly, an improvement from 50th to 80th percentile performance.

Some later intelligent tutoring systems (Gott, Kane, & Lesgold, 1995) were considered just to see how far we are getting with this approach. The average effect size of 1.05 standard deviations for these recent applications is promising. It represents, roughly, an improvement of the performance of 50th percentile students to 85th percentile performance.

The more extensive tailoring of instruction to the needs of individual students that can be obtained through the use of generative, intelligent tutoring systems can only be expected to increase. They may raise the bar for the ultimate effectiveness of technology-based instruction. They may make available far greater efficiencies than we can now obtain from other approaches.

But further, these approaches may provide yet another example of what might be called the Columbus paradox. As readers will recall, Columbus sailed west to find India (and a lucrative spice route). Instead he opened the door to what became a new world for Europeans. Such a result typifies technological progress. Seeking one thing based on a metaphor with common practice, we almost inevitably end up with something at least unforeseen and often unexpected. Wireless telegraph produced something functionally quite different than the telegraph, namely, radio. Similarly, efforts to make a carriage run without a horse produced automobiles, to say nothing of gas stations, motels, and the Santa Monica Freeway. Seeking affordable one-on-one tutoring through automation, we may end up with something no one can envision at present. The existing metaphor is enough to get started, but the result may surprise us all.

Technology Can Be Used to Ensure That All Students Learn

One benefit of technology-based instruction appears to be that fewer students are left behind. Because sequence, pace, difficulty, content, and/or style of technology-based presentations can be tailored to each student's unique needs, some progress by each student can be ensured. Students can achieve the threshold of skill and knowledge required by the work for which they are preparing, thereby shortening the left tail of any distribution of achievement. This possibility is borne out by results. For example, Fletcher (1991) found in a review of 44 empirical comparisons, the spread (variance) of postinstruction measures, such as test scores or time to complete instruction, increased in every case more under conventional instruction than under interactive multimedia instruction. This trend was observed despite an overall increase in relative mean achievement scores of about 0.50 standard deviations under interactive multimedia instruction.

On the other hand, what happens if we open the gates and allow all students to progress as rapidly as they can? The differences noted in the pace with which students can proceed and the capacities of technology-assisted instruction for accommodating to these differences suggest that differences in achievement might well be expected to expand if instructional time is held constant.

Whatever the ultimate results, whether we ultimately decrease or increase the spread of achievement among age-based cohorts of students, instructional technology will help us deal with them. If students are allowed to stretch to their full learning potential, on one hand, and no student is lost in the rush to learn, on the other, we will increase fairness and opportunity equity in instruction at both ends of the spectrum.

Technology Can Be Used to Reduce Time Needed to Reach Instructional Objectives

If instructional time is not spent re-presenting material the student already knows and is concentrated on material the student has yet to learn, learning should occur more quickly. As suggested by Table 4.1, research suggests that it does.

This finding arises repeatedly in reviews of instructional technology. Orlansky and String (1977) found that reductions in time to reach instructional objectives averaged about 54% in their review of CBI used in military training. Fletcher (1991) found an average time reduction of 31% in 6 studies of interactive videodisc instruction applied in higher education. Kulik

TABLE 4.1
Percent Time Savings for Technology-Based Instruction

Study (Reference)	Number of Findings	Average Time Saved (%)
Orlansky and String (1977)	13	54
Fletcher (1991)	6	31
Kulik (1994) (Higher Education)	17	34
Kulik (1994) (Adult Education)	15	24

and his colleagues found time reductions of 34% in 17 studies of CBI used in higher education, and 24% in 15 studies of adult education (Kulik, 1994). These reviews are effectively independent in that they reviewed different sets of evaluation studies. On this basis, reductions of about 30% in the time it takes students to reach a variety of given instructional objectives seem to be a reasonable expectation.

It turns out that 30% is a fairly conservative target. Commercial enterprises that develop technology-based instruction for the Department of Defense (DoD) regularly base their bids on the expectation that they can reduce instructional time by 50%. Noja (1991) reported time savings through the use of technology-based instruction as high as 80% in training operators and maintenance technicians for the Italian Air Force.

Time savings of 30% are not an inconsiderable matter for the Department of Defense. The DoD spends about $4 billion a year on specialized skill training, which is the postbasic training needed to qualify people for the many technical jobs (e.g., wheeled vehicle mechanics, radar operators and technicians, medical technicians) needed to perform military operations. If the DoD were to reduce time to train 20% of the people undergoing specialized skill training by 30%, it would save over $250 million per year. If it were to do so for 60% of the people undergoing specialized skill training, it would save over $700 million per year.

It is harder to assign dollar values to the time that students spend in educational settings, especially K–12 classrooms, but time so spent is not without cost and value. Aside from the obvious motivational issues of keeping students interested and involved in educational material, using their time well will profit both them and any society that depends on their eventual competency and achievement. The time savings offered by technology-based instruction in K–12 education may be more significant and of greater value than those obtained in posteducation training.

Students Prefer Technology-Based Instruction

Many evaluations of technology-based instruction simply ask students if they prefer it to more conventional classroom approaches. Greiner (1991) reviewed these evaluations and found that typically from 70% to 80% of students polled preferred technology-based approaches over those that were not technology based. When students reported that they did not prefer such approaches, the reasons were usually traced to implementation or technical problems with the technology, not the instructional approach itself.

McKinnon, Nolan, and Sinclair (2000) completed a thorough 3-year study of student attitudes toward the use of computers as learning and productivity tools for such applications as spreadsheets, databases, graphics, desktop publishing, and statistical processing in their junior high school English, mathematics, science, and social science courses. The academic performance of the computer-using students remained steadily and significantly superior to that of their noncomputer-using peers throughout the 3 years of the study.

As might be expected, the attitudes of the computer-using students in this study toward computer use slackened and became less positive as the novelty of using the technology wore off. However the attitudes of the computer-using students remained positive and significantly more positive than those of the noncomputer using students throughout all 3 years of the study. After examining their data, McKinnon et al. attributed the decrease in positive attitudes among the computer-using students to "habituation" in using computers rather than any disenchantment with their utility. Computers simply became tools for classroom learning that the students took for granted.

Technology-Based Instruction Can Be Cost-Effective

The central question for researchers often concerns whether or not a new approach is an improvement over current practice. The central question for educational decision-makers, however, must go a step farther. Decision-makers must, of course, be concerned with improving current educational practice, but they must also consider what must be given up to do so. In the practical world, this usually leads to consideration of costs as well as effectiveness. If researchers wish to make a difference in educational practice, they must address decisions of cost-effectiveness.

Cost-effectiveness may be assessed in either of two ways. We may either hold costs constant and assess alternatives for maximizing effectiveness, or we may hold effectiveness constant and assess alternatives for minimizing costs. Adequate models of both costs and effectiveness must be employed in studies using either of these approaches. Few studies using either approach have been performed in education, and more are needed.

One comparison holding effectiveness constant while seeking minimized costs is shown in Table 4.2. The table uses empirical data reported by Jamison, Fletcher, Suppes, and Atkinson (1976), Levin, Glass, and Meister (1987), and Fletcher, Hawley, and Piele (1990). It reports the costs (in constant 2001 dollars) to raise comprehensive mathematics scores on a standardized test one standard deviation using several different instructional approaches: tutors, reduced class size, increased instructional time, and computer-based instruction.

The table suggests that the most cost-effective approaches among all these alternatives are computer-based instruction and peer tutoring. It also suggests that, of the two, computer-based instruction is more cost-effective.

TABLE 4.2
Costs (Constant $2001) to Raise Mathematics
Scores by One Standard Deviation

Alternative	Costs
Tutoring (20 min/day):	
Peer tutors	472
Adult tutors	2,654
Reduce class size from:	
35 to 30	1,619
35 to 20	2,251
Increase instruction time 30 min/day	4,391
Computer-based instruction for 10 min/day:	
- Mini-computer in laboratory (1976)	
Grade 3	382
Grade 5	785
- Microcomputers in classrooms (1990)	
Grade 3	316
Grade 5	339

This result echoes the findings of Niemiec, Sikorski, and Walberg (1989), who compared studies of the costs and effectiveness of peer tutoring with studies of computer-based instruction. They found the two approaches to be equally effective and both to be more effective by about 0.4 standard deviations than conventional classroom instruction. They also found a clear cost-effectiveness superiority (by a factor of about three) for computer-based instruction over peer tutoring.

It is notable that these two approaches are not incompatible and that a strong cost-effectiveness argument can be made for combining peer tutoring with computer-based instruction. Such a combination may be accomplished by presenting instruction to more than one student at a time on a single computer station. This sort of approach has been shown early on by Grubb (1964), and more recently by Shlecter (1990), to be effective.

CAVEATS

A summary of research results must necessarily slide over many issues of intent, design, implementation, and evaluation. These issues may also be summarized.

Assessment of Innovation

One difficulty for any evaluation of an innovative technology is that there is nothing else like it. Each educational approach has its own strengths and limitations. If an evaluation is held to strict instructional and experimental controls based on constraints imposed by one approach, then the other approach will be at a disadvantage. More specifically, in comparisons of older with newer approaches, the older approach may limit application, and assessment, of the newer approach.

New approaches are often not used to best advantage because not enough is understood about how best to use them, they have not matured sufficiently for fair comparison with what's currently available, and/or sufficient infrastructure does not exist to support them adequately. Early horseless carriages were certainly inferior in both costs and effectiveness to horse-drawn carriages if they were viewed strictly as a means for getting from one place to another. They were misused by their drivers, their design and production had not matured sufficiently to make them reliable, and the necessary infrastructure of roads, gas stations, competent mechanics, and so on did not exist. The promise of many instructional technologies and their applications may similarly be masked by our unfamiliarity with them. Despite all the evaluations discussed, instructional approaches that use these technologies to best advantage may not yet exist.

Single Factor Assessment

Empirical evaluations are always subject to one experimental contamination or another. It is rare (i.e., never) that we find comparisons in which the single different factor is the presence or absence of instructional technology. For instance, the instructional content and objectives of the original approach may be revised and incorporated in the new, but not the original, approach. The revised body of materials may then be compared with the original instruction and owe more of its observed success to the revision than to the functionalities that are the object of the evaluation. Problems such as this seem unavoidable. The "trajectory theory" approaches of Suppes et al. (1975, 1976) may provide a way around this problem. Using only the amount of time a new approach is in active use to predict achievement on external measures, such as standard test scores, we may get as close to single factor assessment as we can in field research and assessments.

On the other hand, if we can not be perfect, at least we can be explicit. Careful documentation will ensure that everyone knows what has been done and can weigh conclusions for themselves. Seidel and Perez (1994), many of Reigeluth's (1999) contributors, and others supported this position by emphasizing that candidate innovations for instructional practice must consider the full environment into which an innovation is placed. More attention to full system environments may be needed in evaluations of technology-based instruction. Even when these environments are carefully considered, comprehensive discussions of them are rarely presented in evaluation research literature, which is often constrained by such mundane considerations as publication space. Meta-analytic reviews like those discussed above may provide a partial solution to this problem. If it is impossible to control for all factors, perhaps we can perform and then review enough assessments to ensure that the signal can be separated from the noise of extraneous factors.

Production Quality

Aspects such as the quality of graphics, clarity of instructional text, verisimilitude of simulations, and relevance of tutorial advice may have a substantial impact on the effectiveness of many instructional technology applications, but these issues are rarely addressed. The impact of production quality, especially the impact of its costs on resulting instructional effectiveness, needs to be better understood. It may explain an appreciable portion of the difference in otherwise similar approaches.

Media-Based Assessment

No discussion of technology applications in instruction would be complete without mentioning Clark's (1983) argument that "the best current evidence is that media are mere vehicles that deliver instruction but do not influence student achievement any more than the truck that delivers our groceries causes changes in our nutrition" (p. 445). These concerns may be summed up by the notion that technology alone does not define an instructional approach: What is done with the technology is what counts. This point of view seems unequivocal. The presence of technology is no guarantee that effective instructional content, effective ways to present it, or even that the unique strengths of the technology will be used.

On the other hand, the absence of technology is a reasonable guarantee that its unique capabilities will be missing. It is difficult to imagine approaches that make the intense individualization discussed above affordable or even possible without technology. To take Clark's metaphor directly, improvements in the technology of delivering food from centers of production to markets have had a tremendous impact on the nutrition of nations. The technologies by themselves do not guarantee any impact, but the functionalities they make possible put serious improvements within reach, if not our grasp.

Moreover, arguments such as Clark's are often advanced as blanket recommendations of what should or should not be considered in evaluation research. However, evaluation is performed either explicitly or implicitly to inform a decision. Should we do A or B? How might we improve C? What should our policy be toward D? Should we invest our scarce resources in E? Should we institutionalize the use of F? Aside from technical and methodological quality, blanket prescriptions for what ends an evaluation should or should not serve seem misguided.

But what then should we make of the above meta-analyses of technology-based instruction? What decisions might they inform? These analyses review what has been observed to happen when technology is applied in instruction. They do not address cause and effect, nor do they address how either the technology or the full learning environment should be designed to promote learning or achievement of specific learning outcomes. The state of the art does not seem ready to address these issues, although many individual studies hint at significant possibilities.

These analyses do report data now available from systematic, reasonably well-designed and implemented evaluation studies, and they suggest reasons why we might well expect these data to be favorable. Technology can take on the overwhelming human workload that classroom teachers would need to assume in order to achieve significant new levels of effectiveness in education and to prepare students for the massive, global infusion of technology in the adult working world. If these are our goals, then available data suggest that technology can make their accomplishment both affordable and accessible.

If a decision must be made concerning future investment in these technologies, then the task of the evaluator is to inform the decision as well as possible. Based on the data reviewed above, it seems reasonable, if not imperative, to proceed. Despite the great amount of work that must be done to learn how best to use technology in education, "paralysis by analysis" does not seem to be an acceptable option.

Third-Party Evaluation

Many evaluations of instructional technology applications are performed by their developers or others who have a stake in their success. There are both strengths and weaknesses to such evaluations. Developers are rarely indifferent to the success of their products and may, intentionally or not, bias the results of their evaluation. On the other hand, they also have a stake in honest assessment, and they may understand better than anyone the strengths and limitations of what they have produced. Despite current emphases on the virtues of third-party evaluations, such evaluations should not be sought without question, and evaluations performed by developers and other stakeholders should not be discarded as irrelevant. We should seek to understand better the implications of both sorts of evaluation and the data, findings, and information they provide. Many of the evaluation studies reviewed in the above meta-analyses were performed by developers rather than third parties. Based on the methodological filters applied in selecting the studies and discussions of their results, there seem to be many good reasons to judge their findings as valid.

Antiquity of Applications

By the time an evaluation study is performed, documented, and reported in a form accessible to developers and potential users, the application originally under consideration is likely to be 5 or more years old. By the time it is included in a summary such as this one, the application may be well over 10 years old (or more) and superseded by curriculum requirements, job design, or many other factors that change over time. It is unlikely that the application itself will be of more than historical interest to decision-makers.

However, the principles underlying the design of the applications and their success may well be of continuing interest to designers and potential users. The technologies and media employed in the application are likely to be notable as long as they receive investment. As usual, the value and relevance of the evaluation do not depend as much on the antiquity of the application being considered as on how well it informs the decisions that will be made based on its findings. In a world of rapidly emerging technology and applications, useful information on a specific application is frequently unavailable until the state of the art passes it by. However, the class of applications to which it belongs may persist long enough to be usefully informed by assessments such as those discussed above.

Relation of Instructional Design to Outcomes

Different outcomes, or instructional objectives, must compete for scarce instructional resources. Decisions made in the design of instructional technology programs affect both their costs and their achievement of specific instructional objectives. These relationships should be better understood. How, for instance, should a program be designed to maximize transfer ability, retention, speed of response, accuracy of response, or motivation to continue study? What do the design alternatives cost? To what quantitative degree do they contribute to instructional effectiveness? How should we trade them off against one another, as we invariably must in the practical world of training design?

The individualization of control and student progress that can be exercised in instructional technology applications, raises these issues to a level of both significance and practical payoff that they do not reach elsewhere. Technology offers a degree of control that makes serious engineering of instruction practicable. Raymond Fox (1994) stated that "one of the more difficult problems in dealing with improvement in public education is to replace the notion of teaching as an art form with that of instruction delivery as a systems science" (p. 2). If we are to achieve an engineering of instruction so that predictable results can be reliably obtained by many hands, we must seek an engineering of instructional design that provides predictable outcomes from specific choices among design alternatives. We must seek to learn not only if instructional technology works, but also how it works.

CONCLUSIONS

The results discussed above suggest that applications of technology in education and training are more effective than our current practice. To conclude that they are not would require a substantial flood of findings to the contrary. On the other hand, there remain significant questions to be answered.

How can new technologies best be integrated with existing institutions of instruction? Most change is evolutionary rather than revolutionary, and technology-based approaches to instruction seem no different, despite the immense changes they may ultimately engender. In a constructivist world, we cannot make learning occur, we can only create environments that promote and encourage it (e.g., Mayer, 1999). With or without constructivism, Seidel and Perez (1994) were right. More needs to be done to understand how best to design and implement these environments. The revolution wrought by the horseless carriage was not complete until the infrastructure it required was put into place. The same will be true of technology-based instruction.

Costs must be considered as well as effectiveness. Educational researchers who dedicate their professional lives to improving education by developing new and innovative approaches are well advised to examine effectiveness. Most of them rise responsibly and well to the challenge. For educational decision-makers, however, effectiveness may be only half of the question. Somewhere costs must be considered by someone. Proper consideration of costs depends on the development of adequate models of costs and detailed understanding of the cost consequences arising from any instructional innovation must be developed, especially an innovation involving such an alien approach as technology-based instruction. Few educational decision-makers have time or resources to attend to these matters, and they, like most of us, have a vested interest in maintaining the status quo. That leaves educational researchers to fill the gap. Just as they rise to the challenge in evaluating new approaches to instruction, so they must also begin to address seriously the cost consequences of the new approaches they choose to champion.

How should we design technology-based instruction? The state of the art and practice in technology-based instruction has passed beyond questions of *if* applications using it work to *how* they work. How might instruction and instructional enviroments be designed to bring about specific instructional outcomes? Excellent reviews by Krendl and Lieberman (1988) and Schater and Fagnano (1999) echo earlier recommendations by Suppes (1964) and others to apply advances in cognitive and learning theory to the development of technology-based instruction. Such efforts will both improve the quality of instruction delivered and, probably more importantly, provide feedback to theories of cognition and learning about where they are right, where they might use some improvement, and where they have left gaps that badly need to be filled. This is the traditional interplay of theory and empirical research that has served other areas of systematic investigation so well. Technology-based instruction, with its precise control over inputs and equally precise measurement of outputs, appears to have a unique role to serve in completing the feedback loop between instructional theory and instructional research.

How might we best individualize instruction? If individualization is the key enabling capability of technology-based instruction, then more should be done to determine how best to accomplish it. What cues should be gathered from the interactions of individuals with technology to best tailor sequence, style, content, and pace of the instructional presentations for them? There are bright spots in the research literature. More could and should be done to identify, learn from, and develop them.

This review of technology-based instruction suggests that it will most probably lower costs and increase effectiveness for many applications. It is likely to emerge as the most cost-effective alternative in many settings and applications when considered among all other possibilities in a full systems context. Overall, it is likely to improve both our practice of instruction and theories of learning and cognition. It does not seem unreasonable, then, to argue that the resources needed to realize its potential are well spent. These resources include funding, time, and the effort to effect significant changes in professional practice and in our instructional institutions. The point of the above review has been to suggest that the return on this investment will be sizable and worthwhile.

REFERENCES

Allan, D. M. E. (1989). *The effectiveness of interactive videodisc in clinical medical education.* San Diego, CA: Intelligent Images, DAROX Corporation.

Atkinson, R. C., & Wilson, H. A. (Eds.). (1969). *Computer-assisted instruction.* New York: Academic Press.

Bitzer, D. L., Braunfeld, P. G., & Lichtenberger, W. W. (1962). Plato II: A multiple-student, computer-controlled, automatic teaching device. In J. E. Coulson (Ed.), *Programmed learning and computer-based instruction* (pp. 205–216). New York: Wiley.

Bloom, B. S. (1984). The 2-sigma problem: The search for methods of group instruction as effective as one-to-one tutoring. *Educational Researcher, 13*(6), 4–16.

Carbonell, J. R. (1970). AI in CAI: An artificial intelligence approach to computer-assisted instruction. *IEEE Transactions on Man-Machine Systems, 11,* 190–202.

Clark, R. E. (1983). Reconsidering research on learning from media. *Review of Educational Research, 53,* 445–459.

Crotty, J. M. (1984). *Instruction via an intelligent videodisc system versus classroom instruction for beginning college French students: A comparative experiment.* (AFIT/CI/NR 84-51D). Wright-Patterson AFB, OH: Air Force Institute of Technology/NR. (DTIC No. ADA 145 599). (University Microfilms No. 8513797).

Fletcher, J. D. (1979). The design of computer-assisted instruction in beginning reading: The Stanford projects. In L. B. Resnick & P. A. Weaver (Eds.), *Theory and practice of early reading instruction* (pp. 243–267). Hillsdale, NJ: Lawrence Erlbaum Associates.

Fletcher, J. D. (1991). Effectiveness and cost of interactive videodisc instruction. *Machine Mediated Learning, 3,* 361–385.

Fletcher, J. D. (1997). What have we learned about computer based instruction in military training? In R. J. Seidel & P. R. Chatelier (Eds.), *Virtual reality, training's future?* (pp. 169–177). New York: Plenum.

Fletcher, J. D., Hawley, D. E., & Piele, P. K. (1990). Costs, effects, and utility of microcomputer assisted instruction in the classroom. *American Educational Research Journal, 27,* 783–806.

Fox, R. G. (1994). *A systems approach to education.* Warrenton, VA: Learning Technology Institute.

Gettinger, M. (1984). Individual differences in time needed for learning: A review of the literature. *Educational Psychologist, 19,* 15–29.

Glass, G. V. (1976). Primary, secondary, and meta-analysis of research. *Educational Researcher, 5,* 3–8.

Gott, S. P., Kane, R. S., & Lesgold, A. (1995). *Tutoring for Transfer of Technical Competence* (AL/HR-TP-1995-0002). Brooks AFB, TX: Armstrong Laboratory, Human Resources Directorate.

Graesser, A. C., & Person, N. K. (1994). Question asking during tutoring. *American Educational Research Journal, 31,* 104–137.

Greiner, J. M. (1991). Interactive multimedia instruction: What do the numbers show? In *Proceedings of the Ninth Annual Conference on Interactive Instruction Delivery* (pp. 100–104). Warrenton, VA: Society for Applied Learning Technology.

Grubb, R. E. (1964). *The effects of paired student interaction in the computer tutoring of statistics.* Yorktown Heights, NY: Thomas J. Watson Research Center.

Hedges, L. V., & Olkin, I. (1985). *Statistical methods for meta-analysis.* Orlando, FL: Academic Press.

Heuston, D. H. (1997). *School improvement models: The manual model and the speed of light.* Sandy, UT: Waterford Institute.

Holland, J. G. (1959). A teaching machine program in psychology. In E. Galanter (Ed.), *Automatic teaching: The state of the art* (pp. 69–82). New York: Wiley.

Jamison, D. T., Fletcher, J. D., Suppes, P., & Atkinson, R. C. (1976). Cost and performance of computer-assisted instruction for education of disadvantaged children. In J. T. Froomkin, D. T. Jamison, & R. Radner (Eds.), *Education as an industry* (pp. 201–240). Cambridge, MA: Ballinger.

Krendl, K. A., & Lieberman, D. A. (1988). Computers and learning: A review of recent research. *Journal of Educational Computing Research, 4,* 367–389.

Kulik, J. A. (1994). Meta-analytic studies of findings on computer-based instruction. In E. L. Baker & H. F. O'Neil, Jr. (Eds.), *Technology assessment in education and training* (pp. 9–33). Hillsdale, NJ: Lawrence Erlbaum Associates.

Levin, H. M., Glass, G. V., & Meister, G. R. (1987). Cost-effectiveness of computer-assisted instruction. *Evaluation Review, 11,* 50–71.

Mayer, R. E. (1999). Designing instruction for constructivist learning. In C. M. Reigeluth (Ed.), *Instructional-design theories and models: Vol. II. A new paradigm of instructional theory* (pp. 141–159). Hillsdale, NJ: Lawrence Erlbaum Associates.

McKinnon, D. H., Nolan, C. J. P., & Sinclair, K. E. (2000). A longitudinal study of student attitudes toward computers: Resolving an attitude decay paradox. *Journal of Research on Computing in Education, 32,* 325–335.

Niemiec, R. P., Sikorski, M., & Walberg, H. J. (1989). Comparing the cost-effectiveness of tutoring and computer-based instruction. *Journal of Educational Computing Research, 5,* 395–407.

Noja, G. P. (1991). DVI and system integration: A further step in ICAI/IMS technology. In R. J. Seidel & P. R. Chatelier (Eds.), *Advanced technologies applied to training design* (pp. 161–189). New York: Plenum.

Orlansky, J., & String, J. (1977). *Cost effectiveness of computer-based instruction in military training* (IDA Paper P-1375). Arlington, VA: Institute for Defense Analyses.

Porter, D. (1959). Some effects of year long teaching machine instruction. In E. Galanter (Ed.), *Automatic teaching: The state of the art* (pp. 85–90). New York: Wiley.

Reigeluth, C. (1999). *Instructional design, theories, and models: A new paradigm of instructional theory.* Hillsdale, NJ: Lawrence Erlbaum Associates.

Schacter, J., & Fagnano, C. (1999). Does computer technology improve student learning and achievement? How, when, and under what conditions. *Journal of Educational Computing Research, 20,* 329–343.

Scriven, M. (1975). Problems and prospects for individualization. In H. Talmage (Ed.), *Systems of individualized education* (pp. 199–210). Berkeley, CA: McCutchan.

Seidel, R. J., & Perez, R. S. (1994). An evaluation model for investigating the impact of innovative educational technology. In E. L. Baker & H. F. O'Neil, Jr. (Eds.), *Technology assessment in software applications* (pp. 177–212). Hillsdale, NJ: Lawrence Erlbaum Associates.

Shlechter, T. M. (1990). The relative instructional efficiency of small group computer-based training. *Journal of Educational Computing Research, 6,* 329–341.

Suppes, P. (1964). Modern learning theory and the elementary-school curriculum. *American Educational Research Journal, 1,* 79–93.

Suppes, P., Fletcher, J. D., & Zanotti, M. (1975). Performance models of American Indian students on computer-assisted instruction in elementary mathematics. *Instructional Science, 4,* 303–313.

Suppes, P., Fletcher, J. D., & Zanotti, M. (1976). Models of individual trajectories in computer-assisted instruction for deaf students. *Journal of Educational Psychology, 68,* 117–127.

Tobias, S. (1982). When do instructional methods make a difference? *Educational Researcher, 11*(4), 4–9.

Uttal, W. R. (1962). On conversational interaction. In J. E. Coulson (Ed.), *Programmed learning and computer-based instruction* (pp. 171–190). New York: Wiley.

Verano, M. (1987). *Achievement and retention of Spanish presented via videodisc in linear, segmented, and interactive modes.* (Doctoral dissertation, University of Texas, Austin, TX) (DTIC No. ADA 185 893).

Vinsonhaler, J. F., & Bass, R. K. (1972). A summary of ten major studies on CAI drill and practice. *Educational Technology, 12,* 29–32.

Chapter 5

Presidential Technology Initiative (PTI): A Model for the Integration of Technology in a K–12 Curriculum

Ray S. Perez
Office of Naval Research

Gary Bridgewater
TRW

This chapter describes an innovative technology project initiated and funded by the Department of Defense in partnership with the White House. The project is the Department of Defense (DoD) Presidential Technology Initiative (PTI). The PTI was implemented in the Department of Defense school system that provides kindergarten through Grade 12 educational services to the children of the men and women of the armed forces. The PTI's primary technology innovation was in the development of curriculum-based educational courseware and software management tools developed in collaboration with DoD students, teachers, and staff. The PTI program was conceptualized during the period from 1995 to 1999 at an approximate cost of $19.7 million.

This project was unique in several respects. The project was implemented within an educational system that has schools located worldwide, is managed by a federal agency (the Department of Defense), and has a national reputation for its students' outstanding performance on high-stakes evaluations. This is even more remarkable considering that 40% of its student population is Hispanic and African American and it has a very mobile student population (Department of Defense Education Activity, 2000). This project was launched under the auspices of President Clinton's national educational technology initiatives that are characterized by the "four C's" of computers, connectivity, competency, and curriculum. It focused on the development of content using curriculum-based educational courseware tools.

The agency responsible for the DoD school system is formally titled the Department of Defense Education Activity (DoDEA). Through its headquarters in Arlington, Virginia, the Department of Defense Education Activity manages a school system that provides kindergarten through grade 12 education services similar to those in typical school systems found in any public educational setting. The Department of Defense Education Activity system is divided into two major subordinate organizations: the Department of Defense Dependent Schools and the Defense Dependents Elementary and Secondary Schools. The Department of Defense Dependent Schools is responsible for the school systems outside the continental United States. It serves approximately 85,000 students in 167 schools located in 14 countries and is supported by 12,500 teachers, staff, and other personnel. The Defense Dependents Elementary and Secondary Schools is responsible for the school systems within the United States, Guam, and the Commonwealth of Puerto Rico. It serves approximately 33,000 students in 65 schools and is supported by 5,000 teachers, staff, and other employees. The overall Department of Defense Education Activity school system is comparable in size to the state of Delaware's school system.

The overarching goal of the PTI project was established at the outset by the funding agency, the Personnel and Readiness Office of the Office of the Secretary of Defense (OSD). The charge to the project was to develop effective courseware that improves student learning. The program manager (PM) developed a supporting strategy that focused PTI plans and activities on this central goal. The program strategy consisted of four main components: testbed schools, courseware development, professional development, and evaluation. Early in the program, a testbed environment was established to develop effective courseware, courseware was aligned with the DoDEA curriculum, an approach to encourage commercial developers to build and market effective courseware was instituted, a professional development set of activities was generated, and a series of evaluation activities was initiated.

PTI PROGRAM ACTIVITIES

A Testbed Environment

The DoDEA school system is managed by the federal government and has schools colocated with military bases throughout the world. As a school system, it is similar in many respects to school systems within the United States, but it does have a few unique characteristics:

- The system is more racially diverse than the national average, with 40% of the student population being either Hispanic or African American.

- The classrooms have, on average, more technology than most other schools.
- DoDEA students have a higher mobility rate and are more likely to finish their education in a public education system in the United States.
- The fact that students move from school to school as their parents are reassigned has caused DoDEA to develop a curriculum that adheres to national standards in each of its curriculum areas.

The diversity, technology orientation, and national standards-based curriculum make the DoDEA system an ideal testbed for the development, testing, and evaluation of courseware for grades K through 12. Ten DoDEA school districts were selected to serve as testbeds for the PTI courseware and software tools. The school districts were selected following a formalized process. First, districts interested in participating as testbeds were required to submit an initial proposal to the PTI program manger. It was made clear that participation in the program was voluntary. District proposals had to be accompanied by an endorsement of support for the project from the district superintendent. The endorsement was required to state support for the program's goals and objectives, an agreement to allow for the teachers' participation, and agreement to provide release time for administrators and teachers to engage in professional development activities. The endorsement also stated that the district would provide technical support, participate in the program evaluation, and provide the required number of high-end computers as well as connectivity to the Internet.

The 10 testbed schools selected to participate in the program were from both the Department of Defense Dependent Schools and the Defense Dependents Elementary and Secondary Schools sites. For the Department of Defense Dependent Schools, the sites selected were RAF Alconbury, United Kingdom; Hanau, Kaiserslautern, and Heidelberg, Germany; Aviano and Vicenza, Italy; Iwakuni, Japan; and Osan, Korea. For the Defense Dependents Elementary and Secondary Schools, sites selected were Fort Bragg, North Carolina; Fort Campbell, Kentucky; and Quantico and Dahlgren, Virginia.

The testbeds were used as the environment for the development, testing, and evaluation of the courseware. During the development of the courseware, developers worked in partnership with teachers in an iterative fashion to modify, refine, and test courseware. Courseware and software developers varied in their institutional affiliation from research universities (e.g., University of California at Berkeley) to private companies (e.g., Lockheed-Martin. Inc.) to nonprofit foundations (e.g., Shodor Foundation), and later, three commercial software developers (e.g., Scholastic, Inc.). Many of the software products selected for development were in immature stages of development (preclassroom, beta versions). Typically, teachers volunteered to work with developers to develop products they saw as having potential use in their classrooms.

Once courseware was identified for development, teachers received training in the use of the courseware, tried it out with their students, and provided developers with feedback on how well the courseware worked. In some instances, developers observed the use of their courseware in the classrooms. The feedback was then used to modify and refine the courseware before it was distributed to other DoDEA schools outside of the testbed classrooms. The courseware was subjected to an acceptance procedure. An evaluation of the courseware was conducted at a selected number of testbeds sites in the final year of the program. The results of the evaluation are reported elsewhere (see Klein, Glaubke, Yarnall, & O'Neil, 2000).

Courseware/Software Development Model

Due to the relatively short, planned 4-year life span of the program, a strategy was developed to leverage and take advantage of the many good ideas, concepts, and programs that were already available. This strategy was adopted on the basis of a review of the current literature on courseware development (see, e.g., President's Committee of Advisors on Science and Technology, Panel on Educational Technology, 1997; NSF), the findings of a survey conducted by the PTI program office of the top 10 producers of educational courseware, and the recommendations of the President's Committee of Advisors on Science and Technology, Panel on Educational Technology (1997; also known as the "Shaw Report").

The strategy consisted of two phases of development for two categories of educational software/courseware. The first phase was called "state-of-the-art" development and involved research and development prototypes that had undergone some level of development with government funding. This courseware was commonly referred to as Government Off-the-Shelf software (GOTS). The second phase consisted of the customization of courseware referred to as Commercial Off-the-Shelf software (COTS).

**Government Off-the-Shelf and Commercial
Off-the-Shelf Courseware**

The Phase 1 strategy allowed the program to take advantage of prototype software programs developed under existing government research and development (R&D) educational programs. Examples of these programs include the Defense Advanced Research Project Agency's Computer-Aided Education and Training Initiative (CAETI), the Department of Education's Office of Education Research and Improvement (OERI) technology program, and the National Science Foundation (NSF) educational courseware programs.

The PTI program office reviewed a number of GOTS courseware products as potential candidates for inclusion in the program. However, it was found that whereas some had been designed with the latest learning technologies and the most advanced programing techniques, they were not ready for classroom use. The GOTS products were in an immature stage of development, and were generally unstable, fragile, built on powerful workstations (e.g., Sun Workstations), and programed in demanding operating environments such as UNIX. Additionally, because these products were in their prototype form, they were expensive and difficult to maintain. The maintenance of the courseware/software not only was expensive, but also required a level of technical expertise not typically found in DoDEA or other school systems. School systems generally do not have the budget to purchase the high-end computers and systems to support this type of software. More importantly, many of the GOTS products were difficult to use and required extensive training for use by teachers and students. As a whole, they were not practical for classroom use. Thus, a development effort was begun to refine these GOTS applications and create new courseware.

The selection process to identify courseware for development consisted of teacher and coordinator curriculum comments and suggestions, curriculum priorities, and technical and pedagogical characteristics of the courseware. Based on a needs assessment early in the program, three critical curriculum areas were identified: language arts/reading for grades K–6, mathematics for grades 5–8, and science for grades 9–12.

Teachers and coordinators were requested to evaluate each proposed courseware product on the basis of need, accuracy of content, and design. In addition, three technical design characteristics were used to select candidate courseware products: the use of advanced program techniques, such as object-oriented programing, artificial intelligence, and visual database; the use of advanced learning theory from instructional design, cognitive psychology, or computer science; and the use of advanced design features, such as modularity for ease of maintenance and network-based format for ease of distribution. The PTI staff reviewed more than 40 prototype products before selecting 13 products.

Once these 13 products were identified, PTI engaged the developers in a contractual agreement for 1 year to develop courseware that would meet four stated objectives. (a) Courseware modification was to be hardware independent (JAVA based). Courseware also should (b) be aligned with DoDEA curriculum standards, (c) be user friendly (defined as teachers being able to use the courseware in their classrooms with no more than 2 days of training), and (c) run on standard DoDEA computers with a minimum of technical support and be ruggedized for daily classroom use. The contractual agreement also specified that each developer during the course of development must partner with a DoDEA teacher and test the program in a DoDEA classroom. From these 13 products, teachers selected and used 4 GOTS products for evaluation in their classrooms.

To address a PTI objective of "stimulating the marketplace," noncommercial developers were encouraged to form partnerships with commercial developers to get their products to the marketplace to maximize the distribution and marketing of their finished products. Although PTI supported the development of commercially ready versions of the courseware, the developers maintained all intellectual properties for their own courseware/software. PTI expected to receive from this relation high quality, commercially ready courseware based on the DoDEA curriculum standards.

As for the GOTS software, bringing together the DoDEA educational community and the selected commercial providers with their research-based, newly developed educational courseware was a daunting task. A major impediment for the seamless transition from a research product (prototype) to a viable commercial product was that the initial development began with different objectives between the research and commercial communities. For example, the typical research goal was to develop a prototype, a proof of concept, not a "hardened" for classroom use, commercially ready courseware product. More importantly, developers involved in federal research programs and grants do not have the capability, personnel, or financial resources to bring these research products to a level of maturity where they are commercially ready. In many cases, they (e.g., university personnel working on grants) not only lack the technical know-how to harden their courseware, but also the skills to successfully bring their product to market. The developers in these institutions (e.g., universities and research laboratories) are not provided with incentives to produce products that are commercially viable. Furthermore, many developers in these environments are not intellectually interested in commercialization of their research. However, there were some successes. For example, the PUMP Algebra Tutor (now marketed under Cognitive Tutor™ Algebra I and Cognitive Tutor™ Algebra II by Carnegie Learning, inc.) was evaluated as an "Exemplary Mathematics Program" by the U.S. Department of Education's Mathematics and Science expert panel. PUMP is currently in use not only in the DoDEA schools, but nationwide in eight major school districts (New York City Schools; Norwalk City Schools, Connecticut; Milwaukee Public Schools, Wisconsin; Knox County Schools, Kentucky; Buffalo City Schools, New York; San Diego Unified School District; Escambia County Schools, Florida; and Pittsburgh City Schools, Pennsylvania). Four other software/courseware programs are being developed currently for the marketplace: University of California, Berkeley's Hands-On Universe® (2000), Lockheed-Martin's Online Learning Academy (OLLA, 2000), Fountain Communications'

Multimedia and Thinking Skills (2000), and ISX's Teacher's Associate (1998).

As a result of the GOTS experience, it was decided to develop new courseware that would be implemented by targeting potential suppliers and/or developers at commercial software companies, textbook publishers, multimedia specialists, and courseware specialists rather than university-based providers.

The Commercial Off-the-Shelf Experience

The Shaw Report identified several shortfalls with commercially produced educational courseware currently in the marketplace: (a) Commercial developers are market driven, not needs driven. Decisions of what to produce and market are based on their projected profitability and not on what educational needs should be met. (b) Industry-wide profit margins are typically low, as is return on investment. Thus, availability of internal research and development resources is generally inadequate. (c) The lack of significant R&D investment has impacted on the quality of the educational courseware produced. Quality is not what it should be because of commercial developers' financial inability to invest in their products. The lack of significant investment has caused products to be designed without the latest advanced learning technologies (e.g., theory and practice) and programing techniques (e.g., object-oriented programing). (d) Commercially produced courseware is not designed with the target user in mind (e.g., teachers and students).

The PTI program office's survey of the 10 top commercial producers of educational courseware confirmed many of these findings. The survey found that, on average, the development cycle for courseware varied from 2.5 to 3.0 years, and the majority of the courseware products were aimed at the afterschool market. The afterschool courseware market requires generic skills and general topic areas (e.g., Davidson's Math Blaster, 1992) and would not be likely to include applications that meet the needs of a specific school curriculum.

The COTS strategy focused on accomplishing the following objectives: Stimulate the commercial courseware industry to produce high quality courseware that meets critical curriculum needs that were not being addressed; and leverage available funds to encourage the development of advanced courseware. The strategy encouraged commercial developers to take existing products in their pipeline at various stages of development and customize them to meet curricular needs of the DoDEA system. Ideally, this strategy would bring together members from three distinct communities—the researchers, the commercial developers, and the school personnel—to collaborate on the development of needed courseware. Because the strategy encouraged the selection of existing candidates for customization or COTS, it should have shortened the development cycle from 2.5–3 years to 0.7–1.5 years.

The strategy offered incentives to the commercial developers. For example, it offered a potential successful business model in an area where return on investments and profit margins have been traditionally low. The business model ideally would reduce cost and risk to the developers by having the PTI program underwrite the development, customization, and much of the cost of development. Moreover, a ready market of DoDEA schools (233 schools and over 100,000 students) was made available to commercial developers, ensuring the potential profitability of their product. More importantly, the strategy encouraged collaboration across the various communities to develop curriculum-oriented and standards-based courseware.

The PTI contract with the commercial developers required that they conduct a front-end analysis. This analysis should have identified specific student learning objectives and curriculum standards to be addressed during the COTS customization process. Once these requirements were implemented in the courseware, two "tryouts" were required to be conducted within the DoDEA testbed sites. These tryouts consisted of training teachers in the use of the courseware, implementing the courseware in their classrooms, and collecting data from teachers and students to determine how well the courseware performed. The data collected during the tryouts were used not only to determine how well the courseware worked, but also to collect feedback for needed modification. As in the GOTS phase, the COTS phase encouraged developers to develop their courseware to be platform independent, to use an architecture that was modular in design, and to be aligned with DoDEA's curriculum standards.

The courseware products selected for initial refinement during the COTS phase varied in stages of development. Products ranged from very immature but innovative alpha versions, such as the integration of a sophisticated speech recognition program with storyware, to beta versions requiring field tests and refinement, to commercially ready products requiring minor revisions only. The COTS phase yielded four courseware development products. Three of the products were in reading for grades K–8. One of these was designed for emergent readers in grades K–1, another was aimed at grades 2–4, and one was a remedial reading product using multimedia software with material appropriate for grade 8. Another product selected was a web-based mathematics program designed for grades 5–8. No products were selected for the science area.

Not all of the four products met the PTI project's expectations. Three of the four developers successfully field tested their software products in DoDEA classrooms. The fourth product, a reading aid for emergent readers using cutting edge speech recognition technology, was not field tested and the project was terminated. The developers of the reading aid software were not able to develop a classroom version in time for field testing. The three software products that were successfully field tested are currently in wide use in DoDEA schools today: Scholastic Inc.'s multi-media remedial reading program for grades 4–8 "Read 180" (2000); Computer Curriculum Corporation's reading program, part of "CCC SuccessMaker" (1997), for grades 2–4; and the Shodor Education Foundation's "Project Interactivate" (2000), a web-based middle school math program. All of these programs met the goals of the program.

The improved success rate of the COTS program is possibly due to the fact that commercial courseware developers are oriented to the realities of the marketplace (e.g., profit margins). Expectations for significant changes in commercial developers' business practices and in the design of their courseware were tempered by these realities. If commercial developers are going to have a major impact on the educational marketplace, then it will require a fundamental change in their business models as well as a change in their culture. The COTS phase of the project changed the current business model in three fundamental ways: underwriting the research and development costs; directly linking the commercial developers with the users, teachers, and students; and requiring developers to align their programs with DoDEA curriculum standards.

Training Teachers to Use and Integrate Technology with the Curriculum

The planned development and implementation of the PTI teacher training program was meant to be a major factor in determining the successful integration of technology-based courseware within the DoDEA system. The PTI took advantage of the experiences of a major National Science Foundation (NSF) technology integration program that was ongoing at two of the DoDEA districts: the Vanguard project at Aviano, Italy, and the Model Schools program at Hanau, Germany. Both projects emphasized that teachers needed to be trained in technology-based skills or they would not adopt or use the courseware in their classrooms. The PTI built on this model to satisfy the program's unique needs. Additionally, PTI staff ensured that professional development activities were in alignment with the professional development technology plan developed by the DoDEA Headquarters Professional Development Division.

Before teacher training could begin, training needs had to be established. The PTI staff conducted a "quick look" assessment of all project participants to determine their current technology skill levels. This assessment was used to guide implementation of the professional development plan for all project participants during the first major workshop, Summer Institute I. As a minimum, the assessment was designed to determine the participant's ability to manage multitasks for activities in the classroom, integrate courseware into the curriculum, use common workstation application software (i.e., word processing, spreadsheets, graphics), and use higher level software for research and instructional purposes (i.e., Internet access, browsers, database transfer, HyperStudio).

The training plan for the participants was built around two major activities. One activity included formal workshops conducted at a single facility during the summer that provided teachers, administrators, and support staff training on technology skills, courseware and software, and a process for integrating the courseware with the curriculum. The second activity provided follow-up training during the school year at the testbed sites to address those specific training needs identified by the participants. The onsite training was presented by mobile training teams who worked with the teachers in their classrooms providing hands-on training in the teacher's particular area of curriculum expertise. The planning for this training was formalized through a site implementation plan developed between the PTI staff member responsible for that site and the testbed's site administrator. The site implementation plan proved to be a successful means in Year 1 for planning and conducting required training and was expanded to include the technical needs and support agreed on for the site as well. During the course of this site-based training, it was observed that training had to be content based in order for it to be successful. As a result of the training, the testbed teachers reported they also needed more training in their content areas.

There was substantial funding allocated for staff development workshops with a summer institute planned in each fiscal year to train the testbed teachers, administrators, and other specialists prior to the beginning of the school year. The first summer institute required funds for the travel and per diem expenses of more than 200 participants, as well as the costs for instructors, courseware, software, connectivity, equipment, material, supplies, and contractor technical support for the 2-week workshops. The workshops were designed to train selected DoDEA educational specialists and other technology support personnel so that they could return to their own sites to create and sustain an in-house capability for technology implementation.

The initial formal training workshop, Summer Institute I, was conducted during summer 1997. The 200 PTI participants included mostly teachers, but also administrators and support staff. The workshop was hosted by the Department of Defense Dependent Schools school complex located at the Aviano Air Base, Italy. The Aviano school system was selected because of the presence of the NSF Vanguard Project (Hunter, 1998) and a technology integration program that had adopted many of the lessons learned, insights, and experiences that were valuable as models for PTI professional development activities. Participants from the testbed sites were presented with 2 weeks of hands-on instruction for developing technology skills, planning for technology integration with curriculum content areas, and focusing on at least one tool that would assist in the process.

Subsequent technology training locations for school year 1998–1999 and school year 1999–2000 (Summer Institutes II and III) were planned, but subsequently were canceled because of the perception by DoDEA management that the workshops were duplicative of other DoDEA professional development training activities. The 1998 summer training was reduced to a short, 1-week exposure of technology for the educational technologists. The training also included small, separate workshops for a few selected teachers (three to four) that were presented by the PTI courseware developers to train the teachers to be trainers. The model of "train the trainers" was not entirely successful, in part, because teacher trainers based outside the United States could not be provided with incentives (e.g., additional pay, increased status, or compensatory time off) to encourage them to train teachers outside of their school district. However, for teachers located in the United States, offering them a trip to Europe was enough of an incentive for them to train other teachers. Thus, although training was planned and conducted, an insufficient number of teachers were actually trained in the use of the GOTS or COTS.

An important planned outcome of the training program was the process for integrating educational technology with the DoDEA K–12 curriculum. This process adopted a system developed by Educational Support Systems (a commercial company) that was labeled the Curriculum Technology Integration Process (CTIP; Coley, Cradler, & Engel, 1997). The CTIP was introduced to all 200-plus initial program participants at Summer Institute I. The process was subsequently carried forward to the on-site informal training aspects of the program and served as the cornerstone for the individual teachers' plans for integrating courseware with their curriculum areas. The CTIP is a template that lays out logical steps for teachers to plan for using technology-based courseware in their curriculum. The CTIP allows teachers to address in detail the desired outcomes, instructional design, evaluation plan, courseware, resources needed, professional development requirements, identification of follow-up support, and implementation plans. It was clear that although this was a time-consuming process, it provided the teachers who accomplished their CTIPs with a structured means and clear path for how to best meet the challenge of integrating technology with their curriculum.

Another major advantage of the CTIP process was that a variation was available for administrators to use. This process, the ATIP, gave the administrators an appreciation for what the teachers must do to plan for technology integration with their curriculum as well as a tool for aligning teacher programs with the school improvement program. The CTIP and ATIP working together were recommended to be used for the minimal follow-up training at the testbed sites.

The PTI project staff realized that teachers had to develop technology skills and know-how to review and evaluate the adequacy and usefulness of the courseware in order to select and use it. Thus, the PTI staff also funded the nonprofit California Instructional Technology Clearinghouse to be the agents for jump-starting the process of training the staff and participants on how to evaluate effective educational courseware. The PTI contracted with the California Instructional Technology Clearinghouse to provide initial training on the selection of courseware for the headquarters staff (education division) and for teachers and administrators during Summer Institute I. The training was also presented during follow-up training sessions at each of the testbed sites. The PTI staff developed plans for coordination with the education division and all PTI participants to ensure training on the use and evaluation of the selected courseware provided. Additionally, the California Instructional Technology Clearinghouse was contracted to work closely with the education division to jointly develop courseware criteria to ensure that the evaluation, development, and selection of educational courseware were driven by the DoDEA curriculum.

The California Instructional Technology Clearinghouse was also given the critical task of establishing a DoDEA list of evaluated, commercially available courseware that could be used by PTI participants (and subsequently by all of DoDEA) to select courseware that met the DoDEA curriculum standards. California Instructional Technology Clearinghouse used their established process for evaluating courseware for the California state system and modified the criteria so that the DoDEA curriculum standards were included. Their review produced a list of some 650 courseware products sanctioned for DoDEA use. This list was provided online and was titled the "DoDEA On-Line Clearinghouse." The process was publicized as a key element of the PTI program.

Selecting and Providing Technology-Based Courseware/Software to Meet the Teacher's Curriculum Needs

It was determined early on that the key to the success of integrating leading-edge, technology-based courseware with the curriculum was to have teachers trained on the selection, use, and integration of quality software. However, it became apparent that because of the delayed timing of the deliverables in the PTI program and the canceling of the remaining summer institutes for teacher training, the new courseware (GOTS and COTS) being developed would not be available to teachers to support their training. The solution was to find and select the latest, best quality courseware available in the commercial sector that addressed DoDEA curriculum standards.

Off-the-Shelf Courseware Acquisition

To start the teacher technology integration process, evaluated courseware needed to be immediately available. But the overall goal of the program, the development of new, effective courseware using state-of-the-art technology, had to also be considered. These parameters led to the establishment of a courseware acquisition plan. The plan included the purchase of commercial off-the-shelf courseware, as well as taking advantage of government-developed courseware that was available through other government sources (e.g., the DoD training and education base). Commercial off-the-shelf courseware was made available to the testbed sites through the PTI office as a one-time purchase to jump-start the teachers' training and use. The courseware was needed to ensure the teachers knew how to use and integrate it with their curriculum (CTIP process described earlier).

The courseware purchases were based on teacher CTIPs constructed during the initial summer institute. It was agreed that courseware listed on the teacher CTIPs would be acquired by the PTI program and delivered to the teachers within a few months after Summer Institute I. The PTI acquisition of courseware was expected to produce collateral benefits for all of the DoDEA schools and the education community as a whole. Through the investment of substantial PTI funds for courseware that complies with standards established by the project, it was anticipated that the software developers and publishers would be motivated to develop meaningful, quality educational software. The software would meet DoDEA curriculum needs and be available to other educational systems in the K–12 setting. Unfortunately, communication between the PTI staff and staff of the California Instructional Technology Clearinghouse broke down, causing delays and errors in processing courseware orders that were executed by commercial vendors who were unfamiliar with the logistics of sending software/courseware to military bases outside of the United States. They failed to keep good records, deliver what was promised, or deliver the courseware in a timely manner.

Management and Distribution System

The PTI team established a system for the management, distribution, and maintenance of courseware to the testbeds. This approach appeared to have all the ingredients for success—identification of needs, a structured acquisition system, and a management and tracking system for communication and control. The system called for the purchasing of three types of courseware. The PTI staff identified a set of management, production-enhancing software called the *basic toolkit*. It was determined that all PTI participating teachers should have this basic toolkit regardless of their curriculum area (i.e., HyperStudio, 1997; MS Office, 1995; Netscape Communicator Pro (1997); and a teacher productivity tool, The Teacher's Associate, 1998). Second, toolkits were designed for the PTI teachers relative to their specific curriculum areas (e.g., Science toolkit, Math toolkit, and so on). Third, the identification of courseware specific to the individual teacher needs was derived from the CTIPs. It was in the purchasing of this third type of courseware that the system broke down and resulted in perhaps one of the greatest problems for the program. An analysis of the problem uncovered the following issues: The identification of this software was done through two means.

Each participating teacher at the initial summer institute generated a CTIP. Teachers selected the courseware they intended to use in the classroom. Teachers formalized their selections through the CTIP, and the PTI staff used this as the "ordering" document. The CTIP-based courseware requests were reviewed by the PTI staff for feasibility and affordability, and a list was prepared for ordering. The teachers were left with the impression that they would receive all the courseware they had identified on their individual CTIPs regardless of appropriateness, type, or cost.

As was discussed earlier, the California Instructional Technology Clearinghouse was responsible for acquiring and delivering commercial courseware identified by the PTI staff to the teachers. Unfortunately, due to communication problems between the PTI staff, PTI teachers, and staff of the California Instructional Technology Clearinghouse, software/courseware was not delivered in a timely manner or, in some cases, was not delivered at all.

However, despite many obstacles, mistakes, and delays, over 150 courseware titles were ordered and subsequently delivered to the PTI teachers for their use in the classroom. The delivery of this courseware continued to be one of the major benefits of the program as recognized throughout the testbed districts. In addition, the DoDEA On-Line Clearinghouse developed by the California Instructional Technology Clearinghouse, provided approximately 650 titles of exemplary courseware that were evaluated and ready for the teachers to use in the classroom.

Institute a System to Provide Technical Support to Testbed Schools for Technology Integration Activities

It was recognized in the formative stages of the PTI program that a key element for success would be the establishment of cooperative, responsive, and credible testbed schools. The testbeds were to be a critical factor in the development, integration, and evaluation of the PTI courseware. The testbeds were to provide an operational learning environment wherein the developer, in partnership with the teachers, could test the courseware, determine shortcomings, and modify and try the courseware again until it met the teachers' needs. The testbeds would give the courseware process credibility, which in turn would provide numerous and valuable lessons for all of the DoDEA schools as they began to adopt technology-based courseware throughout the system.

It became apparent that the existing technical personnel for the selected PTI testbeds, although considered technically qualified and motivated for their current workload, would be overwhelmed by the additional demand placed on the system by the expected massive influx of PTI program courseware. To assist the in-place technical support personnel, PTI provided funding for a commercial contractor to provide technical support teams to be responsive on-site at each testbed. In addition, a back-up capability of highly qualified personnel was available as needed to attack a hot spot at a site or at DoDEA headquarters to solve any problem that developed. This "SWAT" team approach was used sparingly but effectively to address problems such as server installations, critical training needs, software evaluation, or establishing LAN/WAN networks that were beyond the scope of the local support teams. It was made clear that the mission of all the contractor support elements was to assist the in-place support and not supplant it. The goal was for the support contractor to assist, train, and transition support activities to the in-house, existing support as the courseware integration project matured.

The testbed sites were pleased with the additional assistance provided by the support contractor, and each site developed its own unique way of using the added support. Some contractor staff concentrated on purely technical areas; others helped teachers with the courseware or work on computers, or in some cases, conducted training for professional development activities. Whereas the teams were expected to work primarily with only the PTI-related hardware, software, and courseware, it became impossible to draw a line on what was and what was not exclusively in the PTI domain. This ambiguity resulted in support to the entire site in some instances. The DoDEA indigenous support personnel dictated in most part how the contractor support personnel were used.

Contractor technical support was even more important in those testbeds where it was discovered that the supporting infrastructure was not always as robust or stable as described in the testbed school proposals. Unexpectedly, some testbed sites had limited access to the Internet, did not have functional local area networks, did not have the computers available in the numbers required for the teachers or students, and did not have the electrical power required to support the equipment. The contractor technical support teams were able to assist these sites in meeting the original testbed selection criteria. In those cases where they were unsuccessful, they reported to the PTI project manager so that the program office could adjust its expectation of participation for those sites. Based on comments from teachers and administrators, the on-site contractor technical support was one of the major successes of the program and was a key element for keeping the program moving at many of the testbed schools.

COMPREHENSIVE EVALUATION OF THE OVERALL PTI PROGRAM

The PTI staff, in cooperation with the DoDEA Research and Evaluation Branch, planned an evaluation that would assess project outcomes in three target areas: student learning by subject area (math, science, language arts, and reading), teacher technology skills, and changes in the learning environment's infrastructure. The PTI staff agreed that the evaluation of the project would compare its expected findings with the National Science Foundation school reform projects. In coordination with the DoDEA Headquarter's Research and Evaluation Branch, the PTI plan was to develop evaluation metrics and technology-based tools to instrument, collect, and organize data for analysis of the evaluated outcomes.

In coordination with the education division, the PTI staff also planned to document and publish findings from the evaluation of the project to describe best practices for integrating meaningful courseware within the DoDEA curriculum. It was hoped these findings would serve as models for the DoDEA schools and would include clear guidance for "scaling up" to full system use. As a part of the analysis process, the PTI staff also worked closely with the NSF school reform projects personnel to identify and document the impact of technology on those programs, their impact on the PTI program, and how they could be incorporated into models for the DoDEA schools.

The original plan was to task one private company, Educational Support Systems (ESS), to be responsible for the evaluation planning and conducting the evaluation. It was later determined that because ESS was also active in conducting PTI on-site teacher training activities as well as having responsibility for the CTIP process, they had too much operational responsibility for the PTI program to be an independent evaluator for the program. The PTI staff then established an evaluation panel composed of nationally recognized experts in education and education technology to review PTI evaluation plans and provide recommendations on how best to conduct the evaluation. The panel members had no direct or indirect connection to the PTI program. The panel reviewed the ESS draft evaluation plan and recommended a third-party evaluation, with an independent agency to take responsibility for the program evaluation.

This recommendation was accepted by the PTI staff, and the UCLA Center for Research on Evaluation, Standards, and Student Testing (CRESST) was funded to take the overall lead for assessment of student learning. ESS, along with another company, Interactive Media (who had responsibility for designing and collecting data on teacher technology skill levels), agreed to work together as a team with CRESST to produce a comprehensive evaluation of the PTI program. The team was based on goodwill and not a contractual agreement (i.e., a prime with two subcontractors).

The specific results of the program evaluation are not reported in this chapter because they are reported elsewhere (Klein et al., 2000). There were some major lessons to be learned from the evaluation of the PTI program. For example, the late availability of the courseware, given the limited time remaining in the program, was not conducive to a thorough evaluation. The developed ("hardened") courseware was delivered well into the first semester of school year 1998–1999. Teachers indicated that they needed at least one full semester of the school year to become proficient in the use of this courseware and to integrate it into their classrooms, so the effectiveness of the courseware was judged in some cases with poorly trained teachers and limited student exposure to it. Furthermore, because the courseware was not ready for classroom use, data collection for the evaluation did not begin until the first semester of school year 1999. Unexpectedly, the program was terminated at the start of school year 1999–2000 requiring the evaluation be abbreviated and compressed into the second semester of school year 1998–1999. Thus, the PTI program ran from January 1997 through September 30, 1999, rather than 4 years as planned. In summary, the evaluation, although planned reasonably appropriately, was a lost opportunity.

CONCLUSIONS

Program Goals, Strategies, and Objectives

The PTI program sponsors made it clear that the program was to provide technology-based courseware aligned with the DoDEA curriculum in ways that would improve student learning. The funds were aligned to these program goals, and the majority of the funds (approximately 70%) were spent on courseware development. However, the DoDEA leadership was never convinced that such technology per se would improve student learning. There was never a clear understanding of and commitment to the systemic changes that would be required to accompany the full implementation of integrating technology into DoDEA.

The PTI program office failed to convince DoDEA's leadership that the PTI program was meeting a critical need or fixing a problem. Critical learning needs were hard to "sell" when the DoDEA schools have a reputation as a very successful system that offers a quality education to its students. These positive perceptions were based, in part, on the fact that these students perform at or above the median on measures of school success such as Scholastic Assessment Test (SAT) scores, achievement tests, the National Assessment of Educational Progress, and percent of students going on to higher education. In summary, many felt that "if it was not broken, then there was no need to fix it."

Management Activities

The lack of DoDEA leadership's commitment to systemic change needed to support the PTI technological innovation was hypothesized to be caused by several factors. First, during this time period, DoDEA experienced an inordinate amount of turbulence at the upper levels of DoDEA management. The associate director of Management Support Services, an ardent sponsor of the PTI, left during the second year of the program. This was the first of many personnel changes in leadership positions that occurred during the life of the program. During the course of the program, the PTI program manager reported to five different supervisors. Second, changing DoDEA priorities captured the attention of the leadership. For example, DoDEA's need for more school counselors to meet the increased stress as a result of military deployments to Bosnia and Kosovo competed for attention with the PTI project. Other priorities deflecting attention away from PTI included the implementation of a full-day kindergarten and reduced class size initiatives.

Third, there was a lack of clear communication between the PTI team and upper management, the district leadership, and the other components in DoDEA created by the dissolution of the DoDEA Technology Task Force in Year 1. This gap in communications created misunderstanding among all leadership levels regarding the expectations and importance, direction, and priorities of the program. Finally, although the use of support contractors at the school sites was effective, management was never comfortable with the use of contractors in this role.

Testbed Selection and Use

The testbeds were proposed to be central to the potential success of the program. Not only were they to provide an environment for developing, testing, and evaluating PTI courseware, but they also would serve as a linchpin for consolidating the teachers', principals', district staff's, and superintendents' commitment to the PTI program and its goals. The formal process for selecting districts and schools to participate as PTI testbeds emphasized that participation as voluntary. The process required the districts to commit to specified support (computers, connectivity, etc.) and to support from the participants themselves. The testbeds were to provide an operational learning environment wherein the developer, in partnership with the teacher, could install the courseware, determine shortcomings, and fix and reinstall the courseware until it met the teacher and student needs. Due to multiple reasons (e.g., optimistic district proposals, little teacher training, late delivery of courseware, etc.), the potential of most of the testbeds was not realized.

Professional Development

The DoDEA teachers, staff, and administrators have a wide range of technology skills ranging from beginner to master level, with the majority at the beginner level. It is clear that the development of the teachers' technology skills and their understanding of how to integrate technology with their curriculum would be essential for successful technology deployment.

Although the PTI training was conducted in both formal and informal settings, the PTI team believed that the most effective training for developing or improving teacher technology skills was the informal approach. The informal approach included a PTI staff member managing the training on-site at the district or school and following a training plan developed specifically for the school or district needs. The training was best when the PTI staff member precoordinated with the district and schools to determine exactly the training desired and to tailor the material to their specific needs. It was not important that a world class instructor provide the instruction, as long as there were small, individual training sessions to demonstrate support for the teachers' needs.

The general software toolkit was an excellent training vehicle for beginner teachers in the first year. The toolkit consisted of administrative and classroom management software tools that allowed the teachers to get comfortable with the workings of a computer and general software applications before content courseware was addressed. The teachers were more favorably disposed to progressing from the software toolkit to understanding and adopting content courseware and integrating it with their classroom use.

Technical Support, Hardware, and Connectivity

The PTI program provided additional on-site technical support for the testbeds to bolster the normal, on-site technical support. It was clear in all the testbed sites, and particularly true in the overseas sites, that the internal

DoDEA technical support was not staffed with enough manpower and resources to meet the demands of a technology-based curriculum. To add further to this personnel support shortfall, an analysis of two key positions, the administrative and the educational technologists, showed that those job duties were not well defined, even though the attempt to clarify them was made several times. As a result, the roles and responsibilities of the administrative technologists and the educational technologists were ill defined and too compartmentalized to address systemic technology problems.

The DoDEA purchasing and acquisition system is restricted by DoD regulations for acquiring hardware, software, and connectivity. This is quite different from most public educational systems that have control of purchases. The DoDEA approach has resulted in purchases from a broad range of vendors with all the quirks and idiosyncrasies that go with a "shotgun" approach to buying computers and associated equipment. The DoDEA Information Technology Division has not established a firm set of minimum hardware requirements for computers, servers, software, and connectivity, exacerbating an already difficult problem. This, coupled with the normal cycle of hardware buys, results in a plethora of aging equipment, equipment types, and equipment capabilities.

This wide variety of equipment type and capability created difficulties for PTI courseware development and courseware purchases. The courseware developers funded by the PTI program developed to one set of standards, only to find that their courseware would work only in certain settings and was not universally available unless it was a web-based, browser-interfaced program. This caused concern on the part of the districts and schools as to the functionality of the new courseware and discouraged teachers from adopting new courseware because of the difficulties in hosting it.

The PTI experience in this area is obvious, if painful: Hardware and software stability must be in place before courseware is introduced and the educational needs and use of the courseware should drive connectivity and bandwidth, not the other way around.

PTI Courseware and Software

Perhaps the most important contribution of the PTI project was the development of educational software under Phases 1 and 2 of the program. The PTI strategy for the development of high quality, curriculum-based courseware/software consisted of two phases of development for two categories of educational software/courseware. The Phase 1 "state-of-the-art" development involved research and development prototypes, GOTS, and the Phase 2 customization of commercial courseware, COTS. Phase 1 achieved modest success with 13 GOTS products identified for development; however, only 5 achieved classroom-ready status. These are PUMP Algebra Tutor (now marketed under Cognitive Tutor™ Algebra I and Cognitive Tutor™ Algebra II, 2000, by Carnegie Learning, inc.), which is currently in use in the DoDEA schools and in eight major school districts nationwide; University of California, Berkeley's Hands-On Universe®, 2000; Lockheed-Martin's Online Learning Academy (OLLA); Fountain Communications' Multimedia and Thinking Skills; Shodor Education Foundation's Project Interactivate; and ISX's Teacher's Associate. Phase 2 of the PTI strategy was somewhat more successful with 3 of the 4 products currently being used in DoDEA schools: Scholastic Inc.'s multimedia remedial reading program for grades 4–8, "Read 180"; Computer Curriculum Corporation's reading program, part of "CCC SuccessMaker," for grades 2–4; and the Shodor Foundation's "Project Interactivate," a web-based middle school math program.

All of these educational software products met the initial goals established by the PTI program: Courseware should be hardware independent (JAVA based) or have two versions (MAC & PC); courseware should be aligned with DoDEA curriculum standards; courseware should be user friendly (defined as teachers being able to use the courseware in their classrooms with no more than 2 days of training); courseware must run on standard DoDEA computers with a minimum of technical support and be ruggedized for daily classroom use; and courseware architecture must be modular in design. The last goal, if successfully implemented, would enable developers to easily customize their software products to meet the unique curriculum requirements of individual school districts. Perhaps more important was the development of an innovative business model used to create the software. Using this model, the PTI project was able to bring together three distinct communities—researchers, commercial developers, and school personnel—to create high quality, curriculum-based educational software. A business model where research and development is underwritten by state or federal agencies may be the only way to improve the quality of educational courseware.

ISSUES FOR THE CLASSROOM
OF THE 21ST CENTURY

The issues and conclusions presented in this chapter are derived from the PTI program experiences over approximately 3 years. The PTI program implemented a project with its focus on the development, testing, evaluation, and implementation of courseware aligned with curriculum requirements in an educational system. Based on PTI experiences, several research issues need to be addressed to support the development of and use of technology in the classrooms of the 21st century.

The overriding research issue with respect to the use of technology in classrooms is the design of courseware. What are the computer-based tools to ensure that content is accurate, up to date, and comprehensive? Is the design instructionally sound? Does the design reflect current understanding (knowledge base) of what is known about how to teach and how students learn?

Most of what is known about the impact of technology on learning is based on earlier research efforts using earlier generation courseware (e.g., Fletcher, chap. 4, this vol.; Kulik, 1994; Schacter & Fagnano, 1999; Wenglinsky, 1998). These research findings have been useful as a foundation for understanding the role of technology in learning in the classroom. However, due to the rapidly changing nature and introduction of new technologies (e.g., increased computational power, increased memory, connectivity, visual and multimedia capacities, and miniaturization), these advances have, according to Honey, McMillian, and Carrigg (1999), radically increased the potential educational use of technology in the classroom.

Not only have the elements of the technology changed, but the efforts of the federal, state, and local governments also have created a rapid increase in the number of computers and connectivity to the Internet in the schools. These changes call for new research on the effectiveness of technology (Tally, 1998), new research questions and new assessment instruments, and at a general level, new model(s) of research that can keep pace with the rate of technology change.

ACKNOWLEDGMENT

The opinions expressed herein are the personal opinions of the authors and do not necessarily represent the official policy or position of the Office of the Secretary of Defense, the Department of Defense Education Activity, or the Office of Naval Research.

REFERENCES

CCC SuccessMaker. (1997). [Multimedia]. Sunnyvale, CA: Computer Curriculum Corporation.

Cognitive Tutor™ Algebra I; Cognitive Tutor™ Algebra II. (2000). [Computer software]. Pittsburgh, PA: Carnegie Learning, Inc.

Coley, R. J., Cradler, J., & Engel, P. K. R. (1997). *Computers and classrooms: The status of technology in U.S. schools.* Princeton, NJ: Educational Testing Service.

Department of Defense Education Activity. (2000, September). DODEA. Available: http://www.odedodea.edu [November 2, 2000].

Hands-On Universe®. (2000). [Computer software]. Berkeley: University of California, Lawrence Berkeley Laboratory.

Honey, M., McMillian, K., & Carrigg, F. (1999, July). *Perspectives on technology and education research: Lessons from the past and present.* Paper presented at the Secretary's (U.S. Department of Education) Conference on Educational Technology: Evaluating the Effectiveness of Technology, Washington, DC.

Hunter, B. (1998, June). *Building capacity for innovation: The Vanguard for Learning Model.* Paper presented at the National Educational Computing conference, San Diego, CA.

HyperStudio. (1997). El Cajon, CA: Roger Wagner Publishing.

Klein, D. C., Glaubke, C., Yarnall, L., & O'Neil, H. F., Jr. (2000). *Student outcomes: Findings in the evaluation of the Department of Defense Presidential Technology Initiative* (Final Report to DODEA). Los Angeles: University of California, National Center for Research on Evaluation, Standards, and Student Testing.

Kulik, J. (1994). Meta-analytic studies of findings on computer-based instruction. In E. L. Baker & H. F. O'Neil, Jr. (Eds.), *Technology assessment in education and training* (pp. 9–33). Hillsdale, NJ: Lawrence Erlbaum Associates.

Math Blaster. (1992). Torrance, CA: Davidson & Associates, Inc., Knowledge Adventure.

Microsoft Office. (1995). Redmond, WA: Microsoft Corporation.

Multimedia and Thinking Skills. (2000). [Computer software]. Oakton, VA: Fountain Communications, Inc.

Netscape Communicator Pro. (1997). Mountain View, CA: Netscape Communications Corporation.

Online Learning Academy. (2000). [Multimedia]. Beachwood, OH: NetForce Development, Inc.

President's Committee of Advisors on Science and Technology, Panel on Educational Technology. (1997). *Report to the President on the use of technology to strengthen K–12 education in the United States.* Washington, DC: USGPO. Available: http://www.whitehouse.gov/WH/EOP/OSTP/NSTC/PCAST/k-12ed.html [2000, November 2].

Project Interactivate. (2000). [Multimedia]. Durham, NC: The Shodor Education Foundation, Inc.

Read 180. (2000). [Multimedia]. New York: Scholastic Inc.

Schacter, J., & Fagnano, C. (1999). Does computer technology improve student learning and achievement? How, when, and under what conditions? *Journal of Educational Computing Research, 20,* 329–343.

Tally, B. (1998, October). *State of research on new media and children.* Paper presented at the Center for Media education's conference "Ensuring a Quality Media Culture for Children in the Digital Age," Washington, DC.

Teacher's Associate. (1998). Westlake Village, CA: ISX.

Wenglinsky, H. (1998). *Does it compute? The relationship between educational technology and student achievement in mathematics* (ETS Policy Information Report). Princeton, NJ: Educational Testing Service. Available: http://www.ets.org/research/pic/dic/preack.html [2000, November 4].

Part II

LEARNING FOUNDATIONS

Chapter 6

Theories of Learning and Their Application to Technology

Richard E. Mayer
University of California, Santa Barbara

Early in the 20th century, E. L. Thorndike, the world's first educational psychologist, envisioned a future in which educational practices in teaching would be guided by a psychological theory of learning (Mayer, in press-b). However, throughout the 20th century, psychologists and educators struggled to devise a theory of learning that is both educationally relevant and research based (Mayer, in press-a). At last, as the field of educational psychology enters its second century, it has become clear that much progress has been made in understanding how students learn in educationally relevant settings (Berliner & Calfee, 1996; Bransford, Brown, & Cocking, 1999; Bruer, 1993; Lambert & McCombs, 1998; Mayer, 1999c). The development of powerful instructional technologies—particularly based on computer and communication technologies—coupled with the rise of educationally relevant theories of learning offer the exciting opportunity to once again grapple with Thorndike's 100-year-old dream. This chapter is based on the premise that the way technology is used in education depends on the instructor's underlying conception of learning. This chapter proposes to examine current theories of how students learn and their implications for technology. The chapter begins with a introduction to constructivist theories of learning, examines four basic issues in the psychology of academic learning, examines three conceptions of learning, summarizes three varieties of constructivism, presents a cognitive constructivist model of technology-based learning, and provides examples of how the theory can be applied to technology-based instruction.

A CONSTRUCTIVIST CONCEPTION OF LEARNING

Today's dominant theory of learning is constructivism—the idea that learning occurs when learners actively try to make sense of material presented to them. Learners engage in constructivist learning by actively and deeply processing the to-be-learned material in an attempt to understand it. Constructivist learning also can be called *knowledge construction*, because learners actively create their own knowledge, or *active learning*, because learners must apply and coordinate their own cognitive processes while learning (Mayer, 1999c). Constructivist learning has traditionally been referred to as *meaningful learning*, or learning by understanding, and can be distinguished from *rote learning*, or learning by memorizing (Wertheimer, 1959).

The conception of constructivist learning has important implications for instructional technology. Constructivist instruction is aimed at fostering and guiding constructivist learning, that is, it seeks to activate cognitive processing that leads to understanding. In short, constructivist instruction fosters constructive cognitive activity in the learner. Under this conception of learning, instructional technology should serve as a cognitive guide to help learners on authentic academic tasks—such as comprehending a text, solving a challenging mathematics problem, or conducting a scientific experiment.

It is important to recognize that constructivist instruction is not the same as hands-on learning or learning-by-doing, because behavioral activity is not the same as cognitive activity. As Ausubel (1968) and Mayer (1999c) pointed out, instruction that emphasizes behavioral activity (e.g., interactive games) can be designed in ways that either do or do not lead to cognitive activity, whereas instruction that does not emphasize behavioral activity (e.g., viewing a multimedia presentation) can be designed in ways that either do or do not lead to cognitive activity. For example, Mayer (in press-b) showed how the apparently passive task of viewing a multimedia presentation can lead to constructivist learning, whereas the apparently active task of answering questions can lead to rote learning. The crucial aspect of constructivist instruction is that it fosters appropriate cognitive processing in the learner rather than the level of behavioral activity that it requires.

Constructivist assessment focuses on the quality of learners' understanding rather than the quantity of knowledge they have acquired. The challenge of constructivist assessment is to develop techniques that assess students' ability to use what they have learned in new situations (i.e., transfer) in addition to their ability to remember what they have learned (i.e., retention).

ISSUES IN LEARNING, TEACHING, ASSESSMENT, AND TECHNOLOGY

How do students learn? How should teachers teach? How should learning be assessed? How should technology be used in education? In this section, four classic distinctions are examined: rote learning versus meaningful learning, curriculum-centered versus child-centered education, retention versus transfer assessments, and technology-centered versus learner-centered applications.

Learning by Memorizing Versus Learning by Understanding

Wertheimer (1959) provided an entertaining example of the distinction between two types of learning: learning by memorizing (rote learning) and learning by understanding (meaningful learning). In learning how to find the area of a parallelogram, one student learns to measure the height of the parallelogram, measure the base of the parallelogram, and multiply the height by the base using the formula, Area = Height × Base. According to Wertheimer, learning to blindly use a formula is an example of rote learning (learning by memorizing). The steps in the procedure are arbitrary to the learner and do not seem to fit with any existing knowledge. Wertheimer showed that students who learn by memorizing are able to solve problems that appear to be similar to those used during instruction (i.e., retention problems), but they are generally unable to solve problems that seem different even though the same principle applies (i.e., transfer problems).

In contrast, another student learns to find the area of a parallelogram by seeing that it is possible to cut off a triangle from one side of the parallelogram, connect it to the other side, and produce a rectangle. This student can use existing knowledge of how to find the area of a rectangle to compute the area of a parallelogram. According to Wertheimer, this student is learning by understanding, thereby showing structural insight into the relation between a parallelogram and a rectangle—namely, that a parallelogram is simply a rectangle in disguise. The steps in the solution procedure make sense because the learner can relate them to the familiar task of finding the area of a rectangle. Wertheimer showed that students who learn by understanding perform well both on retention and transfer problems.

Wertheimer's parallelogram example suggests that when the goal of instruction is retention, then learning by memorizing is an effective approach; but, when the goal of instruction is transfer, then learning by understanding is more likely to pay off. According to Wertheimer, learning by memorizing enables reproductive thinking (i.e., being able to reproduce what was taught), whereas learning by understanding enables productive thinking (i.e., being able to create a novel solution to a problem that has not been seen before). Wertheimer's preference for meaningful over rote learning, first articulated more than 50 years ago, foreshadows the current interest in constructivist learning.

Curriculum-Centered Versus Child-Centered Education

How should teachers teach? Almost a century ago, Dewey (1902) made a classic distinction between curriculum-centered and child-centered approaches to education, which foreshadowed the current distinction between nonconstructivism and constructivist visions of education (Lambert & McCombs, 1998). In the curriculum-centered approach, the teacher begins with the material that needs to be covered and determines how best to help the learner master it. The curriculum-centered prescription, according to Dewey (1902, p. 8), is to "subdivide each topic into studies; each study into lessons; each lesson into specific facts and formulae. Let the child proceed step by step to master each one of these parts, and at last he will have covered the entire ground." What is learned consists of new skills and new pieces of information. The theory of learning underlying the curriculum-centered approach is that of the passive learner (Dewey, 1902, p. 8): "The child is simply the immature being who needs to be matured; he is the superficial being who is to be deepened. . . . It is his to receive, to accept." This view is consistent with behaviorism, which dominated the psychology of learning through the 1950s, and which is still the basis of many educational practices today (Burton, Moore, & Magliaro, 1996).

In contrast, in the child-centered approach, the teacher begins by understanding the characteristics of the learner and proceeds by creating opportunities for the learner to grow intellectually. The prescription for the child-centered approach, according to Dewey (1902, p. 9), is: "The child is the starting-point, the center, and the end. His development, his growth is the ideal." What is learned is a change in the learners' knowledge, including in how children think and control their own learning. The theory of learning underlying the child-centered approach is that of the active learner (Dewey, 1902, p. 9): "Learning is an active. It involves reaching out of the mind. It involves organic assimilation starting from within." This 100-year-old view is remarkably consistent with today's constructivist visions of learning and instruction, including learner-centered cognitive theories (Lambert & McCombs, 1998).

Assessment of Retention Versus Transfer

How should learning be assessed? The most thorough attempt to answer this question culminated in the publication of the *Taxonomy of Educational Objectives* (Bloom, Engelhart, Furst, Hill, & Krathwohl, 1956). Based on conference participation from dozens of the top scholars over a 5-year period and input solicited from a thousand reviewers, the taxonomy's analysis of academic learning outcomes into categories has stood the test of time (L. W. Anderson & Sosniak, 1994). According to the authors, the taxonomy was "intended to provide for classification of the goals of our educational system" (Bloom et al., 1956, p. 1). At its most fundamental level, the taxonomy distinguishes between two broad goals—remembering material that was taught (i.e., which can be called *retention*) and being able to use it in new situations (i.e., which can be called *transfer*). Importantly, this fundamental distinction between retention and transfer has been retained in a revised version of the taxonomy (Anderson et al., 2001). This focus on transfer is consistent with constructivist principles.

One goal of instruction is remembering "either by recognition or recall of ideas, material, or phenomena" (Bloom et al., 1956, p. 62). A typical retention test item is: "A spaniel is a type of: (a) sword, (b) dog, (c) lace, (d) horse, (e) coin" (Bloom et al., 1956, p. 79). In a retrospective, Bloom (1994, p. 1) estimated that "as much as 90 percent of instructional time was spent at this level with very little time spent on the higher mental processes that would enable students to apply their knowledge."

In contrast, another goal of instruction is understanding. Bloom et al. (1956, p. 1) noted that "some teachers believe their students should really understand, others desire their students to internalize knowledge, still others want their students to grasp the core essence." Perhaps the greatest contribution of the taxonomy is the detailed presentation of multiple ways of assessing understanding, ranging from the ability to summarize the theme of a passage to being able to evaluate the effectiveness of a proposed problem solution. The taxonomy articulated a role for transfer as an important complement to retention:

> Although information or knowledge is recognized as an important outcome of learning, very few teachers would be satisfied to regard this as the primary or the sole outcome of instruction. What is needed is some evidence that the students can do something with their knowledge, that is, that they can apply the information to new situations and problems. (Bloom et al., 1956, p. 38)

The inclusion of understanding as a legitimate educational goal foreshadowed the constructivist emphasis on assessment of learner understanding.

Technology-Based Versus Learner-Based Applications

Two approaches to instructional design with educational technology are technology-based applications and learner-based applications (Mayer, 1999b). Technology-based applications begin with the capabilities of technology—usually cutting edge technology—and ask how these new technology-supported capabilities can be incorporated into education. For example, a technology-centered application would be to figure out how to use virtual reality to improve the delivery of information to students in schools or how to insure all students have access to the World Wide Web. Unfortunately, technology-centered applications in education—ranging from motion pictures to radio to television to computer-assisted instruction—have generally failed to become integrated into the daily practice of schooling (Cuban, 1986) despite research indicating that some forms of technology-based instruction can improve student learning (Kulik, 1994; Schacter & Fagnano, 1999; Wenglinsky, 1998). In each case, strong claims were made for how a particular new technology would revolutionize education, but today schools are not heavily dependent on film, radio, TV, or computer-aided instruction (CAI). What went wrong? One answer is that the focus was on giving people access to the latest technology rather than on promoting human cognition through the aid of technology.

Learner-centered applications begin with a conception of how people learn and ask how technology can be used to foster human learning. In short, technology is seen as an aid to human learning, which Landauer (1995, p. 7) referred to as using computers as "augmentation" to the human mind. Similarly, Norman (1993, p. 12) argued that "technology . . . should complement human abilities, aid those activities for which we are poorly suited, and enhance and help develop those for which we are ideally suited." In short, technology can be used to expand cognitive capabilities, but to accomplish this goal instructional designers need a useful conception of how the human mind works.

In summary, constructivism emphasizes learning that is meaningful rather than rote, instruction that is child centered rather than curriculum centered, assessment based on transfer in addition to retention, and a learner-centered rather than a technology-centered approach to using educational technology. These four distinctions are summarized in Table 6.1.

THREE VIEWS OF HOW STUDENTS LEARN

During its 100-year history, educational psychology has devised three distinct visions of how students learn, reflecting what Mayer (1992a, 1996a,

TABLE 6.1
Four Issues in Education

Educational Area	Educational Issue
Learning	Learning by memorizing vs. learning by understanding
Teaching	Curriculum-centered vs. child-centered education
Assessment	Retention vs. transfer
Technology	Technology-centered vs. learner-centered applications

1999c) referred to as metaphors of learning. The first view of learning is that students learn by strengthening or weakening stimulus–response (S–R) associations; these associationist theories of learning are based on the metaphor of learning as response strengthening. The second view of learning is that students learn by adding new information to their long-term memories; these information-processing theories of learning are based on the metaphor of learning as knowledge acquisition. The third view of learning is that students learn by actively trying to make sense out of their experiences; these constructivist theories of learning are based on the metaphor of learning as knowledge construction.

Leary (1990, p. 1) demonstrated how metaphors "have guided—and sometimes preempted—investigation in selected areas of psychology" so that "metaphorical thinking . . . has helped to constitute, and not just reflect, scientific theory." Consistent with Leary's analysis, the use of educational technology may be guided by the three psychological metaphors of learning, so that an instructional designer's view of how students learn drives the ways that technology is used to promote learning. Key characteristics of each view of student learning and their implications for technology are summarized in Table 6.2.

Learning as Response Strengthening

The first theory of student learning to be developed in educational psychology is the associationist vision of learning as response strengthening. According to this view, student learning involves the strengthening or weakening of responses, or to be more precise, the strengthening or weakening of stimulus–response associations. The learning scenario is as follows: The learner is prompted to make a response. A correct response is rewarded,

TABLE 6.2
Three Views of How Students Learn

Learning Is	Teacher's Role	Learner's Role	Role of Technology
Response strengthening	Dispenser of rewards and punishments	Recipient of rewards and punishments	To provide drill and practice on basic skills
Knowledge acquisition	Dispenser of information	Recipient of information	To provide access to information such as databases or hypermedia
Knowledge construction	Cognitive guide	Sense maker	To allow guided participation in academic tasks

whereas an incorrect response is punished, and this process is repeated many times.

The mechanism underlying learning is that rewards automatically strengthen S–R connections, whereas punishments automatically weaken S–R connections. For example, based on research with cats, dogs, and chicks, Thorndike (1911, p. 294) proposed what came to be known as the law of effect:

> Its general law is that when in a certain situation [a learner] acts so that pleasure results, that act is selected from all those performed and associated with that situation, so that, when the situation recurs, the act will be more likely to follow than it was before; that, on the contrary the acts which, when performed in a certain situation, have brought discomfort, tend to be dissociated from that situation.

The law of effect simply states that when a learner's response to a situation is followed by comfort or satisfaction, the learner will be more likely to make the same response to that situation in the future; and, when a learner's response to a situation is followed by discomfort or dissatisfaction, the learner will be less likely to make the same response to that situation in the future. According to Thorndike, the strengthening or weakening of the association between the situation and the response is automatic, working the same way in lab animals on contrived tasks as in humans on academic tasks. Although Skinner (1938, 1968) and others improved on Thorndike's research methodology and enriched his theory, they retained the essential vision of learning as response strengthening. Coupled with the law of exercise, which called for practice, the law of effect came to dominate educational practice and psychological theory during the first half of the 20th century, and continues to be a driving force today.

The response-strengthening view was based largely on research involving laboratory animals learning to perform artificial laboratory tasks. For example, Thorndike's (1911) classic research included the study of cats learning to escape from a cage by performing some response. In a typical study, a hungry cat was placed in a wooden cage called a puzzle box. If the cat performed a certain act, such as pulling a loop of string that was hanging overhead, then a trap door would open allowing the cat to escape and have access to some nearby food. Thorndike found that the first time the cat was put in the box, it engaged in many extraneous behaviors such as pouncing against the bars, thrusting its paws between the bars, and meowing. Eventually, its paw accidentally caught the loop of string and opened the door, allowing the cat to escape. On subsequent trials, the cat tended to engage in fewer and fewer extraneous behaviors, so it took less and less time for the cat to perform the correct response and escape. The gradual decrease across trials in the amount of time required to escape from the puzzle box was consistent with Thorndike's vision of learning as gradually strengthening the successful response (pulling the loop of string) and gradually weakening the unsuccessful responses (e.g., pouncing, thrusting, or meowing).

The response-strengthening view of learning defines the role of the teacher and the student within an educational setting. Based on the response-strengthening view, the teacher is a dispenser of rewards and punishments, whereas the student is the passive recipient of rewards and punishments. The teacher's role is to create situations in which the student is asked to make short, simple responses. If the response is correct, then the student is rewarded; if the student is wrong, then the student is punished— or, at least, is not rewarded. The teacher completely controls the learning environment by choosing which questions will be asked, and by dispensing rewards and punishments contingent on the student's response. The student's role is to respond to prompts or questions from the teacher, and to receive the ensuing reward or punishment. Thus, learners take a passive role in which their behavior, evoked by questions from the teacher, is shaped automatically by its consequences.

The response-strengthening view suggests that educational technology should employ instructional methods such as drill-and-practice, in which the student performs the same skills over and over, receiving feedback on each trial. Pressey's (1926) classic teaching machine, as well as Skinner's (1968) updated and improved teaching machine, were based on the response-strengthening view and were inspired by Thorndike's theory of learning. For example, with Pressey's (1926) teaching machine, a multiple choice question was presented, the student pressed a key on a keyboard to respond, and the machine determined whether the student needed more instruction. With Skinner's teaching machine, the goal was to present simple questions that the student could answer correctly, to provide immediate reinforcement of correct responses, and to move in small steps. Before the advent of computer-assisted instruction (CAI) in the 1960s, the preferred teaching method was programed instruction, in either linear (Holland, 1965) or branching form (Crowder, 1960). Consistent with the response-strengthening view, programed instruction calls for presenting a frame on the screen, waiting for the learner to respond (usually by pressing a key), and then the presenting the next frame (Burton et al., 1996).

Even modern computer technology can be used to support drill-and-practice teaching. For example, Moreno and Mayer (1999) asked sixth-grade students to solve 64 arithmetic problems involving addition and subtraction of signed numbers, such as $2 - -3 = \underline{\quad}$. Each problem appeared on a computer screen, the student typed in a numerical answer, and then received feedback. The feedback for a correct answer was "Yes, the correct answer is ____" (with the correct answer in the blank), whereas the feedback for an incorrect answer was, "Sorry, this is not the correct answer" (and the student had the option of clicking on "Try Again" to enter a new answer or clicking on "See Solution" to see the correct answer). The training took place over four sessions, with 16 problems given at each session. Consistent with the response-strengthening view, performance increased across the four sessions.

Although the results seem to support the use of technology to support drill-and-practice methods of instruction, a major drawback is that students may fail to understand what they are learning. For example, in the Moreno and Mayer (1999) study, performance increased significantly more for a group of students who were allowed to model the problems in a multimedia computer environment; for each problem, students used a joystick to move the bunny along a number line to simulate the operations in the problem, and then received feedback showing the bunny's movements on the number line, a verbal description of the bunny's movements, and the numerical answer. By helping students actively translate each problem into movements along a number line, they were encouraged to make sense out of the procedures they were learning. In this study, learning by understanding in a multimedia environment proved to be more effective than learning by drill and practice.

What is learned according to the response-strengthening view? The answer is S–R associations. Students learn to give fast, accurate responses. Accordingly, the assessment methods should measure the speed and accuracy of responses to simple cues. How fast and accurate are students when they solve a series of addition problems or spell a set of words? These are the kinds of assessments suggested by the response-strengthening view.

The response-strengthening view has important strengths and weaknesses. On the positive side, it constitutes educational psychology's first and most successfully applied approach to learning. For more than 100 years, psychologists and educators have honed procedures for teaching behavioral and cognitive skills using drill-and-practice methods (J. R. Anderson, 1993; Singley & J. R. Anderson, 1989), and there is ample evidence that drill-and-practice can help students' learning, particularly of basic skills. For these reasons, the response-strengthening view—although no longer dominant—is still a force in educational practice and psychological theory.

On the negative side, the response-strengthening view can be criticized for its reliance on lab animal research (rather than human learning in authentic situations), its emphasis on passive learners (rather than active, self-regulated learners), and its failure to handle the thorny issue of transfer. Where is understanding? Where is the ability to apply what is learned to new situations? Where is student motivation to learn? These are some of the questions that led to the ascendancy of new metaphors of learning, as described in the next two sections.

Learning as Knowledge Acquisition

The Gestalt psychologists mounted the major offensive against the response-strengthening vision of learning, but they failed to offer a compelling alternative (Mayer, 1995; Wertheimer, 1959). The basis of the attack was that response-strengthening constituted one type of learning (what could be called rote learning), but there was another kind of learning that needed to be explained (what could be called meaningful learning). Katona (1940, pp. 4–5) articulated the argument as follows: "The main objection to the prevailing theory, which makes one kind of connection the basis of all learning, is not that it may be incorrect, but that in the course of psychological research it has prevented an unbiased study of other possible kinds of learning." In particular, Katona (1940, p. 5) distinguished between rote learning in which "connections [are] established by the conditioned-reflex technique or by repeating the same . . . responses . . . as in all forms of drill" and meaningful learning in which learners produce "insight into a situation" or "understanding of a procedure." Similarly, Kohler (1925, p. 169) distinguished between learning that "arises out of a consideration of the structure of a situation" (which he claimed requires "insight") and learning that does not require such structural insight.

In what is perhaps the most educationally relevant critique, Wertheimer (1959) argued that qualitatively different learning outcomes occur when a student learns by rote versus by understanding. For example, in learning to find the area of a parallelogram, a rote method involves memorizing how to use the formula, Area = Height × Base, whereas a meaningful method involves realizing that you can cut off the triangle on one end of the parallelogram and put it on the other end to form a rectangle. According to Wertheimer, rote methods lead to reproductive thinking in which students perform well on retention but not transfer, whereas meaningful methods of instruction lead to productive thinking in which students perform well on retention and transfer. How can students be helped to learn in ways that allow them to transfer what they have learned to new situations? This is the classic challenge of the Gestalt psychologists to the response-strengthening view (Mayer, 1995).

Although the Gestalt psychologists attacked the monolithic theory that all learning involved response strengthening, they were unable to offer a completing alternative. That task fell on information-processing psychologists, who shared the Gestaltists' objections to behaviorism but who constructed an alternative based on an information-processing metaphor.

Educational psychology's second major theory of student learning is the information-processing view of learning as knowledge acquisition. According to this view, learning occurs when a learner processes information that is presented. The learning scenario is as follows: Information is input to the learner, the learner applies a series of mental operations (each of which transforms the information in some way), and then the learner stores the output in long-term memory. This view is sometimes referred to as the knowledge transmission metaphor, because the teacher transmits information for the student to receive, or the empty vessel metaphor, because the teacher fills the students' empty heads with information.

The mechanism underlying learning is a series of cognitive process that are applied to mental representations resulting in a transformation of the mental representation. Thus, learning involves taking in information and building a mental representation in short-term (or working) memory, applying a series of cognitive processes to the representation, each of which transforms the representation in some way, and then storing the final result in long-term memory.

Electronic computers, which were invented in the 1940s and commercially produced in the 1950s, exerted a strong influence on learning researchers both as a research tool and as the basis for a new kind of theory. By the 1960s and 1970s, the human–computer metaphor dominated psychological theories of learning, as described in the following passage by R. Lachman, J. L. Lachman, and Butterfield (1979, p. 99): "Computers take symbolic input, recode it, make decisions about it, and give back symbolic output. By analogy, that is what most of cognitive psychology is about. It is about how people take in information, how they transform their internal knowledge states, and how they translate these states into behavioral output."

To understand the information-processing view, it is useful to consider the nature of "processing" and the nature of "information." Processing refers to running a program, a sequence of steps, consisting of successive operations applied to cognitive representations. In contrast to the view of learning as strengthening or weakening associations, according to the information-processing view, the process of learning is like running a computer program: "A program is . . . a recipe for selecting, storing, recovering, combining, outputting and generally manipulating [information]" (Neisser, 1966, p. 8). Information is a commodity that can be transferred from teacher to learner, and that can be manipulated, stored, and retrieved by learners. In contrast to focusing on the S–R association as the unit of learning, the information-processing metaphor focuses on the representation of information: "Information is what is transformed, and the structured pattern of its transformation is what we want to understand" (Neisser, 1966, p. 8).

Unlike the response-strengthening view, which was based largely on research with animals in artificial settings, the information-processing view was based largely on research with humans in artificial settings. The shift from lab animal to human research during the 1950s and 1960s resulted in a clear discovery: When humans where tested in the same kinds of situations used for lab animal research, humans did not appear to learn in the same way as the lab animals (Bruner, Goodnow, & Austin, 1956). For example, when animals were placed in discrimination learning situations (e.g., to choose a black maze path rather than a white one), they tended to learn gradually as predicted by the law of effect (Hull, 1943). However, when humans were placed in concept learning tasks (e.g., to choose a card that had red figures on it rather than green or black), they tended to learn in an all-at-once fashion, suggesting that they were actively testing hypotheses (Bruner et al., 1956). Instead of being passively shaped by their experiences, humans appeared to be processors of incoming information.

The information-processing view of learning defines new roles for the teacher and student. According to the information-processing view, the teacher is a dispenser of information, whose job is to present appropriate information to the learner. The teacher must create situations that expose the learner to the to-be-learned information, and must be concerned with efficient methods for delivering information—such as lectures, videos, books, and computer-based presentations. Similarly, the learner is a recipient of information, whose job is to accept, manipulate, store, and retrieve information. The learner must process large amounts of incoming information, and must be concerned with efficient methods for processing information (e.g., strategies for how to represent and remember incoming material).

Mayer (1996a) distinguished between two versions of the information-processing view—a passive learner version (representing classic information-processing theory as described in this section) and an active learner version (consistent with constructivist views as described in the next section). In the passive learner version, learning involves information processing in the strictest sense: What is learned is information, namely, a measurable commodity that can be transferred directly from mind to mind, and the process of learning is viewed as applying one or more well-defined algorithms that take information as input, apply some transformation, and produce revised information as output. According to the passive version, "the learner performs a series of discrete mental operations on input information and stores the result" (Mayer, 1996a, p. 156). In the active learner version, what is learned is knowledge, a personal representation that is mediated by each learner's existing knowledge, and the process of learning is viewed as an active construction. According to the active version, which is consistent with constructivism, "the learner actively selects, organizes, and integrates incoming experience with existing knowledge" (Mayer, 1996a, p. 156).

The instructional implications of the passive learner version of the information-processing view are straightforward. What is needed is a system for delivering large quantities of information to learners. Instructional technologies based on computers and access to the Internet can meet this challenge of delivering information to learners. Examples of instructional technology that can be adapted to the information delivery view include the development of search engines for large-scale databases (Walster, 1996), the development of hypertext presentations (Vora & Helander, 1997), and multimedia lessons (Mayer, in press-c; Moore, Burton, & Myers, 1996).

In a review of research on multimedia learning, Mayer (in press-c) showed the shortcomings of the information delivery view of instructional technology. For example, in one set of studies, students who received an animation along with concurrent corresponding narration performed much better on transfer tests than did students who received an animation along with concurrent corresponding on-screen text (Mayer, in press-c). In another set of studies, students who received an animation along with concurrent corresponding narration performed much better than did students who received an animation followed or preceded by the same narration (Mayer, in press-c). According to the information delivery view, all students in these studies should learn equally well because they all received the same information. These results suggest that something is wrong with the information delivery view of technology.

Similarly, the implications for assessment are clear. What is needed is a method of assessing how many pieces of information the learner acquired. The focus is on retention tests, including multiple choice items or cued recall items covering the presented information. For example, a test item might ask a history student to state the date of an important historic event, or to select it from a short list. The assessments are aimed at determining "how much" was learned.

The instructional implications of the active learner version mesh somewhat with those described in the next section on learning as knowledge construction. Perhaps the most exciting instructional implication is a focus on cognitive process instruction—that is, directly teaching students how to process information effectively (Lochhead & Clement, 1979; Pressley & Woloshyn, 1995). Cognitive process instruction includes teaching reading comprehension strategies such as how to outline a paragraph, how to generate a summary, or how to distinguish important from unimportant information; or teaching list learning strategies such as how to rehearse, how to organize items by taxonomic category, or how to elaborate on the presented material (Weinstein & Mayer, 1986). In addition to possessing appropriate information-processing strategies, learners need the metacognitive awareness to enable them to know when to use them (Mayer, 1987; Pressley & Woloshyn, 1995). The next section explores the implications of a vision of the learner as an active knowledge constructor, which subsumes the active information-processing view.

The information-processing view has important strengths and weaknesses (Mayer, 1996a). On the positive side, it shifted the focus of learning theory from behavior to knowledge, from strengthening associations to applying cognitive processes, and from animal to human research. On the negative side, the information-processing view initially emphasized information rather than knowledge and automatic processing rather than effortful constructing. It also initially focused on contrived laboratory tasks rather than realistic academic tasks, and ignored the motivational, cultural, and biological bases of learning.

Learning as Knowledge Construction

The third major theory of how students learn is the constructivist view of learning as knowledge construction. According to this view, learning occurs when a learner actively builds meaningful cognitive representations. The mechanism underlying learning is the building of cognitive structures, including the building of mental models, through the strategic application of cognitive processes. In constructivist learning, learners engage in active processing such as paying attention to relevant incoming information, mentally organizing it into a coherent structure, and integrating it with existing knowledge.

The constructivist view of learning offers fundamentally new roles for the teacher and student. According to the constructivist view, the teacher is a cognitive guide who works with students on authentic academic tasks. Rather than promoting drill and practice on fragmented subtasks, the teacher asks students to work on realistic academic tasks such as making sense out a text or composing an essay. The teacher may provide guidance when needed, may demonstrate how to carry out certain parts of difficult tasks, and may offer hints and suggestions for appropriate strategies in other parts. The student takes the role of a sense maker, someone who is working to make meaning out of the incoming information by reorganizing it and connecting it with prior knowledge. Both the teacher and learner are active participants in the learning process.

Like the other two conceptions of learning, constructivism has both strengths and weaknesses. On the positive side, by building on the active learner version of information-processing theory, constructivism provides a broader and more plausible vision of learning that recognizes the learner's contributions to the process. Yet, on the negative side, the constructivist view is not the only viable conception of how learning works, nor does it adequately address the motivational, social, cultural, and biological bases of learning. On balance, the constructivist view of learning can offer some potentially useful suggestions for fostering technology-assisted learning.

What is the role of instructional technology under the constructivist view? According to the constructivist view of learning, instructional technology should help guide learners in their efforts at making sense of new material. Simulations, for example, allow learners to work on an authentic task while receiving appropriate guidance (Gredler, 1996). Multimedia presentations can help them to connect presented material with existing knowledge (Cognition and Technology Group at Vanderbilt, 1996). For example, White (1993) developed a microworld that helped students understand the principles of Newtonian physics, and Dunbar (1993) developed a microworld in which students perform experiments that allow them to discover a principle in biology.

Even the conception of what is learned changes under the constructivist view. Instead of learning S–R associations (as in the response-learning view) or isolated facts and procedures (as in the knowledge-acquisition view), learners build coherent mental structures, including mental models. Thus, the kinds of assessments suggested by the constructivist view include multiple measures of understanding (Hambleton, 1996; White & Gunstone, 1992).

Three Learning Scenarios

What happens when students learn? Over the last 100 years, psychologists have developed three possible answers: (a) Learning is like adding a new skill to one's collection (i.e., based on the response-strengthening view). (b) Learning is like depositing new knowledge in one's memory bank (i.e., based on the information delivery view). (c) Learning is like building a model in which pieces are fit together into a meaningful structure (i.e., based on the knowledge construction view). These accounts of learning are represented in the following three learning scenarios, which involve skill learning, rote learning, and meaningful learning, respectively.

Skill Learning. Alan is reading a textbook lesson on the physics of motion. The material is boring to him, but he focuses on computing values using the key formulas in the lesson, such as $V_a = (V_i - V_f)/2$ (where V_a is average speed, V_i is initial speed, and V_f is final speed). He repeatedly practices computing the value of one of the variables in a formula when given values for the other two, and checks to see if he got the right answer. For example, if initial speed is 20 and final speed is 0, then he computes average speed to be $(20 - 0)/2 = 10$.

Alan seems to assume that his job is to master the skill of using formulas. This scenario is most consistent with the idea that learning involves adding skills to one's collection, such as being able to carry out the steps in a procedure when cued to do so. On a test, Alan is fast and accurate in using the formulas to compute the value of one variable when given the other two. But, he performs poorly on retention questions, which cover the exact facts from the book, and on transfer questions, which ask him to apply what was in the book to new situations. Alan's learning outcome can be classified as skill mastery with no learning of other material.

Skill learning involves learning to produce a response or sequence of responses when cued to do so. The learning outcome is procedural knowledge (i.e., knowledge of how to do something). Skill learning is revealed by tests in which a learner performs the skill in a fast and accurate way.

Rote Learning. Bret reads the same lesson. The material is also boring to him, but he laboriously reads each word because he wants to perform well on the test. He hopes his strong effort in trying to remember all the material will overcome his lack of interest. Bret seems to view his task as adding new information to his memory. His approach most closely fits the vision of learning as knowledge acquisition. On the test, he performs well on retention but he does poorly on transfer questions. Bret's learning outcome could be classified as rote learning.

Rote learning involves acquiring pieces of new information that can be produced on request. The learning outcome is declarative knowledge—factual knowledge about the world. Rote learning is revealed by tests in which learners perform well on retention but poorly on transfer.

Meaningful Learning. Charles is working on a science project in which he wants to build a catapult that will deliver a marble into a cup at a specified distance. In order to build the catapult, he reads the same physics lesson as Alan and Bret. His goal is to use the information to help him build a successful catapult, and to do this he knows he needs to understand the physics of motion. His approach most closely fits the constructivist vision of learning as knowledge construction, because he is working hard to make sense out of the material. On a test of the material, Charles performs well on retention and transfer questions, indicating a meaningful learning outcome.

Meaningful learning (or constructivist learning) occurs when a learner actively makes sense out of presented material. The resulting learning outcome is conceptual knowledge (i.e., knowledge of a coherent system, structure, or principle) and strategic knowledge of how to plan and monitor problem solutions. Meaningful learning is revealed by tests in which learners perform well on retention and transfer.

These examples illustrate three different kinds of learning, each of which involves different learning processes and different learning outcomes. Constructivist learning is illustrated in the third scenario, although the other scenarios illustrate other kinds of academic learning situations.

These examples also point to role of educational objectives in learning. For Alan, the educational objective was to master a procedure, so the appropriate assessment was to measure Alan's speed and accuracy in computing values using the formulas he studied. For Bret, the educational objective was to remember as many facts as possible from a text, so the appropriate assessment was to ask factual questions covering the material in the text. For Charles, the educational objective was to understand how the physics of motion works, so the appropriate assessment was to ask questions that involve transfer to new situations.

The role of instructional technology depends on the desired learning outcome. When the goal is the acquisition of cognitive skill, then drill and practice with feedback may be the most reasonable method to use. When the goal is rote learning, then technology can be used to present information. When the goal is to promote meaningful learning, then technology can be used to provide guidance in a simulation or to provide a multimedia presentation that taps the learner's prior knowledge or models the steps in solving a problem.

A CLOSER LOOK AT CONSTRUCTIVISM

Which Kind of Constructivism Is Best?

Educational researchers devote a lot of energy to searching for the best version of constructivism ranging from cognitive constructivism to social constructivism to radical constructivism (Marshall, 1996; Phillips, 1998; Steffe & Gale, 1995). Phillips (1998) showed how it is possible to analyze constructivism into categories, along a series of dimensions. Some major types of constructivism are individually mediated cognitive constructivism, socially mediated cognitive constructivism, social constructivism, and radical constructivism.

Cognitive Constructivism. It is appropriate to begin with cognitive constructivism because it forms a basis for the learning-as-knowledge construction view presented in the foregoing section. Cognitive constructivism rests on the premise that knowledge construction occurs within the minds of individual learners, so learning is essentially a psychological event. However, cognitive constructivism can be divided into two versions on the basis of conceptions of how knowledge is constructed. What is the process by which knowledge is constructed: individual cognitive processes or social/ cultural processes? Within cognitive constructivism are those who focus on the way an individual constructs knowledge in an individual context (e.g., through reading a book) and those who focus on the way an individual constructs knowledge in a social context (e.g., through a group discussion and negotiation). The former view can be called cognitive constructivism in individual contexts (or individually mediated cognitive constructivism), whereas the latter can be called cognitive constructivism in social contexts (or socially mediated cognitive constructivism). Both cases involve cognitive construction because knowledge is assumed to exist within the minds of individual learners; although, as Phillips (1998) pointed out, the latter approach is sometimes mistakenly called social constructivism.

Acknowledging both individually mediated and socially mediated versions of cognitive constructivism provides a wider vision of constructivist learning. This broadened approach to cognitive constructivism assumes that the process of constructivist learning occurs both within learners and within groups of learners, while retaining the straightforward idea that the outcomes of constructivist learning outcomes are stored within learners. Acknowledging the validity of both versions of cognitive consꞇructivism helps to overcome one of the major criticisms of cognitive constructivism, namely, that it focuses too narrowly on the individual learner.

Social Constructivism. An emerging alternative to cognitive constructivism is social constructivism, which is based on the premise that constructed knowledge is stored within social/cultural groups so learning is essentially a sociocultural event. The major dimension dividing cognitive and social constructivism concerns where knowledge is stored: as individual knowledge in the minds of individual learners, which denotes cognitive constructivism (or psychological constructivism), or as public knowledge that is shared by social communities, which denotes social constructivism. Cognitive constructivists are concerned with how individuals come to possess individual knowledge (e.g., knowing how to summarize a passage), whereas social constructivists are concerned with how social groups create public knowledge (e.g., a cultural vision of what it means to be educated). A distinguishing feature separating cognitive and social constructivists concerns whether or not knowledge exists in individual minds; the answer is yes for cognitive constructivists and no for social constructivists.

Social constructivism can be criticized on the grounds that it is absurd to assume that sociocultural factors are the only factors that determine knowledge construction or that knowledge cannot exist in individual minds. Phillips (1998) argued that social constructivists sometimes spoil their analyses of learning through overstatement. Cognitive constructivism can be criticized on the grounds that it offers too narrow a view of knowledge construction. Phillips argued that cognitive constructivists should add more "social beef" to their analyses of student learning.

A reasonable reconciliation between these two versions of constructivism is that both kinds of knowledge construction can take place (Mayer, 1998). Thus, cognitive constructivists are interested in the psychological issue of how an individual learner comes to possess knowledge—an important issue for those who take a learner-centered approach to education (Lambert & McCombs, 1998)—whereas social constructivists are interested in the anthropological/sociological issue of how the common knowledge and practices of a group come into being, which is an important issue for those who take a sociocultural approach to education (Cole, 1996; Lave & Wenger, 1991).

Radical Constructivism. The dimension of how learning occurs enables the distinction between individually mediated and socially mediated versions of cognitive constructivism, whereas the dimension of where learning outcomes are stored provides the distinction between cognitive and social constructivism. The third dimension cutting across constructivism concerns the degree to which knowledge construction is based on the outside world, ranging from the view that knowledge is discovered to the view that knowledge is invented. For example, within social constructivism are radical constructivists who believe that a group's shared knowledge is constructed entirely out of social negotiation and nonradical constructivists who believe that a discipline's knowledge reflects a consensus of how to interpret agreed on observations about the world. Within cognitive constructivism are radical constructivists, who believe that an individual's knowledge is completely invented by the learner, and nonradical constructivists, who hold that the outcome of learning depends on the creative interaction of both what is presented and what the learner already knows.

Radical constructivism can be criticized for its relativistic view that all knowledge representations are equally valid, instruction is impossible because instructional communications mean entirely different things to different people, and teachers can never determine what their students know (Phillips, 1998). At the present, radical constructivism does not seem to offer useful implications for instruction or assessment.

In summary, the two most viable versions of constructivism are individually mediated cognitive constructivism and socially mediated cognitive constructivism (which is sometimes mistakenly called social constructivism). Together they correspond to the learning-as-knowledge construction view that was presented in the introduction, and their implications for how students learn are described in more detail later. Although constructivist theories now dominate psychology and education, it is worthwhile to heed Dewey's (1938, p. 6) classic warning that reformers "should think in terms of education itself rather than in terms of some ism about education." Dewey's (1938, p. 6) rationale is clear: "Any movement that thinks and acts in terms of an ism becomes so involved in reaction against other isms that it is unwittingly controlled by them." The next section examines a constructivist theory of how students learn in more detail.

A CLOSER LOOK AT COGNITIVE CONSTRUCTIVISM

Learning as Structure Building

According to both the individually mediated and socially mediated versions of cognitive constructivism, learning is a process of structure building in which a learner builds a coherent mental representation. For example, Gernsbacher (1990, p. 1) showed how comprehending printed or spoken prose is essentially a model building activity in which "the goal of comprehension is to build a coherent mental representation or structure of the material being comprehended."

The process of structure building is guided by the learner's desire to make sense out of the material. The consensus among cognitive scientists is that this sense making activity is accomplished by fitting pieces of presented information together into a coherent structure and integrating presented information systematically with existing knowledge. For example, one way of making sense out of a presented explanation is to build a mental model, that is, a mental representation that simulates a cause-and-effect system (Gentner & Stevens, 1983; Halford, 1993; Johnson-Laird, 1983). Constructivist views of learning recognize the intimate relation between understanding and model building: "Understanding . . . consists in your having a working model of the phenomenon in your mind" (Johnson-Laird, 1983, p. 2), "understanding entails mental models" (Halford, 1993, p. 3), and "mental models research is characterized by careful examination of the way people understand some domain of knowledge" (Gentner & Stevens, 1983, p. 1). It follows that the goal of constructivist instruction is "to foster the construction of mental models or representations" (English, 1997, p. 3).

For example, in viewing a multimedia lesson on the formation of lightning, a constructivist learner attempts to build a mental model of the cause-and-effect system for lightning formation (Mayer, 1999a). Instruction aimed at fostering the structure building activity depends on appropriate instructional design, including the use of concrete analogies and signaling of the conceptual structure through headings and outlines (Mayer, 1999a). Constructivist learning outcomes are revealed through transfer tests in which learners are asked to use what they have learned in new situations. For example, transfer problems for the lightning passage could involve asking the learner to explain how to reduce the intensity of a lightning storm or to tell what temperature has to do with lightning.

What cognitive processes are required for constructivist learning? Based on reviews of current theories of cognitive constructivism, Mayer (1996b, 1999c, in press-c) outlined three basic processes involved in constructivist learning: selecting relevant information (including relevant visual and verbal information), organizing the incoming information into a coherent structure (including visual and verbal models), and integrating various sources of the incoming information with each other and with existing knowledge. These processes are summarized in Fig. 6.1, which shows the proposed architecture of the human cognitive system. Following Wittrock's (1990) generative theory of learning, all three cognitive process are required for meaningful learning; following Paivio's (1986) dual coding theory, this model also assumes that humans possess separate processing channels for visual/pictorial processing and auditory/pictorial processing; and following Baddeley's (1986) working memory theory, this model assumes that each channel is limited in processing capacity. In contrast to the information-processing view in which information is added to memory, Fig. 6.1 represents a system for building coherent mental structures.

The cognitive model of learning in Fig. 6.1 contains five boxes representing stages in the active construction of knowledge: In the visual/pictorial channel, visually presented material is held as images, then as a pictorial model, and then as part of an integrated cognitive structure. In the auditory channel, auditorily presented material is held as words, then as a verbal model, and then as part of an integrated cognitive structure. It also contains labeled arrows that refer to the cognitive processes of selecting images and selecting words, organizing images into a pictorial model and organizing words into a verbal model, and integrating the visual and verbal models with each other and with prior knowledge, as described later.

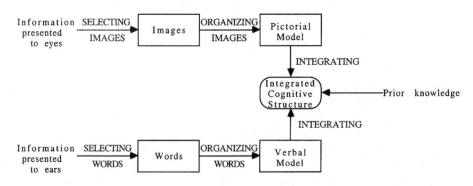

FIG. 6.1.   Cognitive model of learning.

Selecting

Visual and auditory information, such as contained in multimedia instructional messages, enter the cognitive system through the learner's eyes and ears, respectively. The first cognitive process required for constructivist learning is to determine what is important in the incoming sensory information, a cognitive process that can be called *selecting*. This process is represented by the arrow from visual information to images (in the visual/pictorial channel) and by the arrow from auditory information to words (in the auditory/verbal channel), indicating that, as learners pay attention to some of the incoming sensory information, the information is transferred to working memory where it can be processed more deeply. Mayer (1992b, p. 247) defined selecting as "focusing conscious attention on relevant pieces of information" and Sternberg (1985, p. 107) defined it as "sifting out relevant from irrelevant information." In sum, the first component process in constructivist learning is selecting (or paying attention to) relevant information in the instructional message.

An important instructional implication is that students may need help in learning how to guide their attention during instruction. For example, in viewing an animation that depicts the process of lightning formation, students can know where to look when they also hear concurrent narration describing the key actions in words. Some major events in the passage are that cool moist air comes in contact with a warmer surface, the air rises and condenses into a cloud, charges separate within in the cloud, and so on. By highlighting these actions with words, the learner is more likely to pay attention to them in the animation.

Organizing

Once relevant material is held in short-term memory, the next step in the sense-making process is to organize the material into a coherent structure. Thus, the second process in constructivist learning can be called *organizing* because the learner must actively build systematic connections among the selected pieces of information. This process is represented by the arrow from images to pictorial model (in the visual/pictorial channel) and by the arrow from words to verbal model (in the auditory/verbal channel), as mental manipulations occur in working memory. Mayer (1992b, p. 247) defined organizing as "building internal connections among the selected pieces of information" and Sternberg (1985, p. 107) described the process as "combining selected encoded information in such a way as to form an integrated . . . internally connected whole." In sum, organizing occurs when the learner constructs a coherent structure that incorporates the key pieces of presented information.

An important instructional implication is that constructivist learning requires more than just paying attention to relevant pieces of information; the learner may need help in actively organizing the pieces into a coherent structure (Reigeluth, 1999). For example, in the lightning passage, constructivist learners must build a causal chain in which one step in the lightning process (e.g., cool moist air moves over a warm surface) is the cause of the next step (e.g., the air rises). An important implication for instructional design is that instructional messages should include guidance for the construction of internal connections, that is, mentally fitting the pieces of presented information into a coherent structure. Signaling is the most straightforward technique to foster this organizing process in learners (Loman & Mayer, 1983; Meyer, Brandt, & Bluth, 1980). Signaling techniques include the insertion of an outline (including outlines in prose form), headings that are keyed to the outline, and pointer words such as "first, second, third" or "as a result of this." Loman and Mayer (1983) found that students who read signaled versions of a passage performed better on retention of the signaled material and on problem-solving transfer than did students who read the base passage. Overall, text-based techniques for guiding learners' organizing processes can affect both their retention and transfer (Mayer, 1996b).

Integrating

The third cognitive process in constructivist learning is building connections between the visual and verbal representations of the incoming material and with existing knowledge, which can be called the *process of integrating*. The integrating process is represented by the arrow from pictorial model to integrated cognitive structure, from verbal model to integrated cognitive structure, and from prior knowledge to integrated cognitive structure. For meaningful learning to occur, the learner must activate appropriate prior knowledge and bring it into working memory where it can be integrated with new material. Mayer (1992b, p. 249) defined this process as "building external connections between the organized new knowledge and organized existing knowledge" and Sternberg (1985, p. 107) defined it as "relating newly acquired information . . . to old knowledge so as to form an externally connected whole." In sum, integrating involves activating prior knowledge and using that knowledge to help make sense out of new material.

An instructional implication is that, for constructivist learning to occur, students need to know how to activate and use appropriate prior knowledge while they are learning new material and they need to make connections between corresponding visual and verbal representations in working memory. In viewing a multimedia presentation on lightning, students need to see how steps depicted in the animation (e.g., such as a picture of air rising) correspond to steps described in the narration (e.g., such as a sentence stating that the air rises) and to prior knowledge (e.g., previous experience with hot air rising). An important implication for instructional design is that instructional messages should employ techniques that foster the building of external connections by learners, such as the use of concrete analogies as advance organizers (Ausubel, 1968; Mayer, 1983, 1987). For example, Mayer (1983) asked students to read a passage about how radar works that either did or did not have an advance organizer. The advance organizer was a concrete analogy based on the learner's experience with bouncing balls; it consisted of a brief description of a boy throwing a ball, the ball hitting a remote object, the ball bouncing back, and the time it takes being an indication of how far away the object was. Learners performed better on retention of the conceptual information about radar and on problem-solving transfer when they read a passage with the advance organizer than without it (Mayer, 1983). Overall, techniques for fostering the building of external connections can have strong effects both on retention and transfer (Mayer, 1996b).

In summary, constructivist learning (or active learning) requires that the learner engage in three basic cognitive processes: selecting relevant information from what is presented, organizing that information into a coherent structure, and integrating that information with useful existing knowledge. Instruction can be designed to prime each of these processes during learning.

IMPLICATIONS FOR THE DESIGN OF MULTIMEDIA INSTRUCTIONAL MESSAGES

Different conceptions of learning suggest different ways of using technology in education. For example, consider the design of multimedia message intended to explain how some scientific system works, such as how lightning storms develop or how an airplane achieves lift. The multimedia message consists of a short animation along with simultaneous corresponding narration, as in a multimedia encyclopedia. According to a knowledge acquisition view (or information delivery view), a multimedia presentation is a vehicle for presenting information to the learner. The main idea is that more learning occurs when more channels are used for delivering the information. In contrast, according to the knowledge construction view (constructivist view), learners attempt to make sense of a multimedia presentation by selecting relevant words and images to be held in working memory (which is highly limited in capacity), by organizing the words into a verbal model (such as a verbally based cause-and-effect chain) and organizing the images into a visual model (such as a pictorially based cause-and-effect chain), and by integrating the verbal and visual models with each other and with prior knowledge. The main ideas in the constructivist conception of multimedia learning are that learning is an active process involving selecting, organizing, and integrating; humans have separate visual and verbal processing channels; and the capacity of working memory is limited (Mayer, in press-c).

Contiguity Effect in Multimedia Learning

What would happen if instead of presenting the animation and narration simultaneously, they were presented successively—with the narrative given before or after the animation? According to the information delivery view, students should learn as much from successive as from simultaneous presentation, because in both cases information is being delivered via two channels. According to the constructivist view, learners are actively trying to make meaningful connections between the words and pictures; this integration process is fostered when learners hold corresponding visual and verbal material in working memory at the same time. Learners are more likely to hold corresponding visual and verbal material in working memory at the same time when the narration and animation are presented simultaneously rather than successively. Thus, a simultaneous presentation approach should lead to deeper learning than a successive presentation approach. In a series of eight studies, students who received animation and narration simultaneously performed better on subsequent transfer tests than did students who received animation and narration successively (Mayer, in press-c). This *contiguity effect* is inconsistent with the information delivery view and consistent with the constructivist view of learning.

Coherence Effect in Multimedia Learning

One attempt at improving on the simultaneous presentation of animation and narration is to add background music (e.g., a nonintrusive instrumental loop in a multimedia lesson on lightning formation) and environmental sounds (e.g., the crackling sound of lightning in a multimedia message on lightning formation). According to the information delivery view, the addition of these sounds should not hurt learning because the same information is being presented as with the original multimedia message. According to the constructivist view, the sounds must be processed within the auditory/verbal channel, which is limited in capacity. By paying attention to the sounds, the learner may fail to process important verbal information in the narration, such as descriptions of the steps in lightning formation. Students will be less likely to engage in knowledge construction because some key verbal material has been lost. In a set of two studies, students who learned from a multimedia presentation containing irrelevant background music and sounds performed more poorly on transfer tests than did students who received the same presentation without background music and sounds. This *coherence effect* is consistent with the constructivist view and inconsistent with the information delivery view.

Modality Effect in Multimedia Learning

Another modification of the multimedia presentation consisting of simultaneous animation and narration is to change the narration to on-screen text. According to the information delivery view, there are two deliveries of information for animation and narration and there are two deliveries of information for animation and on-screen text, so both presentations should produce equivalent learning. According to the constructivist view, the animation and on-screen text must both be processed initially in the visual/pictorial channel, resulting in an overload that hinders knowledge construction; in contrast, when words are presented as narration, they can be processed in the auditory/verbal channel, freeing the visual/pictorial channel to process only the animation. In a series of four studies, students performed better on transfer tests from animation and narration than from animation and on-screen text. Again the results, which can be called a *modality effect*, support the constructivist view and are inconsistent with the information delivery view.

Redundancy Effect in Multimedia Learning

Finally, what would happen if students received a multimedia message consisting of animation, narration, and on-screen text rather than just animation and narration. According to the information delivery view, three delivery routes are better than two, so presenting animation, narration, and on-screen text should result in the most learning. In contrast, the constructivist view holds that the on-screen text will compete for processing capacity with the animation in the visual/pictorial channel, and thus reduce the chances for knowledge construction. In two studies, adding on-screen text to a narrated animation resulted in poorer transfer performance. This *redundancy effect* is consistent with the constructivist view and inconsistent with the information delivery view.

In each of these four examples, people's conception of how students learn influences how they would design a multimedia instructional message. Importantly, the constructivist conception of learning suggested design principles that were more likely to promote student understanding than was the information delivery conception. This research provides an example of how a conception of how students learn can be used to guide instructional design with educational technology.

CONCLUSIONS

In summary, advances in understanding the nature of human learning provide important implications for the role of educational technology. Constructivist learning is viewed as a process of knowledge construction in which learners seek to make sense out of presented material. Armed with a research-based theory of how students learn, educators are better able to make judgments about appropriate use of technology in education. In particular, constructivist conceptions of learning encourage the use of instructional methods that promote the sense-making process in learners and assessment methods that tap learner understanding. Although constructivist views of learning have been proposed throughout the 20th century, within the last 20 years, there has been an explosion of productive research and theory concerning how students learn. These recent advances in understanding how students learn in academic content areas represents a return to the learner-centered theories of the past and provides exciting opportunities for improving education through technology in the future.

ACKNOWLEDGMENTS

This chapter is a revised and shortened version of a report that was produced under contract with the U.S. Army Research Institute, funded by Department of Defense Education Activity (DoDEA), as part of the Army Research Institute Consortium Research Fellows Program. The report was produced by the author in his capacity as a Senior Consortium Research Fellow. The views expressed are those of the author. Portions of this chapter are based on Mayer (1996a, 1998, 1999b, 1999c). I wish to thank Harold F. O'Neil, Jr. and Ray Perez for their helpful review of this chapter.

REFERENCES

Anderson, J. R. (1993). *Rules of the mind.* Hillsdale, NJ: Lawrence Erlbaum Associates.

Anderson, L. W., Krathwohl, D. R., Airasian, P. W., Cruikshank, K. A., Mayer, R. E., Pintrich, P. R., Raths, J., & Wittrock, M. C. (2001). *A taxonomy of learning for teaching: A revision of Bloom's taxonomy of educational objectives.* New York: Longman.

Anderson, L. W., & Sosniak, L. A. (1994). *Bloom's taxonomy: A forty-year retrospective. Ninety-third yearbook of the National Society for the Study of Education, Part II.* Chicago: National Society for the Study of Education.

Ausubel, D. P. (1968). *Educational psychology: A cognitive view.* New York: Holt, Rinehart & Winston.

Baddeley, A. (1986). *Working memory.* Oxford, England: Oxford University Press.

Berliner, D. C., & Calfee, R. C. (Eds.). (1996). *Handbook of educational psychology.* New York: Macmillan.

Bloom, B. S. (1994). Reflections on the development and use of the taxonomy. In L. W. Anderson & L. A. Sosniak (Eds.), *Bloom's taxonomy: A forty-year retrospective. Ninety-third yearbook of the National Society for the Study of Education, Part II* (pp. 1–8). Chicago: National Society for the Study of Education.

Bloom, B. S., Engelhart, M. D., Furst, E. J., Hill, W. H., & Krathwohl, D. R. (1956). *Taxonomy of educational objectives, The classification of educational goals: Handbook I. Cognitive domain.* New York: McKay.

Bransford, J. D., Brown, A. L., & Cocking, R. R. (Eds.). (1999). *How people learn.* Washington, DC: National Academy Press.

Bruer, J. T. (1993). *Schools for thought: A science of learning in the classroom.* Cambridge, MA: MIT Press.

Bruner, J. S., Goodnow, J. J., & Austin, G. A. (1956). *A study of thinking.* New York: Wiley.

Burton, J. K., Moore, D. M., & Magliaro, S. G. (1996). Behaviorism and instructional technology. In D. H. Jonassen (Ed.), *Handbook of research for educational communications and technology* (pp. 46–73). New York: Macmillan.

Cognition and Technology Group at Vanderbilt (1996). Looking at technology in context: A framework for understanding technology and education research. In D. C. Berliner & R. Calfee (Eds.), *Handbook of educational psychology* (pp. 807–840). New York: Macmillan.

Cole, M. (1996). *Cultural psychology: A once and future discipline.* Cambridge, MA: Harvard University Press.

Crowder, N. A. (1960). Automatic tutoring by intrinsic programming. In A. Lumsdaine & R. Glaser (Eds.), *Teaching machines and programmed learning* (pp. 286–298). Washington, DC: National Education Association.

Cuban, L. (1986). *Teachers and machines: The classroom use of technology since 1920.* New York: Teacher's College Press.

Dewey, J. (1902). *The child and the curriculum.* Chicago: University of Chicago Press.

Dewey, J. (1938). *Experience and education.* New York: Collier.

Dunbar, K. (1993). Concept discovery in a scientific domain. *Cognitive Science, 17,* 397–434.

English, L. D. (Ed.). (1997). *Mathematical reasoning: Analogies, metaphors, and images.* Hillsdale, NJ: Lawrence Erlbaum Associates.

Gentner, D., & Stevens, A. L. (Eds.). (1983). *Mental models.* Hillsdale, NJ: Lawrence Erlbaum Associates.

Gernsbacher, M. A. (1990). *Language comprehension as structure building.* Hillsdale, NJ: Lawrence Erlbaum Associates.

Gredler, M. E. (1996). Educational games and simulations: A technology in search of a research paradigm. In D. H. Jonassen (Ed.), *Handbook of research for educational communications and technology* (pp. 521–540). New York: Macmillan.

Halford, G. S. (1993). *Children's understanding: The development of mental models.* Hillsdale, NJ: Lawrence Erlbaum Associates.

Hambleton, R. K. (1996). Advances in assessment models, methods, and practices. In D. C. Berliner & R. C. Calfee (Eds.), *Handbook of educational psychology* (pp. 899–925). New York: Macmillan.

Holland, J. G. (1965). Research on programmed variables. In R. Glaser (Ed.), *Teaching machines and programmed learning* (pp. 66–117). Washington, DC: Association for Educational Technology Communications and Technology.

Hull, C. (1943). *Principles of behavior.* New York: Appleton-Century-Crofts.

Johnson-Laird, P. N. (1983). *Mental models.* Cambridge, MA: Harvard University Press.

Katona, G. (1940). *Organizing and memorizing: Studies in the psychology of learning and teaching.* New York: Hafner.

Kohler, W. (1925). *The mentality of apes.* New York: Liveright.

Kulik, J. (1994). Meta-analytic studies of findings on computer-based instruction. In E. L. Baker & H. F. O'Neil, Jr. (Eds.), *Technology assessment in education and training* (pp. 9–33). Hillsdale, NJ: Lawrence Erlbaum Associates.

Lachman, R., Lachman, J. L., & Butterfield, E. C. (1979). *Cognitive psychology and information processing.* Hillsdale, NJ: Lawrence Erlbaum Associates.

Lambert, N. M., & McCombs, B. L. (Eds.). (1998). *How students learn: Reforming schools through learner-centered education.* Washington, DC: American Psychological Association.

Landauer, T. (1995). *The trouble with computers.* Cambridge. MA: MIT Press.

Lave, J., & Wenger, E. (1991). *Situated learning: Legitimate peripheral participation.* Cambridge, England: Cambridge University Press.

Leary, D. E. (1990). Psyche's muse: The role of metaphor in the history of psychology. In D. E. Leary (Ed.), *Metaphors in the history of psychology* (pp. 1–78). New York: Cambridge University Press.

Lochhead, J., & Clement, J. (Eds.). (1979). *Cognitive process instruction: Research on teaching thinking skills.* Philadelphia: Franklin Institute Press.

Loman, N. L., & Mayer, R. E. (1983). Signaling techniques that increase the understandability of expository prose. *Journal of Educational Psychology, 75,* 402–412.

Marshall, H. H. (Ed.). (1996). Recent and emerging theoretical frameworks for research on classroom learning: Contributions and limitations. *Educational Psychologist, 31*(3 & 4), 147–240.

Mayer, R. E. (1983). Can you repeat that? Qualitative and quantitative effects of advance organizers on learning from science prose. *Journal of Educational Psychology, 75,* 40–49.

Mayer, R. E. (1987). *Educational psychology: A cognitive approach.* New York: Harper Collins.

Mayer, R. E. (1992a). Cognition and instruction: Their historic meeting within educational psychology. *Journal of Educational Psychology, 84,* 405–412.

Mayer, R. E. (1992b). *Thinking, problem solving, cognition.* New York: Freeman.

Mayer, R. E. (1995). The search for insight: Grappling with Gestalt psychology's unanswered questions. In R. J. Sternberg & J. E. Davidson (Eds.), *The nature of insight* (pp. 3–32). Cambridge, MA: MIT Press.

Mayer, R. E. (1996a). Learners as information processors: Legacies and limitations of educational psychology's second metaphor. *Educational Psychologist, 31,* 151–161.

Mayer, R. E. (1996b). Learning strategies for making sense out of expository text: The SOI model for guiding three cognitive processes in knowledge construction. *Educational Psychology Review, 8,* 357–371.

Mayer, R. E. (1998). Searching for the perfect ism: An unproductive activity for educational researchers. *Issues in Education, 3,* 225–233.

Mayer, R. E. (1999a). Designing instruction for constructivist learning. In C. M. Reigeluth (Ed.), *Instruction design theories and models* (Vol. 2, pp. 141–159). Hillsdale, NJ: Lawrence Erlbaum Associates.

Mayer, R. E. (1999b). Instructional technology. In F. Durso (Ed.), *Handbook of applied cognition* (pp. 551–569). Chichester, England: Wiley.

Mayer, R. E. (1999c). *The promise of educational psychology: Learning in the content areas.* Upper Saddle River, NJ: Prentice-Hall.

Mayer, R. E. (2001a). Changing conceptions of learning: A century of progress in the scientific study of education. In L. Corno (Ed.), *100th Yearbook of the National Society for the Study of Education* (pp. 34–75). Chicago: National Society for the Study of Education.

Mayer, R. E. (2001b). *Multimedia learning.* New York: Cambridge University Press.

Mayer, R. E. (in press). The enduring contributions of E. L. Thorndike to educational psychology. In B. J. Zimmerman & D. H. Schunk (Eds.), *Educational Psychology: A century of progress*. Washington: American Psychological Association.

Meyer, B. J. F., Brandt, D. H., & Bluth, G. J. (1980). Use of top-level structure in text: Key for reading comprehension of ninth-grade students. *Reading Research Quarterly, 16*, 72–103.

Moore, D. M., Burton, J. K., & Myers, R. J. (1996). Multiple channel communication: The theoretical and research foundations of multimedia. In D. H. Jonassen (Ed.), *Handbook of research for educational communications and technology* (pp. 46–73). New York: Macmillan.

Moreno, R., & Mayer, R. E. (1999). Multimedia-supported metaphors for meaning making in mathematics. *Cognition & Instruction, 17*, 215–248.

Neisser, U. (1966). *Cognitive psychology*. New York: Appleton-Century-Crofts.

Norman, D. A. (1993). *Things that make us smart*. Reading, MA: Addison-Wesley.

Paivio, A, (1986). *Mental representations: A dual-coding approach*. Oxford, England: Oxford University Press.

Phillips, D. C. (1998). How, why, what, when, and where: Perspectives on constructivism in psychology and education. *Issues in Education, 3*, 151–194.

Pressey, S. L. (1926). A simple apparatus which gives tests and scores—and teaches. *School and Society, 36*, 35–41.

Pressley, M., & Woloshyn, V. (1995). *Cognitive strategy instruction that really improves children's academic performance*. Cambridge, MA: Brookline Books.

Reigeluth, C. M. (Ed.). (1999). *Instructional-design theories and models: Vol. II. A new paradigm of instructional theory*. Hillsdale, NJ: Lawrence Erlbaum Associates.

Schacter, J., & Fagnano, C. (1999). Does computer technology improve student learning and achievement? How, when, and under what conditions? *Journal of Educational Computing Research, 20*, 329–343.

Singley, M. K., & Anderson, J. R. (1989). *The transfer of cognitive skill*. Cambridge, MA: Harvard University Press.

Skinner, B. F. (1938). *The behavior of organisms: An experimental analysis*. Englewood Cliffs, NJ: Prentice-Hall.

Skinner, B. F. (1968). *The technology of teaching*. Englewood Cliffs, NJ: Prentice-Hall.

Steffe, L. P., & Gale, J. (Ed.). (1995). *Constructivism in education*. Hillsdale, NJ: Lawrence Erlbaum Associates.

Sternberg, R. J. (1985). *Beyond IQ: A triarchic theory of human intelligence*. Cambridge, England: Cambridge University Press.

Thorndike, E. L. (1911). *Animal intelligence*. New York: Hafner.

Vora, P. R., & Helander, M. G. (1997). Hypertext and its implications for the internet. In M. G. Helander, T. K. Landauer, & P. V. Prabhu (Eds.), *Handbook of human-computer interaction* (pp. 877–914). Amsterdam: Elsevier.

Walster, D. (1996). Technologies for information access in library and information centers. In D. H. Jonassen (Ed.), *Handbook of research for educational communications and technology* (pp. 720–754). New York: Macmillan.

Weinstein, C. E., & Mayer, R. E. (1986). The teaching of learning strategies. In M. C. Wittrock (Ed.), *Handbook of research on teaching* (3rd ed., pp. 315–327). New York: Macmillan.

Wenglinsky, H. (1998). *Does it compute? The relationship between educational technology and student achievement in mathematics*. Princeton, NJ: Educational Testing Service.

Wertheimer, M. (1959). *Productive thinking*. New York: Harper & Row.

White, B. (1993). ThinkerTools: Causal models, conceptual change, and science education. *Cognition and Instruction, 10*, 1–100.

White, R., & Gunstone, R. (1992). *Probing understanding*. London: Falmer Press.

Wittrock, M. C. (1990). Generative processes in comprehension. *Educational Psychologist, 24*, 345–376.

Chapter 7

Learning and Technology:
A View From Cognitive Science

John T. Bruer
James S. McDonnell Foundation

Cognitive science is a mature science, now nearly five decades old. In considering what the future contributions of this science might be to theories of learning and to the design of instructional technology, briefly recall what cognitive science has already revealed about how people's minds work and how they learn. Any future contributions to education and instructional technology certainly will build on this 50-year history (Bruer, 1993; McGilly, 1994).[1]

The fundamental tenet of cognitive science is that humans actively process information. Then, nearly 50 years ago, the founders of this new discipline argued that to understand language, memory, and learning, it is necessary to develop psychological theories that go beyond observed behavior to include theoretical constructs and hypotheses that refer to covert mental processes. (For a concise history, see Gardner, 1987.) For example, Chomsky introduced the notion of *deep structures*, internal representations of language not always evident in speech behavior, as a theoretical construct to understand grammar. Miller argued that individuals overcome intrinsic limitations on working memory capacity by recoding knowledge into more complex mental symbol structures that he called *chunks*. Cognitive research on long-term memory developed an insight advanced earlier by Bartlett (1932). Bartlett's insight was the experiences that cohere with organized

---

[1]The references cited in this chapter are not exhaustive, but are intended to provide readers from outside the field with some pointers to literature useful in pursuing topics of interest.

memory traces of prior experience are easier to recall than experiences that fit poorly prior memory traces. Tulving (1983), for example, developed the encoding specificity principle. To remember a percept or experience, specific encoding operations are performed that determine how that percept is stored in long-term memory. Successful recall depends not only on the strength of the mental representation of that percept, but also on the relation or coherence between encoding and retrieval processes. The utility and efficacy of an encoding process depends on, and interacts with, the eventual retrieval conditions. The value of an encoding process, or a learning activity, then can be assessed only relative to what instructors want a student to do with the material they are expected to encode or learn.

Furthermore, if memory and learning are active processes, then students could be made aware of some of these processes. The ability to monitor and control one's own mental activity should thus also contribute to improved learning and understanding. In this way, cognitive science has also pointed to the importance of imparting not only content knowledge, but also metacognitive monitoring and self-awareness skills (Brown, Bransford, Ferrara, & Campione, 1983). Finally, Simon and Newell showed that human problem solving can be modeled computationally (Newell & Simon, 1972). Careful analysis of tasks, like solving number puzzles or playing chess, can be represented as rules in a computer program that, when given input from a problem environment, could produce, as output, a solution to the problem. If these computational programs model human cognition, then these models can be used to formulate and test hypotheses about the covert mental processes employed in complex problem solving.

In the subsequent decades, as cognitive research moved out of the laboratory and began to address complex problem-solving activity, as it occurs in instruction, training, and schooling, researchers have accumulated research-based insights that can guide teaching, learning, and the development of instructional technology. The assumptions and methods of cognitive science have been applied to learning in numerous subject domains— arithmetic, reading, computer programing, algebra, geometry, to name just a few. Some of these domains have detailed models of problem solving and learning. These models provide blueprints and framework for research-based curricula and intelligent tutoring systems (Reigeluth, 1999). Fifty years of research have shown that learning is an active, constructive process and that efficient instruction must be sensitive to students' prior knowledge, current learning conditions, and future application conditions.

How might cognitive science contribute to education and instructional design in the future? The consensus is that cognitive science will contribute by refining and extending on these core ideas. In a web-based discussion that I conducted as background for this chapter among cognitive scientists interested in education, four major themes emerged:

1. There is a need for continued cognitive analyses of problem solving and learning, where the analyses include both individual and group performance.
2. There is a need to exploit more efficiently what is known about memory and learning in instructional contexts.
3. There is a need to recognize that technology itself is generating new problem-solving and representational tools that require careful cognitive study, if these new tools are to be used efficiently.
4. Cognitive research should address and attempt to understand complex, real-world problem solving.[2]

COGNITIVE ANALYSES OF PROBLEM SOLVING AND LEARNING

Although cognitive science was committed to formulating theories that went beyond, or beneath, observed behavior, as a science, cognitive research relied on exacting analyses of observed behavior to construct and test hypotheses about the covert workings of the human mind. To do this, cognitive scientists engage in careful analyses of tasks, problem-solving performances, and behavior. Cognitive scientists, within this research tradition, attempt to analyze logically a problem-solving task to frame initial hypotheses about the knowledge and skills the task requires and about how the knowledge and skills might best be organized to solve the problem. Initially, the problems were simple, puzzlelike problems, but as research advanced, the problem-solving cognitive scientists studied became more complex. For example, cognitive scientists studied how children solved Piagetian developmental tasks. In this way, they began to study how problem solving changed over time as children both matured and learned. Studying how problem solving changed over time, as problem-solvers acquired new knowledge, resulted in the ability to understand learning trajectories within subject domains (how knowledge and skills were acquired and organized) as students gradually made the transition from novice to expert in the domains. One educationally significant application of the understanding learning trajectories was the development of intelligent tutoring systems for disciplines like geometry, algebra, and computer programing. These tutoring systems facilitate student learning by providing appropriate problems and learning activities that help students construct more appro-

---

[2]Ideas in this chapter are derived from a web-based discussion involving cognitive scientists interested in instructional technology. The following individuals participated in the discussion: Melinda Bier, Gerhard Fischer, Jon Frederiksen, Robert Glaser, Earl Hunt, David Klahr, Danielle McNamara, Anthony Petrosino, Joseph Polman, Leona Schauble, and Amy Shapiro.

priate knowledge structures based on their preexisting, often partial, understanding (see Larkin & Chabay, 1992).

A simple, but elegant, example of how cognitive analyses of a subject domain can guide the design of instructional technology is DIAGNOSER, a computer-based assessment and instructional tool developed by Earl Hunt, Jim Minstrell, and their colleagues at the University of Washington (Hunt & Minstrell, 1994). Minstrell, a high school physics teacher, observed that his students had preexisting misconceptions, or understandings—often of how the physical world worked—that affected not only how they solved physics problems, but also how they responded to instruction. Minstrell set out to catalog his students' preexisting conceptions and misconceptions about the physical world. He called these pieces of prior knowledge "facets." On Minstrell's view, effective instruction must build on students' correct facets, to help them correct or eliminate their incorrect facets.

DIAGNOSER is a computerized program that, through a series of multiple choice questions, elicits students' facets as they attempt to answer and reason about physics problems. After completing a DIAGNOSER session, the program gives the student advice and instruction that is tailored to the student's facets as elicited in the session. Thus, the program combines assessment with instruction and tailors subsequent instruction to build on students' current understanding. All the responses a student makes during a DIAGNOSER session are recorded. A set of teacher's utilities allows the instructor to analyze these responses and to assess an individual student's, or an entire class' understanding as a guide for the design of future lessons. Interested readers can experiment with a web-based version of DIAGNOSER (www.depts.washington.edu/huntlab/diagnoser/web/index.html).

Cognitive scientists agree that there is need for continued, careful analyses of problem solving and learning in other subject domains. Most importantly, they see a need to conduct cognitive analyses of student learning and performance that move beyond single subject matter domains, that extend over longer developmental time periods, and include group or social factors that might contribute to successful classroom learning.

For example, there has been considerable cognitive analysis of problem solving in both arithmetic and algebra. But, only recently have cognitive scientists begun to look carefully at how students make the transition from arithmetic to algebra. How do students use their prior understanding of arithmetic to learn algebra?

Koedinger, Nathan, studied this question with some interesting initial results (Nathan & Koedinger, 2000a, b). There is a conventional view among middle-school mathematics teachers that algebra is more difficult for students than arithmetic and solving word problems is more difficult for students than solving symbolic equations. Based on this view, mathematics

texts, curricula, and lesson plans move from teaching symbolic arithmetic
(4 + 2 = ?), to teaching arithmetic word problems (If you have 4 golf balls
and I give you 2 more, how many do you have?), to teaching symbolic algebra (4 + x = 6), to teaching verbal algebra (You have four golf balls. After
digging to the bottom of your golf bag you ended up with 6 balls. How
many balls did you find in your bag?).

After analyzing student problem-solving performance, Koedinger, Nathan, and Tabachneck found a different pattern of difficulty. Students do
find algebra problems more difficult than arithmetic problems, as would be
expected and as the normative view maintained. However, contrary to the
normative view, students find symbolic problems significantly more difficult than verbally presented, or word, problems. As a result, students find
symbolic arithmetic problems as difficult as algebra word problems and
symbolic algebra problems the most difficult of all. If so, curricula based on
the normative view do not effectively build on students' prior knowledge
and preexisting expertise. Also, contrary to conventional math teaching
wisdom, verbal presentation of problems facilitates rather than impedes
problem solving. Thus, a cognitive understanding of the transition from
the domain of arithmetic to that of algebra reveals pedagogical misconceptions about what is difficult for students and about how instruction might
best be sequenced to facilitate learning. Teaching and learning could well
benefit from similar analysis across other school subject domains. This research would also, of course, contribute to the design of effective instructional technology.

Another important future dimension for cognitive analysis in education
is to move beyond the study of individual learners to study social factors
that can influence learning. How does learning occur within communities
of learners and how can people build effective learning communities
(Brown & Campione, 1994)? Furthermore, computer and communication
technology itself creates the possibility of creating communities of learners
within classrooms, as well as the ability to study, guide, and facilitate learning within these communities.

An example that illustrates this new dimension for cognitive analysis and
research is Scardamalia and Bereiter's (1994) computer-supported intentional learning environment (CSILE). CSILE might best be described as an
information management system for classroom instruction. CSILE allows
students to pursue their learning by doing individual research, entering
their findings and questions in a communal database, and extending their
learning by engaging in discussions of material in the database with their
fellow students. The system encourages children to write, to think, and to
communicate about their learning, all of which can deepen students' understanding of the subject matter. Furthermore, utilities designed to analyze the communal databases and patterns of student dialogue provide

teachers and researchers with tools to trace learning, to redirect student discussions if they become bogged down or enmeshed in misconceptions, and more importantly to study and observe learning, problem solving, and student performance within the wider community context.

FEATURES OF MEMORY AND LEARNING

Basic cognitive research on memory has contributed to what Resnick and Klopfer (1989) called one of the organizing themes of cognitive instructional theory: "We learn most easily when we already know enough to have organizing schemas that we can use to interpret and elaborate upon new information" (p. 5). As cognitivists have long known given how human memory works, prior knowledge effects learning, as does how well the learning situation coheres with the situation in which students are expected to apply their learning. Another organizing theme in cognitive instructional theory is that effective learning requires metacognitive knowledge and skills, the ability to monitor and control mental processing (Brown et al., 1983). Effective learners are aware of their own learning strengths and weaknesses, are sensitive to what they know and what they do not know, and employ strategies to monitor and guide their own learning. Cognitive research has also shown that it is possible to teach metacognitive strategies and teaching such strategies can help weak learners become stronger learners. A good example is reciprocal teaching of reading comprehension in which weak readers are taught the metacognitive skills that expert readers commonly use, skills like summarizing while reading, predicting what might happen next in a story, taking time to clarify difficult points, and formulating questions to aid comprehension (Palincsar & Brown, 1984).

Future research should strive to better understand how encoding processes, retrieval, prior knowledge, and metacognition interact. Some research suggests that they interact in interesting and sometimes counterintuitive ways.

McNamara's (1998) research on how to improve students' comprehension of science texts provides one interesting example. Her studies revealed an interesting interaction between students' maturity, their prior knowledge, and their ability to benefit from using metacognitive reading comprehension strategies.

Research on text comprehension has shown that skilled readers are more active processors of information than are nonskilled readers. Skilled readers employ metacognitive strategies while they read, as shown, for example, in the successful use of reciprocal teaching. One such metacognitive strategy is self-explanation. Readers who attempt to formulate an explanation of material as they read tend to have better text comprehension. However, self-explanation strategies (i.e., trying to explain the meaning of the text to yourself as you read) requires some amount of background or prior knowledge about the text's topic.

McNamara wondered if she could improve students active processing of science texts, and hence their comprehension, by teaching them to use self-explanation skills. She found that self-explanation, when compared to merely reading the text aloud, did not increase middle school students' comprehension of science texts. Furthermore, even after giving students explicit training in self-explanation strategies, she found no reliable differences in science text comprehension when she compared students who used these newly learned skills with students who merely read the texts aloud. In her studies, the best predictor of reading comprehension for science texts among middle school students was students' prior knowledge of the subject area.

However, she did find that teaching adult readers metacognitive self-explanation strategies did increase their comprehension of science texts. Among adults, even low background knowledge readers improved their comprehension when they were taught and used these metacognitive strategies. Low background knowledge adult readers, who used self-explanation, comprehended science texts as well as the high background knowledge readers. It would seem then that background knowledge and metacognitive strategies that depend on background knowledge interact in very different ways for middle school students and adults.

UNDERSTANDING AND USING NEW REPRESENTATIONAL TOOLS

One very important trend to keep in mind when thinking about cognition and instructional technology is that technology itself is creating new representational tools to support thinking and problem solving. Something as simple as spreadsheet software allows for modeling of data, test assumptions, and running of "what-if scenarios" that would have been difficult if not impossible 25 years ago. More recently, technology has also provided additional representational tools such as data mining, visual presentation of complex data sets, and, more commonly, hypertext. These computational and technological tools can expand and strengthen human cognitive capacities.

Currently, these tools—hypertext, for example—are widely available in schools and in the marketplace. Yet, relatively little is known about the cognitive demands or payoffs of this technology. In order to benefit from new technology-driven representational tools, it will be necessary to gain understanding of how the tools interact with, and extend, cognitive capabilities.

Before looking at hypertext more closely, it is instructive to look briefly at how cognitive science has helped in an understanding, comparatively recently, of how to teach a technology that is now nearly 17 centuries old. Hindu-Arabic numerals were a technological invention of 3rd century A.D. India. This technology reached Western Europe via Moorish Spain in the 14th century. Hindu-Arabic numerals provide written, symbolic representations for numbers that allow the use of standard, simple algorithms to carry out complex calculations. Historically, the written representations of number problems replaced physical representations of such problems, as used on abacuses and counting boards, for doing calculations. The new calculating technology spread throughout the world because it provides a representational tool that enhances cognitive skills. It now allows almost everyone, including schoolchildren, to solve computational problems that only masters of the counting board could solve prior to the 14th century.

Despite its power and appeal, teaching this technology has always presented problems. In 14th-century Europe, teachers noticed that students who had previous experience with counting boards often learned the new written algorithms more quickly. In the last few years, cognitive research on this technology has found that there are cognitive difficulties and hurdles that modern-day schoolchildren must overcome to master this technology. There is a set of typical mistakes or misunderstandings—often involving counting, carrying, and using the symbol 0—that children make (Brown & Burton, 1978; Von Lehn, 1983). Furthermore, cognitive research on teaching this technology has found that students learn more readily if they are taught the written algorithms using physical representations (i.e., blocks, sticks) of the problems (Resnick, 1982). Contemporary cognitive research allows for an understanding of the 14th-century teacher's insight about how familiarity with physical representations of quantity can facilitate learning of the written representations and algorithms. Research has created pedagogical methods with which to better teach this ancient technology to some children, who have difficulty learning it.

Hypertext is a new representational tool that is widely available in the modern world. People use it every time they search the Web, going from link to link between pages or documents. It appears to give some advantages in navigating texts or processing information, but everyone has at one time or another lost their way in hyperspace (How far back was that page on single malt scotch? How did I get there?). However, like those 14th-century masters of written calculation, relatively little is known about hyperliteracy, how to teach it, and even how best to use it. As Rich Lehrer and Leona Schaubel noted in our Internet discussion, "We are still largely ignorant of how to best exploit hypermedia, but this is not surprising in light of the centuries of rhetorical development that preceded modern text." The present

understanding of hyperliteracy does not begin to approach the understanding of traditional literacy. The centuries of rhetorical development
that accompanied the uses of written text are lacking, a development that
defines ideas of literacy, as well as ideas of what effective written communication requires. Cognitive research on this technology-based representational tool can facilitate the development of "hyper-rhetoric."

Shapiro's (1998) current research on hypertext provides an example of
the kinds of questions that must be asked and answered to develop a theory
of hypertext literacy. The departure point for Shapiro's research, as might
be expected, is previous cognitive research on text processing. She began
by applying cognitive theories of text processing to hypertext processing
and then looked for similarities and dissimilarities between how people
learn from text and how they learn from hypertext. Research on text processing has shown that texts that are less coherent and less structured—
maybe less well written, more telegraphic, or that require the reader to
make more inferences—promote more active cognitive information processing in the reader than do coherent, well-structured texts. Less structured
texts require the reader to work harder.

Consistent with what is already known about memory, increased active
cognitive processing of a text results in acquiring a deeper level of understanding of the text and better retention of the material. Of course, this assumes that the reader has the requisite prior knowledge to fill the gaps and
make the necessary inferences required by a less coherent text. Shapiro
found the same to be true for hypertext learning systems. Systems that are
less structured promote more active processing and deeper learning. However, also like text, she found that less structured hypertext systems require
that the students have a deeper, prior understanding of subject domain for
learning to occur. It is exactly this deep, prior understanding that weaker
students lack. Weaker students, deficient in background knowledge, learn
better from more highly structured hypertext systems.

If the intent is to use hypertext in instructional tools, be aware that these
tools should ideally be designed to incorporate different degrees of hypertext coherence (be sensitive to students' background knowledge prior to
instruction). Shapiro also found that the hypertext links used in a system—
its linking structure—do affect students' internal mental representations of
the subject matter and the concept maps that students form of the subject
domain. So far, however, Shapiro's studies, which have been limited primarily to the use of hypertext systems to teach social studies, showed that
these systems have only limited educational benefits over traditional texts.
Hypertext is an appealing technology and it may be a powerful one, on the
order of Hindu-Arabic numerals, but to exploit its potential as a learning
tool, and to discover how to communicate with it most effectively, will require considerably more cognitive research.

THE IMPORTANCE OF REAL-WORLD PROBLEMS

Cognitive scientists have advanced from working on simple puzzle problems in the laboratory (e.g., Tower of Hanoi) to working on learning and problem solving in complex domains (e.g., medical decision making, electronic troubleshooting, and physics problem solving) as these activities occur in clinics, repair shops, and classrooms.

This maturation has resulted in the beginnings of an applied science of learning. Cognitive scientists agree that they should continue and extend work on complex, real-world problems, recognized that such work will not only advance applied pedagogical science, but will also provide an opportunity to test cognitive theories and hypotheses.

Current research by Tom Carr, a cognitive psychologist, and Jacqueline Hinckley, a rehabilitation scientist, at Michigan State University is an illustrative example in the area of aphasia (Carr and Hinckley, personal communication). Aphasia (loss or partial loss of speech production or comprehension skills following stroke or traumatic brain injury) affects one million people in United States. Each year, in the United States alone, there are 85,000 new cases. Aphasia is much more prevalent than Parkinson's disease and results in considerable personal pain and financial cost. Aphasia is a substantial real-world problem. It presents an authentic learning problem in that the goal of aphasia rehabilitation is to restore the patient's ability to function in the complex world of daily life.

Carr and Hinckley observed that there are two general approaches to aphasia therapy. The first they call the *part-task*, or the *neuropsychological*, approach. In this approach, therapy consists of analyzing tasks that the patient should master into subcomponents and then helping the patient practice and master these subcomponents separately. It is a "divide and conquer" approach. This rehabilitation strategy assumes that the task subcomponents are easier to learn in isolation and subcomponents so learned can be recombined to solve other different tasks. It assumes that practicing subcomponents reduces cognitive load, this is best way to automatize the subcomponents, and part-task learning will facilitate transfer to related tasks in other contexts.

Carr and Hinckley called the second approach to aphasia therapy the *whole-task*, or the *contextual* approach. This therapeutic strategy uses authentic real-world tasks in patient therapy and teaches those tasks in the real-world contexts in which patients will eventually have to function on their own. This approach assumes that it is preferable to provide the patient with real-world skills in real-world contexts. Making the therapy as much as possible like everyday situations will assure that the learning transfers from the therapeutic context to the real-world of the patient's daily life.

Both approaches to aphasia rehabilitation have some commonsense appeal and are pursued religiously, but largely atheoretically, within different segments of the rehabilitation community. However, it is interesting to note that these two therapeutic approaches have at least family resemblances to two contrasting theoretical perspectives within educational psychology, the cognitive and the situated perspective.

The *cognitive perspective*, like the part-task rehabilitation strategy, assumes that tasks or problems can be legitimately factored or decomposed into subtasks or subproblems, students can learn these tasks in relative isolation, and once such subtasks are overlearned and become automatized, they are available as units that can be recombined to solve difference problems in different contexts. In this way, knowledge acquired in one situation can be transferred to new learning and problem-solving situations.

Within the situated perspective, like the whole-task or functional approach to rehabilitation, learning occurs in contexts or situations and these learning tasks or situations cannot be legitimately analyzed or decomposed. On the situated view, one learns within specific contexts and transfer occurs—if it can be said to occur at all—by successfully solving authentic, whole, real-world problems in a variety of different contexts or situations. On the situated view, learning is highly context specific.

One future challenge for cognitive science will be to consider how, or whether, these different theoretical perspectives can be integrated or to specify how each perspective might best be suited to answer different, but complementary, questions about cognition and learning. Within the cognition and education literature, there is active discussion and constructive debate concerning these and related issues (Anderson, Reder, & Simon, 1996, 1997; Greeno, 1997; see also Mayer, chap. 6 in this vol.).

Carr and Hinckley see research on aphasia rehabilitation as providing an experimental context within which they might be able to test claims and theories emanating from these contrasting theoretical perspectives. They are developing and assessing two aphasia rehabilitation protocols, one grounded in the part-task perspective and the other in the whole-task perspective. They will develop two training regimens for a variety of tasks, such as ordering items from a mail order catalog, that might be used in rehabilitation and assess patient outcomes under the different regimens. They will also assess their patient-subjects on severity of injury, age at injury, premorbid cognitive function, and the stage of recovery at which therapy begins. They may find that the part-task or whole-task approach is superior for all patients or they may find that certain patient subgroups fare better under one of the therapeutic approaches than they do under the other. Either result will provide important insights into how to improve aphasia rehabilitation programs. Either result will also provide interesting evidence from a clinical, real-world context with which to assess theoretical claims and with which to revise and refine cognitive theory. Other real-world settings and authentic problems will no doubt also prove opportunities to advance both basic cognitive science and an applied science of learning.

CONCLUSIONS

Although cognitive research can contribute to more refined theories of learning and more effective instructional technology, several practical problems should not be ignored.

First, there is a widespread, at least implicit, assumption afoot that technology will make education more efficient, where "efficient" means "less expensive." This may not be the case. Rather than looking to save dollars and/or person-hours, it might be better to look at instructional technology as a means whereby more students can be helped to reach higher and more broadly distributed levels of expertise. This is a worthwhile goal, but achieving it, even with the help of technology, may well increase educational costs.

Second, developing instructional technology is expensive. Developers of technology, like publishers of textbooks, are often more interested in a return on their investment than in educational effectiveness. Thus, it is essential to confront the problem that commercial applications of technology may not always reflect the best theories of teaching and learning. If textbooks can serve as a guide, then theories will be sacrificed to the usability and marketability of products.

Third, adopting technology in schools is most often based on popular perceptions, not on research, or on the demonstrated value of the technology. One reason is the scarcity of sound evaluation data. Although some school systems may have substantial discretionary budgets for technology, and research agencies may have substantial budgets to support development of technology, there is little willingness to invest in evaluating the educational effectiveness of technology.

Finally, researchers, educators, and the public must avoid what Fischer called the "gift wrapping problem." Fisher meant taking one's favorite, and often traditional, view of schooling or learning and gift wrapping it in technology. For example, drill-and-practice software is gift-wrapped behaviorist learning theory. The challenge is to move beyond gift wrapping to see how the best understanding of teaching and learning can be combined with the potential of technology in ways that do justice to both theory and technology. How might technology change or enhance the theory? How might the theory shape and inform technology?

Klahr posed this challenge via a thought experiment. He wrote: "Imagine such new technology as was available hundred fifty years ago, before we constructed the school systems we have today. What would we design and how would it differ from what we have now? How much of what we currently have in our schools is only an unintended side effect of the lack of any technology beyond blackboard and printing press when the system was created?" Teasing out the consequences of Klahr's thought experiment can help to think creatively about how to combine cognitive science, educational engineering, and instructional technology to design new, improved learning environments. By thinking and doing so, researchers have an opportunity to make education demonstrably better, not just superficially different.

REFERENCES

Anderson, J. R., Reder, L. M., & Simon, H. A. (1996). Situated learning and education. *Educational Researcher, 25*(4), 5–11.

Anderson, J. R., Reder, L. M., & Simon, H. A. (1997). Rejoinder: Situative versus cognitive perspectives: Form versus substance. *Educational Researcher, 26*(1), 18–21.

Bartlett, F. C. (1932). *Remembering: A study in experimental and social psychology.* New York: Macmillan.

Brown, A. L., Bransford, J. D., Ferrara, R. A., & Campione, J. C. (1983). Learning, remembering and understanding. In P. H. Mussen (Ed.), *Handbook of child psychology: Vol. 3. Child development* (pp. 77–166). New York: Wiley.

Brown, A. L., & Campione, J. C. (1994). Guided discovery in a community of learners. In K. McGilly (Ed.), *Classroom lessons: Integrating cognitive theory and classroom instruction* (pp. 229–272). Cambridge, MA: MIT Press.

Brown, J. S., & Burton, R. R. (1978). Diagnostic models for procedural bugs in basic mathematical skills. *Cognitive Science, 2,* 155–192.

Bruer, J. T. (1993). *Schools for thought: A science of learning in the classroom.* Cambridge, MA: MIT Press.

Gardner, H. (1987). *The mind's new science: A history of the cognitive revolution.* New York: Basic Books.

Greeno, J. (1997). Response: On claims that answer the wrong questions. *Educational Researcher, 26*(1), 5–17.

Hunt, E., & Minstrell, J. (1994). A cognitive approach to the teaching of physics. In K. McGilly (Ed.), *Classroom lessons: Integrating cognitive theory and classroom instruction* (pp. 51–74). Cambridge, MA: MIT Press.

Larkin, J. H., & Chabay, R. W. (Eds.). (1992). *Computer-assisted instruction and intelligent tutoring systems.* Hillsdale, NJ: Lawrence Erlbaum Associates.

McGilly, K. (Ed.). (1994). *Classroom lessons: Integrating cognitive theory and classroom instruction.* Cambridge, MA: MIT Press.

McNamara, D. S. (1998, August). *Training self-explanation strategies: Effects of prior domain knowledge and reading skill.* Paper presented at the 20th annual meeting of the Cognitive Science Society, Madison, WI.

Nathan, M. J., & Koedinger, K. R. (2000a). Teachers' and researchers' beliefs about the development of algebraic reasoning. *Journal for Research in Mathematics Education, 31*(2), 168–190.

Nathan, M. J., & Koedinger, K. R. (2000b). An investigation of teachers' beliefs of students' algebra development. *Cognition and Instruction, 18*(2), 209–237.

Newell, A., & Simon, H. A. (1972). *Human problem solving.* Englewood Cliffs, NJ: Prentice-Hall.

Palincsar, A. S., & Brown, A. L. (1984). Reciprocal teaching of comprehension-fostering and comprehension-monitoring activities. *Cognition and Instruction, 1,* 117–175.

Reigeluth, C. M. (Ed.). (1999). *Instructional-design theories and models: Vol. II. A new paradigm of instructional theory.* Hillsdale, NJ: Lawrence Erlbaum Associates.

Resnick, L. B. (1982). Syntax and semantics in learning to subtract. In T. P. Carpenter, J. M. Moser, & T. A. Romberg (Eds.), *Addition and subtraction: A cognitive perspective* (pp. 136–155). Hillsdale, NJ: Lawrence Erlbaum Associates.

Resnick, L. B., & Klopfer, L. E. (1989). Toward the thinking curriculum: An overview. In L. B. Resnick & L. E. Klopfer (Eds.), *Toward the thinking curriculum: Current cognitive research, 1989 ASCD Yearbook* (pp. 1–18). Association for Supervision and Curriculum Development, Arlington, VA.

Scardamalia, M., Bereiter, C., & Lamon, M. (1994). The CSILE project: Trying to bring the classroom into world 3. In K. McGilly (Ed.), *Classroom lessons: Integrating cognitive theory and classroom instruction* (pp. 201–208). Cambridge, MA: MIT Press.

Shapiro, A. M. (1998). Promoting active learning: The role of system structure in learning from hypertext. *Human Computer Interaction, 13*(1), 1–35.

Tulving, E. (1983). *Elements of episodic memory.* New York: Oxford University Press.

Von Lehn, K. (1983). On the representation of procedures in repair theory. In H. P. Ginsburg (Ed.), *The development of mathematical thinking* (pp.). Academic Press.

Chapter 8

Connecting Learning Theory and Instructional Practice: Leveraging Some Powerful Affordances of Technology

Cognition and Technology Group at Vanderbilt

Many educators have argued that the kinds of learning required for the 21st century go well beyond those required for the last century. In particular, there is a need for all students, not just a select few, to develop their abilities to think, solve problems, and become independent learners (e.g., Bruer, 1993; CTGV, 1997; L. B. Resnick & D. P. Resnick, 1991). This is consistent with new standards for instruction recommended by groups such as the National Research Council (1996) and the National Council of Teachers of Mathematics (1989, 2000). These standards, based on social constructivist principles of learning, emphasize the importance of teaching in ways that promote deep understanding by students. Learning is no longer viewed solely as the accretion of new information (Bransford, Brown, & Cocking, 1999). Instead, it is viewed as a transformational process wherein conceptual representation and understanding slowly evolves. In this milieu, teachers are being asked to adopt a more "cognitive" stance to teaching, which includes being aware of the preconceptions that their students bring to new learning situations, teaching in ways that make students' thinking "visible" to other students, and helping students reflect on and reconcile their conceptions with those of others. Frequent opportunities for students to display their understanding are necessary if teachers are expected to adapt instruction to current levels of student understanding.

Teaching for understanding by all students demands different approaches to the design of curriculum, instruction, and assessment than those required by teaching for memorization (e.g., Bransford & Stein,

1993; CTGV, 1997, 2000; Resnick & Klopfer, 1989). Students need opportunities to explore topics in depth rather than simply skim the surface and memorize a set of facts about particular subject areas. Knowledge of what it means to teach for understanding is important but not sufficient for guiding learning. Teachers and students also need frequent opportunities for feedback on their own progress toward meeting these goals. Many classrooms that are changing their practices from memorizing textbooks to "doing projects" are not systematically evaluating what students learn as they pursue these projects. In many cases, what is learned is often disappointing (see Barron et al., 1998; CTGV, 2000; Vye et al., 1998). Learning, by students or teachers, occurs best when there are frequent opportunities to receive feedback, reflect on that feedback, and revise. Relatively small-scale pilot studies and "design experiments" consistent with these ideas, such as "Fostering a Community of Learners" (Brown & Campione, 1994) and "Schools for Thought" (e.g., CTGV, 2000; Lamon et al., 1996; Secules, Cottom, Bray, Miller, & the Cognition and Technology Group, 1997; Williams et al., 1998), have shown some of the exciting possibilities when new theories of learning are combined with information technology resources to restructure curriculum, instruction, and assessment.

It is not a coincidence that many different "actors" in the educational context have come to share common perspectives about the nature of learning and instruction and the design of effective learning environments. Much of the confluence of perspectives can be traced to the past three decades of research on cognition and instruction, which has produced an extraordinary outpouring of scientific work on the processes of thinking and learning and on the development of competence. Much of this work has also been shown to have important implications for the design of learning environments and for the nature of the instructional practices that maximize individual and group learning outcomes in such environments (see, e.g., Bransford, Brown, & Cocking, 1999; Donovan, Bransford, & Pellegrino, 1999). Simultaneously, information technologies have advanced rapidly and now render it possible to design much more complex, sophisticated, and potentially more powerful learning and instructional environments. Although much is now possible given theoretical, empirical, and technological advances, many questions remain regarding the principles that need to be considered in connecting together learning theory, instructional practice, and information technologies in powerful ways.

This chapter considers how contemporary learning theory can be connected to instructional practice to build better learning environments through capitalizing on some of the many affordances of information technologies. The current thinking about these matters results from over 10 years of work attempting to forge such a linkage. The discussion begins by examining some of the principal findings from research on learning that have clear implications for instructional practice. This discussion includes four important principles for the design of powerful learning and instructional environments that can be enabled and enhanced by various information technologies. The chapter then illustrates examples of the use of technology to support one or more of these critical components of effective learning environments by considering design examples from past work with K–12 populations. As this work evolved, it became increasingly clear that multiple, definable characteristics of powerful learning environments need simultaneous attention. If possible, they should be linked together for maximal benefit. A technology-based design for helping to realize such an integration, the STAR.Legacy software shell, is presented, and the principles are discussed underlying its design and operation for populations ranging from K–12 students through adult learners in university, business, and school settings. Finally, the utility of this technology-based approach to integrating learning and instruction relative to future technologies and educational goals is considered.

IMPORTANT PRINCIPLES ABOUT LEARNING AND TEACHING

Two National Academy of Sciences reports on "How People Learn" (Bransford, Brown, & Cocking, 1999; Donovan et al., 1999) provided a broad overview of research on learners and learning and on teachers and teaching. Although there are many important findings that bear on issues of learning and instruction, three of the findings described in those reports are highlighted here. Each has a solid research base to support it, has strong implications for how teachers teach, and helps in thinking about ways in which technology assists in the design and delivery of effective learning environments.

The first important principle about the way people learn is that students come to the classroom with preconceptions about how the world works, which include beliefs and prior knowledge acquired through various experiences. In many cases, the preconceptions include faulty mental models about concepts and phenomena. If their initial understanding is not engaged, then they may fail to grasp the new concepts and information that are taught, or they may learn them for purposes of a test but revert to their preconceptions outside the classroom. Research on early learning suggests that the process of making sense of the world begins at a very young age. Children begin in preschool years to develop sophisticated understandings (whether accurate or not) of the phenomena around them (Wellman, 1990). Those initial understandings can have a powerful effect on the integration of new concepts and information. Sometimes those understandings are accurate, providing a foundation for building new knowledge. But sometimes they are inaccurate (Carey & Gelman, 1991). In science, students often have misconceptions of physical properties that cannot be easily observed. In humanities, their preconceptions often include stereotypes or simplifications, as when history is understood as a struggle between good guys and bad guys (Gardner, 1991). A critical feature of effective teaching is that it elicits from students their preexisting understanding of the subject matter to be taught and provides opportunities to build on, or challenge, the initial understanding. Minstrell (1989), a high school physics teacher, described the process as follows

> Students' initial ideas about mechanics are like strands of yarn, some unconnected, some loosely interwoven. The act of instruction can be viewed as helping the students unravel individual strands of belief, label them, and then weave them into a fabric of more complete understanding. Rather than denying the relevancy of a belief, teachers might do better by helping students differentiate their present ideas from and integrate them into conceptual beliefs more like those of scientists. (pp. 130–131)

The understandings that children bring to the classroom already can be quite powerful in the early grades. For example, some children have been found to hold onto their preconception of a flat earth by imagining a round earth to be shaped like a pancake (Vosniadou & Brewer, 1989). This construction of a new understanding is guided by a model of the earth that helps the child explain how people can stand or walk on its surface. Many young children have trouble giving up the notion that one eighth is greater than one fourth, because 8 is more than 4 (Gelman & Gallistel, 1978). If children were blank slates, telling them that the earth is round or that one fourth is greater than one eighth would be adequate. But because they already have ideas about the earth and about numbers, those ideas must be directly addressed in order to transform or expand them.

Drawing out and working with existing understandings is important for learners of all ages. Numerous research experiments demonstrate the persistence of preexisting understandings even after a new model has been taught that contradicts the naïve understanding. Students at a variety of ages persist in their beliefs that seasons are caused by the earth's distance from the sun rather than by the tilt of the earth (Harvard-Smithsonian Center for Astrophysics, 1987), or that an object tossed in the air has both the force of gravity and the force of the hand that tossed it acting on it, despite training to the contrary (Clement, 1982). For the scientific understanding to replace the naïve understanding, students must reveal the latter and have the opportunity to see where it falls short.

The second important principle about how people learn is that to develop competence in an area of inquiry, students must have a deep foundation of factual knowledge, understand facts and ideas in the context of a conceptual framework, and organize knowledge in ways that facilitate retrieval and application. This principle emerges from research that compares the performance of experts and novices, and from research on learning and transfer. Experts, regardless of the field, always draw on a richly structured information base; they are not just "good thinkers" or "smart people." The ability to plan a task, to notice patterns, to generate reasonable arguments and explanations, and to draw analogies to other problems are all more closely intertwined with factual knowledge than was once believed.

But knowledge of a large set of disconnected facts is not sufficient. To develop competence in an area of inquiry, students must have opportunities to learn with understanding rather than memorizing factual content. Key to expertise is a deep understanding of subject matter that transforms factual information into "usable knowledge." A pronounced difference between experts and novices is that experts' command of concepts shapes their understanding of new information: It allows them to see patterns, relationships, or discrepancies that are not apparent to novices. They do not necessarily have better overall memories than other people. But, their conceptual understanding allows them to extract a level of meaning from information that is not apparent to novices, and this helps them select and remember relevant information. Experts are also able to fluently access relevant knowledge because their understanding of subject matter allows them to quickly identify what is relevant. Hence, their attention is not overtaxed by complex events.

Geography can be used to illustrate the manner in which expertise is organized around principles that support understanding. A student can learn to fill in a map by memorizing states, cities, countries, and so on, and can complete the task with a high level of accuracy. But if the boundaries are removed, then the problem becomes more difficult. There are no concepts supporting the student's information. An expert who understands that borders often developed because natural phenomena (like mountains or water bodies) separated people, and large cities often arose in locations that allowed for trade (along rivers, large lakes, and at coastal ports), will easily outperform the novice. The more developed the conceptual understanding of the needs of cities and the resource base that drew people to them, the more meaningful the map becomes. Students can become more expert if the geographical information they are taught is placed in the appropriate conceptual framework.

A key finding in the learning and transfer literature is that organizing information into a conceptual framework allows for greater "transfer"; that is, it allows the student to apply what was learned in new situations and to learn related information more quickly. The student who has learned geographical information for the Americas in a conceptual framework approaches the task of learning the geography of another part of the globe with questions, ideas, and expectations that help guide acquisition of the new information. Understanding the geographical importance of the Mississippi River sets the stage for the student's understanding of the geographical importance of the Nile. And as concepts are reinforced, the student will transfer learning beyond the classroom, observing and inquiring about the geographic features of a visited city that help explain its location and size (Holyoak, 1984; Novick & Holyoak, 1991).

A third critical idea about how people learn is that a metacognitive approach to instruction can help students learn to take control of their own learning by defining learning goals and monitoring their progress in achieving them. In research with experts who were asked to verbalize their thinking as they worked, it was revealed that they monitored their own understanding carefully, making note of when additional information was required for understanding, whether new information was consistent with what they already knew, and what analogies could be drawn that would advance their understanding. These metacognitive monitoring activities are an important component of what is called *adaptive expertise* (Hatano, 1990).

Because metacognition often takes the form of an internal conversation, it can easily be assumed that individuals will develop the internal dialogue on their own. Yet many of the strategies used for thinking reflect cultural norms and methods of inquiry (Brice-Heath, 1981, 1983; Hutchins, 1995; Suina & Smolkin, 1994). Research has demonstrated that children can be taught these strategies, including the ability to predict outcomes, to explain to themselves in order to improve understanding, as well as to note failures to comprehend, activate background knowledge, plan ahead, and apportion time and memory. Reciprocal teaching, for example, is a technique designed to improve students' reading comprehension by helping them explicate, elaborate, and monitor their understanding as they read (Palincsar & Brown, 1984). The model for using the metacognitive strategies is provided initially by the teacher, and students practice and discuss the strategies as they learn to use them. Ultimately, students are able to prompt themselves and monitor their own comprehension without teacher support.

The teaching of metacognitive activities must be incorporated into the subject matter that students are learning (White & Frederiksen, 1998). These strategies are not generic across subjects, and attempts to teach them as generic can lead to failure to transfer. Teaching metacognitive strategies in context has been shown to improve understanding in physics (White & Frederiksen, 1998), written composition (Scardamalia, Bereiter, & Steinbach, 1984), and heuristic methods for mathematical problem solving (Schoenfeld, 1983, 1984, 1991). And metacognitive practices have been shown to increase the degree to which students transfer to new settings and events (Palincsar & Brown, 1984; Scardamalia et al., 1984; Schoenfeld,

1983, 1984, 1991). Each of these techniques shares a strategy of teaching and modeling the process of generating alternative approaches (to developing an idea in writing or a strategy for problem solving in mathematics), evaluating their merits in helping attain a goal, and monitoring progress toward that goal.

The three core learning principles described earlier, although simple, have profound implications for the enterprise of teaching and the potential of technology to assist in that process. Teachers must draw out and work with the preexisting understandings that their students bring with them. This requires that the model of the child as an empty vessel to be filled with knowledge provided by the teacher must be replaced. Instead, the teacher must actively inquire into students' thinking, creating classroom tasks and conditions under which student thinking can be revealed. Students' initial conceptions then provide the foundation on which the more formal understanding of the subject matter is built. The roles for assessment must be expanded beyond the traditional concept of "testing." The use of frequent formative assessment helps make students' thinking visible to themselves, their peers, and their teacher. This provides feedback that can guide modification and refinement in thinking. Given goals of learning with understanding, assessments must tap understanding rather than the mere ability to repeat facts or perform isolated skills.

Teachers must teach some subject matter in depth, providing many examples in which the same concept is at work and providing a firm foundation of factual knowledge. This requires that superficial coverage of all topics in a subject area must be replaced with in-depth coverage of fewer topics that allows key concepts in that discipline to be understood. The goal of coverage need not be abandoned entirely, of course. But there must be a sufficient number of cases of in-depth study to allow students to grasp the defining concepts in specific domains within a discipline. Moreover, in-depth study in a domain often requires that ideas be carried beyond a single school year before students can make the transition from informal to formal ideas. This requires active coordination of the curriculum across school years, something that is typically done only at a very shallow and superficial level, which typically includes overlapping or repeated topic coverage without any serious attempt to build on the prior concepts and information.

Assessment for purposes of accountability (e.g., statewide assessments) must test deep understanding and not just surface knowledge. Deep understanding means evidence of an understanding of conceptual organization and conceptual relations as well as the ability to apply knowledge of a topic, whereas surface knowledge includes disconnected simple factual or procedural knowledge based primarily on topic memorization. Assessment tools are often the standard by which teachers are held accountable. Teachers are put in a bind if they are asked to teach for deep conceptual understanding, but in doing so produce students who perform more poorly on standardized tests. Unless new assessment tools are aligned with new approaches to teaching, the latter are unlikely to muster support among the schools and their constituent parents. This goal is as important as it is difficult to achieve. The format of standardized tests can encourage measurement of factual knowledge rather than conceptual understanding, but it also facilitates objective scoring. Measuring depth of understanding can pose challenges for objectivity. Much work needs to be done to minimize the trade-off between assessing depth and assessing objectively.

The teaching of metacognitive skills should be integrated into the curriculum in a variety of subject areas. Because metacognition often takes the form of an internal dialogue, many students may be unaware of its importance unless the processes are explicitly emphasized by teachers. An emphasis on metacognition needs to accompany instruction in each of the disciplines because the type of monitoring required will vary. In history, for example, students might be asking themselves, "who wrote this document, and how does that affect the interpretation of events," whereas in physics they might be monitoring their understanding of the underlying physical principle at work. Integration of metacognitive instruction with discipline-based learning can enhance student achievement and develop in students the ability to learn independently. It consciously should be incorporated into curricula across disciplines and age levels.

THE DESIGN OF LEARNING ENVIRONMENTS

Findings from contemporary research on cognitive and social issues in learning, such as those described in the preceding section and in the "How People Learn" reports, suggest that four important characteristics of powerful learning environments overlap with the following four major design principles for instruction that are critically important for achieving learning with understanding:

> *Effective learning environments are knowledge centered:* Attention is given to what is taught (central subject matter concepts), why it is taught (to support "learning with understanding" rather than merely remembering), and what competence or mastery looks like.
>
> *Effective learning environments are learner centered:* Educators must pay close attention to the knowledge, skills, and attitudes that learners bring into the classroom. This incorporates preconceptions regarding subject matter and it also includes a broader understanding of the learner. Teachers in learner-centered environments pay careful attention to what students

know as well as what they do not know, and they continually work to build on students' strengths.

Effective learning environments are assessment centered: Especially important are efforts to make students' thinking visible through the use of frequent formative assessment. This permits the teacher to grasp the students' preconceptions, understand where students are on the "developmental corridor" from informal to formal thinking, and design instruction accordingly. They help both teachers and students monitor progress.

Effective learning environments are community centered: This includes the development of norms for the classroom and school, as well as connections to the outside world, that support core learning values. Teachers must be enabled and encouraged to establish a community of learners among themselves. These communities can build a sense of comfort with questioning rather than knowing the answers and can develop a model of creating new ideas that builds on the contributions of individual members.

Consistent with the ideas about the multiple and interacting elements of a powerful learning environments are four principles for the design of instruction within such a contextual perspective:

1. To establish knowledge-centered elements of a learning environment, instruction is organized around meaningful problems with appropriate goals.
2. To support a learner-centered focus, instruction must provide scaffolds for solving meaningful problems and supporting learning with understanding.
3. To support assessment-centered activities, instruction provides opportunities for practice with feedback, revision, and reflection.
4. To create community in a learning environment, the social arrangements of instruction must promote collaboration and distributed expertise, as well as independent learning.

Each principle is considered in turn and is briefly described in terms of how technology can support its realization. A more complete discussion of these ideas and the variety of technology-based tools available to support these design principles can be found in Goldman et al. (1999). The focus is on specific technology tools and applications rather than technology in general or its general or specific effects on student learning outcomes. For those interested in learning outcomes, a variety of analyses have appeared in recent years of the impact of technology on instruction, including discussions and evidence of when technology applications appear to be most effective in producing student learning gains (see, e.g., CTGV, 1996; Kulik, 1994; Schacter & Fagnano, 1999; Wenglinsky, 1998).

Instruction Is Organized Around the Solution
of Meaningful Problems

When students acquire new information in the process of solving meaning-ful problems, they are more likely to see its potential usefulness than when they are asked to memorize isolated facts. Meaningful problems also help students overcome the "inert knowledge" problem, defined by Whitehead (1929) as knowledge previously learned but not remembered in situations where it would be potentially useful. Seeing the relevance of information to everyday problems helps students understand when and how the informa-tion may be useful.

When students see the usefulness of information, they are motivated to learn (McCombs, 1991, 1994). Research on the relation between interest and learning indicates that personal interest in a topic or domain positively impacts academic learning in that domain (Alexander, Kulikowich, & Jet-ton, 1994). New approaches to motivation emphasize motivational en-hancement through authentic tasks that students perceive as real work for real audiences. This emphasis contrasts with earlier emphases on elaborate extrinsic reinforcements for correct responding (see for discussion Collins, 1996).

Problem solving is at the core of inquiry- or project-based learning. Stu-dents will work on problems that are interesting and personally meaningful (Brown & Campione, 1994; CTGV, 1997; Hmelo & Williams, 1998; Resnick & Klopfer, 1989). Several contemporary educational reform efforts use di-lemmas, puzzles, and paradoxes to "hook," or stimulate, learners' interests in the topic of study (Brown & Campione, 1994, 1996; CTGV, 1997; Gold-man et al., 1996; Lamon et al., 1996; Scardamalia, Bereiter, & Lamon, 1994; Secules et al., 1997; Sherwood, Petrosino, Lin, Lamon, & the Cognition and Technology Group, 1995).

One major challenge for inquiry-based learning environments is devel-oping problems that are rich and complex enough to engage students in the kinds of sustained inquiry that will allow them to deeply understand im-portant new concepts. Bringing complex problems into the classroom is an important function of technology. Unlike problems that occur in the real world, problems that are created with graphics, video, and animation can be explored again and again. These multimedia formats capture children's interest and provide information in the form of sound and moving images that is not available in text-based problems and stories. Multimedia formats are more easily understood and allow the learner to concentrate on high level processes such as identifying problem-solving goals or making impor-tant inferences (Sharp et al., 1995).

Although technology-based problem environments come in many forms, an important characteristic is that they are under the learner's control: Stories on interactive videodisc, CD-ROM, or DVD can be reviewed many times and specific frames or pictures can be frozen and studied. Problems presented via the World Wide Web or in hypermedia allow students to search easily for the parts that interest them most. Exploratory environments called "microworlds," or simulations, allow students to carry out actions, immediately observe the results, and attempt to discover the rules that govern the system's behavior. No matter what form of technology is involved, the student is primarily responsible for deciding how to investigate the problem and the technology creates an environment in which flexible exploration is possible. A subsequent section elaborates on some specific examples of technology-based multimedia materials for bringing meaningful problems and learning resources into the classroom.

Instruction Provides Scaffolds for Achieving Meaningful Learning

The previous section briefly described the benefits of giving students the opportunity and responsibility of exploring complex problems on their own. This is clearly a way to support the implementation of knowledge-centered elements in a learning environment. The mere presence of these opportunities, however, does not lead to learning with understanding, nor will it enhance a learner-centered approach. Because of the complexity of the problems and the inexperience of the students, scaffolds must be provided to help students carry out the parts of the task they cannot yet manage on their own. Cognitive scaffolding assumes that individuals learn through interactions with more knowledgeable others, just as children learn through adult–child interactions (Bakhtin, 1981; Bruner, 1983; Vygotsky, 1962). Adults model good thinking, provide hints, and prompt children who cannot "get it" on their own. Children eventually adopt the patterns of thinking reflected by the adults (Brown, Bransford, Ferrara, & Campione, 1983; Wood, Bruner, & Ross, 1976). Cognitive scaffolding can be realized in a number of ways. Collins, Brown, and Newman (1989) suggested modeling and coaching by experts, and providing guides and reminders about the procedures and steps that are important for the task.

Technologies can also be used to scaffold the solution of complex problems and projects by providing resources such as visualization tools, reference materials, and hints. Multimedia databases on CD-ROM, videodisc, or on the World Wide Web provide important resources for students who are doing research. Technology-based reference materials provide several advantages over those in book format. Most importantly, they allow the presentation of information in audio or video format. In many cases, students can see an actual event and create their own analysis rather than reading someone else's description. Electronic references are easy to search and provide information quickly while students are in the midst of problem solving. For example, definitions of words and their pronunciations are readily available while a student is reading or writing a story. Hints and demonstrations can be effortlessly accessed when a student is stuck while setting up a math problem. The knowledge acquired in these "just in time" situations is highly valued and easily remembered, because learners understand why it is useful to them.

Technology can help learners visualize processes and relations that are normally invisible or difficult to understand. For example, students might use spreadsheets to create a graph demonstrating a trend or showing if one result is out of line with the rest. These graphs are useful in initial interpretations of numerical data and also valuable for reporting it to others. Graphs, maps, and other graphic representations can be created by students or automatically generated by simulation programs to depict the changes brought about by student actions.

Instruction Provides Opportunities for Practice
With Feedback, Revision, and Reflection

Feedback, revision, and reflection are aspects of metacognition that are critical to developing the ablity to regulate one's own learning. Many years ago, Dewey (1933) noted the importance of reflecting on one's ideas, weighing ideas against data and predictions against obtained outcomes. In the context of teaching, Schön (1983, 1988) emphasized the importance of reflection in creating new mental models. Content-area experts exhibit strong self-monitoring skills that enable them to regulate their learning goals and activities. Self-regulated learners take feedback from their performance and adjust their learning in response to it. Self-monitoring depends on deep understanding in the domain because it requires an awareness of one's own thinking, sufficient knowledge to evaluate that thinking and provide feedback to oneself, and knowledge of how to make necessary revisions. In other words, learners cannot effectively monitor what they know and make use of the feedback effectively (in revision) unless they have deep understanding in the domain. The idea that monitoring is highly knowledge dependent creates a catch-22 for novices. How can they regulate their own learning without the necessary knowledge to do so? Thus, the development of expertise requires scaffolds for monitoring and self-regulation skills so that deep understanding and reflective learning can develop hand in hand.

Analyses of expert performance indicate that the development of expertise takes lots of practice over a long period of time (e.g., Bereiter & Scardamalia, 1993; Glaser & Chi, 1988). Cycles of feedback, reflection, and opportunities for revision provide students with opportunities to practice using the skills and concepts they are trying to master. Cognitive theories of skill acquisition place importance on practice because it leads to fluency and a reduction in the amount of processing resources needed to execute the skill (e.g., Anderson, 1983; Schneider, Dumais, & Shiffrin, 1984; Schneider & Shiffrin, 1977). Practice with feedback produces better learning than practice alone. Thorndike provided a simple but elegant illustration of the importance for learning of practice with feedback. He spent hundreds of hours trying to draw a line that was exactly 4 inches long. He did not improve until he took off his blindfold. Only when he could see how close each attempt had come to the goal was Thorndike able to improve. Unless learners get feedback on their practice efforts, they will not know how to adjust their performance to improve.

An early and major use of technology was providing opportunities for extended practice of basic skills. It is important to distinguish between two stages to basic skill development, these are *acquisition* and *fluency*. Acquisition refers to the initial learning of a skill and fluency refers to being able to access this skill in a quick and effortless manner (e.g., math facts). If basic skills are not developed to a fluent level, then the learning process is incomplete and the student will not be able to function well in the real world.

Although there is no question that the nature of a drill-and-practice application makes it ideal for providing endless practice in almost any curricular area, when a student is in an acquisition phase of learning, the use of drill and practice is inappropriate. As the names implies, computer-based drill and practice is designed to reinforce previously learned information rather than to provide direct instruction on new skills. If technology is to be used during the acquisition phase of a new skill or concept, then the tutorial is more appropriate than drill and practice. A technology-based tutorial differs from a drill-and-practice application in that a tutorial attempts to play the role of a teacher and provide direct instruction on a new skill or concept. The tutorial presents the student with new or previously unlearned material in an individualized manner, providing frequent corrective feedback and reinforcement.

It is important to remember that tutorials and drill-and-practice software came into existence at a time when teacher-led lecture and recitation was widely accepted and these applications frequently mirror this instructional approach. For some, the mere mention of this type of software evokes a negative response; however, when students encounter difficulties in the process of solving meaningful problems, the opportunity for individualized instruction and practice can be very valuable. This is especially true when the curriculum provides students a chance to apply what they have learned by revising their solutions to the problem that caused them difficulty.

Fortunately, there are now multiple examples that support a wide range of formative assessment practices in the classroom. They include exciting new technology-based methods such as the "Diagnoser" software for physics and mathematics (Hunt & Minstrell, 1994), "Latent Semantic Analysis" for scoring essays (e.g., Landauer, Foltz, & Laham, 1998), the IMMEX system for providing feedback on problem solving (Hurst, Casillas, & Stevens, 1998), as well as the "Curriculum Based Measurement" system (L. S. Fuchs, D. Fuchs, Hamlett, & Stecker, 1991) and Knock Knock environments (CTGV, 1998) for feedback on literacy skills to young children. Such software can also be used to encourage the kind of self-assessment skills that are frequently seen in expert performance.

The Social Arrangements of Instruction Promote Collaboration and Distributed Expertise, as Well as Independent Learning

The view of cognition as socially shared rather than individually owned is an important shift in the orientation of cognitive theories of learning. It reflects the idea that thinking is a product of several heads in interaction with one another (Bereiter, 1990; Hutchins, 1991). In the theoretical context of cognition-as-socially-shared, researchers have proposed having learners work in small groups on complex problems as a way to deal with complexity. Working together facilitates problem solving and capitalizes on distributed expertise (Barron, 1991; Brown & Campione, 1994, 1996; CTGV, 1992a, 1992b, 1992c, 1993a, 1993b, 1994a; Pea, 1993; Salomon, 1993; Yackel, Cobb, & Wood, 1991). Collaborative environments also make excellent venues for making thinking visible, generating and receiving feedback, and revising (Barron et al., 1995; CTGV, 1994a; Hatano & Inagaki, 1991; Vye et al., 1997, 1998).

A number of technologies support collaboration by providing venues for discussion and communication among learners. Through the use of computer networks, many schools today are connecting their computers to other computers often thousands of miles away. By networking computers within a room, building, or larger geographic area, students can send and receive information from other teachers or students not in their physical location. By networking computers, teachers and students are freed from the constraints of location and time. For example, students can "log on" to a network at any time that is convenient to send or receive information from any location attached to their network. Also, given the heavy dependence on text in most networked systems, students have a reason to use text to read, write, and construct thoughts and ideas for others to read and respond to. In addition, a vast amount of information is available through the Internet.

A vast array of communications services are rapidly becoming available to schools. For example, two-way video and two-way audio systems are now being used to allow students and teachers at remote sites to see and hear each other. In this way, face-to-face interactions can take place over great distances in real time. Communal databases and discussion groups make thinking visible and provide students with opportunities to give and receive feedback, often with more reflection because the comments are written rather than spoken. Networked and web-based communications technologies such as e-mail, List Serves, and more sophisticated knowledge building software, such as Knowledge Forum (Scardamalia & Bereiter, 1994), can also help students form a community around important ideas. Such technology helps capture ideas that otherwise can be ephemeral and supports communication that is asynchronous as well as synchronous.

EXAMPLES OF TECHNOLOGY-BASED LEARNING ENVIRONMENTS

Current thinking regarding technology-supported learning environments derives from over 10 years of research with students and teachers on ways to motivate and assess exceptional learning (Barron et al., 1995; CTGV, 1994a, 1994b, 1997, 2000). The initial work focused on the problem of learning with understanding in middle school mathematics. The focus of efforts was on ways in which cognitive theory and research on problem solving might be connected with mathematics instruction. The result was development of an approach called "anchored instruction" within which teaching and learning are focused around the solution of complex problems or "anchors." The anchors are stories on videodisc (or CD-ROM) that each end with a challenge to solve. All of the data needed to solve the challenges are contained in the stories. The problems are complex and require extended effort to solve (at a minimum, in the range of 3–5 hours for most middle school students), are relatively ill-defined and require significant formulation prior to solving, and have multiple viable solutions. The anchors are designed to engage students in authentic problem-solving activities that highlight the relevance of mathematics or science to the world outside of the classroom. The design of anchored instruction problem-solving environments was a very explicit way to focus on using technology in instructional design to emphasize the knowledge-centered and learner-centered components of powerful learning environments. The next section briefly describes one such set of anchored instruction materials and the types of learning they afforded relative to the components of effective learning environments and principles of instruction discussed earlier.

The Jasper Adventures

The cumulative work on *The Adventures of Jasper Woodbury Problem Solving Series* (CTGV 1994a, 1997, 2000) is the single best example of our attempt to engage in the process of instructional design based on cognitive theory.

Through the process of implementing those designs in multiple classrooms, researchers came to understand the complexities of designing and managing powerful learning environments. For descriptions of this body of work and data, see CTGV (1992a, 1992b, 1992c, 1993a, 1993b, 1994a, 1997, 2000); Goldman, Zech, Biswas, Noser, and the Cognition and Technology Group (1997); Pellegrino et al. (1991); Vye et al. (1997, 1998); and Zech et al. (1994, 1998).

The Jasper series consists of 12 interactive video environments that invite students to solve authentic challenges, each of which requires them to understand and use important concepts in mathematics. For example, in the adventure known as *Rescue at Boone's Meadow* (RBM), which focuses on distance–rate–time relationships, Larry is teaching Emily to fly an ultralight airplane. During the lessons, he helps Emily learn about the basic principles of flight and the specific details of the ultralight she is flying, such as its speed, fuel consumption, fuel capacity, and how much weight it can carry. Not long after Emily's first solo flight, her friend Jasper goes fishing in a remote area called Boone's Meadow. Hearing a gunshot, he discovers a wounded bald eagle and radios Emily for help in getting the eagle to a veterinarian. Emily consults a map to determine the closest roads to Boone's Meadow, then calls Larry to find out about the weather and see if his ultralight is available. Students are challenged to use all the information in the video to determine the fastest way to rescue the eagle.

After viewing the video, students review the story and discuss the setting, characters, and any unfamiliar concepts and vocabulary introduced in the video. After they have a clear understanding of the problem situation, small groups of students work together to break the problem into subgoals, scan the video for information, and set up the calculations necessary to solve each part of the problem. Once they have a solution, they compare it with those that other groups generate and try to choose the optimum plan. Like most real-world problems, Jasper problems involve multiple correct solutions. Determining the optimum solution involves weighing factors such as safety and reliability, as well as making the necessary calculations.

The Jasper series focuses on providing opportunities for problem solving and problem finding. It is not intended to replace the entire mathematics curriculum. Frequently, while attempting to solve these complex problems, students discover that they do not have the necessary basic skills. Teachers use these occasions as opportunities to conduct benchmark lessons in which they review the necessary concepts and procedures. Solutions to RBM clearly require mathematical knowledge. For example, students have to solve distance–rate–time problems, such as how long it would take to fly from point A to point B given the cruising speed of the ultralight. But, there are big ideas about mathematics (e.g., concepts such as rate) that are not necessarily revealed by simply solving problems such as RBM.

Three strategies were devised to help students abstract important mathematical ideas from their experiences with Jasper adventures. The first was meant to encourage teachers to use two similar Jasper adventures rather than one, and to help students compare the similarities in solution strategies required to solve them. Gick and Holyoak's (1983) work on abstraction and transfer illustrates advantages of this approach. Often, however, teachers wanted to use dissimilar Jasper adventures (e.g., one involving distance–rate–time, one involving statistics); this reduced the chances of abstraction. Additional strategies were needed to help students conceptualize powerful mathematical ideas.

A second strategy for making the use of Jasper Adventures more knowledge centered while also scaffolding student learning was to develop analog and extension problems for each adventure that invited students to solve "what if" problems that changed parameters of the original problems. For example, given the RBM adventure already discussed: "What if the ultralight had travelled at a speed of 20 rather than 30 miles per hour? How would that affect the solution?" Or "What if Emily flew to Boone's Meadow with the help of a 10 mph tailwind and flew back with a 10 mph headwind? Would these two cancel each other out?" (The answer is "no" and it is instructive for students to explore the reason.)

Analog problems for *The Big Splash* (TBS), a Jasper statistics adventure, further illustrate the importance of promoting what-if thinking. When solving the adventure, students see a particular method used to obtain a random sample and extrapolate the findings to a larger population. Analog problems help students think about alternative randomization procedures that might have been used. Data indicate that the use of analog problems increases the flexibility of students' transfer. Students benefited greatly from opportunities to develop a more general understanding of sampling and statistical inferencing after solving TBS (Schwartz et al., 1998). Similarly, students who solved analog problems after solving RBM showed more flexibility in their thinking than students who solved RBM without analogs. For example, they were more likely to modify their original solution strategies when presented with transfer problems that could be solved more elegantly with a change in strategy (e.g., CTGV, 1997; Williams, 1994).

A third strategy for helping students understand big ideas in mathematics and scaffolding their learning takes the idea of analog and extension problems one step further. Instead of presenting students with environments that involve only "one shot" problem solving, they are helped to conceptualize environments where problems tend to reoccur and it becomes useful to invent ways to deal with these reoccurrences. Theorists, such as Lave (1988), Norman (1993), Pea (1993), Rogoff (1990), and others, argued that people become smart, in part, by learning to eliminate the need to laboriously compute the answer to important problems that tend to reoccur in their environments. One way to do this is through the invention of "smart" tools. Examples of smart tools that can eliminate cumbersome computations include charts, graphs, computer programs, and gadgets such as watches, speedometers, and proportion wheels. Researchers did not want to simply give students tools because these can often be applied without understanding, causing people to fail to adapt when situations change (e.g., see Resnick, 1987). They wanted to help students invent, test, and refine their own smart tools.

The development of smart tools has been pursued in the context of Jasper Adventures such as *Rescue at Boone's Meadow* (RBM). Instead of receiving a challenge where they are asked to solve a single problem (rescuing the eagle as quickly as possible), students are invited to imagine that Emily becomes an entrepreneur who sets up a pickup and delivery service for people who go camping in her area. She has several different planes to choose from depending on the needs (e.g., some can carry more payload, fly faster, etc.). When customers call to ask for assistance, Emily asks where they are (or where they want to go) and what they want to carry; she then needs to tell them the trip time and fuel costs as quickly as possible. Different requests involve problems that vary in terms of the location of the destination, windspeed conditions, payload limits that determine which plane must be used, costs due to fuel consumption, and so forth. To calculate the answer to each individual problem is cumbersome, and Emily needs to be as efficient as possible. The challenge for students in the classrooms is to invent smart tools that allow people to solve such problems with efficiency. A simple but elegant smart tool for determining travel time for one of Emily's planes (the one that cruises at a speed of 45 mph) is illustrated in Fig. 8.1.

In summary, the Jasper Adventures provide one example of using cognitive theory and technology to assist in the design of learning environments that demonstrate knowledge-centered and learner-centered features. In developing the problems and then designing instructional strategies and tools to support learning from these materials, steps were taken to adhere to the principles that instruction should be organized around the solution of meaningful problems and the environment should provide scaffolds for support of meaningful learning. Technology has been a significant component in attempts to achieve these objectives.

Beyond Jasper—SMART Environments

The development, implementation, and evaluation of Jasper materials was coincident with and impacted other related curricular design projects. For example, a second set of curriculum designs was constructed, designated by the title "Scientists in Action" (Goldman et al., 1996; Sherwood et al., 1995). In response to student, teacher, and researcher feedback, these curriculum

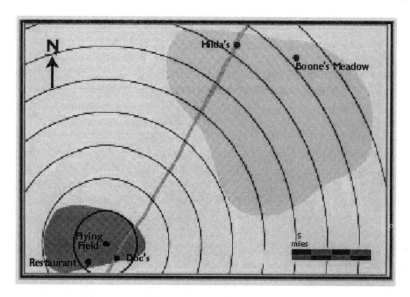

FIG. 8.1. An example of a SMART tool developed for assisting in problem-solving extensions for the Jasper Adventure "Rescue at Boone's Meadow."

materials have undergone development along distinct but somewhat parallel lines to those in the Jasper Adventure series. Once again, designs evolved to incorporate sophisticated forms of scaffolding to enhance effective student learning. But increasingly, the focus was on the two dimensions of an effective learning environment that many of the Jasper projects had not yet focused on deeply—formative assessment and community building.

Various methods have been explored in the context of working with both the Scientists in Action series and the Jasper Adventures to provide frequent and appropriate opportunities for formative assessment (Barron et al., 1995, 1998; CTGV, 1994a, 1997, 2000). These include assessment of student-generated products at various points along the way to problem solution, such as blueprints or business plans, and assessment facilitated by comparing intermediate solutions with those generated by others around the country who are working on similar problem-based and project-based curricula. In these examples, assessment is both teacher and student generated and it is followed by opportunities to revise the product that has been assessed. The revision process is quite important for students and seems to lead to changes in students' perspectives of the nature of adult work as well as conceptual growth.

Different ways of organizing classrooms can also have strong effects on the degree to which everyone participates, learns from one another, and makes progress in the cycles of work (e.g., Brown & Campione, 1996; Collins, Hawkins, & Carver, 1991). It is beneficial to have students work collaboratively in groups, but to also establish norms of individual accountability. One way to do this is to set up a requirement that each person in a group has to reach a threshold of achievement before moving on to collaborate on a more challenging project, for example, to be able to explain how pollution affects dissolved oxygen and hence life in the river; to create a blueprint that a builder could use to build some structure. Under these conditions, the group works together to help everyone succeed. The revision process is designed to ensure that all students ultimately attain a level of understanding and mastery that establishes a precondition for moving from the problem-based to project-based activity.

The larger model is known as SMART, which stands for Scientific and Mathematical Arenas for Refining Thinking. The SMART model incorporates a number of design features to support the four features of an effective learning environment mentioned earlier. For example, a variety of scaffolds and other technology-based learning tools were developed to deepen the possibilities for student learning:

1. *Smart Lab:* A virtual community for students in which they are exposed to contrasting solutions to problems in the context of being able to assess the adequacy of each.

2. *Toolbox:* Various visual representations that can be used as tools for problem solving.

3. *Kids-on-Line:* This features students making presentations. By using actors who make presentations based on real students' work, it was possible to seed the presentations with typical errors. This design feature allows students to engage in critical analysis of the arguments, and see same-age peers explaining their work in sophisticated ways.

As part of this process of providing resources, breaking down the isolation of the classroom can also be a powerful way to support learning through social mechanisms. It has proven useful to provide students and teachers with access to information about how people outside their classroom have thought about the same problem that they are facing (CTGV, 1994a, 1997, 2000). Such access can help students be more objective about their own view and realize that even with the same information, other people may come to different conclusions or solutions. In addition, discussion of these differences of opinion can support the development of shared standards for reasoning. This can have a powerful effect on understanding the need for revising one's ideas and as a motivator for engaging in such a process. Internet and web-based environments now provide excellent mechanisms to incorporate these processes within the overall SMART model. Some of these mechanisms include interactive Web sites with database components that are dynamically updated as students from multiple classrooms respond to items or probes on the Web site. An example of this use of the Internet and the Web is described later in the context of implementing the SMART model with a Scientists in Action adventure.

Reviewing the evolution of one Scientists in Action curriculum, the *Stones River Mystery*, will demonstrate the increasing attention paid to embodying all four elements, especially the assessment-centered and community-centered elements, while further refining the learner- and knowledge-centered dimensions already present in the Jasper-anchored instruction designs. It also illustrates how web-based resources were introduced into the learning environment.

In the *Stones River Mystery* video, students are presented with the challenge of understanding the complexities of river pollution. In its early form, students engaged in this curriculum watched a video story of a team of high school students who are working with a hydrologist and a biologist to monitor the quality of the water in Stones River. The team travels in a specially equipped van to various testing sites, and can electronically submit test results to students back at school. The video shows the team collecting and sorting samples of macroinvertebrates from the river's bottom. They also measure dissolved oxygen, temperature, and other water quality indicators. The video anchor poses various challenges to students: First, test and evaluate the water quality at a particular river site to determine if pollution is present, then localize the source of the pollution, and finally, determine the best method to clean up the pollution.

Students use a Web site as they solve each challenge. The site has three components. One component gives individualized feedback to students about the problem solving that they can use to revise their work. For example, when working on the challenge of how to clean up the pollution in Stones River, students access the web-based "Better Business Bureau." This site contains proposals submitted by various companies for how to clean up the pollution in Stones River. Students using the site are asked to select the best company to hire based on the information provided in the proposals and to chose a rationale for their selection. They also indicate their rationale for not selecting each of the other companies. Some proposals contain deliberately erroneous scientific information and clean up solutions. Students' selections and rationales are submitted online and they receive individualized online feedback (that can be printed out for later reference) about their submissions. The feedback contains information on any problems with their selections and rationales and suggestions for offline resources for learning more about key concepts.

In addition to the formative feedback component, the site has two other components that are designed to draw on the community building potential of the Internet as well as serve a formative assessment function. The site contains a backend database that collects the data submitted by all student users. Information from the database is used to dynamically build graphs that display aggregate data on the choices and reasons that students selected. These graphs are viewed and discussed by the class. Because students' opinions often differ on which company is best and why, the graphs are "conversations starters" that make this evident and invite discussion about the merits of various choices and about key concepts that support or argue against a specific choice and/or rationale. Students are motivated to take part in discussions about the aggregate data because they understand that it represents the input of students in their class and other participating classes. Finally, the site contains presentations (text plus audio) by actors in which they explain their ideas on which company to hire and why. As mentioned earlier, these presentations purposely contain misconceptions that students often have about the underlying science content. The actors ask students to give them feedback on their thinking (they submit this feedback, which is then posted online). In this way, the classroom discussion is seeded to focus on understanding important content by bringing the input of the broader learning community into the classroom.

SMART learning environments were designed to foster the development of high standards, rich content, and authentic problem-solving environments. But, as compared to earlier curriculum units, special attention is paid to assessment and community building. Included in the former category are assessments of student-generated products, such as blueprints or business plans, and assessment facilitated by comparing solutions to problems with others around the country who are working on similar problem- and project-based curricula. The second category included a number of tools that enable students to get feedback from a variety of external communities, including parents, community leaders, expert practitioners, and academics. As they have evolved, SMART learning environments embody the four instructional design principles discussed earlier: a focus on learning goals that emphasize deep understanding of important subject matter content, the use of scaffolds to support both student and teacher learning, frequent opportunities for formative self-assessment, revision, and reflection, and social organizations that promote collaboration and a striving for high standards. Each characteristic is enabled and supported through the use of various technologies for the delivery of resources and the exchange of information. The ability of students and teachers to make progress through the various cycles of work and revision is dependent on the various resource materials and tools that assist the learning and assessment process. Research indicates that students who use these tools learn significantly more than students who go through the same instructional sequence for the same amount of time without using the tools (Barron et al., 1995, 1998; Vye et al., 1998).

A SOFTWARE SHELL FOR CREATING AND MANAGING
EFFECTIVE LEARNING ENVIRONMENTS

The anchored instruction designs described in the preceding two sections are very much focused on carrying out an extended inquiry process within regular classrooms with reasonable technology capability. They can be executed at varying levels of sophistication depending on access to specific technology infrastructure. In the course of pursuing these designs, it became apparent that the most effective learning and instruction was transacted in situations where all four elements of powerful learning environments were present. Doing so demands a wide range of resources and tools and also the capacity to organize and manage the instructional and learning process in a way that is faithful to learner exploration and support. One of the things discovered along the way, especially as SMART inquiry environments were implemented, was the need for externalization of the overall process. As a result, a software shell was developed for helping people visualize and manage inquiry in a manner that is learner, knowledge, assessment, and community centered. Called STAR.Legacy (STAR stands for Software Technology for Action and Reflection), the environment provides a framework for anchored inquiry. Chances to solve important problems, assess progress, and revise when necessary play a prominent role in the Legacy cycle. The environment can also easily be adapted to fit local needs, in part, by having teachers and students "leave legacies" for future students (hence the name Legacy).

The STAR.Legacy design grows out of collaborations with teachers, students, curriculum designers, educational trainers, and researchers in learning and instruction. One of its virtues is that it makes explicit the different components of an instructional event focused around an inquiry process. Furthermore, it connects the events with learning theory and the four components of powerful learning environments. STAR.Legacy formalizes those components and their rationale within a learning cycle that is easy to understand and follow. Figure 8.2 shows the home page of STAR.Legacy (Schwartz, Brophy, Lin, & Bransford, 1999; Schwartz, Lin, Brophy, & Bransford, 1999). The software features learning cycles anchored around successive challenges that are represented as increasingly high mountains. As learners climb each mountain, they progressively deepen their expertise. Within each challenge, students generate ideas, hear perspectives from experts, conduct research, and receive opportunities to "test their mettle" and revise before "going public." The structure of STAR.Legacy is designed to help balance the features of learner, knowledge, assessment, and community centeredness.

The home page of STAR.Legacy helps students become more active and reflective learners by being able to see where they are in a research cycle.

FIG. 8.2.   The STAR.Legacy reference diagram illustrating the organization and sequencing of the components of a multiple challenge inquiry learning cycle.

The importance of this feature became apparent during research that was discussed earlier (Barron et al., 1995, 1998; CTGV, 1994a, 1997; Vye et al., 1998). When working on complex units, students often got lost in the process. Earlier research created a visual map of a curriculum unit that was placed in the classrooms; this helped students and teachers understand where they were in the process and where they were going (see Barron et al., 1995, for more information). STAR.Legacy provides a model of inquiry that represents an advance on these earlier designs. It too helps students see where they are and where they are trying to go. White and Fredricksen's (1998) inquiry model for science (which is more specific than Legacy, but definitely compatible with it) provides an additional illustration of the importance of helping people visualize the processes of inquiry. Teachers can use STAR.Legacy to organize whole class work (by projecting the software on a big screen), or students can work individually or in groups.

The "overview" section of Legacy (see the top left of Fig. 8.2) allows teachers or students to begin by exploring the purposes of the unit and what they should accomplish by the end. Overviews frequently include pretests that let students assess their initial knowledge about a topic. Teachers can use the pretest to make the students' thinking visible and identify beliefs about the subject matter that may need careful attention (for examples of the value of beginning with students' assumptions, see Hunt & Minstrell, 1994). At the end of the unit, students can revisit the pretest and see how much they have learned; the benefits of this are discussed in Schwartz, Brophy et al. (1999) and Schwartz, Lin et al. (1999).

Pretests that are problem based or design based, rather than simply multiple choice or true and false, are encouraged. The former are more interesting to students initially, and they better reveal students' assumptions about phenomena because their answers are not constrained by predetermined choices provided on the tests. A pretest for a unit on "rate" may ask students to help a small private flying company design a way to efficiently give people trip time estimates from their airport depending on wind speeds, aircraft speed, and their destination. On a pretest, middle school and even college students usually try to remember formulas and almost never think of inventing "smart" tools like the one illustrated in Fig. 8.1.

A pretest for one unit on monitoring rivers for water quality introduces students to Billy Bashinall (a cartoon character), who acts in ways that reveal his assumptions (many are wrong) about water; the students' job is to assess Billy's understanding and prepare to teach him. Students also assess Billy's attitude toward learning (which is quite negative) and discuss their thoughts about how it might be changed.

Overall, the overview component of Legacy is learner centered in the sense that students are encouraged to state their initial ideas about the overview problem and define learning goals; knowledge centered in the sense that units are designed to focus on important ideas in a discipline; assessment centered in the sense that teachers can gather information about students' beliefs, students can discover that they hold conflicting beliefs as a group, and students can eventually assess their progress when they return to the overview problem after completing the unit. The overview also supports the development of community-centered environments in the sense that teachers can present the pretest as a challenge that all will work on collaboratively (although there can still be individual accountability) in order to communicate their ideas to an outside group (e.g., by "going public" through live presentations or publishing on the Web).

Following the overview to a unit, students are introduced to a series of challenges (represented as increasingly high mountains in Fig. 8.2) that are designed to progressively deepen their knowledge. This way of structuring challenges reflects lessons learned about knowledge-centered curricula that were discussed earlier. For example, the first challenge for a unit on "rate" in mathematics may ask students to solve the Jasper adventure "Rescue at Boone's Meadow," where Emily uses an ultralight to rescue a wounded eagle. It's a calm day, so headwinds and tailwinds do not have to be taken into the account. What is the best way to rescue the eagle and how long will that take? (issues of fuel consumption and capacity come into play in determining this).

The second challenge uses footage of Charles Lindbergh and asks students to decide if he could make it from New York to Paris given particular data such as his fuel capacity and plane speed. Interestingly, Lindbergh could not have made the trip without a substantial tailwind. This helps students extend their thinking of rate by considering ground speed versus air speed.

The third challenge invites students to build tools that help them solve entire classes of problems rather than only a single problem. The challenge features Emily's rescue and delivery service. Students are challenged to create a set of smart tools that help Emily quickly determine how long it will take to get to various destinations and what the fuel costs will be (see Fig. 8.1 for an example). Attempts to build tools eventually introduce students to linear and nonlinear functions; for example, changes in wind speeds on different parts of a route introduce students to piecewise linear functions. Examples are provided in Bransford et al. (1996, 1999).

Within each challenge cycle, Legacy engages students in activities that encourage them to use their existing knowledge, assess their learning, and develop a sense of community with their classmates and the teachers. First, students generate their own ideas about a challenge, either individually, in small groups, or as a whole class. Teachers can listen to students' ideas in whole class sessions and students get a chance to hear the ideas of their classmates. Electronic notebooks in Legacy let teachers capture the thinking of the whole class, or let students who are working in groups capture their thinking and keep it with them as they work through the unit. Teachers can access these notebooks to see how students are approaching the challenges.

After generating their own ideas, students can open "multiple perspectives" and see experts discussing ideas that are relevant to the challenge. An important goal of multiple perspectives is to help students (and in some instances teachers) begin to see the relation between their personal thinking about an issue and the thinking that is characteristic of experts from a scientific community. For example, middle school students may have intuitions that tailwinds can help a plane fly faster, but few will have a well-worked out understanding of how to quantify this intuition and how to differentiate air speed and ground speed. In addition, experts can help students understand the value of thinking about the rate of airplane fuel consumption from the perspective of hours of flying time rather than miles per hour.

Opportunities to see multiple perspectives have been especially well-received by students. Because they first get to generate their own ideas about a topic (in Generate Ideas), they are able to contrast their own thinking with the thinking of experts. Opportunities to experience contrasting cases are important for helping students develop a deeper understanding of new areas of inquiry (e.g., see Bransford, Franks, Vye, & Sherwood, 1989; Bransford & Schwartz, 1999; Schwartz & Bransford, 1998). The fact that Legacy is intended to be an authorable environment also means that teachers can add themselves as one of the multiple perspectives. Having a video of the teacher appear in the media appears to have effects on student attentiveness that go beyond simply having the teacher say the same thing in front of the class.

The "research and revise" component of Legacy provides access to resources for learning, including videos, audio, simulations, and access to the Web. Resources can be different for each of the separate Legacy challenges. For example, a resource for the tools needed for the third Jasper challenge noted earlier might involve a simple Java-based simulation for building graphs with student-specified scales.

An especially important feature of each Legacy cycle is the "test your mettle" component that focuses attention on assessment, especially self-assessment. For example, students can assess their thinking before "going public" (e.g., by making oral or written presentations or publishing on the Web). For the first Jasper challenge noted (the Eagle rescue), test your mettle might provide students with a checklist to assess whether they have considered important elements such as payload, availability of suitable landing sites, fuel consumption, and so on. Alternatively, Legacy might link students to the Jasper Adventureplayer software that allows them to enter their answers to the rescue problem and see a simulation of the results (Crews, Biswas, Goldman, & Bransford, 1997).

For the second challenge cycle noted (the Charles Lindbergh example), test your mettle may help students assess their thinking about headwinds and tailwinds (e.g., If Lindbergh takes a test flight where he travels 60 miles to City A with a 10 mph headwind and then flies back with the wind as a tailwind, will the headwind and tailwind cancel each other out?). The Jasper Adventureplayer software (Crews et al., 1997) can also provide feedback on these kinds of variables. The test your mettle for the third challenge cycle (the one dealing with smart tools) may provide students with a variety of "call ins" to Emily asking about trip time and expenses to take them to certain locations. Students test their tools to see how efficiently they permit answers to these questions. If the tools need revising (and they usually do), students can go back to resources, multiple perspectives, or any other part of Legacy. The software is designed to allow flexible back-and-forth navigation—it does not force students into a rigid loop.

At the end of each of the three legacy cycles, students have the opportunity to "go public." This includes a variety of options, such as making oral presentations in the classroom or posting reports, smart tools, simulations, and other artifacts on the Web. The idea of going public helps create a sense of community within the classroom because students' and teachers' ideas are being considered by others. For example, in a Legacy used in a college class, students at Vanderbilt went public by publishing essays on the Web that were then reviewed by students from Stanford (Schwartz, Brophy et al., 1999). In middle school classrooms, students' essays might be read by other classes or by groups of experts from the community.

At the end of the final challenge in a Legacy unit, students can return to "overview" and revisit the pretest that they took initially. This helps students see how much they have learned in a Legacy unit, and it provides feedback that helps them identify any important concepts that they may have missed.

STAR.LEGACY AND FLEXIBLE DESIGN

Most teachers do not have time to create Legacy units from scratch, but they like to adapt existing units so that they better fit the needs of their classrooms. Teachers may want to choose from several different pretests for a unit, choose from among a number of possible challenge cycles, select a subset of the available resources and "test your mettles," and so forth. It was noted earlier that teachers can also place themselves in the software (e.g., as video participants in multiple perspectives, resources, or test your mettle). Over time, Legacy units can be readily adapted to meet teachers' particular goals and needs.

Legacy can also be used to help foster schoolwide and community-wide connections by adding videos of local experts who appear in multiple perspectives and resources, and as friendly critics in test your mettle. The ability for students within a single class to meet (via video) others from the local school community is powerful. Because students see them visually and learn something about their expertise and interests, experiences show that they are much more likely to begin conversations and ask questions when they meet these people. It has also been observed that students are more likely to go to these people for advice when a project they are working on is relevant to their areas of expertise (Schwartz, Brophy et al., 1999; Schwartz, Lin et al., 1999).

Legacy is also designed with the idea of having students add their own information to units. The primary mechanism for doing this is to leave a legacy for the next group that explores a unit. Students can add their ideas to multiple perspectives, resources, or test your mettle. For example, students may provide a clip or two in multiple perspectives that explain that a challenge initially seemed arbitrary to them and a waste of time but they later realized its value—hence the new students should stick with it. Students might also point toward new resources in the research and revise section (e.g., new Web sites) that they found to be particularly valuable. If they wish, students can also add a new challenge. Overall, the opportunity to leave a Legacy is very motivating to students and helps them see themselves as part of a community whose goal is to teach others as well as to learn.

Legacy also helps teachers envision a common inquiry cycle that extends across disciplines. Many teachers have found that this helps them communicate with colleagues in other disciplines. A number have used the Legacy cycle to design their curricula even when it is not computerized. The overview and test your mettle sections of Legacy have been especially important for curriculum development because they focus attention on goals for learning that are more explicit than a mere list of abstract objectives that are often only vaguely defined.

Legacy also provides a shell for dynamic assessment environments that can be used to assess people's abilities to learn new information. Legacy can capture students questions, use of resources, tests, and revisions. Students who are better prepared for future learning (because of well-organized content knowledge as well as attitudes and strategies) should do better in these environments than students who are less prepared (for more discussion, see Bransford & Schwartz, 1999).

The STAR.Legacy design is intended to be flexible and adaptive to the needs of instructors and learners in a variety of contexts. To date it has been employed in both K–12 and adult learning contexts. At the K–12 level, it has been used with inquiry-based science learning and with complex mathematics problem solving at the middle school level. With adults, it has been used in instructional contexts ranging from electrical engineering, educational psychology, and bioengineering education, to teacher professional development. For some examples, see Schwartz, Brophy et al. (1999) and Schwartz, Lin et al. (1999). Across these varied contexts, it has proven to be a highly usable design and development environment. It can be as simple or as "high tech" as someone wants or needs. It has the capacity to support complex learning because it links activities to purposes and makes things explicit and manageable. As discussed earlier, it includes all four components of effective and powerful learning environments. With regard to other technology tools and resources, it can support the use and integration of multiple technology tools and products, including multimedia, Internet resources, simulations, automated assessments, virtual reality, and communication and dialog systems. Finally, it is highly compatible in its design features with future technology tools and developments in education.

CONCLUSIONS

This chapter has tried to illustrate how contemporary learning theory can be connected to instructional practice to build powerful and effective learning environments, most especially through capitalizing on some of the many affordances of information technologies. The discussion began by examining some of the principal findings from research on learning that have clear implications for instructional practice, including four important characteristics of effective learning environments (knowledge centered, learner centered, assessment centered and community centered) and four important design principles for their attainment. Each design principle can be enabled and enhanced by various information technologies. For example, technology makes it easier to organize instruction around the solution of meaningful problems and to provide scaffolds for the support of learning with understanding. Various new resources and materials, embedded in technology delivery and support systems, such as multimedia, simulations and visualizations, and virtual reality environments are examples of capitalizing on this affordance. Technology also makes information accessible when needed and enables embedded assessment strategies so that instruction can be designed to provide ongoing opportunities for practice with feedback, reflection, and revision. Finally, technology supports communication and collaboration and makes it possible to design instruction to capitalize on social arrangements that enhance cooperative and distributed expertise together with independent learning.

It is often noted that technology is really just a tool to support learning and instruction, but it is less often noted or made clear that the nature of the technology tools and their manner of use matters deeply (see CTGV, 1996). Thinking about these issues is the product of over 10 years of work attempting to forge a linkage between learning theory and instructional practice, mediated by advances in technology. As work has evolved over time, it has became increasingly clear that multiple characteristics of powerful learning environments are needed for maximal payoff. Technology allows for this possibility, but it also adds levels of complexity. Fortunately, one of technology's affordances is that it is simultaneously capable of supporting the structuring and management of that complexity in ways that also enhance the instructional process. The STAR.Legacy software shell, a technology-based design for inquiry learning, was presented as one example of how to connect learning theory, instructional design and management, and the deployment of multiple technologies. Researchers look forward to exploring these issues further and to exploring the affordances that future technologies will hold for the enhancement of learning and instruction.

ACKNOWLEDGMENTS

Members of the Cognition and Technology Group whose work contributed to this chapter include Jan Altman, Jill Ashworth, Brigid Barron, Linda Barron, Helen Bateman, Kadira Belynne, John Bransford, Melinda Bray,

Sean Brophy, Kay Burgess, William Corbin, Nathalie Coté, Carolyn Cottom, Elizabeth Goldman, Susan R. Goldman, Ted S. Hasselbring, Peggy Hester, Daniel Hickey, Cindy Hmelo, Ron Kantor, Charles Kinzer, Xiaodong Lin, Delessa McNair, Cynthia Mayfield-Stewart, Linda Miller, Allison Moore, Tom Noser, Jay Pfaffman, James Pellegrino, Victoria Risko, Anthony Petrosino, Daniel Schwartz, Teresa Secules, Diana Sharp, Robert Sherwood, Keisha Varma, Nancy Vye, Rick Weise, Susan Williams, and Linda Zech. The content of this chapter draws from several published works by members of the CTGV, including CTGV (2000); Donovan et al. (1999), Goldman et al. (1999), and Schwartz, Brophy et al. (1999).

The research of the Cognition and Technology Group on issues in the application of learning theory and information technology to instructional design has been supported by grants from the James S. McDonnell Foundation, the Mellon Foundation, the National Science Foundation, and the Office of Educational Research and Improvement of the U. S. Department of Education. We are grateful for the support provided by these groups. The opinions expressed in this chapter are those of the authors and not of the granting agencies.

REFERENCES

Alexander, P. A., Kulikowich, J. M., & Jetton, T. L. (1994). The role of subject-matter knowledge and interest in in the processing of linear and non-linear texts. *Review of Educational Research, 64*, 201–252.

Anderson, J. R. (1983). A spreading activation theory of memory. *Journal of Verbal Learning and Verbal Behavior, 22*, 261–296.

Bakhtin, M. (1981). Discourse in the novel. In M. Holquist (Ed.), *The dialogic imagination* (pp. 259–422). Austin: University of Texas Press. (Original work published 1935)

Barron, B. (1991). *Collaborative problem solving: Is team performance greater than what is expected from the most competent member?* Unpublished doctoral dissertation, Vanderbilt University, Nashville, TN.

Barron, B. J., Schwartz, D. L., Vye, N. J., Moore, A., Petrosino, A., Zech, L., Bransford, J. D., & the Cognition and Technology Group at Vanderbilt. (1998). Doing with understanding: Lessons from research on problem and project-based learning. *Journal of Learning Sciences, 7*, 271–312.

Barron, B., Vye, N. J., Zech, L., Schwartz, D., Bransford, J. D., Goldman, S. R., Pellegrino, J., Morris, J., Garrison, S., & Kantor, R. (1995). Creating contexts for community-based problem solving: The Jasper Challenge Series. In C. N. Hedley, P. Antonacci, & M. Rabinowitz (Eds.), *Thinking and literacy: The mind at work* (pp. 47–71). Hillsdale, NJ: Lawrence Erlbaum Associates.

Bereiter, C. (1990). Aspects of an educational learning theory. *Review of Educational Research, 60*, 603–624.

Bereiter, C., & Scardamalia, M. (1993). *Surpassing ourselves: An inquiry into the nature and implications of expertise.* Chicago, IL: Open Court.

Bransford, J. D., Brown, A. L., & Cocking, R. R. (1999). *How people learn: Brain, mind, experience, and school.* Washington, DC: National Academy Press.

Bransford, J. D., Franks, J. J., Vye, N. J., & Sherwood, R. D. (1989). New approaches to instruction: Because wisdom can't be told. In S. Vosniadou & A. Ortony (Eds.), *Similarity and analogical reasoning* (pp. 470–497). New York: Cambridge University Press.

Bransford, J. D., & Schwartz, D. (1999). Rethinking transfer: A simple proposal with multiple implications. *Review of Research in Education, 24,* 61–100.

Bransford, J. D., & Stein, B. S. (1993). *The IDEAL problem solver* (2nd ed.). New York: Freeman.

Bransford, J. D., Zech, L., Schwartz, D., Barron, B., Vye, N., & the Cognition and Technology Group at Vanderbilt. (1996). Fostering mathematical thinking in middle school students: Lessons from research. In R. J. Sternberg & T. Ben-Zeev (Eds.), *The nature of mathematical thinking* (pp. 203–250). Hillsdale, NJ: Lawrence Erlbaum Associates.

Bransford, J. D., Zech, L., Schwartz, D., Barron, B., Vye, N., & the Cognition and Technology Group at Vanderbilt. (1999). Designs for environments that invite and sustain mathematical thinking. In P. Cobb (Ed.), *Symbolizing, communicating, and mathematizing: Perspectives on discourse, tools, and instructional design* (pp. 275–324). Hillsdale, NJ: Lawrence Erlbaum Associates.

Brice-Heath, S. (1981). Toward an ethnohistory of writing in American. In M. F. Whiteman (Ed.), *Writing: The nature, development, and teaching of written communication* (Vol. 1, pp. 25–45). Hillsdale, NJ: Lawrence Erlbaum Associates.

Brice-Heath, S. (1983). *Ways with words: Language, life and work in communities and classrooms.* Cambridge: Cambridge University Press.

Brown, A. L., & Campione, J. C. (1994). Guided discovery in a community of learners. In K. McGilly (Ed.), *Classroom lessons: Integrating cognitive theory and classroom practice* (pp. 229–272). Cambridge, MA: MIT Press/Bradford Books.

Brown, A. L., & Campione, J. C. (1996). Psychological theory and the design of innovative learning environments: On procedures, principles, and systems. In L. Schauble & R. Glaser (Eds.), *Innovations in learning: New environments for education* (pp. 289–325). Hillsdale, NJ: Lawrence Erlbaum Associates.

Brown, A. L., Bransford, J. D., Ferrara, R. A., & Campione, J. L. (1983). Learning, remembering, and understanding. In J. Flavell & E. M. Markman (Eds.), *Handbook of child psychology: Vol. 3. Cognitive development* (Vol. 1, pp. 77–166). New York: Wiley.

Bruer, J. T. (1993). *Schools for thought.* Cambridge, MA: MIT Press.

Bruner, J. S. (1983). *Child's talk: Learning to use language.* New York: Norton.

Carey, S., & Gelman, R. (1991). *The epigenesis of mind: Essays on biology and cognition.* Hillsdale, NJ: Lawrence Erlbaum Associates.

Clement, J. (1982). Student preconceptions of introductory mechanics. *American Journal of Physics, 50,* 66–71.

Cognition and Technology Group at Vanderbilt. (1992a). An anchored instruction approach to cognitive skills acquisition and intelligent tutoring. In J. W. Region & V. J. Shute (Eds.), *Cognition approaches to automated instruction* (pp. 135–170). Hillsdale, NJ: Lawrence Erlbaum Associates.

Cognition and Technology Group at Vanderbilt. (1992b). The Jasper experiment: An exploration of issues in learning and instructional design. *Educational Technology Research and Development, 40,* 65–80.

Cognition and Technology Group at Vanderbilt. (1992c). The Jasper series as an example of anchored instruction: Theory, program description, and assessment data. *Educational Psychologist, 27,* 291–315.

Cognition and Technology Group at Vanderbilt. (1993a). The Jasper series: Theoretical foundations and data on problem solving and transfer. In L. A. Penner, G. M. Batsche, H. M. Knoff, & D. L. Nelson (Eds.), *The challenge in mathematics and science education: Psychology's response* (pp. 113–152). Washington, DC: American Psychological Association.

Cognition and Technology Group at Vanderbilt. (1993b). Toward integrated curricula: Possibilities from anchored instruction. In M. Rabinowitz (Ed.), *Cognitive science foundations of instruction* (pp. 33–55). Hillsdale, NJ: Lawrence Erlbaum Associates.

Cognition and Technology Group at Vanderbilt. (1994a). From visual word problems to learning communities: Changing conceptions of cognitive research. In K. McGilly (Ed.), *Classroom lessons: Integrating cognitive theory and classroom practice* (pp. 157–200). Cambridge, MA: MIT Press/Bradford Books.

Cognition and Technology Group at Vanderbilt. (1994b). Multimedia environments for developing literacy in at-risk students. In B. Means (Ed.), *Technology and educational reform: The reality behind the promise* (pp. 23–56). San Francisco: Jossey-Bass.

Cognition and Technology Group at Vanderbilt. (1996). Looking at technology in context: A framework for understanding technology and education research. In D. C. Berliner & R. C. Calfee (Eds.), *The handbook of educational psychology* (pp. 807–840). New York: Simon & Schuster MacMillan.

Cognition and Technology Group at Vanderbilt. (1997). *The Jasper Project: Lessons in curriculum, instruction, assessment, and professional development.* Hillsdale, NJ: Lawrence Erlbaum Associates.

Cognition and Technology Group at Vanderbilt. (1998). Designing environments to reveal, support, and expand our children's potentials. In S. A. Soraci & W. McIlvane (Eds.), *Perspectives on fundamental processes in intellectual functioning* (pp. 313–350). Norwood, NJ: Ablex.

Cognition and Technology Group at Vanderbilt. (2000). Adventures in anchored instruction: Lessons from beyond the ivory tower. In R. Glaser (Ed.), *Advances in instructional psychology: Vol. 5. Educational design and cognitive science* (pp. 35–99). Hillsdale, NJ: Lawrence Erlbaum Associates. `

Collins, A. (1996). Design issues for learning environments. In S. Vosniadou, E. DeCorte, R. Glaser, & H. Mandl (Eds.), *International perspectives on the psychological foundations of technology-based learning environments* (pp. 347–362). Hillsdale, NJ: Lawrence Erlbaum Associates.

Collins, A., Brown, J. S., & Newman, S. E. (1989). Cognitive apprenticeship: Teaching the crafts of reading, writing, and mathematics. In L. B. Resnick (Ed.), *Knowing, learning, and instruction: Essays in honor of Robert Glaser* (pp. 453–494). Hillsdale, NJ: Lawrence Erlbaum Associates.

Collins, A., Hawkins, J., & Carver, S. M. (1991). A cognitive apprenticeship for disadvantaged students. In B. Means, C. Chelemer, & M. S. Knapp (Eds.), *Teaching advanced skills to at-risk students* (pp. 216–243). San Francisco, CA: Jossey-Bass.

Crews, T. R., Biswas, G., Goldman, S. R., & Bransford, J. D. (1997). Anchored interactive learning environments. *International Journal of Artificial Intelligence in Education, 8*(2), 142–178.

Dewey, J. (1933). *How we think, a restatement of the relation of reflective thinking to the educative process.* Boston: Heath.

Donovan, M. S., Bransford, J. D., & Pellegrino, J. W. (1999). *How people learn: Bridging research and practice.* Washington, DC: National Academy Press.

Fuchs, L. S., Fuchs, D., Hamlett, C. L., & Stecker, P. M. (1991). Effects of curriculum-based measurement on teacher planning and student achievement in mathematics operations. *American Educational Research Journal, 28,* 617–641.

Gardner, H. (1991). *The unschooled mind: How children think and how schools should teach.* New York: Basic Books.

Gelman, R., & Gallistel, C. R. (1978). *The children's understanding of number.* Cambridge, MA: Harvard University Press.

Gick, M. L., & Holyoak, K. J. (1983). Schema induction and analogical transfer. *Cognitive Psychology, 15,* 1–38.

Glaser, R., & Chi, M. T. H. (1988). Introduction: What is it to be an expert? In M. T. H. Chi, R. Glaser, & M. J. Farr (Eds.), *The nature of expertise* (pp. xv–xxiix). Hillsdale, NJ: Lawrence Erlbaum Associates.

Goldman, S. R., Petrosino, A., Sherwood, R. D., Garrison, S., Hickey, D., Bransford, J. D., & Pellegrino, J. W. (1996). Anchoring science instruction in multimedia learning environments. In S. Vosniadou, E. De Corte, R. Glaser, & H. Mandl (Eds.), *International perspectives on the psychological foundations of technology-supported learning environments* (pp. 257–284). Hillsdale, NJ: Lawrence Erlbaum Associates.

Goldman, S. R., Williams, S. M., Sherwood, R. D., Hasselbring, T. S., and the Cognition and Technology Group at Vanderbilt. (1999). *Technology for teaching and learning with understanding: A primer.* Boston: Houghton Mifflin.

Goldman, S. R., Zech, L. K., Biswas, G., Noser, T., & the Cognition and Technology Group at Vanderbilt. (1997). Computer technology and complex problem solving: Issues in the study of complex cognitive activity. *Instructional Science,* 1–34.

Hatano, G. (1990). The nature of everyday science: A brief introduction. *British Journal of Developmental Psychology, 8,* 245–250.

Hatano, G., & Inagaki, K. (1991). Sharing cognition through collective comprehension activity. In L. Resnick, J. M. Levine, & S. D. Teasley (Eds.), *Perspectives on socially shared cognition* (pp. 331–348). Washington, DC: American Psychological Association.

Harvard-Smithsonian Center for Astrophysics, Science Education Department. (1987). *A private universe* [video]. Science Media Group: Cambridge, MA.

Hatano, G. (1990). The nature of everyday science: A brief introduction. *British Journal of Developmental Psychology, 8,* 245–250.

Hatano, G., & Inagaki, K. (1991). Sharing cognition through collective comprehension activity. In L. Resnick, J. M. Levine, & S. D. Teasley (Eds.), *Perspectives on socially shared cognition* (pp. 331–348). Washington, DC: American Psychological Association.

Hmelo, C. E., & Williams, S. M. (Eds.). (1998). Learning through problem solving. Special issue of the *Journal of the Learning Sciences* (Nos. 3–4), 265–449.

Holyoak, K. J. (1984). Analogical thinking and human intelligence. In R. J. Sternberg (Ed.), *Advance in the psychology of human intelligence* (Vol. 2, pp. 199–230). Hillsdale, NJ: Lawrence Erlbaum Associates.

Hunt, E., & Minstrell, J. (1994). A cognitive approach to the teaching of physics. In K. McGilly (Ed.), *Classroom lessons: Integrating cognitive theory and classroom practice* (pp. 51–74). Cambridge, MA: MIT Press.

Hurst, K. C., Casillas, A. M., & Stevens, R. H. (1998). *Exploring the dynamics of complex problem-solving with artificial neural network-based assessment systems.* (CSE Tech. Rep. No. 387). Los Angeles, CA: University of California Los Angeles, National Center for Research on Evaluation, Standards, and Student Testing.

Hutchins, E. (1991). The social organization of distributed cognition. In L. Resnick, J. M. Levine, & S. D. Teasley (Eds.), *Perspectives on socially shared cognition* (pp. 283–307). Washington, DC: American Psychological Association.

Hutchins, E. (1995). *Cognition in the wild.* Cambridge, MA: MIT Press.

Kulik, J. (1994). Meta-analytic studies of findings of computer-based instruction. In E. L. Baker & H. F. O'Neill (Eds.), *Technology assessment in education and training* (pp. 9–33). Hillsdale, NJ: Lawrence Erlbaum Associates.

Lamon, M., Secules, T., Petrosino, A. J., Hackett, R., Bransford, J. D., & Goldman, S. R. (1996). Schools for thought: Overview of the project and lessons learned from one of the sites. In L. Schauble & R. Glaser (Eds.), *Innovation in learning: New environments for education* (pp. 243–288). Hillsdale, NJ: Lawrence Erlbaum Associates.

Landauer, T. K., Foltz, P. W., & Laham, D. (1998). Introduction to Latent Semantic Analysis. *Discourse Processes, 25,* 259–284.

Lave, J. (1988). *Cognition in practice: Mind, mathematics, and culture in everyday life.* Cambridge, England: Cambridge University Press.

McCombs, B. L. (1991). Motivation and lifelong learning. *Educational Psychologist, 26,* 117–127.

McCombs, B. L. (1994). Alternative perspectives for motivation. In L. Baker, P. Afflerback, & D. Reinking (Eds.), *Developing engaged readers in school and home communities* (pp. 67–87). Hillsdale, NJ: Lawrence Erlbaum Associates.

Minstrell, J. (1989).Teaching science for understanding. In L. B. Resnick & L. E. Klopfer (Eds.), *Toward the thinking curriculum: Current cognitive research* (pp. 130–131). Alexandria, VA: ASCD.

National Council of Teachers of Mathematics. (1989). *Curriculum and evaluation standards for school mathematics.* Reston, VA: Author.

National Council of Teachers of Mathematics. (2000). *Principles and standards for school mathematics.* Reston, VA: Author.

National Research Council. (1996). *National science education standards.* Washington, DC: National Academy Press.

Norman, D. A. (1993). *Things that make us smart: Defending human attributes in the age of the machine.* New York: Addison-Wesley.

Novick, L. R., & Holyoak, K. J. (1991). Mathematical problem solving by analogy. *Journal of Experimental Psychology: Learning, Memory, and Cognition, 17*(3), 398–415.

Palincsar, A. S., & Brown, A. L. (1984). Reciprocal teaching of comprehension-fostering and comprehension monitoring activities. *Cognition and Instruction, 1,* 117–175.

Pea, R. D. (1993). Practices of distributed intelligence and designs for education. In G. Salomon (Ed.), *Distributed cognitions: Psychological and educational considerations* (pp. 47–87). New York: Cambridge University Press.

Pellegrino, J. W., Hickey, D., Heath, A., Rewey, K., Vye, N. J., & the Cognition and Technology Group at Vanderbilt. (1991). *Assessing the outcomes of an innovative instructional program: The 1990–1991 implementation of the "Adventures of Jasper Woodbury"* (Tech. Rep. No. 91-1). Nashville, TN: Vanderbilt University, Learning Technology Center.

Resnick, L. (1987). Learning in school and out. *Educational Researcher, 16*(9), 13–20.

Resnick, L. B., & Klopfer, L. E. (Eds.). (1989). *Toward the thinking curriculum: Current cognitive research.* Alexandria, VA: ASCD.

Resnick, L. B., & Resnick, D. P. (1991). Assessing the thinking curriculum: New tools for educational reform. In B. R. Gifford & M. O'Connor (Eds.), *New approaches to testing: Rethinking aptitude, achievement and assessment* (pp. 37–76). New York: National Committee on Testing and Public Policy.

Rogoff, B. (1990). *Apprenticeship in thinking.* New York: Oxford University Press.

Salomon, G. (Ed.). (1993). *Distributed cognitions: Psychological and educational considerations.* New York: Cambridge University Press.

Scardamalia, M., & Bereiter, C. (1994). Computer support for knowledge-building communities. *Journal of the Learning Sciences,* 265–285.

Scardamalia, M., Bereiter, C., & Lamon, M. (1994). The CSILE project: Trying to bring the classroom into world 3. In K. McGilly (Ed.), *Classroom lessons: Integrating cognitive theory and classroom practice* (pp. 201–228). Cambridge, MA: MIT Press.

Scarmadalia, M., Bereiter, C., & Steinbach, R. (1984). Teachability of reflective processes in written composition. *Cognitive Science, 8,* 173–190.

Schacter, J., & Fagnano, C. (1999). Does computer technology improve student learning and achievement? How, when, and under what conditions? *Journal of Educational Computing Research, 20,* 329–343.

Schneider, W., Dumais, S. T., & Shiffrin, R. M. (1984). Automatic and controlled processing and attention. In R. Parasuraman & D. R. Davies (Eds.), *Varieties of attention* (pp. 1–27). Orlando, FL: Academic Press.

Schneider, W., & Schiffrin, R. M. (1977). Controlled and automatic human information processing: Detection, search, and attention. *Psychological Review, 84,* 1–66.

Schoenfeld, A. H. (1983). Problem solving in the mathematics curriculum: A report, recommendation and annotated bibliography. *Mathematical Association of America Notes,* No. 1.

Schoenfeld, A. H. (1984). *Mathematical problem solving.* Orlando, FL: Academic Press.

Schoenfeld, A. H. (1991). On mathematics as sense making: An informal attack on the unfortunate divorce of formal and informal mathematics. In J. F. Voss, D. N. Perkins, & J. W.

Segal (Eds.), *Informal reasoning and education* (pp. 331–343). Hillsdale, NJ: Lawrence Erlbaum Associates.

Schön, D. A. (1983). *The reflective practitioner: How professionals think in action.* New York: Basic Books.

Schön, D. A. (1988). Coaching reflective teaching. In P. P. Grimmett & G. L. Erickson (Eds.), *Reflection in education* (pp. 17–29). New York: Teacher's College Press, Columbia University.

Schwartz, D. L., & Bransford, J. D. (1998). A time for telling. *Cognition & Instruction, 16,* 475–522.

Schwartz, D. L., Brophy, S., Lin, X., & Bransford, J. D. (1999). Flexibly adaptive instructional design: A case study from an educational psychology course. *Educational Technology Research and Development, 47,* 39–59.

Schwartz, D. L., Goldman, S. R., Vye, N. J., Barron, B. J., and Bransford, J. D., & the Cognition and Technology Group at Vanderbilt. (1998). Aligning everyday and mathematical reasoning: The case of sampling assumptions. In S. P. Lajoie (Ed.), *Reflections on statistics: Learning, teaching, and assessment in grades K–12* (pp. 233–273). Hillsdale, NJ: Lawrence Erlbaum Associates.

Schwartz, D. L., Lin, X., Brophy, S., & Bransford, J. D. (1999). Toward the development of flexibly adaptive instructional designs. In C. M. Reigeluth (Ed.), *Instructional design theories and models: Vol. II. A new paradigm of instructional theory* (pp. 183–213). Hillsdale, NJ: Lawrence Erlbaum Associates.

Secules, T., Cottom, C. D., Bray, M. H., Miller, L. D., & the Cognition and Technology Group at Vanderbilt. (1997). Schools for thought: Creating learning communities. *Educational Leadership, 54*(6), 56–60.

Sharp, D. L. M., Bransford, J. D., Goldman, S. R., Risko, V. J., Kinzer, C. K., & Vye, N. J. (1995). Dynamic visual support for story comprehension and mental modal building by young, at-risk children. *Educational Technology Research and Development, 43,* 25–42.

Sherwood, R. D., Petrosino, A. J., Lin, X., Lamon, M., & the Cognition and Technology Group at Vanderbilt. (1995). Problem-based macro contexts in science instruction: Theoretical basis, design issues, and the development of applications. In D. Lavoie (Ed.), *Towards a cognitive-science perspective for scientific problem solving* (pp. 191–214). Manhattan, KS: National Association for Research in Science Teaching.

Suina, J. H., & Smolkin, L. B. (1994). From natal culture to school culture to dominant society culture: Supporting transitions for Pueblo Indian students. In P. M. Greenfield & R. R. Cocking (Eds.), *Cross-cultural roots of minority child development* (pp. 115–130). Hillsdale, NJ: Lawrence Erlbaum Associates.

Vosniadou, S., & Brewer, W. F. (1989). *The concept of the earth's shape: A study of conceptual change in childhood.* Unpublished manuscript, Center for the Study of Reading, University of Illinois, Champaign.

Vye, N. J., Goldman, S. R., Voss, J. F., Hmelo, C., Williams, S., & the Cognition and Technology Group at Vanderbilt. (1997). Complex mathematical problem solving by individuals and dyads. *Cognition and Instruction, 15,* 435–484.

Vye, N. J., Schwartz, D. L., Bransford, J. D., Barron, B. J., Zech, L., & the Cognition and Technology Group at Vanderbilt. (1998). SMART environments that support monitoring, reflection, and revision. In D. Hacker, J. Dunlosky, & A. Graesser (Eds.), *Metacognition in educational theory and practice* (pp. 305–346). Hillsdale, NJ: Lawrence Erlbaum Associates.

Vygotsky, L. S. (1962). *Thought and language.* Cambridge, MA: MIT Press.

Wellman, H. M. (1990). *The child's theory of mind.* Cambridge, MA: MIT Press.

Wenglinsky, H. (1998). *Does it compute? The relationship between educational technology and student achievement in mathematics.* Princeton, NJ: educational Testing Service.

White, B. C., & Frederiksen, J. (1998). Inquiry, modeling, and metacognition: Making science accessible to all students. *Cognition and Instruction, 16*(1), 3–118.

Whitehead, A. N. (1929). *The aims of education.* New York: Macmillan.

Williams, S. M. (1994). *Anchored simulations: Merging the strengths of formal and informal reasoning in a computer-based learning environment.* Unpublished doctoral dissertation, Vanderbilt University, Nashville.

Williams, S. M., Burgess, K. L., Bray, M. H., Bransford, J. D., Goldman, S. R., & the Cognition and Technology Group at Vanderbilt. (1998). Technology and learning in schools for thought classrooms. In C. Dede (Ed.), *1998 ASCD year book: Learning with technology* (pp. 97–119). Alexandria, VA: ASCD.

Wood, S. S., Bruner, J. S., & Ross, G. (1976). The role of tutoring in problem solving. *Journal of Child Psyhcology and Psychiatry, 17,* 89–100.

Yackel, E., Cobb, P., & Wood, T. (1991). Small group interactions as a source of learning opportunities in second-grade mathematics. *Journal for Research in Mathematics Education, 22,* 390–408.

Zech, L., Vye, N., Bransford, J. Goldman, S., Barron, B., Schwartz, D., Hackett, R., Mayfield-Stewart, C., & the Cognition and Technology Group at Vanderbilt. (1998). An introduction to geometry through anchored instruction. In R. Lehrer & D. Chazan (Eds.), *New directions in teaching and learning geometry* (pp. 439–463). Hillsdale, NJ: Lawrence Erlbaum Associates.

Zech, L., Vye, N. J., Bransford, J. D., Swink, J., Mayfield-Stewart, C., Goldman, S. R., & the Cognition and Technology Group at Vanderbilt. (1994). Bringing geometry into the classroom with videodisc technology. *Mathematics Teaching in the Middle School Journal (MTMS), 1*(3), 228–233.

Part III

ASSESSMENT ISSUES

Chapter 9

Technology and Assessment

Lawrence T. Frase
George Mason University

Russell G. Almond
Jill Burstein
Karen Kukich
Kathleen M. Sheehan
Linda S. Steinberg
Educational Testing Service

Robert J. Mislevy
University of Maryland

Kevin Singley
International Business Machine

Martin Chodorow
Hunter College and *The City University of New York*

Despite its successful use in selection, placement, and instruction, traditional educational assessment faces more difficult challenges today than ever. Multiple choice tests seem too simple for those who want tests that resemble complex naturalistic settings. The underlying rationales for tests that measure general verbal and mathematical skills seem not to lend themselves enough to instructional applications; thus, tests seem remote from school curricula. Many tests rely on paper-and-pencil technologies when computer delivery would be convenient for testers and test-takers alike. In addition, the need to disclose test items, and hence to produce vastly more of them, coupled with the growth of test volumes over the years, puts a heavy burden on the assessment community. Finally, shifts in the federal demand for assessment services and increased competition in the assessment market, made possible through web-based technologies, constitute other emerging challenges.

To the assessment community, confronted by these many challenges, modern process, psychometric, and computational technologies promise some relief. In response to current challenges, the assessment community, relying on psychological and statistical research, is strengthening the cognitive and psychometric rationales for assessment. By incorporating test items into instructional practice, and by providing more informative diagnostic information from tests, assessment is paving the way for the integration of teaching and learning. In fact, the use of technology promises to improve and make more efficient all phases of assessment. This chapter reviews technologies that are laying the groundwork for improvements in the creation, delivery, interpretation, and use of educational assessments. These technologies are explored within the context of critical assessment activities and, at the end of this chapter, consequences that arise from the use of technology in assessment are considered. The work reported in this chapter was conducted while the authors were affiliated with the Educational Testing Service (ETS). ETS is a nonprofit organization that provides testing and related services, such as research on assessment issues, to educational, government, and business organizations in 181 countries. It develops and annually administers more than 11 million tests worldwide.

As the context for considering the application of technology in assessment, the processes involved in building tests (cf. Frase et al., 1998) are reviewed and consideration is given to how they relate to the different sections of this chapter. A high level, somewhat oversimplified, characterization of the assessment process, as it occurs in large-scale assessment, includes design and management, item construction, tryout and delivery, and scoring, analysis, and reporting. Each stage contains activities that can be made more efficient through the use of technology.

Design and Management

Test design involves the planning of new items, including a rationale for the constructs represented by the test and a context for the collection of human performance data reflective of cognitive or other processes. For instance, an assessment might involve reading, writing, listening, and speaking in integrated social situations, which might then be used to test grammatical, textual, and sociolinguistic competencies. Major activities, needed to design tests, include the transmission of information, meetings among personnel, and the exchange of information in the form of written and graphic materials. How can the planning and implementation of such complex assessment be systematized and better managed? The section "Evidence-Centered Assessment Design," in this chapter, addresses this issue by presenting a model that lays out the critical processes and products needed to develop a well-reasoned test. In a sketch of the ETS Portal project (Almond, Steinberg, & Mislevy, 2000; Mislevy, Steinberg, & Almond, in press), a broad view of technology as a process of managing the critical elements of test planning and implementation is presented. The Portal model can be used to guide the development of tests in a broad range of assessment domains. Other sections describe technologies that support various aspects of the evidence-centered process entailed in the Portal project. Specific technologies, such as the Web, can be used to support these assessment processes, but new business models are sometimes needed to make the most effective use of them (Frase, 2000).

Construction

Test construction includes the collection of information about the content and response characteristics of new items as well as the production of new test items. Much of this activity involves the exchange of information among test developers, training activities, and the revision and redistribution of items. These activities involve the presentation and collection of various kinds of data, such as voice, text, or graphics. In short, the ability to record and produce spoken language and the ability to represent realistic situations could all be prerequisites for the development of a particular test. Test construction is an expensive labor intensive activity. The section "Item Generation" discusses work that involves the automated production of test items. If valid and reliable items can be generated automatically, other stages of the assessment process, such as extensive testing with humans, might be avoided. Another section of this chapter, on the use of natural language processing ("Automated Tools for Test Development"), discusses the development of a wide range of computer tools to support several aspects of the test development process, including the activities of test developers that involve item construction.

Tryout and Delivery

Item tryout includes the distribution and trial of preliminary items, the collection of test scores, and the storing of original items and their data. This stage of test development involves a preliminary version of items as they might be delivered and it requires distribution channels that are sufficient for the various modalities of presentation and response recording. Although there is not enough space to review ETS's Internet-based work related to tryout, delivery, and item management, clearly web-based technologies have great potential (Hansen, Forer, & Mang, 2000). Item and test delivery entail data storage and retrieval activities required to document scores. The process of item management, in the sense of the selection, storage, and updating of item information, must be a rigorous formal procedure for classifying, storing, and retrieving items.

Scoring, Analysis and Reporting

Item scoring requires procedures for deriving a measure of test-taker performance, but not necessarily its deep interpretation. These procedures may be computer algorithms, scoring rubrics, or human evaluations. The section "Automated Essay Scoring" discusses the basis for the automated scoring of essays and it reviews current commercial applications of automated scoring at ETS. Item analysis requires procedures for determining the final interpretable or analyzable score, in whatever form (e.g., administration or instruction). Such scores not only represent a numerical or other characterization of performance, but, if analytic, they relate that characterization to some general educational or developmental scheme. The section "Tree-Based Regression" reports new psychometric techniques for characterizing complex cognitive outcomes. Tree-based psychometric representations of test data help visualize, at an abstract level, the underlying elements of test performance. These techniques are capable of revealing complex interactions (Clark & Pregibon, 1992), which are sometimes difficult to comprehend by other methods. Score reporting is becoming more sophisticated due to the development of complex cognitive models of performance and the availability of psychometric techniques. The assembly, interpretation, and distribution of diagnostic information will no doubt increase in importance. Score reporting is not addressed as a separate issue in the chapter. See Willingham (1999) for information on this issue.

In summary, this chapter describes tools and techniques that have grown out of research on psychometrics, computation, and other assessment technologies. The final part highlights technical, social, and political issues raised by the use of technology in assessment.

EVIDENCE-CENTERED ASSESSMENT DESIGN

Evidence-centered design describes a program of research and application carried out in the research division at ETS (Almond et al., 2000; Mislevy et al., in press; Mislevy, Steinberg, Breyer, Almond, & Johnson, 1999a, 1999b). The work introduces a principled framework for designing, producing, and delivering educational assessments. Special attention is given to assessments that incorporate features (e.g., complex student models and interactive simulations) that lie beyond the rules of thumb and analytic procedures that have evolved over the years to support familiar kinds of assessments.

Rationale

Off-the-shelf assessments and standardized tests are increasingly unsatisfactory for guiding learning and evaluating students' progress. Advances in cognitive and instructional sciences stretch expectations about the kinds of knowledge and skills that should be developed in students, and the kinds of observations needed to evidence them (Glaser, Lesgold, & Lajoie, 1987). Advances in technology make it possible to evoke evidence of knowledge more broadly conceived, and to capture more complex performances. One of the most serious bottlenecks, however, is making sense of the complex data that result.

Fortunately, advances in evidentiary reasoning (Schum, 1994) and in statistical modeling (Gelman, Carlin, Stern, & Rubin, 1995) allow researchers to bring probability-based reasoning to bear on the problems of modeling and uncertainty that arise naturally in all assessments. These advances extend the principles on which familiar test theory is grounded, to more varied and complex inferences from more complex data (Mislevy, 1994). Good tasks cannot simply be constructed in isolation, however, with the hope that someone down the line will figure out "how to score it." A complex assessment must be designed from the very start around the necessary inferences, the observations needed to ground them, the situations that will evoke those observations, and the chain of reasoning that connects them (Messick, 1994).

This project lays out a conceptual design framework for the elements of a coherent assessment at a level of generality that supports a broad range of assessment types, from familiar standardized tests and classroom quizzes, to coached practice systems and simulation-based assessments, to portfolios and student–tutor interaction. The design framework is based on the principles of evidentiary reasoning and the exigencies of assessment production and delivery. Designing assessment products in such a framework ensures that the way in which evidence is gathered and interpreted bears on the underlying knowledge and purposes the assessment is intended to address. The common design architecture further ensures coordination among the work of different specialists, such as statisticians, task authors, delivery-process developers, and interface designers. The project integrates and extends work on evidentiary reasoning in assessment (Mislevy, 1994; Mislevy & Gitomer, 1996), cognitively based intelligent tutoring systems (Steinberg & Gitomer, 1996), theory-based task design (Irvine & Kyllonen, in press), and knowledge-based construction of probability models (Almond, 1995).

Facets of the Assessment Design Work

This assessment design work has taken place at ETS under the project name "Portal." The activities encompass three distinguishable but interrelated aspects: a conceptual framework, an object model, and supporting tools. The evidence-centered Portal conceptual framework explicates the relations among the inferences the assessor wants to make about the student, what needs to be observed to provide evidence for those inferences, and what features of situations evoke that evidence. This is a way of thinking about the purposes and perspectives meant to provide the conceptual foundation of an assessment and what they imply for how tasks are to be designed and data analyzed. This conceptual framework can guide assessment design in the absence of the next two aspects, discussed later. Those aspects, however, are meant to achieve efficiencies and economies by promoting the reuse of assessment elements, processes, and structures.

The second aspect of the project is an object model for creating specifications for particular assessment products. The Portal object model embodies the elements and relationships that any assessment needs to be coherent. Instantiating instances of the objects, as needed for a particular assessment, ensures that an assessment will have the functionality it needs and the components will work together. Further, this framework promotes reusability of objects and processes (Almond et al., 2000). A key idea is that different kinds of objects are not defined for different kinds of tests; rather, the same general kinds of objects are tailored and assembled in different ways to meet different purposes.

The third aspect of the work is developing software tools for creating and managing the design objects. A first generation of software tools is now available to create, manipulate, and coordinate a structured database that contains the elements of an assessment design, which then serves as a blueprint to develop the application.

Several publications discuss the Portal conceptual model and its implications, although details of the object-model and software tools remain proprietary. Various papers highlight different interconnecting facets of designing and implementing complex assessments, including cognitive psychology (Steinberg & Gitomer, 1996); probability-based reasoning (Almond et al., 2000), task design (Almond & Mislevy, 1999; Mislevy et al., in press), and computer-based simulation (Mislevy et al., 1999a). Mislevy et al. (1999a, 1999b) applied this machinery to design a simulation-based assessment of problem solving in dental hygiene. Almond et al. (2000) applied the ideas to the challenge of defining standards for the interoperability of assessment/instructional materials and processes.

The Conceptual Assessment Framework

The important design concepts are made explicit in the conceptual assessment framework. The objects and specifications created here provide a blueprint for the operational aspects of work, including the creation of assessments, tasks, and statistical models; delivery and operation of the assessment; and analysis of data fed back from the field. Figure 9.1 is a high level

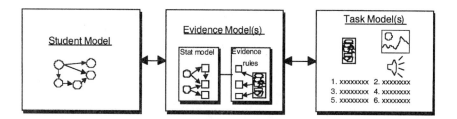

FIG. 9.1. The three central models of the conceptual assessment framework.

schematic of the three central models in the conceptual assessment framework and objects they contain. This is the evidentiary-reasoning argument, from task design to observations to scoring to inferences about students.

The Student Model: What Complex of Knowledge, Skills, or Other Attributes Should Be Assessed? Configurations of values of student-model variables approximate selected aspects of the infinite configurations of skill and knowledge that real students have, as seen from some perspective about skill and knowledge in the domain. These are the terms in which researchers want to determine evaluations, make decisions, or plan instruction—but they do not get to see the values directly. Instead, they see what students say or do, and must interpret that as evidence about these student-model variables. The number and nature of student model variables in an assessment also depend on its purpose. A single variable characterizing overall proficiency might suffice in an assessment meant only to support a pass–fail decision. But a coached practice system to help students develop the same proficiency might require a finer grained student model in order to monitor how a student is doing on particular facets of skill and knowledge for which anyone can offer advice or suggest practice.

The student model in Fig. 9.1 depicts student-model variables as circles. The arrows represent important empirical or theoretical associations. A statistical model is used to manage knowledge about a given student's unobservable values for these variables at any given point in time, expressing current knowledge as a probability distribution that can be updated in light of new evidence. In particular, the student model takes the form of a fragment of a Bayesian inference network, or Bayes net (Spiegelhalter, Dawid, Lauritzen, & Cowell, 1993).

Evidence Models: What Behaviors or Performances Should Reveal Those Constructs, and What Is the Connection? An evidence model lays out the argument about why and how the observations in a given task situation constitute evidence about student-model variables.

Figure 9.1 shows that there are two parts to the evidence model. The *evaluative submodel* concerns extracting the salient features of whatever the student says, does, or creates in the task situation—the "work product" represented by the jumble of shapes in the rectangle at the far right of the evidence model. It is a unique human production, perhaps as simple as a response to a multiple choice item, or as complex as repeated evaluation and treatment cycles in a patient-management problem. The three squares coming out of the work product represent "observable variables," evaluative summaries of whatever the designer has determined are the key aspects of the performance in light of the assessment's purpose. Evaluation rules map unique human actions into a common interpretative framework, effectively laying out the argument about what is important in a performance. These rules can be as simple as determining whether the response to a multiple choice item is correct, or as complex as an expert's holistic evaluation of multiple aspects of an unconstrained patient-management solution. There can be several stages of evaluation and synthesis. The rules can be automated, demand human judgment, or require both in combination. Here the project connects with educational measurement research concerning models for rating and for automated scoring (e.g., Clauser et al., 1997).

The *statistical submodel* of the evidence model expresses how the observable variables depend, in probability, on student-model variables. This is effectively the argument for synthesizing evidence across multiple tasks or from different performances. Figure 9.1 shows that the observables are modeled as depending on some subset of the student-model variables. Familiar models from test theory, such as item response theory and latent class models, are examples of statistical models in which values of observed variables depend probabilistically on values of unobservable variables. These familiar models can be expressed as special cases of Bayes nets, and extend the ideas as appropriate to the nature of the student model and observable variables (Almond & Mislevy, 1999). Here the project connects with research concerning broader ranges of psychometric models, including those for cognitively diagnostic assessment (e.g., Adams, Wilson, & Wang, 1997) and the work on tree-based regression reported later in this chapter.

Task Models: What Tasks or Situations Should Elicit Those Behaviors? A task model provides a framework for constructing and describing the situations in which examinees act. Task model variables play many roles, including structuring task construction, focusing the evidentiary value of tasks, guiding assessment assembly, implicitly defining student-model variables, and conditioning the statistical argument between observations and student-model variables (Mislevy et al., 2000). A task model includes specifications for the environment in which the student will say, do, or produce something—for example, characteristics of stimulus material, instructions, help, tools, affordances. Here the project connects with research in theoretically based task construction (e.g., Embretson, 1998) and automated item generation (Irvine & Kyllonen, in press). The task model also includes specifications for the work product (i.e., the form in which what the student says, does, or produces will be captured).

Implementation and Delivery

Figure 9.2 sketches four principal processes that take place in an assessment. Some are compressed or implicit in familiar forms of assessment. Explicating them makes it easier to design reusable, interoperable components. The *Activity Selection Process* selects a task (or other activity) and instructs the *Presentation Process* to display it. When the examinee has finished interacting with the item, then the Presentation Process sends the results (a work product) to the *Evidence Identification Process*. This process identifies key observations about the results and passes them to the *Evidence Accumulation Process* that updates the examinee record. The Activity Selection Process then makes a decision about what to do next based on the current beliefs about the examinee.

Ensuring that these processes interact coherently requires standards for the messages they must pass from one to another. The protocols for defining the forms and the contents of the messages in a given assessment—importantly, not the forms or the content themselves—are specified in the evidence-centered object model. In this way, designing an assessment within the common evidence-centered framework ensures the coordination of operational processes. Analogously, fully specifying the assessment objects in the object model helps the assessment designer lay out specifications for task creation and statistical analyses.

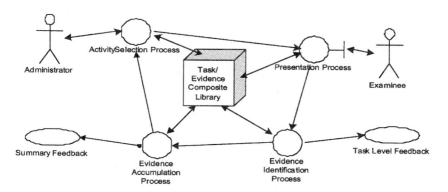

FIG. 9.2. Processes in the assessement cycle.

Summary of Evidence-Centered Assessment Design

Opportunities are borne of new technologies, and desires are borne of new understandings of learning—a new generation of assessment beckons. To realize the vision, it will be necessary to reconceive the present ways of thinking about assessment, from purposes and designs to production and delivery. The approach outlined here links assessment designs more explicitly to the inferences researchers want to draw and to the processes they need to create and deliver them. It provides a flexible framework for developing wide ranges of assessments for many purposes, while ensuring the coherence of contributions of the different bodies of expertise that are needed to make them work.

TREE-BASED REGRESSION: A NEW TOOL FOR UNDERSTANDING COGNITIVE SKILL REQUIREMENTS

Examinees who receive high test scores are expected to know more, or to be able to do more, than examinees who receive low test scores. But what are the additional aspects of knowledge or skill that the higher scoring examinees have mastered and the lower scoring examinees have failed to master? For some existing tests, especially tests that have been developed from cognitive design frameworks, information about the patterns of skill mastery that underlie strong and weak performances is likely to be readily available (cf. Embretson, 1998; Mislevy, Almond, Yan, & Steinberg, 1999). For a large number of established tests, however, processing characteristics are not specified during test development, so information about underlying skill mastery patterns may not be readily available.

A new procedure for distinguishing the increases in knowledge and capabilities that characterize performances at increasingly advanced levels on a test's reported score scale was introduced by Sheehan (1997). This new approach employs tree-based regression techniques to develop detailed descriptions of the observable item stimulus features that signal particular required skills. As demonstrated in Sheehan (1997), accurate information about the skills underlying performance on individual test items can lead to similarly accurate information about the skills underlying performance at successive score points. This new approach is described next. A subsequent section details an application of the approach to the problem of understanding the cognitive skills underlying performance on the Reading Comprehension Section of the Test of English as a Foreign Language (TOEFL).

The problem of evaluating hypotheses about required cognitive skills may be described in terms of its two functional subtasks: model development and model validation. Although it is useful to think of these two subtasks as two distinct activities occurring at two distinct points in time, in practice a large number of repeated development/validation cycles are likely to be needed. Within each cycle, hypotheses concerning the observable item stimulus features that signal particular required skills are refined and validated. Validation is accomplished by considering the extent to which hypothesized similarities in required skills are reflected in observed item performance data. The item performance data that is likely to be most useful for this purpose is the estimated item trace line or item characteristic curve (ICC).

Why should validation analyses be focused on explaining variation in estimated item trace lines? Experience has shown that instability in item performance characteristics is the exception rather than the rule. That is, most verbal and quantitative reasoning items exhibit relatively stable trace lines. The standard explanation for this stability is that the ICC has not changed because the skills needed to respond correctly to the item have not changed. In fact, when significant changes in an item's estimated trace line are observed, investigations aimed at evaluating alternative explanations for what is presumed to be a change in the item's profile of required skills are often initiated.

The stability results summarized suggest that it is appropriate to think of an item's observed trace line as a reflection of its underlying skill mastery requirements. Consequently, the validity of an assumed proficiency model may be investigated by considering the extent to which items classified as requiring similar combinations of skills are found to have exhibited similar trace lines.

In many large-scale educational assessments, item response theory (IRT) methods (Lord, 1980) are used to develop parametric representations for the observed item trace lines. The availability of a parametric representation vastly simplifies the problem of evaluating ICC similarity. In particular, when a parametric representation is available, ICC similarity may be approximated by considering the degree of similarity found in the sets of item parameters selected to represent each curve. When the relevant IRT model is unidimensional, these sets contain at most three parameters: the item difficulty parameter $(\hat{b})$, the item discrimination parameter $(\hat{a})$, and the item guessing parameter $(\hat{c})$. The item difficulty parameter characterizes variation in the horizontal location of the point of inflection, the item discrimination parameter characterizes variation in the slope of the curve at the point of inflection, and the item guessing parameter characterizes variation in the height of the lower asymptote. Of these three possibilities, the item difficulty parameter is most useful for evaluating ICC similarity because it anchors the curve at a particular proficiency level and numerous recovery studies have demonstrated that it is more accurately estimated than any of the other parameters. Thus, in the tree-based analysis, the response variable is the $(n \times 1)$ vector of IRT item difficulty parameters estimated for the n items considered in the analysis.

Tree models are fit in a forward stepwise fashion. The analysis begins with all items classified as measuring a single undifferentiated skill. Potential improvements to this model are evaluated by using a recursive partitioning algorithm to estimate the reductions in unexplained variation resulting from all possible splits of all possible hypothesized skills (Brieman, Friedman, Olshen, & Stone, 1984). This evaluation is accomplished using deviance, a statistical measure of the unexplained variation remaining after each new variable is added to the model. In the particular application described here, deviance is calculated as the sum of squared differences between the observed and predicted values of item difficulty.

At the conclusion of the model fitting process, the mean value of the response within each terminal node is taken as the predicted value of the response for each of the items in each of the nodes. The more homogeneous the node, the more accurate the prediction. Thus, the terminal node definitions resulting from a tree-based regression analysis provide an item clustering scheme that minimizes within cluster variation while simultaneously maximizing between cluster variation.

Application to the TOEFL Reading Comprehension Section

The TOEFL Reading Comprehension Section is a passage-based multiple choice test designed to assess the English language reading proficiency of nonnative English-speakers wishing to attend North American universities. A detailed analysis of the skills underlying performance on different types of TOEFL reading items was reported in Sheehan, Ginther, and Schedl (1999). This section summarizes the results obtained for items classified as measuring comprehension of explicitly stated information.

The tree-based regression model developed to explain difficulty variation among Explicit items is shown in Fig. 9.3. In this particular display, each node is plotted at a horizontal location determined from its estimated difficulty value and a vertical location determined from its estimated deviance value. The skills selected to define each split are listed on the edges connecting parent nodes to offspring nodes. The number of items assigned to each node is plotted as the node label. The root node at the top of the tree provides the total number of items considered in the analysis. Subsequent nodes detail a process whereby the items at each node are divided into smaller and smaller subsets, such that each new subset is defined in terms of a specified combination of hypothesized skills and contains items that are increasingly more homogeneous with respect to observed item difficulty. The six terminal nodes shown at the base of the tree define an item

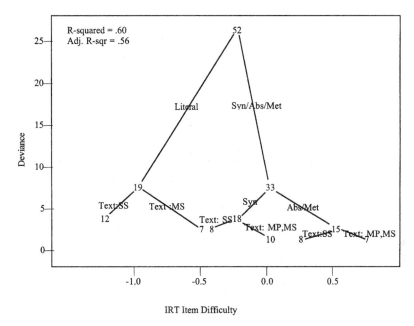

FIG. 9.3. A graphical representation of the regression tree estimated for items testing comprehension of explicitly stated information.

clustering scheme that can be used to classify any new or previously written item into one of the identified skill categories.

The tree confirms that two of the hypothesized skills are significantly related to observed variation in item difficulty. The first significant skill is the Level of Language Processing needed to complete the item. This skill has three levels: Literal, Synonymous, and Abstract/Metaphorical. As indicated by the first two splits shown in the tree, items classified at the Literal level tend to be clustered at the low end of the proficiency scale, items classified at the Synonymous level tend to be clustered near the middle of the proficiency scale, and items classified as requiring an understanding of abstract or metaphorical word use tend to be clustered at the high end of the proficiency scale. Illustrative items at each these three different proficiency levels are shown in Fig. 9.4.

The estimated regression tree also highlights the influential role of the Amount of Text variable. This variable distinguishes among items that only require processing of a Single Sentence (Text = SS), and items that require processing of Multiple Sentences Within the Same Paragraph (Text = MS), or Multiple Sentences that Span Different Paragraphs (Text = MP). Note that all three of the items in Fig. 9.4 only require processing of a Single Sentence. Thus, all three were classified as Text = SS, and, as indicated in the tree, all three were situated at the low end of their respective clusters.

Item E.03:

For how many [months of the year] were [temperatures below freezing] in the circumpolar region?

(A) 4-5 months

(B) 6 months

* (C) 8-9 months

(D) 12 months

Relevant Section of Text:

[Temperatures] in the northern lands were [below freezing] for eight or nine [months of the year].

Item C.17:

According to the passage, which of the following posed [the biggest obstacle to the development of military forts]?

(A) Insufficient shelter

(B) Shortage of materials

(C) Attacks by wild animals

* (D) Illness

Relevant Section of Text:

From the earliest colonial times throughout the nineteenth century, disease ranked as [the foremost problem in defense].

Item E.48:

[Neap tides occur when]

* (A) the Sun counteracts the Moon's gravitational attraction

(B) the moon is full

(C) the Moon is farthest from the sun

(D) waves created by the wind combine with the Moon's gravitational attraction

Relevant Section of Text:

Twice each month, at the quarters of the moon, [when] the Sun and Moon lie at the apexes of a triangular configuration and the pull of the Sun and the Moon are opposed, the moderate tidal movements called [neap tides occur].

FIG. 9.4. Sample explicit items requiring literal (Item E.03), synonymous (Item C.17), and abstract/metaphorical (Item E.48) comprehension skills. Correspondences between the item stem and the text are enclosed in brackets. Correspondences between the item key and the text are underlined.

Why should additional text contribute to additional difficulty? A further analysis of the items classified at each level of the Amount of Text variable revealed that items classified as Text = SS tend to be easier not because processing is limited to a single sentence, but rather because the reader encounters the correct information before having a chance to encounter any incorrect information. Similarly, items classified as Text = MS or Text = MP tend to be more difficult, not because more text has to be processed, but rather, because the additional text opens the door, so to speak, for distracting information to enter. This distracting information may come in either of two different forms: a noun phrase that matches literally or synonymously to one of the incorrect options, or a text feature, for example, a paragraph break or an organizing phrase such as "on the other hand," which erroneously signals that it is time to develop a new substructure.

Summary of Tree-Based Regression

The analysis of TOEFL reading comprehension items described yielded a great deal of useful information about the combinations of cognitive skills that underlie performance at increasingly advanced levels on the TOEFL reading comprehension scale. This information can be used to develop feedback about students' underlying strengths and weaknesses, write new test items that are optimally configured to yield accurate diagnostic inferences, and provide the collateral information needed to reduce pretest sample size requirements.

AUTOMATED ESSAY SCORING

The ability to score essays by computer has been examined since the early 1960s (Page, 1966). In the past year, based on new computational linguistic approaches, computer-based essay scoring has been used in commercial applications in assessment. ETS has been successfully using an automated essay scoring system, Electronic Essay Rater (e-rater), as one of the two readers for the Graduate Management Admissions Test (GMAT) Analytical Writing Assessment. This section reviews the components of this intelligent scoring system (Burstein et al., 1998; Burstein & Chodorow, 1999).

E-rater's current scoring performance is comparable to agreement between two human readers for scoring GMAT essays. Performance is approximately 92% for exact plus adjacent agreement between two readers (i.e., two human reader scores, based on a 6-point rating scale, differ by no more than a single point). This is also approximately the performance measured between a single human reader and e-rater scores. The comparable performance between human readers and e-rater on GMAT essays has lead to continued research in e-rater essay scoring for essay items on the Graduate Record Exam (GRE), the Test of English as a Foreign Language (TOEFL), and the College Board's Advanced Placement examination (AP).

E-rater was designed to score essays based on holistic scoring guides (scoring rubrics) (for sample GMAT scoring rubrics, see http://www.gmat. org).[1] Holistic scoring guides instruct the human reader to evaluate the es-

---

[1]The score range for GMAT essays is from 0–6, where 6 indicates essays with the highest competency.

say based on the quality of writing characteristics in an essay. For instance, the reader is to assess the quality of the writer's organization of ideas, syntactic variety, and appropriate vocabulary use. Holistic scoring requires the reader to evaluate the essay to ensure that the response answers the question (i.e., the writer is "on-topic"), but the reader is not looking for specific facts about the topic of the essay. Unlike the holistic rubric, a scoring rubric for a subject-based exam, like the AP essay exam, requires the reader to consider, not only the general quality of the writing in the response, but also the examinee's knowledge about the topic of the question.

Over the past year, e-rater research has taken new directions. Earlier GRE research examined the general use of e-rater for essays written by the GRE test-taking population and for e-rater performance on gender and ethnic subgroups. The GRE study indicated that e-rater scores were as reliable as human reader scores for the general and subgroup populations. Research for TOEFL is examining e-rater performance on nonnative English-speakers. In addition to scoring research, e-rater can be used to examine characteristics of writing that occur in nonnative-speaker essays that might influence reader scores. E-rater features can be used to facilitate an understanding of possible language or prompt-based affects that might be reflected in reader scores. Research using nonnative-speaker essay responses is examining the e-rater features selected to score nonnative-speakers across several native language groups. In addition, features selected by e-rater to score essays written by native speakers of specific language groups, such as Arabic, Spanish, and Japanese, are being examined. Examination of e-rater features used to score specific prompts can yield information about possible increased difficulty of prompts for specific language groups. Current research, using essay writing samples from the AP English Literature and U.S. History essay, evaluates the e-rater performance on subject-based essays.

Current E-rater Methodology and Heuristics

E-rater was designed to model holistic scoring rubric features, so that the e-rater score prediction is based on the same kinds of features that human readers use to score essays. Features in e-rater can be mapped to writing qualities such as organization of ideas, syntactic variety, and vocabulary usage. There are approximately 52 features used currently in e-rater that characterize discourse and syntax information, and vocabulary (or topical) content. These features are combined for operational e-rater scoring. However, for research purposes, the system is flexible in that features can be used to score, independently, and new features can also be easily added to e-rater.

Model Building and Essay Scoring. E-rater builds a new model for each test question. A set of 270 essays scored by at least two human readers is used for the training sample.[2] The distribution at each score point in the 270 training essays is as follows: five 0's, fifteen 1's, and fifty 2's through 6's.[3]

The syntactic, discourse, and topical analysis features to be described are identified for each of the 270 essays. Vectors of raw counts and ratios of occurrences are generated for syntactic and discourse structure information. Scores generated for the two topical analysis components are also generated. All of the feature information is submitted to a stepwise linear regression. For each prompt, the regression selects the subset of predictive features. Typically, from 8 to 12 features are selected. Although every model has a different combination of features, in the 75 models that are currently being used, the five most frequently occurring features are the topical analysis score by argument, the topical analysis score by essay, the number of subjunctive auxiliary words, the ratio of subjunctive auxiliary words to total words in the essay, and the total number of argument development terms. The coefficient weightings for each of the predictive features generated from the regression for each prompt are then used to score essays from that prompt.

Discourse Cues and Organization of Ideas. Organization of ideas is a criterion that the GMAT scoring guide asks human readers to consider in assigning essay score. E-rater contains a lexicon based on the conceptual framework of conjunctive relations from Quirk, Greenbaum, Leech, and Svartik (1985) in which cue terms, such as "In summary" and "In conclusion," are classified as conjuncts used for summarizing. The conjunct classifiers contain information about whether or not the item is a kind of discourse "development" term (e.g., "for example" and "because"), or whether it is more likely to be used to begin a discourse statement. It also contains heuristics that define the syntactic or essay-based structures in which these terms must appear to be considered as discourse markers. For example, in order for the word "first" to be considered a discourse marker, it must not be a nominal modifier—as in the sentence, "The first time I went to Europe was in 1982," in which "first" modifies the noun "time." Instead, "first" must occur as an adverbial conjunct to be considered a dis-

---

[2]Essays are scored by two human readers if the readers' scores differ by no more than a single point. A third human reader is used in the case where the first two scores are discrepant (i.e., the readers disagree by more than a single point).

[3]To date, this sample composition has given us the best cross-validation results. Some previous studies, experimenting with smaller training samples with this fairly flat distribution, or samples that reflect more directly the natural distribution of the data at each score point, have shown lower performance in scoring cross-validation sets of 500–900 essays.

course marker, as in the sentence, "First, it has often been noted that length is highly correlated with essay score." The cue term lexicon and the associated heuristics are used by e-rater to automatically annotate a high level discourse structure of each essay. These annotations are also used by the system to partition each essay into its separate arguments, which are used by the system's topical analysis component to analyze the topical content of the essay.

Syntactic Structure and Syntactic Variety.   The GMAT rubric criteria specify that the syntactic variety used by a candidate should be directly related to the essay score. The e-rater system uses an ETS-enhanced version of the CASS syntactic chunker (Abney, 1997), referred to here as the *parser*. The parser identifies several syntactic structures in the essay responses, such as subjunctive auxiliary verbs (e.g., would, should, might), and complex clausal structures, such as complement, infinitive, and subordinate clauses. Recognition of such features in an essay yields information about its syntactic variety.

Topical Analysis and Vocabulary Usage.   Vocabulary usage is another criterion listed in human reader scoring guides. To capture use of vocabulary, or identification of topic, e-rater uses content vector analyses based on the vector-space model commonly found in information retrieval applications. The content vector analyses are done at the level of the essay (big bag of words) or the argument.

Training essays are converted into vectors of word frequencies, and the frequencies are then transformed into word weights.[4] These weight vectors populate the training space. To score a test essay, the essay is converted into a weight vector and a search is conducted to find the training vectors most similar to it, as measured by the cosine between the test and training vectors. The closest matches among the training set are used to assign a score to the test essay.

E-rater uses two different forms of the general procedure sketched here. In one form, for looking at topical analysis at the essay level, each of the 270 training essays is represented by a separate vector in the training space. The

---

[4]Word (or term) weight reflects not only a word's frequency in the essay but also its distribution across essays. E-rater's formula for the weight of word w in essay j is:

$$\text{weight}_{wj} = (\text{freq}_{wj}/\text{maxfreq}_j) * \log(\text{nessays}/\text{essays}_w)$$

where freq_{wj} is the frequency of word w in essay j, maxfreq_j is the frequency of the most frequent word in essay j, nessays is the total number of training essays, and essays_w is the number of training essays that contain w. The first part of the formula measures the relative importance of the word in the essay. The second part gauges its specificity across essays, so that a word that appears in many essays will have a lower weight than one that appears in only a few. In the extreme case, a word that appears in all essays (e.g., "the") has a weight of 0.

score assigned to the test essay is a weighted mean of the scores for the six training essays whose vectors are closest to the vector of the test essay. This score is computed using the following formula, rounded to the nearest integer:

$$\text{Score for test essay } t = \Sigma(\text{cosine}_{tj} * \text{score}_j)/\Sigma(\text{cosine}_{tj})$$

where j ranges over the six closest training essays, score_j is the human rater score for training essay j, and cosine_{tj} is the cosine between test essay t and training essay j.

The other form of content vector analysis in the system combines all of the training essays for each score category and populates the training space with just six "supervectors," one each for scores 1–6. This method is used to evaluate the vocabulary usage at the argument level. The test essay is evaluated one argument at a time. Each argument is converted into a vector of word weights and compared to the six vectors in the training space. The closest vector is found and its score is assigned to the argument. This process continues until all the arguments have been assigned a score. The overall score for the test essay is an adjusted mean of the argument scores using the following formula, rounded to the nearest integer:

$$\text{Score for test essay } t = (\Sigma\text{argscore}_j + \text{nargs}_t)/(\text{nargs}_t + 1)$$

where j ranges over the arguments in test essay t, argscore_j is the score of argument j, and nargs_t is the number of arguments in t. Using this adjusted mean has the overall effect of reducing, slightly, the score for essays with few arguments, and of increasing somewhat the score of essays with many arguments.

E-rater Performance for GMAT.   Although several research studies are underway that evaluate e-rater performance, the most comprehensive results are from GMAT data, because e-rater is in operational use for GMAT. Recent results for GMAT essay data show the following agreement between humans and e-rater. Two humans show approximately 50% exact agreement and 92% exact-plus-adjacent agreement. One human and e-rater show approximately 46% exact agreement and 92% exact-plus-adjacent agreement.

Summary of Automated Essay Scoring

Although e-rater began as an automated essay scoring technology limited to numerical essay rating for holistic essay ratings, its potential as an assessment tool for broader applications has grown considerably.

The e-rater scoring engine is continually being worked on to better understand and improve its current performance. In addition, e-rater's uses can be expanded through its continually expanding feature set. Features in e-rater models are being used to examine both machine and human essay scoring of ethnic, gender, and language subgroups. Additionally, the feasibility of e-rater scoring for subject-based exams is being evaluated.

Research is also being done to design computational models for automatic generation of diagnostic information about essays. A current study for the College Board is experimenting with the use of features generated from the current version of e-rater and hierarchical rhetorical relation features for modeling diagnostics for English composition tests. These essay data were collected and scored by human readers for overall quality of writing, and also on individual features of writing (e.g., rhetorical strategy and organization of ideas) (Burstein, Breland, Kubota, Wolff, & Marcu, submitted for publication). Experiments are also being done with the use of automatically generated essay summarization for use with e-rater scoring and modeling of diagnostic information. Essay summaries could be instructive for test-takers in that the summaries theoretically contain the essence of the writer's essay. Test-takers might use summarization text to evaluate how the essential information in their own essay compares to an essay that received a higher score (Burstein & Marcu, 2000).

LANGUAGE PROCESSING TOOLS
FOR TEST CONSTRUCTION

Natural Language Processing (NLP) research is helping to increase the productivity and creativity of test developers. This section reviews tools that automate item review processes as well as tools that aid in item generation and item difficulty estimation.

A Lexical Overlap Detection Tool

Detecting lexical overlap among items in a test pool is a process that has been fully automated. Screening for lexical overlap is necessary to avoid the possibility of having the same word appear in two items on the same exam. When each new item is written, the root forms of all the words in the item must be recorded. Determining those root forms and inserting them in the right fields was a laborious task that test developers once had to do manually. Today, a lexical overlap detection tool does it for them automatically. This tool uses a word morphology grammar to produce a list of root forms of words in stems, keys, and distracters for each test item, thus freeing the test developer from the need to perform this task.

Analogy and Antonym Helper Tools

An Analogy/Antonym Helper tool set was developed to help verbal test item writers during the process of creating novel analogy and antonym items and variants. The tool set includes two online lexical databases, WordNet (Fellbaum, 1998) and the Breland word frequency database (Breland & Jenkins, 1997), and it provides three functions to assist test developers—the *WordNet browser*, a WordNet *definition search tool*, and a lexical *difficulty index tool*.

The WordNet database contains definitions of over 80,000 nouns, verbs, adjectives, and adverbs organized in a network to indicate a variety of relations among words, including synonyms, hyponyms, antonyms, and others. The Breland word frequency database contains standardized frequency indices for over 100,000 words. The WordNet browser allows item writers to navigate the lexical network to find words that stand in specific relations to others (e.g., synonyms and antonyms). The definition search tool allows item writers to search for words with specific attributes in their definitions. For example, one test developer suggested that in creating an analogy around the word "plummet," meaning "to drop sharply," he might want to search for other words whose definition contains the attribute "sharply." The definition search tool returns the words "swerve," "chop," "pluck," and others. The difficulty index tool gives verbal item writers two pieces of information they can use to judge the difficulty level of a word—the word's Breland frequency index and the word's total number of senses in WordNet. Research has shown these measures to be highly predictive of difficulty levels for antonyms.

An even stronger predictor of difficulty is the frequency of the specific sense of a word in a given context. However, disambiguating word senses automatically is a nontrivial task. Basic research is being conducted in this area to produce additional tools to aid verbal item writers.

Item Difficulty Estimation and Item Variant Generation Tools

Additional language processing tools are being designed to help test developers identify certain linguistic features in passages and items that correlate with item difficulty levels and specific reading comprehension skills. Test developers can then manipulate these features to create items and variants with specific difficulty levels and language skill requirements.

Vocabulary Difficulty Estimation. Good estimates of vocabulary difficulty can help test developers in creating items that fill the need for items with specific difficulty levels. A somewhat more sophisticated tool has been developed for estimating vocabulary difficulty. This tool, which incorporates a part-of-speech tagger, provides a composite measure computed from the word's frequency index and its number of senses when used as a particular part of speech. Knowing how a word is used in context (e.g., as a noun, adjective or verb) helps to refine its vocabulary difficulty estimate. For example, without any context, the word "marked" would be assigned a relatively low difficulty level based on its high frequency index and its high number of senses (14 senses). But in the sentence "Citizens of prosperous middle-class republics have always shown a 'marked' taste for portraiture," its use as an adjective limits its number of senses (three senses), which results in a relatively high difficulty level.

Synonym Generation Help. A tool that generates synonyms for a word in a test item, along with difficulty levels and definitions for those synonyms, can help test developers produce variants of the item with prespecified difficulty estimates. For example, the test developer's synonym tool produces over 30 synonyms, along with their difficulty estimates and definitions, for the verb "carry" in the sentence, "Some of the lithospheric plates *carry* ocean floor and others *carry* land masses . . ." Examples of those synonyms and corresponding difficulty levels include: transport (4), hold (1), pack (1), take (3), channel (4), conduct (4), run (1), bear (1), contain (4), hold (4), convey (4), express (4), . . . , where, on a 5-point scale, 1 indicates least difficult and 5 indicates most difficult. Note that the synonym tool returns synonyms for all senses of the verb "carry," so the test developer must choose synonyms that match the appropriate sense of the term in its given context when creating an item variant.

Literal-Synonymous-Metaphorical Reasoning. An important goal of research is to unobtrusively capture the expert judgments made by test developers as they work, annotating the database of test items so that the information can be used to help devise future tools for automating the sense disambiguation process. The NLP tool set for reading comprehension also contains tools for highlighting literal and synonymous overlap between words in items and words in the text of the reading passage. Research has shown that items exhibiting literal matches between the key (i.e., the correct option) and the text of a passage tend to be less difficult, whereas literal word matches between a distracter (i.e., an incorrect option) and the passage tend to increase the difficulty of an item. Research has also shown that items exhibiting literal overlap with text in the passage tend to be less difficult than those with synonymous overlap. Furthermore, items that have no overlap with text in the passage (i.e., items that require metaphorical or other inferential reasoning) are invariably more difficult.

Summary of Language Processing Tools for Test Construction

The current NLP tool set helps test developers determine whether items require literal reasoning, synonymous reasoning, or some undetermined higher level of inferential reasoning, such as the use of metaphor. As with the synonym tool, another important goal of ETS's language processing research is to unobtrusively capture test developers' expert judgments about these skill levels as they create items. The resulting annotated items can then be linked to skill level proficiency scales, thus providing the potential for giving diagnostic or instructional feedback to examinees.

AUTOMATIC ITEM GENERATION

Large-scale testing organizations are in the midst of an item capacity crisis. To stem potential breaches of security brought on by the adoption of continuous computer-based testing, as well as respond to legislative calls for disclosure (Linn, 1989, p. 8), the demand for items has grown markedly in the last several years. By all indications, the demand for calibrated, operational-ready items will continue to grow in the near future (Hattie, Jaeger, & Bond, 1999, p. 410).

The use of automatically generated item variants has been put forth as one potentially attractive way to respond to the item capacity problem. In full flower, the item variant vision involves the automatic or semi-automatic generation of items in accord with some principled theory that can be used to predict the performance of the generated items (Bejar, 1993; Singley & Bennett, in press). The deployment of such variants is attractive from a cost standpoint because, presumably, they would be cheaper to produce than handcrafted singleton items and, if accompanied by predictions of difficulty, could be calibrated using smaller pretest sample sizes. Aside from these potential cost savings, there is the intellectual appeal of having the clarity of understanding and level of control that such a principled generation of items would entail. Thus, such an approach has the promise of moving us toward a more principled and deliberate design of tests.

This integrated vision, involving the coupling of automatic item generation and the model-based prediction of item performance, has already been realized and successfully deployed for item types that might be characterized as well-circumscribed and knowledge lean (e.g., the British Army Recruit Battery aptitude tests used by the British military and developed at the University of Plymouth in the UK; Dann, Tapsfield, & Collis, 1997). But the item types for many large-scale admissions tests, such as the SAT and the GRE, have more of an achievement component and therefore tend to be knowledge rich and range widely across broadly defined domains such as language and mathematics. Such item types present formidable challenges to principled item generation. Nevertheless, some progress has been made in realizing this full vision, most notably in the relatively well-structured areas of quantitative reasoning, analytical reasoning, antonyms, and analogies.

An Example: The Math Test Creation Assistant

In the Test Creation Assistant project at ETS, a system has been developed for the principled semi-automatic generation of math item variants. The cornerstone underlying this thinking with respect to item generation is the notion of a problem schema (see VanLehn, 1989, p. 545), which consists of a set of variables and constraints that defines a problem's deep structure. Given this notion of a schema, a wide spectrum of item generation possibilities exists, ranging from the deep to the superficial. For instance, given a set of primitive equations (e.g., distance = rate × time, part + part = whole), generate a set of interesting problem schemas. These schemas could be arranged into a taxonomy of sorts and could serve as a repository of ideas for test developers. Some possibilities of schema use include the following: (a) Given a particular schema (e.g., the motion or rate schema defined earlier), generate interesting structural elaborations. This involves adding one or more constraints. For example, in the motion schema, some relation could be added between the rate for one leg of a trip and the second (e.g., the rate uphill is half the rate downhill). (b) Given a particular schema, generate all the possible problem structures. A problem structure is defined as a particular configuration of given and goal variables. (c) Given a problem structure, generate and/or select a problem context. Thus, the motion schema could be instantiated in a hiking context, a boating context, and so forth. (d) Given a context, vary the noun referents for problem variables and generate different sets of values for given variables. For example, "Juanita" becomes "Tom" and the total time changes from 10 to 20 hours. And (e) Given a context, noun referents and variable values, generate a natural language cover story.

The Mathematics Test Creation Assistant is an initial attempt at fleshing out the vision described. The Test Creation Assistant contains an editor and facilities for model browsing, model creation, and variant generation. The editor uses Microsoft Word. In the Test Creation Assistant, a model represents a schematized description of a class of questions from which draft test items are automatically generated for the test developer to review and revise. To begin, the developer selects an existing model or creates a new one either from an existing test item or anew. Existing models can be varied by the developer to form a model "family;" that is, a collection of models that shares variables, constraints, and invariant text.

Within a family, models can be hierarchically organized by their underlying schematic structures. The hierarchy is defined in terms of shared schema equations, such that a child schema inherits all the equations of its parent schema, and perhaps supplies one or two more. Parent–child relationships between schemas are designated in the interface by indentation in the list of models, as is done in many displays of directory-subdirectory structures for computer file systems.

Table 9.1 is a schematic summary of the contents of the window seen by a test developer. The table represents the elements of the Test Creation Assistant's Model Workshop, where the test developer creates and edits item models. These models are created within Microsoft Word templates designed around particular item types. Currently, the Test Creation Assistant supports three such templates: standard multiple choice (as shown in Table 9.1), quantitative comparison (used on the GRE General Test and the SAT I), and data sufficiency (a GMAT item type). Figures, charts, tables, pictures, audio, and video—indeed, any Microsoft Word object—can be incorporated.

Creating an item model from an existing item is basically a two-step process: First, the user replaces literal strings of text and/or numbers in the original stem and options with variables. Second, the user defines constraints that tell the system something about how the variables should be instantiated. A critical feature of the system is that these constraints are defined declaratively: The user simply states the constraints and it is the system's responsibility to figure out how to solve them simultaneously.

The Test Creation Assistant screen shows the test developer the results of this process for a word problem. In the top left section of the screen is the item stem with the variables in the problem clearly identified. These are ele-

TABLE 9.1
Contents of the Computer Display Seen by a Test Developer

Left Portion of Window	Right Portion of Window
Item stem: e.g., a distance–rate–time word problem requiring distance to be calculated from rate and time	*Variables*: e.g., the distance or time specified in the problem.
Key or correct answer: e.g., 100 miles.	*Variation constraints*: e.g., equations for calculating relations between distance, rate, and time.
Distractor 1: e.g., 50 miles.	*Distractor constraints*: e.g., the relations leading to incorrect alternatives.
Distractor 2: e.g., 10 miles.	*Test developer comments*: e.g., comments on item difficulty.
Distractor 3: e.g., 5 miles *Distractor 4*: e.g., 75 miles.	

ments that the test developer can alter to produce different items. All remaining elements are literals that remain constant across variants. Some
variables are *ntuples*, that is, string variables whose values change in syn-
chrony, thereby allowing the situational context to be changed from one
variant to the next in a substantively coordinated way.

In the right-hand pane, the test developer sees the variable definitions,
variation constraints, and the distracter constraints. Variables are defined
by indicating their type (string, real, integer, untyped) and specifying the
values they can take on. For string variables, the test developer may either
type in a list of values or import them from a library of files built specifically
to support the instantiation of nonnumeric variables. In the case of numeric variables (which will be the only variables for pure mathematical
problems), the user can define a range for the variable, as well as step size
(e.g., the variable may be specified as ranging from 1 to 100 in steps of 5).
By specifying the range and step size, the user can control critical features
of the variants that may affect problem difficulty. Another way to specify the
values for a numeric variable is by writing new equations that derive the
value of the current variable from the values of others.

The variation-constraints window contains the schema equations for the
problem being constructed (e.g., a distance–rate–time problem). The
distracter-constraints window shows how each of the distracters is computed, for example, by adding or subtracting a constant from the key (correct response). Thus, the system automatically defines, as constraints, the
equations that characterize the item's schema. The variables in the schema
equations automatically become variables that can be referenced in the
template, and any values supplied by the system for these variables will necessarily satisfy the schema equations.

One important feature of the system is that it is quite easy to modify the
templates themselves and thus greatly increase the range of variation associated with a particular parent item. By switching information between the
stem and the options, it is easy to create a new template that asks the
examinee to solve a modified version of the same problem. For instance, in
a distance–rate–time problem, in which the constraints of the problem are
defined by the relations among distance and rate and time, test variants
might ask for responses that require time or rate or distance calculations, or
distance calculations incorporating a test-developer modified time variable.
This amounts to changing the configuration of givens and goals across
problems. When the developer believes the model is ready for generating
variants, the model can be tested to make sure that it is sufficiently constrained. To aid in model debugging, variables, variation constraints, and
distracter constraints can be tested simultaneously (as classes or individually). When the model tests successfully, the system is prepared to generate
variants. Variants can, of course, be edited by hand. The developer may

wish to change specific words, so as to make the item more realistic, or to adjust various values of the problem, such as distance, rate, or time required in a methematics word problem.

A preliminary Test Creation Assistant tool has also been built that allows the test developer to estimate item difficulty. This tool incorporates initial models for both the GRE and the GMAT. At present, all model variables are entered by the test developer. The GRE model includes the domain (arithmetic, algebra, geometry), whether the item is real or pure, the type of computation required, cognitive demand (procedural, conceptual, higher order), and whether certain concepts are involved (e.g., probability, percent of a percent, percent change, linear equality).

Summary of Automatic Item Generation

Full and proper use of automatically generated item variants will require answers to some thorny theoretical questions. The complete vision will only be realized when there are robust models of item difficulty based on collateral information. Also, currently there is a lack of any systematic understanding of the long-term impact of variant use on test validity: How does exposure to (or coaching on) one variant effect performance on another? To what extent will the adoption of variants systematize and/or constrict the sampling of the domain, that is, the representation of the construct? These questions need answers before moving forward with complete confidence.

CONCLUSIONS

This chapter has described several uses of technology in assessment, including new methods for planning, designing, and implementing assessments (evidence-centered design), computer tools that assist test developers in creating valid and reliable test items (language processing tools for test construction; automatic item generation), psychometric techniques that provide informative conceptions of human performance (tree-based regression), and automated techniques for the scoring of complex written responses (automated essay scoring). For instance, the work on tree-based regression shows how information from new psychometric techniques can be used to develop feedback about students' underlying strengths and weaknesses and thus to help write effective diagnostic test items. The work on language tools for test developers suggests how annotation systems can help link test items to skill level proficiency scales, thus improving their use for instructional purposes. All of these techniques support various elements in the evidence-centered design approach, which was reviewed. Beyond the work reported here, promising developments in computer applications, such as authoring systems, make it possible to construct multimedia instruction rapidly. Important human activities in assessment, such as collaborative decision making and exchange of test results (writing and speech samples), can also be enhanced through technology.

Clearly there has been progress. Along with that progress, new social, technical, and political challenges have emerged (cf. Rochlin, 1997). The indirect effects of technology in assessment are only too apparent to those who develop tests. Radical changes in the environment of test development affect many in the assessment community; those who score tests, those who use tests, and those who do research on tests. At the project level, for instance, a focus on team-oriented activities dominates. People whose work was once relatively independent now work mostly in task-oriented group sessions. Work is often done within the context of computer-based item development systems that seem to constrain creativity. The business of essay scoring is increasingly taken over by computers. Human test scorers worry that they may be replaced by computers. Competition is growing. Significant growth in the number of organizations that promise to deliver and manage assessment creates pressure for more rapid test production and delivery. As test technologies multiply, there is increased need to establish and maintain recognized assessment standards through training and collaborative efforts among academics, corporations, and the public.

The lack of technology integration is perhaps the greatest weakness in assessment if researchers want to have more realistic tests (Frase, 1997). Technologies, such as speech recognition and speech production, are poorly integrated in current teaching and testing systems. For instance, language instruction systems often rely on self-evaluation, or on preconstructed multiple choice tests, to provide feedback to learners. An automated naturalistic learning system might include some combined assessment of reading, writing, speaking, and listening. To construct such a system would require integrating elements of technology, psychometrics, and instructional design. The Conceptual Assessment Framework, described in this chapter, has the potential to manage important aspects of this integration.

The rapidity of technological change has created disparities among elements of the assessment community. These disparities affect the ways that research and development are done. Consider the time scales within which progress takes place in technology. Computing speed and miniaturization advance rapidly. The development of software, to make use of those capabilities, lags behind. Research on software usability and models for educational implementation lag even more. Developments in educational and testing theory lag even more. To meet the growing demand for new and different technology-based tests, the pace of research and development must quicken. The idealized model of scientific research, as long-term controlled experimentation leading to the resolution of major theoretical issues, is clearly the wrong focus for education and assessment in an age of rapid technology change. An engineering approach, using the tools and techniques of science to evaluate evolutionary changes in educational products and processes (cf. Landauer, 1995), seems the better model. Such a model is consistent with the Conceptual Assessment Framework described in this chapter.

There are many things that remain a mystery. In the area of test generation, as discussed in the section on item generation, there is currently a lack of systematic understanding of the long-term impact of the use of item variants on test validity: How does experience with one variant affect performance on subsequent tests? Will computational models overly constrain further test development? On the other hand, in attempting to automate human processes, researchers may come to a better understanding of the strengths and weaknesses of the constructs that humans use to assess writing and other complex tasks.

The projects described herein can be used to create a broader range of options for those who develop tests and those who take them. Ultimately, there should be some concern for the effects of assessment on teaching and learning. Are the right concepts being tested? Will technology-based assessments reveal and encourage the highest levels of human accomplishment, or will they merely be improved means to unimproved ends (Postman, 1993)?

ACKNOWLEDGMENTS

We are grateful to Dennis Quardt, Eiji Muraki, Catherine Hombo, Brenda Lim, and Liane Patsula for their work in alternative modeling techniques for e-rater scoring. We thank Daniel Marcu of the Information Sciences Institute of the University of Southern California for generating rhetorical parses and summarizations of essays, and for numerous discussions that contribute to the expansion of e-rater research. We gratefully acknowledge GMAT, GRE, TOEFL, College Board, and ETS for their continued support of this research.

REFERENCES

Abney, S. (1997). Part-of-speech tagging and partial parsing. In S. Young & G. Bloothooft (Eds.), *Corpus-based methods in language and speech* (pp. 118–136). Dordrecht: Kluwer.

Adams, R., Wilson, M. R., & Wang, W.-C. (1997). The multidimensional random coefficients multinomial logit model. *Applied Psychological Measurement, 21,* 1–23.

Almond, R. G. (1995). *Graphical belief modeling.* London: Chapman & Hall.

Almond, R. G., & Mislevy, R. J. (1999). Graphical models and computerized adaptive testing. *Applied Psychological Measurement, 23,* 223–237.

Almond, R. G., Steinberg, L. S., & Mislevy, R. J. (2000). *A sample assessment using the four process framework.* White paper prepared for the IMS Working Group on Question and Test Inter-Operability. Princeton, NJ: Educational Testing Service.

Bejar, I. I. (1993). A generative approach to psychological and educational measurement. In N. Frederiksen, R. J. Mislevy, & I. I. Bejar (Eds.), *Test theory for a new generation of tests* (pp. 323–359). Hillsdale, NJ: Lawrence Erlbaum Associates.

Breland, H., & Jenkins, L. (1997). *English word frequency statistics: Analysis of a selected corpus of 14 million tokens.* New York: College Entrance Examination Board.

Brieman, L., Friedman, J. H., Olshen, R., & Stone, C. J. (1984). *Classification and regression trees.* Belmont, CA: Wadsworth.

Burstein, J., Breland, H., Kubota M., Wolff, S., & Marcu, D. (submitted for publication). *An evaluation of computational modeling of writing features in essays.* New York: College Entrance Examination Board.

Burstein, J., & Chodorow, M. (1999). Automated essay scoring for nonnative English speakers. In *Joint Symposium of the Association of Computational Linguistics and the International Association of Language Learning Technologies, Workshop on Computer-Mediated Language Assessment and Evaluation of Natural Language Processing* (pp. 68–75). College Park, MD: Association for Computational Linguistics.

Burstein, J., Kukich, K., Wolff, S., Lu, C., Chodorow, M., Braden-Harder, L., & Harris, M. D. (1998, August). Automated scoring using a hybrid feature identification technique. In the *Proceedings of the 36th Annual Meeting of the Association of Computational Linguistics, and 17th International Conference on Computational Linguistics* (pp. 206–210). Montreal, Canada. San Francisco, CA: Morgan Kaufmann.

Burstein, J., & Marcu, D. (2000, August). Benefits of modularity in an automated scoring system. In *Proceedings of the Workshop on Using Toolsets and Architectures to Build NLP Systems, 18th International Conference on Computational Linguistics* (pp. 44–50). Saarbrucken, Germany. San Francisco, CA: Morgan Kaufmann.

Clark, L. A., & Pregibon, D. (1992). Tree-based models. In J. M. Chambers & T. J. Hastie (Eds.), *Statistical models in S* (pp. 377–419). Pacific Grove, CA: Wadsworth.

Clauser, B. E., Ross, L. P., Clyman, S. G., Rose, K. M., Margolis, M. J., Nungester, R. J., Piemme, T. E., Chang, L., El-Bayoumi, G., Malakoff, G. L., & Pincetl, P. S. (1997). Development of a scoring algorithm to replace expert rating for scoring a complex performance-based assessment. *Applied Measurement in Education, 10,* 345–358.

Dann, P., Tapsfield, P., & Collis, J. (1997). *The theory, research and development of the British Army Recruit Battery.* Plymouth, UK: University of Plymouth Human Assessment Laboratory.

Embretson, S. E. (1998). A cognitive design system approach to generating valid tests: Application to abstract reasoning. *Psychological Methods, 3,* 380–396.

Fellbaum, C. (Ed.). (1998). *WordNet: An electronic lexical database.* Cambridge, MA: MIT Press.

Frase, L. T. (1997). Integrating technology and test design. In V. Kohonen, A. Huhta, L. Kurki-Suonio, & S. Luoma (Eds.), *Current developments and alternatives in language assessment—Proceedings of LTRC 96* (pp. 538–542). Finland: University of Jyvaskyla.

Frase, L. T. (2000). Adapting to change in the new millennium. *T.H.E. (Technological Horizons in Education), 27*(6), 47.

Frase, L. T., Gong, B., Hansen, E., Kaplan, R., Katz, I., & Singley, K. (1998). *Technologies for language testing* (TOEFL Monograph Series MS-11). Princeton, NJ: Educational Testing Service.

Gelman, A., Carlin, J. B., Stern, H. S., & Rubin, D. B. (1995). *Bayesian data analysis.* London: Chapman & Hall.

Glaser, R., Lesgold, A., & Lajoie, S. (1987). Toward a cognitive theory for the measurement of achievement. In R. Ronning, J. Glover, J. C. Conoley, & J. Witt (Eds.), *The influence of cognitive psychology on testing and measurement: The Buros-Nebraska Symposium on measurement and testing* (Vol. 3, pp. 41–85). Hillsdale, NJ: Lawrence Erlbaum Associates.

Hansen, E. G., Forer, D. C., & Mang, L. S. (2000, February). Making movies on the Web accessible to people with disabilities. In *Proceedings of the international meeting of M/SET (Mathematics/Science Education & Technology) 2000* (pp. 197–201). Charlottesville, VA: Association for the Advancement of Computing in Education.

Hattie, J., Jaeger, R. M., & Bond, L. (1999). Persistent methodological questions in educational testing. In A. Iran-Nejad, & P. D. Pearson (Eds.), *Review of research in education* (Vol. 24, pp. 393–446). Washington, DC: American Educational Research Association.

Irvine, S., & Kyllonen, P. (Eds.). (in press). *Generating items for cognitive tests: Theory and practice.* Hillsdale, NJ: Lawrence Erlbaum Associates.

Landauer, T. (1995). *The trouble with computers.* Cambridge, MA: MIT Press.

Linn, R. L. (1989). Current perspectives and future directions. In R. L. Linn (Ed.), *Educational measurement* (pp. 1–10). New York: Macmillan.

Lord, F. M. (1980). *Applications of item response theory to practical testing problems.* Hillsdale, NJ: Lawrence Erlbaum Associates.

Messick, S. (1994). The interplay of evidence and consequences in the validation of performance assessments. *Educational Researcher, 23*(2), 13–23.

Mislevy, R. J. (1994). Evidence and inference in educational assessment. *Psychometrika, 59*, 439–483.

Mislevy, R. J., Almond, R. G., Yan, D., & Steinberg, L. S. (1999). Bayes nets in educational assessment: Where do the numbers come from? In K. B. Laskey & H. Prade (Eds.), *Proceedings of the Fifteenth Conference on Uncertainty in Artificial Intelligence* (pp. 437–446). San Francisco, CA: Morgan Kaufmann.

Mislevy, R. J., & Gitomer, D. H. (1996). The role of probability-based inference in an intelligent tutoring system. *User-Modeling and User-Adapted Interaction, 5*, 253–282.

Mislevy, R. J., Steinberg, L. S., & Almond, R. G. (in press). On the roles of task model variables in assessment design. In S. Irvine & P. Kyllonen (Eds.), *Generating items for cognitive tests: Theory and practice* (pp. 97–128). Hillsdale, NJ: Lawrence Erlbaum Associates.

Mislevy, R. J., Steinberg, L. S., Breyer, F. J., Almond, R. G., & Johnson, L. (1999a). A cognitive task analysis, with implications for designing a simulation-based assessment system. *Computers and Human Behavior, 15*, 335–374.

Mislevy, R. J., Steinberg, L. S., Breyer, F. J., Almond, R. G., & Johnson, L. (1999b, September). *Making sense of data from complex assessments.* Paper presented at the 1999 CRESST Conference, Los Angeles, CA.

Page, E. B. (1966). The imminence of grading essays by computer. *Phi Delta Kappan, 48*, 238–243.

Postman, Neil. (1993). *Technopoly.* New York: Vintage.

Quirk, R., Greenbaum, S., Leech, G., & Svartik, J. (1985). *A comprehensive grammar of the English language.* New York: Longman.

Rochlin, G. I. (1997). *Trapped in the net: The unanticipated consequences of computerization.* Princeton, NJ: Princeton University Press.

Steinberg, L. S., & Gitomer, D. G. (1996). Intelligent tutoring and assessment built on an understanding of a technical problem-solving task. *Instructional Science, 24*, 223–258.

Schum, D. A. (1994). *The evidential foundations of probabilistic reasoning.* New York: Wiley.

Sheehan, K. M. (1997). A tree-based approach to proficiency scaling and diagnostic assessment. *Journal of Educational Measurement, 34*, 333–352.

Sheehan, K. M., Ginther, A., & Schedl, M. (1999). *Development of a proficiency scale for the TOEFL Reading Comprehension Section* (TOEFL Research Report). Princeton, NJ: Educational Testing Service.

Singley, M. K., & Bennett, R. E. (in press). Item generation and beyond: applications of schema theory to mathematics assessment. In S. Irvine & P. Kyllonen (Eds.), *Generating items for cognitive tests: Theory and practice* (pp. 361–384). Hillsdale, NJ: Lawrence Erlbaum Associates.

Spiegelhalter, D. J., Dawid, A. P., Lauritzen, S. L., & Cowell, R. G. (1993). Bayesian analysis in expert systems. *Statistical Science, 8,* 219–283.

VanLehn, K. (1999). Problem solving and cognitive skill acquisition. In M. I. Posner (Ed.), *Foundations of cognitive science* (pp. 527–579). Cambridge, MA: MIT Press.

Willingham, W. W. (1999). A systematic view of test fairness. In S. Messick (Ed.), *Assessment in higher education* (pp. 213–242). Hillsdale, NJ: Lawrence Erlbaum Associates.

Chapter 10

Technological Fluency:
Needed Skills for the Future

Eva L. Baker
University of California, Los Angeles/
National Center for Research on Evaluation,
Standards, and Student Testing (CRESST)

Harold F. O'Neil, Jr.
University of Southern California/CRESST

How can we help create a productive link between technology and learning? Will we be able to tell if we have been successful? Unfortunately, there are no simple recipes to guide us. We believe that part of the answer resides in technological fluency or understanding people's ability to apply, explore, and adapt technology to serve important purposes. Are there building blocks to this competence? Can they be measured? These fundamental questions underlie the task of this chapter—to explore the concept of technological fluency, the ways it can be defined, and the creation of strategies to assess the developing technological fluency of students. In the future, this skill will be required of students to be successful in school as well as in the world of work.

The term *technological fluency* is not widely used; it comes to us most directly from Kathleen Fulton's (1997) excellent analysis of technological skills and was generally described earlier by Papert (1996). Although we will spend considerable time in this chapter discussing operational definitions of the term, even without much thought most of us could quickly generate common language interpretations of technological fluency. For now, accept our definition that technological fluency denotes an individual's well-developed skills, propensities, and knowledge that are required to use, design, and develop electronic and bionic hardware and software to enhance various aspects of life. Let us also pause to consider the meaning of technology. Throughout the chapter, we use the term technology in an encompassing way. By it, we mean the set of products that amend or amplify a broad range of sensory and cognitive resources available to an individual or group (Baker, 2000).

A major component task of this chapter is to formulate and evaluate the ways in which we can tell whether and how much technological fluency has been developed. Our language will focus on "students" as the target of fluency, but we could just as easily include teachers or workers in various job settings as well. We will pursue this task in five steps. First, because the crux of the analysis balances on the definition and assessment of technological fluency, we will develop a description of the technological fluency construct and determine how widely or narrowly we should draw our definition of technological fluency, and we will try to imagine alternative futures for our society, the workplace, and educational systems—the actual contexts in which technological fluency will be developed and exercised. We do so as a heuristic, a safeguard against proposing an assessment strategy with too short a shelf-life. We believe that analyzing and betting on characteristics of our future society should lead us to specific clarifications of this construct. As a result, we hope to clarify choices regarding expectations, goals, constraints, loci, and beliefs about technology and learning, so that we can best decide how to measure technological fluency.

Second, we will describe components of the technological fluency construct through the use of literature, experience, and some targeted interviews. This section will close with a tentative model of technological fluency. Third, we will reprise the core ideas in the field of testing and assessment. This summary is intended to help the reader judge our recommendations fairly. Fourth, practical approaches to the measurement of aspects of the model will be proposed, based on the assessment purposes and constraints we adopt. Fifth and finally, we will make some recommendations about what to do now and in the near future regarding its management.

TECHNOLOGICAL FLUENCY

What does technological fluency mean? Our working definition is again relatively broad: An individual's well-developed skills, propensities, and knowledge required to use, design, or develop electronic and bionic hardware and software in order to enhance various aspects of life.

Fluency means expertise exercised in a flowing manner or with automaticity. Papert (1996) used language expertise as an analogy to help us in understanding what he meant by technological fluency, and like all analogies, it has its limits. A person fluent in one language can converse across a range of topics with comfort and expertise. A person fluent in multiple languages can converse both across a range of topics *and* in different languages. In contrast, switch the analogies to music. A good musician develops fluency with practice. What musicians practice makes a difference. They might be fluent (comfortably expert) in playing wind instruments but not percussion instruments. They might be great performers of short pieces, but may not possess the stamina for extended symphonic music. They might be good at heavy metal but inept at improvisational jazz. Papert (1996) promoted the idea that technological fluency is a "main effect" capacity—if you have it, it works everywhere. In fact, a good many human competencies are conditional—how good you are depends on the breadth or focus of the domain—be it all of music or classical guitar. We define technological fluency as limited by domain knowledge.

To pursue boundaries of technological fluency, we have to consider in more detail what we mean by technology and define the types of technology we are considering in a way analogous to different languages (or types of music). Our definition of technology is the set of products that amend or amplify a broad range of sensory and cognitive resources available to an individual or group. This definition only makes sense with a set of examples to illustrate our meaning.

These examples include multidimensional models to assist in visualization of the unseeable, or electronic music or hearing aids as auditory sensory extenders. Another list includes the growing set of powerful software tools—including search engines and spreadsheets, virtual memory, and multitasking—to illustrate the extension of cognitive resources. Excellent reviews of using technology to support education have been provided by Fletcher (this volume, chap. 4), Means et al. (1993), Kulik (1994), Schacter and Fagnano (1999), and Wenglinsky (1998).

THE TIME DIMENSION AND TECHNOLOGY DEVELOPMENT

All examples are time bound, and prognostication with respect to the future is tricky. How bound by the present is our vision of future technology? That is, how free can we be in imagining the technologies with which our students will be expected to be "fluent?" The answers to these questions depend both on the push of technology (Glennan, 1967) and on the pull of societal requirements. Technology push means that inventions and innovations find new applications and adaptations. We already know the direction of technology development, in cost, speed, size, and assimilation. Think about the Borg in Jean-Luc's *Star Trek*. The negative valence of the analogy is not our intention, but it is helpful to think about how substantial technology will be integrated on the person of the individual. Although starting for the most part with compensatory purposes (e.g., hearing devices), specific technology is now commonly available as enhancements, for example, night vision goggles. In a virtual minute we will have on the mass market special-purpose products already in existence: visual enhancers, virtual reality walkmen, electronic/chemical clothes that change color and texture to be consistent or to contrast with the environment. Not all of these rapid developments are worthy of the attention of educational systems, although they will set the context in which learners will live. Technology that is second nature now (e.g., cellular phones, answering machines, and pagers) has not yet found its way into school curriculum. What this kind of technology does accomplish is to change the nature of our students' expectations and experience and raise questions about how these enhancements can be accepted as part of legitimate educational experiences. For an example of the public policy downside, think calculators and the controversy about their use in mathematics instruction and testing.

Certainly, the use of technology has massively and subtly influenced us all. Twenty years ago we were repeatedly interviewed by troubled journalists worried about whether early technology experiences would damage young children. To show the distance we've come since this time, let's recount two telling examples. A friend reports that her 11-month-old son routinely selects his choice of videotapes, and inserts and plays them in the VCR, without assistance. A colleague describes a crisis that occurred around age 2 for each of her three young children—the confusion experienced when they discovered that broadcast television did not permit them to fast forward commercials. The recognition that broadcast TV was not under their direct control created surprise and frustration (of course, that is no longer a restriction). Both of these examples illustrate components of technological fluency, skill development, choice, and the need to manage affective states. As it happens, these component behaviors developed because of the push of technology—they could not have occurred without the availability of the VCR technology. It so happens, we will argue, that they respond to the pull of societal needs and requirements as well.

REQUIREMENTS PULL: VISIONS OF LEARNING SOCIETIES

The contrast to technology push is the analysis of societal needs—the requirements-pull side of the equation. Requirements derive from answering questions such as these: How will work be structured? How will society change? What will learning and schools be like in 30 years—a reasonable period if we are planning to impact kindergarten children today? How can we anchor in reality potential flights of fancy? One way is to look at how far we have come.

A typical approach to planning work, societal, and school requirements involves empirical procedures, like needs assessment surveys of experts or key constituencies, or analyses of current deficiencies or shortfalls in workforce skills. Most of these studies are conducted in the anticipation of what the world will be like in a decade or less from the present.

As an exercise, let's think about what the future might hold for today's children. To make this thought experiment more concrete, we'll connect it to real people and deeply personal interests. In 2027, our grandchild Jacob will be 30 years old. His first child (or our great-grandchild) may be ready to begin school. Although this seems far distant, Jacob himself has two great-grandparents who were in school in the 1920s. In real life, we have a 100-year span between them and Jacob's future child. Even if we are less futuristic, is it possible to project the competence Jacob should acquire over the next 18 years? What will he need to be prepared to enter the workforce or to continue his education? We can't defer the task, because he will be in kindergarten in just a year from now.

To answer these questions, we need to think about the reality of the future. What will the future be like? Let's subdivide the future into three interacting arenas: the demands of the workplace, the nature of educational settings, and broader options for the future of society.

Workplace of the Future

Many books are marketed annually depicting the workplace of the future. All focus on the need for most individuals to participate in organizations. Almost all forecast multiple settings and multiple careers for individuals. All put a premium on the individual understanding and managing his or her own learning and contributing to the organization's learning. In Table 10.1, we provide a series of relevant trends developed from a national job survey conducted by the American Society for Training and Development (see Bassi, Benson, & Cheney, 1996, pp. 29–40) that is representative of many of these analyses. Table 10.1 emphasizes the continuing interaction of technology and training in future business environments. Although many of the trends relate to technological improvements, Trend 9 enumerates a set of characteristics that directly imply technological fluency requirements. These include systems thinking, continuous learning, and group involvement in tasks and decisions.

Visions of the Educational System

What trends do we see today that are likely to influence the shape of the educational system? In fact, many of the changes in learning and teaching projected 30 years ago have yet to occur, although pundits annually opine that we are "poised" to make dramatic improvements. Richard E. Schutz

TABLE 10.1
Learning Requirements of the Future Workplace

Trend 1:	Skill requirements will continue to increase in response to rapid technological change.
Trend 2:	The American workforce will be significantly more educated and more diverse.
Trend 3:	Corporate restructuring will continue to reshape the business environment.
Trend 4:	Corporate training departments will change dramatically in size and composition.
Trend 5:	Advances in technology will revolutionize the way training is delivered.
Trend 6:	Training departments will find new ways to deliver services via outsourcing and partnerships.
Trend 7:	Training professionals will focus more on interventions in performance improvement.
Trend 8:	Integrated high-performance work systems will proliferate as there is some evidence that they impact the bottom line.
Trend 9:	Companies will transform into learning organizations. • A belief that systems thinking is fundamental • A climate that encourages, rewards, and enhances individual and collective learning • A view that surprises, mistakes, and failures are learning opportunities • Widely available access to information and resources • A desire for continuous improvement and renewal • Learning integrated with work
Trend 10:	Organizational emphasis on human performance management will accelerate. Testing will be used at every critical juncture in employment, including hiring, training (what kind and how much), promotions, transfers, and firing.

(1970), writing for the now defunct *Journal of Research and Development,* created a table in which he compared classrooms now to classrooms 30 years in the future. He characterized 1970 classrooms on a variety of attributes, including the dominance of the teacher, the presentation of information in a lock-stepped fashion, common goals, and fixed seating. The future classroom involved students working on individual goals at their own rates, flexibility, high-quality curriculum, and so on.

If past projections about changes in classrooms have hardly been fulfilled, there are alternative futures we may posit now in order for us to imagine what requirements and constraints will operate in the future.

First, there is policy agreement that high content standards are important for students to learn, but disagreement about how they are operationalized. There is increasing focus on the use of measurement and testing as a policy tool, despite mixed evidence of impact. There is a movement intended to reduce the central control of education at the school district level through legislative mandate, partly to control spending on administration. There is diversification in providers, by private schools and franchises, by charter schools, and by home schoolers. There is a continued and un-equally distributed need for high-quality teachers and for strategies to prepare and renew a turbulent teaching staff. As prices drop and software and hardware markets are increasingly linked, technology has already become widely available in schools. Computer technology has become integrated with wireless and cable systems, and multimedia computers are common in homes as well. The platforms will be there. Some may ultimately be worn as clothing or accessories.

Despite the tendency toward decentralization and diversification, common conflicting values and goals exist: the desire for coherent programs in individual schools, the need to prepare all individuals for a mobile society, and the expectation that schools or other agencies will provide extended care in safe, educational environments for children of working parents.

We believe that the private sector will respond to and lead development to respond to this changing educational environment. One obvious initiative is to shore up concerns about the quality and credibility of educational services. We see that educational software, for use in the home, in after-school environments and day care, and in schools, will be developed as a default curriculum, in order to provide safety nets for students enrolled in institutions perceived to be inadequate. Similarly, privately controlled testing systems will be available to assess or confirm students' academic status.

Visions of the Future of Society

Can pictures be projected of the way the future will look to Jacob and his children? Independent of perspectives or forecasts on the balance between private sector and government initiative, between dominance of mega-corporate entities and highly energized, disposable organizations, between continued globalization or nationalism, or on the leadership of the United States or of its competitors, we can be sure of at least a few things. Americans will value education. Unforeseen societal problems will always spring up and need to be solved. Problems and solutions will diffuse more rapidly because of technology and the media. These problems will usually have both social and technical components. They will be urgent. Their solutions will depend on individuals who can mobilize themselves, who have sets of compatible skills, and who can access deep understanding of knowledge—knowledge in fields that have yet to be well defined, using technology not yet conceived.

Regrettably, there is no prescience of these specific problems, so our strategy to meet this future must focus on what we believe to be the enduring, generalizable human capacities that can thrive in a context of changing technology. These human capacities form the core of our analysis of technological fluency and have three major components: performance in families of cognitive demands, core propensities reflecting affective and social components, and focused technology skills.

BUILDING THE CONSTRUCT OF TECHNOLOGICAL FLUENCY

Families of Cognitive Demands

No one advocates technological prowess absent content to which it is applied. One question that comes up is whether technological fluency should be assessed only within particular subject matter constraints. For a mundane example, should spreadsheets be used as an integrated approach to assess algebra competence? Can the judgment of the quality of historical essays be determined by explicitly measuring students' approaches to knowledge acquisition, composition, and document design? Although instructionally it is clear to us that the integration of technological fluency and subject matter is essential, on the measurement and evaluation side, many difficulties are presented if one is attempting to infer technological fluency as well as subject matter content attainment. One major problem is the degree to which prior knowledge, the students' existing breadth and depth of understanding of disciplines and topics, influences their ability to use technology wisely—to profit from search, to organize writing by important themes and principles, and to recognize essential and nonessential instances of major concepts. Almost all writers in the field of psychology emphasize the impact of specific prior knowledge on the ability to perform at varying levels of expertise (e.g., Bransford & Johnson, 1972; Mayer & Wittrock, 1996).

Another problem with technology fluency assessment is simple practicality. It is not possible (given short-term constraints) to create, validate, and administer a sufficient number of separate subject-matter-by-technology measures to allow a solid inference to be made.

Our approach to this problem is to adopt a model used in our research and development in testing (Baker, 1995, 1997) that identifies the key families of cognitive demands that need to be incorporated in school (and workplace) learning. These are represented in Fig. 10.1. We assert three strong statements about this model: First, it will be practically impossible to think of educational goals that do not use one or a combination of these sets of cognitive demands. Second, these demands should be the infrastructure outcomes of formal education. Third, these families of demands can be implemented validly in different subject matter. For example, in content understanding families, we consider typical analyses of the nature of knowledge: declarative knowledge, procedural knowledge, system knowledge—

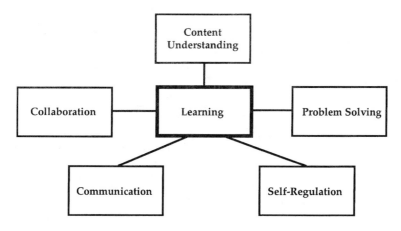

FIG. 10.1. Families of cognitive demands.

in other words, what, how, and the big picture of knowledge (Rumelhart & Norman, 1989). What and how can involve general ideas, like the concepts of estimation or principles of macroeconomics, or they may be formulated at more specific levels, like the names of U.S. allies in World War II or the formula for computing compound interest. The cognitive demands in the content understanding family involve not only the class of what is to be measured—for instance, disciplinary knowledge in biology, literature, or mathematics, or interdisciplinary studies like American culture, technology, or media and politics—but the general ways in which the knowledge can be displayed and assessed (Baker, Freeman, & Clayton, 1991; Niemi, 1996). This knowledge may be a goal in itself or may be required in order to develop comprehension (e.g., Bransford & Johnson, 1972; Mayer & Wittrock, 1996).

For this family, and the others as well, we have provided limited examples of assessment methodologies that we believe can be implemented in multiple domains, as shown in Table 10.2. In fact, we have more than 10 years worth of data in support of our theory that these families generalize to other content areas (Baker et al., 1996; Niemi, 1997; O'Neil, Chung, & Brown, 1997). We will illustrate the idea with a second important family of cognitive demands: problem solving. The justification for problem solving as a core demand can be found in analyses of both the workplace and academic learning. O'Neil, Allred, and Baker (1997) reviewed five major studies from the workplace readiness literature. Each of these studies identified the need for higher order thinking skills, teamwork, and some form of technological fluency. In four of the studies, problem-solving skills were specifically identified as essential. The Conference Board of Canada (1993) identified problem solving as part of key foundation skills. When individuals

TABLE 10.2
Types of Learning and Assessment Methodology

Types of learning	Assessment methodology
Content understanding	
Facts, concepts, procedures, principles	Explanation tasks, knowledge mapping, multiple-choice tests
Problem solving	
Domain-specific knowledge, domain-specific strategies, metacognition, motivation	Augmented knowledge mapping with search task, transfer tasks, motivation (effort, self-efficacy, anxiety) search strategies (analytic, browsing)
Teamwork and collaboration	
Adaptability, communication, coordination, leadership, decision making, interpersonal	Collaborative simulation, self-report, observation techniques
Self-regulation	
Planning, self-checking, effort, self-efficacy	Self-report
Communication	
Comprehension, expression, communication, use of conventions	Explanation scored for communication; collaborative simulations scored for communication

(e.g., employees, graduates, or students) are asked to rate the relative importance of skill sets, problem solving is usually rated the highest.

Researchers have been exploring the components of problem solving for many years, and there now appears to be an agreement on a subset of attributes. Using the work of Glaser, Raghaven, and Baxter (1992), Mayer and Wittrock (1996), Sugrue (1995), and Baxter, Elder, and Glaser (1996), we have synthesized a model of problem solving that includes three elements: content understanding of the problem domain; domain-specific or domain-independent problem-solving strategies; and self-regulation, which includes metacognition or self-management of learning and motivation (O'Neil, 1999). This model differs from problem-solving models in earlier epochs, which tended to define this area in terms of generic skills without a corresponding connection to the domain or content of the problem and solutions.

An example of a domain-dependent cognitive strategy in a problem-solving search task would be the "use of Boolean operators" (search for *problem solving* and *technology*). An example of a domain-independent strategy would be the use of analogies; for example, "a tire pump is like a syringe." The model suggests that to be successful problem solvers, individuals must know content, possess strategies to analyze and evaluate options (some of which apply specifically to the content in question), be able to plan and monitor their progress toward the solution, and be motivated to find the solution to the problem. This definition of problem solving invokes two other of the families of cognitive demands: content understanding and self-regulation. When collaborative problem solving is a focus or when a team solution is desired, then three other families are incorporated into the model of problem solving.

A number of rationales can be offered in support of the cognitive model approach. First, the National Educational Technology Standards (NETS) Project offers a set of goals that focus on these areas: basic operations and concepts; social, ethical, and human issues; productivity tools; technology tools for communications; research, problem solving, and decisions making (National Educational Technology Standards, n.d., p. 1). Analyses by Sternberg (1996) describing components of successful intelligence (i.e., the practical application of intelligence) support, in part, this line of argument. It is also a far more economical approach than designing a separate set of items or measures for every combination of content and cognitive demand. More relevant to our task here, at the National Center for Research on Evaluation, Standards, and Student Testing (CRESST) we have implemented these models in integrated simulations that provide us, to date, with approaches to assess students' content understanding (through knowledge representation and explanation), their ability to find information and evaluate its appropriateness to solve problems, and their ability to collaborate and communicate effectively with one another (Baker & Mayer, 1999; Chung, O'Neil, & Herl, 1999; Herl et al., 1996; Klein, O'Neil, & Baker, 1996; Schacter & Fagnano, 1999). The components of the CRESST simulations, originating with funding from Apple Computer, were developed with support from the Departments of Defense and Education, and with private foundation support.

Our formulation of families of cognitive demands argues for the centrality of subject matter knowledge and the strategies that embed cognitive demands into particular content domains. How does technology understanding fit with these models? Much of the writing in the area of technology understanding focuses on the cognitive components of the tasks (Fulton, 1997; National Educational Technology Standards, n.d.). In fact, the domain of technology knowledge can be conceived as merely another specific domain, rapidly growing as it is. Its content is formed by understanding the systems, particular technology problems in use or design, technical procedures to manage resources and apply or invent software, and the criteria to discern a productive, elegant solution.

Affective Propensities

Despite the preceding argument for cognitive families, almost everybody—from research psychologists to foreign car technicians—will recognize that high performance has strong affective components as well. To col-

People who can activate practical intelligence . . .

- are self-motivating   • accept fair blame

- are independent   • delay gratification

- control impulses   • know when to persevere

- complete tasks and follow through   • don't procrastinate

- have reasonable levels of self-   • put forth effort
  confidence and a belief in their ability
  to accomplish goals

FIG. 10.2.   Behaviors to activate practical intelligence.

laborate well and to be good team players, individuals need to know how, but also they must be motivated and sensitive to interpersonal feedback. To be good metacognitive thinkers, individuals must know not only how to plan, but also how to overcome personal dispositions that might lead them to rush or procrastinate or to get hopelessly distracted from the task. Psychologists have been studying the affective components of learning for years and are beginning to converge on a limited number of attributes that connect to learning (Snow, Corno, & Jackson III, 1996). For example, Sternberg (1996, pp. 251–266) enumerated a set of key traits that activate practical intelligence (see Fig. 10.2). People who can activate practical intelligence engage in multiple behaviors (Fig. 10.2).

On-the-Ground Confirmation

In our pursuit of understanding the components of technological fluency, we decided to go to real people operating at high levels of performance. One of us interviewed four early career individuals, who all, we are certain, would be classified as having the high end of technological fluency skills. All were well educated, either holding doctorates or about to obtain them. Their areas of training included computer science, game design, psychometrics, and cognitive psychology, although each now is committed to the field of education. All were interviewed individually about what they thought technological fluency was, whether they thought that they possessed it or its components, and what experience contributed to their ability. The generalizations from this group are limited, because of sampling and because of the obvious problem of selection; that is, they each had chosen to work in branches of the technology field itself. Although our interviews touched on topics related to the families of cognitive demands above (particularly teamwork, metacognition, problem solving, and system knowledge), by far the most interesting points emerged in relation to affective components of technological fluency. The following are some unelaborated quotes from those interviewed:

> Most problems are solvable in the technology area given time. You try a different approach—do a perspective shift. Lack of progress says you're overlooking something basic. (Cognitive Scientist)

> There's a difference between people who can set long-term goals and those who don't use them. When structuring out tasks, some will get emotional support by [achieving] minor goals. Others won't get that . . . support unless they achieve their ultimate goal. The first group will be more persistent and will shift when they reach an impasse. (Game Designer)

> Hackers don't look beyond the goal, despite what trouble may be at the goal, and they aren't self-protective. They just want to get there. At [Corporation X], they give hands-on computer problems to potential employees to see how they approach problems, whether they are more like hackers or designers. It's better to be one or the other in different situations. (Cognitive Scientist)

> We have a high level of self-efficacy. When things don't happen right, you have to figure out why they didn't, understanding the goals you've set. You improvise and figure out what to do. When you're without the tools to do things, you approximate or substitute. You need to get people in different environments to think about problems in different ways. (Psychometrician)

> Deadlines are good to focus efforts, but if the deadlines are too short, it can become chaotic. (Cognitive Scientist)

> You need to know about systems in such a way that you can use the analogy of one system when approaching a new one. This way you can use different systems and know what they are. You need to know the structures and key functions such as hardware. With experience, the fear of new things goes away. Give kids lots of experience with different things. Some expertise in a few things is good but lots of generalized experience will help them learn to transfer those skills. (Computer Scientist/Courseware Designer)

> You need to realize you should be using the old information for solving the new problems. (Psychometrician)

> They don't need to be a designer or creator. Being a user is also being a creator when they do their work on the computers. (Psychometrician)

Our interpretation of these interviews reemphasized the importance of a subset of affective skills. Our reviews of the literature lead us to believe that propensities, or affective propensities, go hand in hand with cognitive and technical skills in building fluency. We believe that at least four of these

Type	Operational Statement
Self-Efficacy	I can make this work
Effort, Persistence	I need to keep at it
Risk-Taking, Curiosity	Let me try this
Anxiety	I worry about my ability to use this technology
Success-Seeking	I want to be the best at this
Interpersonal Skills	I am able to help others

FIG. 10.3.   Affective components of technological fluency.

propensities should be systematically measured, studied, and, if substantiated, developed to improve technological fluency (see Fig. 10.3).

We include the construct of anxiety not because it is desirable. It is, rather, an anticipated negative side effect for some people who use technology; for instance, some teachers are anxious about their ability to use technology to help students in the classroom. Anxiety is a potential cost of developing technological fluency. It should be collaterally measured and mitigations should be sought.

Near-Term User Skills

Although few would believe computer fluency is wholly limited to the particular competencies exhibited in using commonly available software tools, these skills are important to our analysis for four reasons. First, skills are the most common way people presently think about acquiring expertise in technology. Second, skills can be plausibly measured and evaluated, or at least approximated. Third, in the light of the recent investments in computer technology in schools, skills have been emphasized and therefore are most likely to show impact. There are several good examples of such an approach to assessment. Educational Testing Service (ETS) has developed a self-report measure of computer familiarity (Eignor, Taylor, Kirsch, & Jamieson, 1997). Another interesting self-report approach to measure the ways that people use computers is provided by Panero, Lane, and Napier (1997).

Fourth, skills may be an important stepping stone or launching pad for true fluency development. Let us expand on the fourth point for a moment. In the pursuit of musical virtuosity, repeated practice with particular pieces is required before nuanced performance is attained and before the performer is able to demonstrate high levels of performance over a range of instances.

In attempting to master particular school goals or to reach given standards, students will be involved on many occasions with the same or similar software applications. A short list would include word processing software, e-mail programs, databases, spreadsheets and search engines, photography kits, video editors, and drawing and design programs. Although the platforms, software providers, and school tasks may vary, there are standard protocols that users learn about straight-ahead uses of the software, help options, customization, and level of risk in exploring the environment. If students are able to synthesize these understandings, then each time they approach a new software package, they will bring to it the set of skills learned from prior experience. A minimum set of operational skills would be the following: (a) ability to transfer technology applications to various content areas, (b) ability to transfer between applications to accomplish a goal, (c) ability to self-teach a new version or product in a software application family (e.g., spreadsheet, word processor), and (d) ability to teach a novice how to use a product.

This set of skills is focused on a major role in technological fluency, that of a proficient user of software for a range of purposes. We have not specifically discussed the requirements of roles of repair, design, and development of software. In some ways, these represent problem domains where domain-specific strategies, for example, troubleshooting approaches, graphic design, or systems analysis, would come into play much in the same way as an engineer would need to have specific model building strategies to represent a process in software. For that reason, we won't break out specific understanding required in user-centered design, use of programming tools, or the husbanding of technological resources. Neither will we explore the very interesting and believable configuration of propensities and skills that go with a systems-oriented designer as opposed to a "hacker," even though there are provocative differences in putative strategy, goal setting, gratification, and motivation between the two types of software creators.

A Preliminary Model of the Construct of Technological Fluency

In Fig. 10.4, we present a preliminary model of the construct, our operational definition of technological fluency. The model consists of three major subcomponents of the technological fluency construct (i.e., cognitive demands, affective propensities, and skills within content domains). All components are arrayed against a background of content. There is no implication that they should be measured external to the assessment of a topic or subject matter. The component *cognitive demands* includes intellectual skills and functions as follows: problem solving, content understanding, collaboration and teamwork, communication, and self-regulation. These subcomponents interact with one another in most cases.

Technological Fluency (TF)

Goal: Enhance All Aspects of Life Through Technology

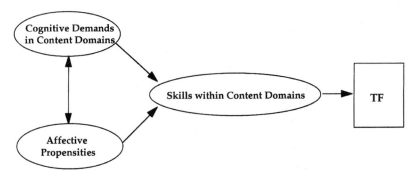

FIG. 10.4.   Preliminary model of technological fluency construct.

Most have domain- (or content-) specific components as well. A second component, *affective propensities,* incorporates the most powerful attributes that we believe contribute to the exhibition of technological fluency. These include self-efficacy, effort, risk-taking, and, negatively, anxiety. The reciprocal arrows in the model imply that cognitive demands and affective propensities interact. Together, these components become focused on the skill area of technology. The model is to be read from left to right and has the potential of being subject to verification by data obtained to measure each component.

ASSESSMENT OF TECHNOLOGICAL FLUENCY

We have not yet considered an additional, unspoken goal of most testing: to make a prediction. When we give the SAT, we clearly intend to use results to make a prediction about success in higher education (based on studies of first-year college grades). We certify doctors on the Medical Board Specialty Examinations because we think those who pass will have greater proficiency in future practice. We require tests for high school diplomas because we believe students will be more ready for the workplace and higher education if they succeed on these tests, and therefore they will succeed in jobs or in higher education at higher rates than those who do not pass such tests. The predictive function lies underneath almost every test purpose, and it should be very much a subtext in this chapter. Our problem is that we need to think about testing that can predict technological fluency for technologies and environments not yet conceived.

Interim Conclusions

For which purposes should we consider the design and development of our technological fluency measures? Four areas suggest themselves: system monitoring, program evaluation, instructional improvement, and individual progress monitoring of student learning. System monitoring and program evaluation purposes will be relevant to the policy communities, because assessment results may help answer relatively short-term and pressing questions about the general acquisition of broad competence in the system as well as the differential impact of specific programs or initiatives on the technological fluency domain. Instructional improvement implies that information will be developed and reported so that it could guide or at least influence the instructional strategies used by teachers, curriculum designers, software producers, and other educational service providers. If assessments are intended to provide progress in the monitoring of student learning, then they should help students to assess their own competencies and thereby focus student attention on developing those areas of greatest need.

None of these purposes would be expected to have special sanctions attached to it, thus allowing us to sidestep the difficulties associated with having stable measures of individual performance. However, we expect it is possible that students would not put forth their best effort and an underestimate of actual competency might result. We believe we can determine the degree to which such performance occurs by measuring effort simultaneously. Moreover, because we are not as yet clear on how fluency could be developed, holding individuals accountable for their performance at this time makes little sense.

To summarize our recommendations, we present one last figure (Fig. 10.5) representing the short-term decisions that we believe will push this area ahead. Taken together, the properties of technical and practical quality form a set of essential standards or criteria, standards that we will use to judge the acceptability of various technological fluency assessment options. Each assessment choice will need to meet standards of validity for every intended use of results. Standards of reliability, fairness, credibility, and utility will also be applied (American Educational Research Association, American Psychological Association, and National Council on Measurement in Education, 1999, see chaps. 1, 13, and 15).

What Else?

Will we have to measure technology addiction, distractibility, or stimulus seeking and find mitigating approaches sooner than we think? Do we have the interest to move these concerns beyond the relatively primitive conceptions of technology use we have found in today's schools? Where is this activity and focus to be located now in the schools, many of which are failing

Decision	Method
Create model to operationalize construct	Literature, experience, and musing
What to measure	Cognitive demands, affective propensities, and skills implemented in content
Purposes	System monitoring, program evaluation, instructional improvement, monitoring student learning
Assessment approaches	Sampling with questionnaires; computer simulations
Formats	Multiple-choice, knowledge maps; complex performance tasks
Unit	Individual
Stakes	Low
Age	Grades 4-12
Testing time	TBD
Costs	TBD

FIG. 10.5.   Blueprint for the assessment of technological fluency.

to provide minimum competencies for students? Who will make sure it occurs? Should the educational purposes of technology keep up with the expansion expected in other sectors? Or should education try to do a few things well—such as demonstrate the systematic link of content mastery and technology prowess?

SUMMARY

In this chapter, we have provided a story about a plausible definition of the construct of technological fluency. The gist of our position is that the construct should be defined as consisting of essential cognitive and affective components. These components will be important and resilient despite the shape of future society or the shock and wonder of new technologies. Each component operates within the broader context of content. Content domains may be academic or derive from work environments. We do not advocate the measurement of technological fluency apart from a realistic problem in a believable setting. We have also provided a discussion of testing and assessment purposes to lead the reader to conclude that creating an all-purpose instrument is neither desirable nor technically acceptable.

Certain purposes can be addressed by large-scale methods, using paper-and-pencil approximations. More interesting approaches involve the recommendation of technology contests (to continue the definition of the construct and to promote public awareness) and the support of integrated simulations measuring the construct. Taken together, they will lay a foundation that will allow us not only to recognize technological fluency when we see it, but to help our students develop high performance in technological fluency for real problems needing real solutions.

AUTHOR NOTE

The work reported herein was supported principally by the Milken Family Foundation and also by the Department of Defense Education Activity (DoDEA). The work reported herein was also supported in part under the Educational Research and Development Centers Program, PR/Award No. R305B60002, as administered by the Office of Educational Research and Improvement, U.S. Department of Education. The findings and opinions expressed in this report do not reflect the positions or policies of the National Institute on Student Achievement, Curriculum, and Assessment, the Office of Educational Research and Improvement, the U.S. Department of Education, the Milken Family Foundation, or DoDEA.

We wish to thank Gregory Chung, Katharine Fry, Howard Herl, Davina Klein, Derrick Mitchell, and David Westhoff for their contributions.

REFERENCES

American Educational Research Association, American Psychological Association, and National Council on Measurement in Education. (1999). *Revision of the standards for educational and psychological testing.* Washington, DC: American Psychological Association.

Baker, E. L. (1995, September). *Finding our way.* Presentation at the annual conference of the Center for Research on Evaluation, Standards, and Student Testing, University of California, Los Angeles.

Baker, E. L. (1997). Model-based performance assessment. *Theory Into Practice, 36,* 247–254.

Baker, E. L. (2000). *Understanding educational quality: Where validity meets technology* (William Angoff Memorial Lecture Series, November 8, 1998). Princeton, NJ: Educational Testing Service.

Baker, E. L., Freeman, M., & Clayton, S. (1991). Cognitive assessment of history for large-scale testing. In M. C. Wittrock & E. L. Baker (Eds.), *Testing and cognition* (pp. 131–153). Englewood Cliffs, NJ: Prentice-Hall.

Baker, E. L., & Mayer, R. E. (1999). Computer-based assessment of problem solving. *Computers in Human Behavior, 15,* 269–282.

Baker, E. L., Niemi, D., Herl, H., Aguirre-Muñoz, A., Staley, L., & Linn, R. L. (1996). *Report on the content area performance assessments (CAPA): A collaboration among the Hawaii Department of Education, the Center for Research on Evaluation, Standards, and Student Testing (CRESST) and the teachers and children of Hawaii* (Final Deliverable). Los Angeles: University of California, National Center for Research on Evaluation, Standards, and Student Testing.

Bassi, L. J., Benson, G., & Cheney, S. (1996). The top ten trends. *ASTD Journal T&D,* December, 28–42.

Baxter, G. P., Elder, A. D., & Glaser, R. (1996). *Assessment and instruction in the science classroom* (CSE Tech. Rep. No. 418). Los Angeles: University of California, National Center for Research on Evaluation, Standards, and Student Testing.

Bransford, J. D., & Johnson, M. K. (1972). Contextual prerequisites for understanding: Some investigations of comprehension and recall. *Journal of Verbal Learning and Verbal Behavior, 6,* 717–726.

Chung, G. K. W. K., O'Neil, H. F., Jr., & Herl, H. E. (1999). The use of computer-based collaborative knowledge mapping to measure team processes and team outcomes. *Computers in Human Behavior, 15,* 463–493.

Conference Board of Canada. (1993). *Employability skills profile.* Ottawa, Ontario, Canada: Author. (The Conference Board of Canada, 255 Smyth Road, Ottawa, Ontario, K1H 8M7, Canada, 10/93)

Eignor, D., Taylor, C., Kirsch, I., & Jamieson, J. (1997, April). *Development of a scale for assessing the level of computer familiarity of TOEFL examinees* (Draft Report). Princeton, NJ: Educational Testing Service.

Fulton, K. (1997). *Learning in a digital age: Insights into the issues. The skills students need for technological fluency.* Santa Monica, CA: Milken Family Foundation, Milken Exchange on Education Technology.

Glaser, R., Raghaven, K., & Baxter, G. (1992). *Cognitive theory as the basis for design of innovative assessment: design characteristics of science assessments* (Deliverable to CRESST/OERI). Los Angeles: University of California, Center for Research on Evaluation, Standards, and Student Testing.

Glennan, T. K., Jr. (1967). Issues in the choice of development policies. In T. Marschak, T. A., Glennan, Jr., & R. Summers (Eds.), *Strategies for research and development* (pp. 13–48). New York: Springer-Verlag.

Herl, H. E., O'Neil, H. F., Jr., Dennis, R. A., Chung, G. K. W. K., Klein, D. C. D., Lee, J. J., Schacter, J., & Baker, E. L. (1996). *Measurement of learning across five areas of cognitive competency: Design of an integrated simulation approach to measurement. Year 1 report* (Report to ISX/DODEA). Los Angeles: University of California, Center for Research on Evaluation, Standards, and Student Testing.

Klein, D. C. D., O'Neil, H. F., Jr., & Baker, E. L. (1996). *A cognitive demands analysis of innovative technologies* (Report to ISX/DODEA). Los Angeles: University of California, Center for Research on Evaluation, Standards, and Student Testing.

Kulik, J. (1994). Meta-analytic studies of findings on computer-based instruction. In E. L. Baker & H. F. O'Neil, Jr. (Eds.), *Technology assessment in education and training* (pp. 9–33). Hillsdale, NJ: Lawrence Erlbaum Associates.

Mayer, R. E., & Wittrock, M. C. (1996). Problem-solving transfer. In D. C. Berliner & R. C. Calfee (Eds.), *Handbook of educational psychology* (pp. 47–62). New York: Simon & Schuster Macmillan.

Means, B., Blando, J., Olson, K., Middleton, T., Morocco, C. C., Remz, A. R., & Zorfass, J. (1993). *Using technology to support education reform.* Washington, DC: U.S. Government Printing Office.

National Educational Technology Standards. (n.d.). *Performance domains. Profiles of technology literate students*. The National Educational Technology Standards (NETS) Project, International Society for Technology in Education. Available: http://www.cnets.iste.org/pdf/nets_brochure.pdf [2000, August 15].

Niemi, D. (1996). Assessing conceptual understanding in mathematics: Representation, problem solutions, justifications, and explanations. *Journal of Educational Research, 89*, 353–363.

Niemi, D. (1997). Cognitive science, expert-novice research, and performance assessment. *Theory Into Practice, 36*, 239–246.

O'Neil, H. F., Jr. (1999). Perspectives on computer-based performance assessment of problem solving: Editor's introduction. *Computers in Human Behavior, 15*, 255–268.

O'Neil, H. F., Jr., Allred, K., & Baker, E. L. (1997). Review of theoretical frameworks for workforce competencies of high school graduates. In H. F. O'Neil, Jr. (Ed.), *Workforce readiness: Competencies and assessment* (pp. 3–25). Mahwah, NJ: Lawrence Erlbaum Associates.

O'Neil, H. F., Jr., Chung, G., & Brown, R. (1997). Use of networked simulations as a context to measure team competencies. In H. F. O'Neil, Jr. (Ed.), *Workforce readiness: Competencies and assessment* (pp. 411–452). Mahwah, NJ: Lawrence Erlbaum Associates.

Panero, J. C., Lane, D. M., & Napier, H. A. (1997). The computer use scale: Four dimensions of how people use computers. *Journal of Educational Computing Research, 16*, 297–315.

Papert, S. (1996). *The connected family: Bridging the digital generation gap*. Atlanta, GA: Longstreet Press.

Rumelhart, D. E., & Norman, D. A. (1989). Representations in memory. In R. C. Atkinson, R. J. Herrnstein, G. Lindzey, & R. D. Luce (Eds.), *Stevens' handbook of experimental psychology. Volume 2: Learning and cognition* (2nd ed., pp. 511–587). New York: Wiley.

Schacter, J., & Fagnano, C. (1999). Does computer technology improve student learning and achievement? How, when, and under what conditions? *Journal of Educational Computing Research, 20*, 329–343.

Schutz, R. E. (1970). The nature of educational development. *Journal of Research and Development in Education, 3*(2), 39–64.

Snow, R. E., Corno, L., & Jackson III, D. (1996). Individual differences in affective and conative functions. In D. C. Berliner & R. C. Calfee (Eds.), *Handbook of educational psychology* (pp. 243–310). New York: Simon & Schuster Macmillan.

Sternberg, R. J. (1996). *Successful intelligence: How practical and creative intelligence determine success in life*. New York: Simon & Schuster.

Sugrue, B. (1995). A theory-based framework for assessing domain-specific problem-solving ability. *Educational Measurement: Issues and Practice, 14*(3), 29–36.

Wenglinsky, H. (1998). *Does it compute? The relationship between educational technology and student achievement in mathematics* (ETS Policy Information Report). Princeton, NJ: Educational Testing Service. (ERIC Document Reproduction Service No. ED 425 191)

Chapter 11

An Electronic Infrastructure
for a Future Generation of Tests

Randy Elliot Bennett
Educational Testing Service

Represented by such tests as the Graduate Record Examinations (GRE) General Test (for graduate school admissions) and the Graduate Management Admission Test (GMAT; for business school admissions), the first generation of computer-based testing (CBT) offers several advantages over traditional paper-and-pencil measures. To start, CBT has changed the pragmatics of high stakes test administration dramatically. Instead of taking the test on one of only a few dates per year in a large group at a temporary center, the advent of permanent CBT centers allows examinees to test when they want, in small groups, and in more comfortable environments specifically designed for testing. Because responses are scored immediately, the examinee may see the results as soon as the test concludes. In computer-adaptive implementations, tests can be considerably shorter than their paper-and-pencil counterparts, without any sacrifice in reliability. In addition, because adaptive tests are dynamically built to match the examinee's skill level, substantially equal precision can be attained throughout the score scale, giving better measurement of those whose abilities fall outside the more limited target range of the conventional linear test.

This first generation of CBT, however, must be regarded as an initial step. First, this generation is limited primarily to multiple choice questions, with all the potential negative consequences this limitation implies (see Bennett, 1993, for a review of these consequences). Open-ended formats such as those that constitute the core of the performance assessment movement are minimally represented. Second, the first generation focuses on measuring traditional constructs and does not take full advantage of the computer's potential to present stimuli and track information, for example, through dynamic displays or recording of response latencies (Bennett et al., 1999). Finally, because the existing infrastructure is not yet optimized, high stakes computer-based testing is still considerably more costly to conduct than paper-and-pencil assessment (Bennett, 2001).

What this initial manifestation does provide is the outline of an electronic infrastructure for a future generation of tests. This chapter presents one conception of this scheme. Key to this conception is combining the best of traditional approaches with new technology to form an integrated "distance" assessment system. This idealized system will employ performance tasks modeling good instructional practice, include important skills not well-measured in current examinations, sample behavior more frequently, and give feedback to facilitate individual growth. As a consequence, the system should help improve student learning and educational decision making.

AN INFRASTRUCTURE FOR THE FUTURE

What capabilities might this infrastructure be expected to provide? Figure 11.1 depicts test development, test delivery, response processing, and reporting, with the order of events primarily proceeding from left to right.

Beginning with test development, it is interesting to note that until very recently, computer-based test developers wrote items using a process similar to the "word processing center" model that characterized the U.S. workplace in the early to middle 1980s. In this model, the professional sent a handwritten manuscript to the center, the manuscript was processed, and a printed copy was returned. The professional then made notations on the copy and gave it back to the center, the notated copy was processed, a clean document was returned, and so on. As in the word processing center model, the CBT developer roughed out the item by entering text into the computer and drawing graphics on paper, sending both to a test production center where a CBT production specialist redrew the graphics and integrated the text to make a functioning item. The item was then returned to the test developer who reviewed it, communicated corrections verbally or on paper, and sent the result back to the production center. Iterations continued until the item was as the developer, the production specialist, and reviewers desired. In a world characterized by increasing demands for faster turnaround and multiple parallel item pools to increase test security, this process was cumbersome at best.

To improve efficiency, test developers are beginning to use more sophisticated item processing tools. These tools will help them build, try out, re-

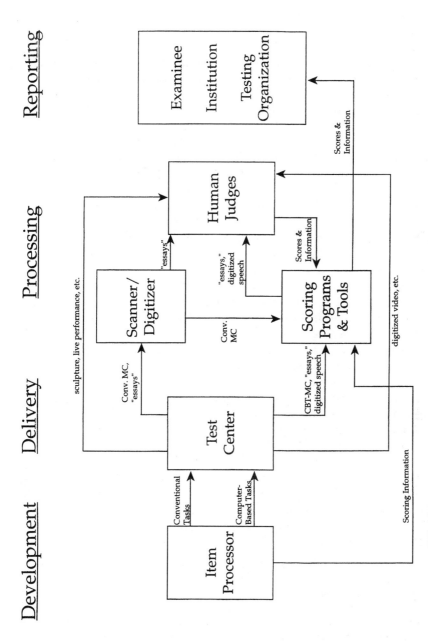

FIG. 11.1. An infrastructure for a future generation of tests. Conv. MC = response to a conventional multiple choice task; CBT-MC = response to a computer-based multiple choice task.

vise, and package items into functional, although not necessarily operational, tests.

These item processing tools will have several important characteristics. First, the tools will have multimedia capabilities that permit the developer to insert, not only graphics, but animation, sound, and video (much like Powerpoint® allows today for slide presentations). Second, low level screen formatting, which production specialists now spend significant time on, will be taken over by software, either as part of the item-processor interface or as postprocessing.[1] Third, CBT items authored in this environment will be fully functional, permitting the developer to take the item as would the examinee, or pilot test it in its draft form. Fourth, the item processor would have generative capabilities for some item classes: Given parameters specified by the test developer, the tool would automatically rough out a question for editing. For item classes where the domain structure and the determinants of difficulty are understood, developers could create items to assess critical aspects of that structure, more confidently pitching them at desired difficulty levels (see Bejar, 1993, or Irvine and Kyllonen, 2002, for more on automatic item generation). Fifth, for open-ended items, there would be rubric creation aids. These aids would help the developer specify a score scale, as well as describe the features of responses falling at each scale point. In some instances, this information would also be electronically encoded for subsequent use by automated scoring programs. Finally, the item processor would be capable of authoring conventional, as well as computer-based, questions. This dual capability is important as conventionally delivered tasks will continue to play an important role in assessment, not only because universal access to computers will take time but because some important tasks cannot be authentically replicated in the CBT environment.

Moving to the right in Fig. 11.1 shows that delivery will occur in test centers. This nomenclature covers several arrangements. Students may test in large assemblages, as is common for paper-and-pencil admissions tests today, in small CBT centers, or in their classrooms. In technologically capable centers, they may take computer-based tests, conventional tests, or combinations of the two. The particular arrangement will depend on the testing program and the availability of technology.

---

[1] In this vein, an intriguing innovation is the potential for separating item format from content. Markup languages like XML (extensible markup language) now enable such separation (Hunter, 2000). In this approach, item content is stored as text-based data and formatting (i.e., item presentation) is managed by a template. One advantage of this structure is that the same item content can be delivered on monitors with different screen sizes and resolutions, as well as in different media (e.g., on paper, through synthesized speech), without changing the content. This flexibility should make it possible to deliver computerized tests to many more locations and to create alternate versions more cost-effectively. The potential disadvantage is that such variations in presentation may affect examinee performance in irrelevant ways.

Responses to conventionally delivered (i.e., noncomputer-based) tasks, fall into two classes: Those that can be adequately converted to digital form and transmitted electronically, and those that cannot (see the top of Fig. 11.1). The former would include all paper-and-pencil responses, whether multiple choice or open ended. Examples that might be too complex for digital capture and transmission are sculptures and live performances, although even here solutions such as digital holography, digital video, and broadband transmission (for rapidly moving large response files), may soon prove practical. (Note that, as collections of responses, student portfolios also could be handled in this framework; whether their contents could be easily digitized would depend on the form those contents take.)

Responses that can be digitized are scanned, either at the test center or after being received at a central location. The digitized multiple choice responses are then scored by a conventional program and the results reported to the examinee, one or more designated institutions, and testing organization files. Digital representations of open-ended responses (e.g., essays, mathematical proofs, diagrams) are handled differently. These are sent to computer terminals, where human judges grade them, possibly with the aid of built-in electronic tools (e.g., calculator, protractor, ruler, symbol manipulator). The judges may be at the same site as the scanner or at a site in another city, region, or country. Judges may be collocated so that they can train together and interact directly about unusual responses and changes to the rubric, or they may be distributed, communicating by e-mail or by personal video-teleconferencing utilities. Real-time moderation could occur too by having judges blindly score a common set of "anchor" responses, identifying the discrepancies, and resolving them socially or adjusting for them statistically (e.g., Braun, 1988).

Responses to tasks that cannot be digitized are handled in the usual manner. Those recorded on paper or some other nondigital medium (e.g., analog videotape) are physically moved from test centers to a processing location and given to human judges to adjudicate by hand. (Responses delivered live may be judged in real time, with the evaluations recorded and sent on for processing.) Last, judgments are converted to machine-readable form for use by a program that computes scores for the total test and reports the results.

As the infrastructure for computer-based testing becomes widespread, more examinees will take tests on computer and fewer through conventional means. By definition, responses to these computer-delivered tasks will be captured digitally; as a consequence, it may be possible to score some immediately at the point of capture. Certainly, immediate scoring occurs now for responses to multiple choice and related items (e.g., those that require entering a numeric response). But increasingly, it will become true for more complex responses (e.g., mathematical expressions, words, and phrases). (For a description of the scoring of mathematical expressions, see Bennett, Steffen, Singley, Morley, & Jacquemin, 1997.) Responses to other items will need to be transmitted electronically to a location that could, in principle, be across town or, in the case of international assessments, on the other side of the world. These responses may take the form of extended mathematical proofs, speech captured by microphone, diagrams constructed with a pen and tablet, or essays typed on the computer.

Whereas these responses may not all be fully machine scorable in real time, some may be scorable semiautomatically. Several approaches might be taken toward such processing. In one approach, the computer could be used as a quality control mechanism for human raters. That is, instead of scoring each response with two human raters (as many testing programs now do), each might be scored by machine and human, with a second human called in to adjudicate discrepancies. (A variation on this theme is to score all responses by machine, having humans check a random sample.)

A second approach is for the machine to process all responses, passing to human raters only those that it could not accurately evaluate. Where scoring accuracy is associated with score level or some related computable feature, that feature might be used to assign responses. In other instances, the grading program may be capable of making reasonable judgments throughout the score scale. Here, it would transfer for resolution only those cases of which it was unsure. This assignment strategy presumes a scoring program that can make judgments about its own performance.

A third approach to semiautomatic scoring might use machine and human graders in complementary fashion, for example, with each judging different dimensions. The machine might be used to award an overall score and the humans to give diagnostic feedback (or vice versa, depending on the particular capabilities of each).

Other responses will be too complex for even semiautomatic processing. These responses will be treated similarly to digitized conventional tasks. As an illustration, imagine a test to certify teachers of children with hearing impairment. The candidate sits down at the computer and sees on the screen a video of a person posing a question in American Sign Language. As the candidate signs a response, it is recorded by a miniature digital TV camera sitting atop the computer monitor. The response is stored, then electronically transmitted and displayed at a judge's terminal for evaluation.

When responses can be automatically scored, reporting to the examinee can be immediate. Even when responses must be transmitted electronically to another location, it may be possible to report scores unofficially by the end of the testing session if the constructed response portions are administered first and if graders are readily available.

Regardless of when reporting occurs, it will be done electronically. In principle, it could be delivered to an examinee's e-mail address, or simply made accessible via the Internet or interactive telephony (i.e., using the telephone keypad to manipulate a remote computer). Computer-based reports will bring with them the capacity for multiple views, perhaps showing how the examinee's performance compares to established content standards or to user-defined reference groups (e.g., those with similar background characteristics, those applying to particular institutions). Finally, for those individuals who want it, technology should make possible detailed information on the kinds of problems they were able to solve or the constellation of skills they appear to possess.

IMPROVING LEARNING AND DECISION MAKING

How might this infrastructure make assessment contribute to learning and decision making? First, the infrastructure makes more practical the use of measurement methods like performance assessment. Performance assessment is common to the educational systems of many countries (Feuer & Fulton, 1994), and has found increasing favor in the United States. One of its defining attributes is the use of tasks that closely resemble good instructional exercises. Once reified in assessment, these tasks can become positive models for teaching practice (J. R. Frederiksen & Collins, 1989).

A major impediment to using performance assessment more widely has been cost (U.S. Congress, 1992, p. 243). The proposed conception makes large-scale deployment more feasible by providing an integrated structure for five classes of performance task roughly arrayed by operational cost (and, not incidentally, response complexity). These are computer delivered and automatically scored, computer delivered and semiautomatically scored, computer delivered and human scored on computer terminal, conventionally delivered and human scored on terminal, and conventionally delivered and conventionally scored by human judges. Testing programs can opt to use whatever combination of performance tasks their educational goals require and their fiscal resources allow.

A second way this infrastructure might contribute to learning and decision making is by making it easier to measure important constructs that conventional testing programs do not now assess and that correlate only modestly with existing indicators. Including such constructs in making postsecondary admissions decisions, for example, would broaden the definition of talent and, consequently, the pool of eligible applicants.

One such construct might be "learning-to-learn," or how effectively students profit from instruction (Lidz, 1987). Attempts to measure this construct have shown promise in identifying potentially capable students who have not achieved because they have come from extremely deprived environments or have never been adequately taught (Feuerstein, 1979; Grigorenko & Sternberg, 1998). Also, these measures appear to add independently to the prediction of scholastic achievement over what traditional tests provide (Campione & Brown, 1987). The general method for measuring this construct, known as "dynamic assessment," involves presenting the student with a task just above that individual's level, providing hints or other instruction, and retesting performance (Lidz, 1987). For any cost-effective large-scale implementation, computer technology would be required to identify the examinee's current skill level, select appropriate tasks, control the presentation of hints, and capture the sequence of responses.

Another example might be the ability to generate alternative explanations. This skill has been judged important to success in graduate education (Powers & Enright, 1987). It also has been found to overlap only minimally with the competencies measured by existing admissions tests and to add independently over those measures to the prediction of academic performance (Bennett & Rock, 1995; Enright, Rock, & Bennett, 1999; N. Frederiksen & Ward, 1978). This ability, too, could only be assessed cost-effectively on a large scale with technology.

A third way this infrastructure might contribute to learning and decision making is by allowing frequent behavior sampling. Conventional testing programs, whether for institutional or individual accountability, typically assess performance at one point in time. For some students, this single sampling may misrepresent current capability and prospects for future accomplishment. These estimates—be they too high or too low—may encourage wrong decisions. Some decisions may involve learning, as in choosing between academic and technical tracks or, within tracks, among courses of study. Better skill estimates derived from frequent behavior sampling would allow students to make more informed decisions (e.g., to pursue learning in areas best suited to them) and, consequently, to increase their chances for success.

One means of implementing frequent behavior sampling is through curriculum-embedded assessment; that is, administering tasks periodically, which because of their fit with the course syllabus, serve both institutional testing program and classroom instructional purposes (Bennett, 1998). To facilitate such assessment, schools could be linked to the proposed infrastructure through the Internet. Curriculum-embedded tasks might be done on computer or in paper and pencil and scanned before being uploaded. Responses that could not be automatically scored would be processed, perhaps by teachers at other schools (using the same online mechanisms for rater calibration described earlier). These data would be retained by the institutional testing program for its purposes (e.g., institutional accountability, postsecondary admissions), and could potentially become part of local, regional, national, or international databases. Schools and students would benefit from the relative unobtrusiveness of this approach, the relevance of its tasks, and the representativeness of the information it provided. All involved would gain from its faster, more cost-effective processing.

A final instance of how this infrastructure might support learning and decision making is through the type of feedback it enables. For example, through this infrastructure, many responses, all scores, and much other relevant information will be put into electronic form. Once in that form, these data would be available for generating individualized reports containing such elements as student profiles and digitized "work" samples illustrating standing in important areas. These reports should provide a richer picture of student accomplishment from which to gauge progress and design instruction.

BUILDING THE INFRASTRUCTURE

Creating an infrastructure of this magnitude is likely to require a multi-organizational effort. Rather than being built anew, it would use computer networks created for more general purposes. In all probability, this assessment infrastructure would be only part of a larger, integrated series of services. The other services might include test registration, information, and preparation; career and academic guidance; application to postsecondary education; and instruction. These additional services would be accessible from school and at home.

Whereas this next-generation infrastructure is not yet here, rudimentary portions already exist, some in prototype and some in operational form (see Frase et al., chap. 9, in this vol.). Looking first at the part of Fig. 11.1 that deals with computer-based tests, the most substantial extant component is the test center network. Center networks have been established by several organizations, including ETS in partnership with Prometric, ACT in partnership with Electronic Data Systems, Computer Adaptive Technologies (CAT, Inc.) in partnership with HQ Global Workplaces, and NCS Pearson. The first of these networks delivered tests to physical locations (e.g., Sylvan Learning Centers) via dedicated telephone line. This distribution route was chosen for security and reliability. More recently, organizations (e.g., CAT, Inc., NCS Pearson) have begun using the Internet instead. This mechanism allows tests to be delivered to any location with Internet access and the proper machine configuration. The result is a potentially broader distribution, including to locations that may act as centers only for the duration of the test (e.g., the classroom, school computer lab, corporate human resources office, college admissions office).

As of spring 2002, the ETS/Prometric network comprised several hundred operational locations in the United States and abroad. These locations were at both Sylvan Learning Centers and institutions of higher education. Item pools and software updates routinely flowed electronically from ETS to these locations, and responses to multiple choice questions, to simple constructed response items, and essays written on computer passed back to ETS on a daily basis. From ETS, scores were reported electronically to some test sponsors. This network used dedicated connections. Over the next few years, it is expected to move to Internet delivery, which other lower volume testing programs were already doing.

Research underway at ETS is using the Internet to deliver National Assessment of Educational Progress (NAEP) test prototypes directly to classrooms and school computer labs. A nationally-representative trial was completed in 2001, during which mathematics examinations were administered to fourth- and eighth-grade students in 100 schools. Additional trials will follow with the goal of introducing technological delivery in some aspect of operational NAEP by 2004.

In addition to the test center network and delivery components of the proposed infrastructure, remarkable progress has been made in automated scoring. Complex constructed response tasks are now being operationally scored automatically in postsecondary admissions, licensure, and employment tests. The first operational use of automated scoring in a computerized test occurred with the introduction of the Architect Registration Examination (ARE) in February 1997 (Bejar, 1995; Williamson, Bejar, & Hone, 1999). This examination contains questions in which the candidate must use graphical tools to create a design that satisfies given requirements. The design is scored automatically by analyzing it to confirm that all critical features called for in the requirements and in the applicable building code are present.

The second operational use of automated scoring was introduced in the GMAT's Analytical Writing Assessment, now taken on computer. Originally, each of the two essay questions comprising this assessment was graded by two human raters. In February 1999, one grader was replaced with e-rater (1997). For each essay prompt, a regression model is built that relates computable features of essays—including indicators of syntax, discourse organization, and topical content—to the grades assigned by humans. E-rater then computes features for each new essay response and uses the appropriate regression model to generate a score. Research with e-rater has found it to agree about as highly with human graders in assigning scores as those graders agree among themselves (e.g., Burstein et al., 1998). Studies with other essay grading programs used in experimental contexts have produced similar results (Elliot, Burnham, Chernoff, & Kern, 1997; Landauer, Laham, Rehder, & Schreiner, 1997; Larkey, 1998; Page & Petersen, 1995).

Automated scoring was also recently introduced into medical licensure through the United States Medical Licensure Examination (USMLE). This examination includes the Primum Computer-based Case Simulations, which ask the examinee to diagnose and treat a patient (Clauser, Swanson, & Clyman, 1999).

Finally, PhonePass™ uses speech recognition technology to score language samples taken over the telephone. PhonePass™ is used to measure English speaking and listening skills. Research with both PhonePass™ and the Primum Computer-based Case Simulations also shows high agreement with the judgments of human raters (Clauser et al., 1999; Ordinate, 1999).

Moving to the test development segment of Fig. 11.1, the ETS network now supports computer-based tools that allow the developer to rough-out items online, as long as those items conform to a fixed set of question formats. Integrated into this system is a tool for automatically generating mathematics questions, called the Mathematics Test Creation Assistant (TCA) (1998). The TCA allows the test developer to describe items abstractly in the form of an item model, from which draft item variants can be generated for review and revision (Singley & Bennett, 2002). A model can be thought of as a test item in which certain elements have been recast as variables, with constraints imposed on the values those variables can take and on how the variables relate to one another. Models can be developed from scratch, or can be based on "parent" items of known psychometric characteristics. Such models can be created for traditional multiple choice items, constructed response questions, or extended performance tasks, and can include charts, graphs, or multimedia objects. A given model can be written to produce variants that differ only in surface features or variants that have no obvious connection to one another. The TCA is being used operationally to generate items for the GRE General Test, GMAT, and the Uniform Certified Public Accountant Examination.

Turning to the portion of Fig. 11.1 that represents conventionally delivered tests, many organizations have well-honed processes for scoring paper-and-pencil, as well as more complex, performance tasks. These processes center around gatherings of human judges to develop rubrics and evaluate responses. NCS Pearson has automated part of the process and has used it operationally to score millions of constructed responses to the National Assessment of Educational Progress (NAEP), as well as those from other tests. Paper-and-pencil responses (e.g., to essay prompts, mathematical problems) are shipped to a central facility, where they are scanned, digitized, and uploaded to a wide-area network. The digitized representations are given to human judges at terminals, who are grouped according to discipline. Because the images are digitized, the judge can enlarge any portion of the response. The system can assign to multiple judges every nth response as a means of checking rater agreement, and the table leader can view the results in real time. This real-time analysis allows the table leader to stop the scoring to clarify elements of the rubric with individuals, or with the group, as needed. Because each group is composed of about a dozen individuals housed in a private room, the collegial interaction is much the same as it is in a paper-based scoring session, with frequent exchange about such things as unusual responses and the rubric modifications needed to accommodate them. Results of using the system with NAEP responses suggest that, although rater reliability levels are comparable to the conventional method, more responses are scored per unit time and much less labor is needed to manage the movement and storage of responses (J. Goodison, personal communication, September 9, 1994).

ETS expanded on this model with an online scoring system intended to handle input from both paper and computer-based tests (Odendahl, 1999). Originally, essays entered on computer were sent electronically from the test center to one of several scoring locations. At the scoring center, judges sitting at terminals did the grading (as in the NCS Pearson model). Here, too, rater accuracy appeared to be unaffected by having to mark responses on a computer (Powers, Farnum, Grant, & Kubota, 1997). As of summer 2000, student responses were available over the Internet, so that graders can work individually from anywhere in the world. Grader reliability is maintained by requiring each individual to reach an accuracy criterion on a calibration set before beginning each scoring session, by having a scoring leader available for telephone consultation during scoring hours, and by monitoring grading results.

With respect to the reporting end of Fig.11.1, the GMAT was perhaps the first major program to include performance samples as part of its score reports ("New GMAT," 1994). As noted, in addition to its computer-based multiple choice verbal and quantitative sections, the GMAT includes two word processed essay tasks. The examinee's response to each is appended to the numerical test results, allowing admissions committees to evaluate the quality of the candidate's reasoning and writing skills directly.

CONCLUSIONS

This chapter presented one conception of a multiorganizational infrastructure for a future generation of tests in which conventional and new technological capabilities are combined to form an integrated "distance" assessment system. This is a distance system in that examinees, graders, test developers, CBT production specialists, response-processing programs, and score recipients may reside at different locations but are linked electronically.

This infrastructure should help assessment contribute to learning and decision making. These assessments will make that contribution in several ways. First, they will employ performance tasks modeling good instructional practice. Second, they will include important skills not well-measured in current examinations, thus broadening the criteria on which assessment decisions are made. Third, they will sample behavior more frequently, providing proficiency estimates that help students to better plan their schooling. Finally, they will give feedback to facilitate individual growth.

This electronic network might be part of a larger arrangement delivering additional, but integrated, educational services—test registration, information, and preparation; career and academic guidance; application to postsecondary education; and instruction. Making it easier for examinees to take tests, helping them perform in a manner that accurately reflects their capabilities, giving them the guidance needed to make good decisions, and making the application process as painless as possible can only further improve assessment.

Significant portions of the proposed assessment infrastructure exist, but in a fragmented and often experimental state. The major challenges are clear. Computerized tasks measuring a wider range of relevant skills must be created, along with routines for automatically scoring the responses. Measurement models must be developed to help make meaningful inferences from performance on complex tasks, and these models and tasks must be embedded in computer-delivered curricula. New capabilities must be prototyped and they must be moved to production quickly and efficiently. And finally, the various infrastructure components must be integrated into a coherent, efficient whole that ultimately helps institutions and individuals make better educational choices.

ACKNOWLEDGMENTS

This chapter is adapted from a presentation at the annual meeting of the International Association for Educational Assessment, Wellington, New Zealand, October 1994, and from an ETS Research Report (Bennett, 1994).

Appreciation is expressed to David Kuntz, Kevin Singley, Len Swanson, and Bill Ward for their helpful reviews of an earlier version of this chapter.

REFERENCES

Bejar, I. I. (1993). A generative approach to psychological and educational measurement. In N. Frederiksen, R. J. Mislevy, & I. Bejar (Eds.), *Test theory for a new generation of tests* (pp. 323–357). Hillsdale, NJ: Lawrence Erlbaum Associates.

Bejar, I. I. (1995). From adaptive testing to automated scoring of architectural simulations. In E. L. Mancall & P. G. Bashook (Eds.), *Assessing clinical reasoning: The oral examination and alternative methods* (pp. 115–130). Evanston, IL: American Board of Medical Specialties.

Bennett, R. E. (1994). *An electronic infrastructure for a future generation of tests* (RR-94-61). Princeton, NJ: Educational Testing Service.

Bennett, R. E. (1993). On the meanings of constructed response. In R. E. Bennett & W. C. Ward (Eds.), *Construction vs. choice in cognitive measurement: Issues in constructed response, performance testing, and portfolio assessment* (pp. 1–27). Hillsdale, NJ: Lawrence Erlbaum Associates.

Bennett, R. E. (1998). *Reinventing assessment: Speculations on the future of large-scale educational testing.* Princeton, NJ: Policy Information Center, Educational Testing Service. (Also available: ftp://ftp.ets.org/pub/res/reinvent.pdf)

Bennett, R. E. (2001). How the Internet will help large-scale assessment reinvent itself. *Educational Policy Analysis Archives* [on-line], *9*(5), Available: http://epaa.asu.edu/epaa/v9n5.html

Bennett, R. E., Goodman, M., Hessinger, J., Ligget, J., Marshall, G., Kahn, H., & Zack, J. (1999). Using multimedia in large-scale computer-based testing programs. *Computers in Human Behavior, 15,* 283–294.

Bennett, R. E., & Rock, D. A. (1995). Generalizability, validity, and examinee perceptions of a computer-delivered formulating-hypotheses test. *Journal of Educational Measurement, 32,* 19–36.

Bennett, R. E., Steffen, M., Singley, M. K., Morley, M, & Jacquemin, D. (1997). Evaluating an automatically scorable, open-ended response type for measuring mathematical reasoning in computerized-adaptive tests. *Journal of Educational Measurement, 34,* 162–176.

Braun, H. I. (1988). Understanding scoring reliability: Experiments in calibrating essay readers. *Journal of Educational Statistics, 13,* 1–18.

Burstein, J., Braden-Harder, L., Chodorow, M., Hua, S., Kaplan, B., Kukich, K., Lu, C., Nolan, J., Rock, D., & Wolff, S. (1998). *Computer analysis of essay content for automated score prediction* (RR-98-15). Princeton, NJ: Educational Testing Service.

Campione, J. C., & Brown, A. L. (1987). Linking dynamic assessment with school achievement. In C. S. Lidz (Ed.), *Dynamic assessment: An interactional approach to evaluating learning potential* (pp. 82–115). New York: Guilford.

Clauser, B. E., Swanson, D. B., & Clyman, S. G. (1999). A comparison of the generalizability of scores produced by expert raters and automated scoring systems. *Applied Measurement in Education, 12,* 281–299.

Elliot, S., Burnham, W., Chernoff, M., & Kern, K. (1997, March). *Computerized scoring of open-ended Bar Examination questions.* Paper presented at the annual meeting of the American Educational Research Association, Chicago.

Enright, M. K., Rock, D. A., & Bennett, R. E. (1999). Improving measurement for graduate admissions. *Journal of Educational Measurement, 35,* 250–267.

E-rater (1997). [Computer software]. Princeton, NJ: Educational Testing Service.

Feuer, M. J., & Fulton, K. (1994). Educational testing abroad and lessons for the United States. *Educational Measurement: Issues and Practice, 13*(3), 31–39.

Feuerstein, R. (1979). *The dynamic assessment of retarded performers: The Learning Potential Assessment Device, theory, instruments, and techniques.* Baltimore: University Park Press.

Frederiksen, N., & Ward, W. C. (1978). Measures for the study of creativity in scientific problem-solving. *Applied Psychological Measurement, 2(1),* 1–24.

Frederiksen, J. R., & Collins, A. (1989). A systems approach to educational testing. *Educational Researcher, 18*(9), 27–32.

Grigorenko, E. L., & Sternberg, R. J. (1998). Dynamic testing. *Psychological Bulletin, 124,* 75–111.

Hunter, D. (2000). *Beginning XML programming.* Chicago, IL: Wrox Press.

Irvine, S., & Kyllonen, P. (Eds.). (2002). *Item generation for test development.* Hillsdale, NJ: Lawrence Erlbaum Associates.

Landauer, T. K., Laham, D., Rehder, B., & Schreiner, M. E. (1997). How well can passage meaning be derived without using word order? A comparison of Latent Semantic Analysis and humans. In G. Shafto & P. Langley (Eds.), *Proceedings of the 19th Annual Meeting of the Cognitive Science Society* (pp. 412–417). Hillsdale, NJ: Lawrence Erlbaum Associates.

Larkey, L. S. (1998, August). *Automatic essay grading using text categorization techniques.* Paper presented at the 21st international conference of the Association for Computing Machinery-Special Interest Group on Information Retrieval (ACM-SIGIR), Melbourne, Australia.

Lidz, C. S. (1987). Historical perspectives. In C. S. Lidz (Ed.), *Dynamic assessment: An interactional approach to evaluating learning potential* (pp. 3–32). New York: Guilford.

Mathematics Test Creation Assistant (1998). [Computer software]. Princeton, NJ: Educational Testing Service.

"New GMAT adds essay component." (1994, November). *ETS Access,* pp. 1–2.

Odendahl, N. (1999, April). *Online delivery and scoring of constructed-response assessments.* Paper presented at the annual meeting of the American Educational Research Association, Montreal.

Ordinate. (1999). *Validation summary for PhonePass Set-10* [online]. Available: http://www.ordinate.com [January 3, 2001].

Page, E. B., & Petersen, N. S. (1995). The computer moves into essay grading: Updating the ancient test. *Phi Delta Kappan, 76,* 561–565.

Powers, D. E., & Enright, M. K. (1987). Analytical reasoning skills in graduate study: Perceptions of faculty in six fields. *Journal of Higher Education, 58,* 658–682.

Powers, D., Farnum, M., Grant, M., & Kubota, M. (1997). *A pilot test of online essay scoring* (RM-97-7). Princeton, NJ: Educational Testing Service.

Singley, M. K., & Bennett, R. E. (2002). Item generation and beyond: Applications of schema theory to mathematics assessment. In S. Irvine & P. Kyllonen (Eds.), *Item generation for test development* (pp.). Hillsdale, NJ: Lawrence Erlbaum Associates.

U.S. Congress, Office of Technology Assessment. (1992). *Testing in American schools: Asking the right questions* (OTA-SET-519). Washington, DC: U.S. Government Printing Office.

Williamson, D. M., Bejar, I. I., & Hone, A. S. (1999). "Mental model" comparison of automated and human scoring. *Journal of Educational Measurement, 36,* 158–184.

Chapter 12

Assessment of Teamwork Skills Via a Teamwork Questionnaire

Harold F. O'Neil, Jr.
University of Southern California/CRESST

Shuling Wang
Charlotte Lee
University of California, Los Angeles/CRESST

Jamie Mulkey
Hewlett-Packard

Eva L. Baker
University of California, Los Angeles/CRESST

Almost all of the new standards for educational outcomes rely heavily on the use of groups and collaborative learning approaches in content domains (e.g., National Council of Teachers of Mathematics, 1989, 1991). These approaches are assumed to be even more prevalent in schools in the future. Much progress has been made in the specification of what outcomes should be targeted in K–12 content areas. However, less progress has been made in the assessment of collaborative or teamwork processes and outcomes. Similarly, in the world of work, teamwork or collaboration skills are deemed critical now and in the future. Teamwork is a common, desired characteristic of many work environments, particularly high performance, high paying ones (O'Neil, 1997). These skills have become important because, as responsibility is shifted further down the management hierarchy to groups of workers, the average worker needs to communicate and cooperate with other members of the organization to an increasing degree. However, the measurement of teamwork for selection, credentialing, promotion, training outcomes, and so on, is primitive. Currently, the ideal assessment of teamwork is based on think-aloud protocols (Ericsson & Simon, 1993; Voss & Post, 1988) or observational information. However, such assessments are expensive and time consuming.

The model of teamwork presented here is adapted from the Salas, Dickinson, Converse, and Tannenbaum (1992) model in which teamwork skills are defined as team process skills that influence how effective an individual member will be as part of a team. They are domain independent and are assumed to be present in all teams in varying degrees. Such skills have been measured in a team context using computer simulation (e.g., collaborative concept mapping techniques; see Chung, O'Neil, & Herl, 1999). However, there is no feasible way to measure teamwork skills directly without having individuals participate in a team. What would be desirable is to have some indirect, cost-effective means of measuring an individual's potential contribution to a team or collaborative group. The use of a questionnaire technique is one way to accomplish this indirect measurement. This chapter is based on prior reports on this topic (O'Neil, Lee, Wang, & Mulkey, 1999; O'Neil, Wang, Chung, & Herl, 1998). When appropriate, text from the technical reports is used. In some cases, O'Neil and colleagues' (O'Neil et al., 1998; O'Neil et al., 1999) results were recomputed to ensure comparability of samples and statistical analyses. Where there are slight differences, this chapter should be considered the more accurate measure.

The measurement approach is to view teamwork skills as a trait of the individual that predisposes the individual to act as a team member. A *trait* is a characteristic in a person that is relatively enduring (e.g., intelligence or personality). This trait of teamwork skills would be measured by a 5- to 10-minute, multiple choice rating scale and could be administered via paper and pencil or computer.

What, then, is a team? There are various definitions of teams. The following are some useful ones: (a) Teams are composed of two or more people who share a common goal. (b) Teams are composed of members of a working group identified as a "team." (c) A team is a set of two or more people who interact dynamically, interdependently, and adaptively in working toward a common and valued goal, who have each been assigned specific roles or functions to perform, and who have a limited life span of membership (Baker & Salas, 1992).

This model of teamwork skills is adapted from several sources. For example, Salas et al. (1992) characterized teams in terms of two kinds of skills: taskwork skills and teamwork skills. *Taskwork team skills* influence how well a team performs on a particular task. *Teamwork skills*, or *team process skills*, influence how effective an individual member will be as part of a team and are assumed to be common (although they may vary in frequency or intensity) for all team tasks. Experience with teams could occur at work, or when individuals play (athletic teams), or when they contribute time on a team in their community or collaborative groups in school.

The taxonomy (O'Neil, Chung, & Brown, 1997) is made up of six teamwork processes. These skills include (a) adaptability—recognizing problems and responding appropriately; (b) coordination—organizing team activities to complete a task on time; (c) decision making—using available information to make decisions; (d) interpersonal—interacting cooperatively with other team members; (e) leadership—providing direction for the team; and (f) communication—clear and accurate exchange of information.

During the research, successive versions of the teamwork questionnaire were revised. The original plan was to create a 20-item scale that would be unidimensional. The process began with an existing set of teamwork items (developed but not used in an evaluation of collaborative courseware [for the CAETI project]). These teamwork skills items were expanded by writing a set of items based on the interpersonal skills of the Secretary's Committee on Achieving Necessary Skills (SCANS; U.S. Department of Labor, 1991, 1992a, 1992b), the New York Standards for Interpersonal Skills (New York State Education Department, 1990), and the Conference Board of Canada (1993) Employability Skills Profile. This expansion of items resulted in a new questionnaire. This questionnaire was reviewed by a colleague, Dr. Trevor Williams of Westat.

Williams' classification of items in this teamwork questionnaire revealed a disproportionate number of interpersonal items, with the resulting questionnaire being mainly a measure of team cooperation. This is not surprising, as the number of similar interpersonal items is consistent with integrating multiple frameworks (in this case, SCANS, Conference Board of Canada, CRESST, New York) that all have an interpersonal flavor. Another person was asked (a collaborator on the teamwork research at UCLA) to classify the same items, without knowledge of Williams' classification. Then items with poor interjudge reliability were dropped. Thus, the version of the questionnaire used in the study to be reported here has dramatically fewer interpersonal items. New items were written to provide breadth of coverage consistent with the framework. These changes resulted in a 23-item revised questionnaire.

This chapter reports the reliability and validity of the multiple versions of the teamwork skills questionnaire. The teamwork measure was revised by using multiple samples and resulted in a 12-item teamwork skills questionnaire.

PARTICIPANTS

The reliability of the teamwork skills questionnaire was investigated by using multiple samples (total $N = 545$) from four different environments. There were 167 participants from a high technology electronics firm. There were also 153 participants from a (U.S.) Los Angeles-based union. The third data set, which had 108 participants, was drawn from two temporary workers' agencies. The fourth data set, from a Canadian union, had 117 participants.

Electronics Firm

Most participants were males; only 10 participants were female. This firm in Silicon Valley, California, is well known for emphasizing teamwork skills in its environment and is perceived as a high performance workplace. The mean age for these participants was 36.69 years (SD = 8.62); ages ranged from 20 to 58 years.

U.S. Air Conditioning and Refrigeration Union

In order to promote skillful service in the air conditioning and refrigeration industry, an industry/union training program in southern California is conducted in a training center for those union members who are journeymen and apprentices. Of the 153 participants from the training center, only 3 participants were female. Participants' ages ranged from 21 to 65 years, and the mean age was 32.03 years (SD = 7.48).

Temporary Workers' Agencies

One hundred twenty-nine participants were recruited and paid from two temporary workers' agencies. Fifty-three males and 75 females participated. (As not all participants completed all questions in the study materials, there are slightly different numbers in the resulting analyses.) The mean age for these temporary agency participants was 36.91 years (SD = 11.80), and ages ranged from 18 to 63 years. The ethnic composition for this sample was 41 White/Anglos, 44 African Americans, 17 Hispanic/Latinos, and 5 Asians. Participants' educational levels in general ranged from high school graduates to those with doctorates, including 42 high school graduates, 17 participants with associate of arts degrees, 40 with bachelor's degrees, and 9 with master's or doctoral degrees.

Canadian Construction Union

One hundred seventeen participants were recruited from health and safety training courses for the Canadian construction industry. Ninety-nine males and 18 females participated. The mean age for these Canadian company participants was 35.37 years (SD = 11.02), and ages ranged from 18 to 61 years. All but 10 worked in the construction industry, as was indicated by the transmittal letter that accompanied the data (from Lynda Fownes, Skills Improvement Council, Burnaby, BC, Canada, to Eddy Ross, Statistics Canada, Ottawa, Ont., Canada, October 8, 1998).

REVISED TEAMWORK QUESTIONNAIRE

This 23-item questionnaire consisted of six scales measuring teamwork skills and 14 items asking participants about their work environment and whether or not it was high performance (see Appendix, "Background Questions About Your Company"). The six teamwork scales were adaptability (3 items; e.g., *When I work as part of a team, I help to solve problems by using information provided by the team*), coordination (3 items; e.g., *When I work as part of a team, I focus on completing the team task successfully*), decision making (4 items; e.g., *When I work as part of a team, I identify possible alternatives*), leadership (4 items; e.g., *When I work as part of a team, I exercise leadership*), communication (4 items; e.g., *When I work as a member of a team, I attempt to change incorrect information immediately*), and interpersonal (5 items; e.g., *When I work as part of a team, I interact cooperatively with other team members*). Item responses ranged from (1) "almost never," to (2) "sometimes," (3) "often," and (4) "almost always." The 14 background items asking about participants' work environment focused mainly on participants' general thoughts and feelings about their work environment (e.g., *The work generally goes according to plan*). The background items had the same response options as the teamwork items. These background questions were based on a description of a high performance workplace provided by Nash and Korte (1997).

Procedure

Participants in the electronics firm sample were employees attending internal technical support training courses. During a class break, participants were asked to take 15 minutes to complete a voluntary questionnaire. Participants were told that their participation in the study was completely voluntary and choosing not to participate would not impact their job status. Surveys were then collected by the survey administrator and sent back to the research group.

For the U.S. union sample, the investigators went to the industry/union training center in southern California. The investigators informed the participants that they were conducting a study examining teamwork and negotiation skills. Volunteer participants were given the teamwork skills questionnaire and were asked to complete it before doing a computer-based negotiation task. Participants completed the questionnaire in from 7 to 10 minutes.

For the temporary agency workers sample, participants came to CRESST at UCLA. These participants were informed that they were to be part of a study of teamwork and negotiation skills. Volunteer participants were given the teamwork skills questionnaire, and they completed it in about 10 minutes. Due to a test administrator's error, 21 participants were not given the questionnaire and thus were dropped from the analysis.

Volunteer participants in the Canadian union sample completed the questionnaire in approximately 10 minutes when they were attending their health and safety training courses.

Results

Descriptive Statistics.   Means and standard deviations for the items in the teamwork questionnaire scales are shown in Table 12.1. The interpersonal scale had the highest item mean compared with the other scales across all four samples. The leadership scale had the lowest item mean compared with the other scales across all four samples. The results indicated that participants perceived themselves to have higher interpersonal skills than leadership skills. The performance of each sample was similar to that of other samples.

Because the temporary agency sample and the Canadian union sample included more females than either the electronics firm sample or the U.S.

TABLE 12.1
Item Means and Standard Deviations of Teamwork Skills Scales

Scale (# of Items)	Electronics Firm		U.S. Union		Temporary Agency		Canadian Union	
	M	SD	M	SD	M	SD	M	SD
Adaptability	3.09	.44	3.16	.52	3.16	.53	3.19	.51
(3)	(N = 166)		(N = 150)		(N = 104)		(N = 115)	
Coordination	2.97	.53	3.15	.53	3.07	.57	3.16	.47
(3)	(N = 165)		(N = 152)		(N = 107)		(N = 115)	
Decision making	3.27	.41	3.38	.45	3.37	.49	3.39	.41
(4)	(N = 165)		(N = 153)		(N = 108)		(N = 116)	
Leadership	2.71	.56	2.87	.53	2.75	.75	2.81	.59
(4)	(N = 166)		(N = 150)		(N = 104)		(N = 113)	
Communication	3.29	.42	3.38	.41	3.45	.45	3.47	.41
(4)	(N = 165)		(N = 151)		(N = 107)		(N = 117)	
Interpersonal	3.50	.39	3.54	.42	3.61	.37	3.59	.34
(5)	(N = 155)		(N = 150)		(N = 108)		(N = 114)	

union sample, the descriptive statistics for gender differences on teamwork skills scales were also examined for the temporary agency workers and the Canadian union people. For all of the analyses, listwise deletion was conducted and numbers were truncated, not rounded. The statistical results indicated there were no significant differences between males and females or type of sample on the teamwork skills scales (see Table 12.2).

Reliability of the Teamwork Skills Questionnaire. An estimate of internal consistency (Cronbach's α) of the scales for each sample was performed. A rule of thumb was that the reliability should be over .70. As indicated in Table 12.3, the reliability for the total questionnaire was good to excellent (.84–.90). In contrast, the reliability for the individual scales was not acceptable (.30–.84). The latter results are not surprising given the small number of items that constitute each scale. In general, all samples were similar with respect to alpha reliability.

Exploratory Factor Analyses. Separate exploratory factor analyses were conducted for each sample, initially on the electronics firm and the U.S. union samples. The results of the initial analysis using a principal factor analysis with varimax rotation indicated that the items of the communication scale loaded on multiple factors. For the U.S. union sample, after dropping Item 19, which loaded on two factors, the other three items of the communication scale loaded on three different factors. For the electronics firm sample, the four items of communication scale also loaded on three different factors. Thus, all items in the communication scale (Items 7, 11, 15, and 19) were dropped. It made sense to drop the entire set of communication scale items, because the definition of communication involved the clear and accurate exchange of information. Such exchange of information was always in the context of another process (e.g., decision making). Thus, the data showed that participants were not separating communication from other processes, as the communication items loaded on other factors. In addition, Item 1 (i.e., adaptability) and Item 9 (i.e., decision making) loaded on multiple factors and thus were dropped.

The remaining items were then analyzed by principal factor analysis with varimax rotation (see Table 12.4). The same analysis is provided for the Canadian union sample, for the reader's inspection. The results based on the electronics firm and the U.S. union samples indicated that Item 13 loaded on two factors for the electronics firm and the U.S. union sample. Also, the factor loadings of Item 3 for the U.S. union sample and Item 17 for the electronics firm sample were less than .40. As a result, these three items were dropped. The Canadian union sample data were very similar.

After dropping the items loading on two factors or loading less than .40 based on the second analysis, the third analysis on the same samples (elec-

TABLE 12.2
Item Means and Standard Deviations for Gender on Teamwork Skills Scales for Temporary Agency Workers and Canadian Union Participants

| | Temporary Agency | | | | | | Canadian Union | | | | | |
| | Male | | | Female | | | Male | | | Female | | |
Scale	M	SD	N	M	SD	N	M	SD	N	M	SD	N
Adaptability	3.20	.53	42	3.12	.54	58	3.23	.49	98	2.98	.56	17
Coordination	3.13	.60	42	3.05	.55	61	3.18	.46	98	3.00	.54	17
Decision making	3.33	.52	43	3.40	.46	61	3.40	.39	98	3.31	.50	18
Leadership	2.86	.74	42	2.68	.75	58	2.85	.58	95	2.58	.62	18
Communication	3.40	.48	43	3.50	.42	60	3.51	.40	98	3.29	.37	18
Interpersonal	3.58	.36	43	3.65	.37	61	3.57	.35	96	3.68	.23	18

TABLE 12.3
Reliability of the Subscales of the Teamwork Skills Questionnaire

Scale (# of Items)	Electronics Firm		U.S. Union		Temporary Agency		Canadian Union	
	α	N	α	N	α	N	α	N
Total scale (23)	.86	(148)	.84	(145)	.90	(102)	.85	(117)
Adaptability (3)	.45	(166)	.53	(150)	.42	(104)	.56	(115)
Coordination (3)	.45	(165)	.49	(152)	.44	(107)	.30	(115)
Decision making (4)	.60	(165)	.67	(153)	.66	(108)	.57	(116)
Leadership (4)	.76	(166)	.68	(150)	.84	(104)	.73	(113)
Communication (4)	.51	(165)	.48	(151)	.58	(107)	.53	(117)
Interpersonal (5)	.66	(155)	.71	(150)	.63	(108)	.58	(114)

TABLE 12.4
Second Item Analysis of the Teamwork Skills Questionnaire,
Electronics Firm, and Two Union Samples

Item #	Electronics Firm (N = 167)		U.S. Union (N = 153)		Canadian Union (N = 117)	
	Factor 1	Factor 2	Factor 1	Factor 2	Factor 1	Factor 2
16 (leadership)	.75		.67		.62	
23 (leadership)	.73		.63		.78	
2 (leadership)	.70		.72		.74	
5 (leadership)	.57		.56		.54	
6 (decision making)	.59		.64		.53	
8 (coordination)	.56		.67		.70	
18 (decision making)	.42		.44		.43	
14 (adaptability)	.48			.51		.58
21 (coordination)	.44		.40			
17 (interpersonal)				.41	.46	
20 (interpersonal)		.73	.71			.68
12 (interpersonal)		.76	.68			.62
10 (interpersonal)		.61	.73			.65
13 (decision making)	.49	.56	.42	.50	.55	
3 (coordination)		.51			.43	
4 (interpersonal)		.55		.59		.60
22 (adaptability)		.44		.49	.46	.46

tronics firm and U.S. union) indicated that, with one exception, all items loaded uniquely on one factor with loadings over .40 for both samples (see Table 12.5). The factor loadings were also very similar for both samples, except for Item 14. Although Item 14 loaded on the first factor for the electronics firm sample, it loaded on the second factor for the union sample. As a result, Item 14 was dropped. Moreover, after dropping Item 14, Item 22 became the only item for the adaptability scale. Thus, Item 22 also was

TABLE 12.5
Third Item Analysis of the Teamwork Skills Questionnaire

Item #	Electronics Firm (N = 167)		U.S. Union (N = 153)		Canadian Union (N = 117)	
	Factor 1	Factor 2	Factor 1	Factor 2	Factor 1	Factor 2
16 (leadership)	.75		.70		.63	
23 (leadership)	.74		.67		.82	
2 (leadership)	.68		.71		.77	
6 (decision making)	.59		.63		.53	
5 (leadership)	.53		.55		.56	
8 (coordination)	.60		.69		.71	
18 (decision making)	.43		.45		.56	
14 (adaptability)	.48			.49		
21 (coordination)	.45		.44		.56	
20 (interpersonal)		.73		.74		.68
10 (interpersonal)		.67		.72		.68
12 (interpersonal)		.66		.70		.62
4 (interpersonal)		.60		.62		.59
22 (adaptability)		.52		.50	.45	.49

dropped from the study. The Canadian union sample was not used to make this decision, but the same analysis is provided for this sample in Tables 12.4 and 12.5. As may be seen in Tables 12.4 and 12.5, basically the same decisions would have been made if based on results for the Canadian sample.

Based on these exploratory factor analyses, the revised teamwork skills questionnaire consisted of 12 items and was defined with two dimensions: (a) a cognitive teamwork dimension that consisted of items from leadership (4 items), decision making (2 items), and coordination (2 items) processes, and (b) an interpersonal teamwork dimension that was defined by the 4 items from the interpersonal process scale. This revised questionnaire was refined by using principal factor analysis with varimax rotation based on successive analyses of the electronics firm and U.S. union samples.

After data collection was completed for all samples, the 12-item revised questionnaire was tested for all four samples (see Table 12.6). Not surprisingly, the results indicated the factor loadings were nearly identical for both the electronics firm and the U.S. union samples, as the questionnaire was revised using these samples, but slightly different for the two other samples. With few exceptions, all items loaded on the expected factors for the revised questionnaire. However, for the temporary agency worker and Canadian union samples, although almost all items loaded on expected factors with loadings over .40, the factor loading of Item 21 was less than .40 (factor loadings less than .40 are not displayed) and Item 18 loaded on both the interpersonal and cognitive dimensions.

TABLE 12.6
Factor Loadings of the Revised Teamwork Questionnaire for All Samples

Item #	Electronics Firm		U.S. Union		Temporary Agency		Canadian Union	
	Cognitive	Interpersonal	Cognitive	Interpersonal	Cognitive	Interpersonal	Cognitive	Interpersonal
16	.76		.72		.75		.62	
23	.76		.67		.79		.80	
6	.71		.62		.64		.58	
2	.59		.71		.83		.79	
5	.57		.55		.80		.58	
18	.55		.47		.40	.69	.41	.40
8	.43		.70		.71		.75	
21	.40		.43					
12		.72		.75		.67		.68
10		.70		.77		.79		.66
20		.69		.71		.60		.71
4		.62		.65		.51		.60

293

TABLE 12.7
Reliability of the Revised Teamwork Skills Scales

Scale (# of Items)	Electronics Firm	U.S. Union	Temporary Agency	Canadian Union
Total revised questionnaire (12)	.76	.73	.83	.69
Cognitive teamwork scale (8)	.77	.77	.84	.75
Interpersonal teamwork scale (4)	.69	.72	.60	.60

Reliability of the Revised Teamwork Skills Questionnaire. For the revised questionnaire (12 items; see Appendix) alpha reliability was acceptable (.69–.83). The alpha reliabilities for the two dimensions were .60 and greater (see Table 12.7), with alpha reliability for the cognitive teamwork dimension ranging from .75 to .84. However, reliability for the interpersonal teamwork dimension was not acceptable, ranging from .60 to .72. Because there are only four items in the interpersonal teamwork dimension, more items will need to be written if a score for this dimension is desired.

Confirmatory Factor Analysis. A confirmatory factor analysis using EQS (Bentler, 1997) was used to investigate the adequacy of the model (see Table 12.7). EQS (or "Equations") is a structural equation modeling program. The measurement model consisted of two latent factors (scales): a cognitive and an interpersonal teamwork dimension. The items of each scale were assigned to the three indicators of the latent factors, because according to Anderson and Gerbing (1988), it is better to have three indicators per latent factor. Thus, the model had six indicators.

Single-Group Analysis. The model was tested separately for each sample (group). The results are shown in Table 12.8. For the electronics firm sample, the results indicated that the model was reasonably supported by all the fit indices: Bentler-Bonett Non-Normed Fit Index (NNFI) = .96, Comparative Fit Index (CFI) = .98, chi-square ratio = 2.17, and Root Mean Square Er-

TABLE 12.8
Fit Indices for the Model

	Electronics Firm	U.S. Union	Temporary Agency	Canadian Union
Bentler-Bonett Non-Normed Fit Index	.96	.97	.90	.92
Comparative Fit Index	.98	.98	.95	.96
Chi-square/degrees of freedom/p value	13.44/8/ $p > .05$	11.38/8/ $p > .05$	18.57/8/ $p < .05$	11.97/8/ $p > .05$
Chi-square ratio	2.17	1.42	2.32	1.50
RMSEA	.06	.05	.11	.07

ror of Approximation (RMSEA [ε]) = .06, with a 90% confidence interval of $0 < \varepsilon < .121$. A RMSEA of .05 or less is a rule of thumb indicating an excellent fit. Moreover, every indicator significantly loaded on its assigned factors ($p < .05$). The loadings were .45 and above.

For the U.S. union sample, results indicated the Bentler-Bonett Non-Normed Fit Index = .97. The model was supported by most indices: Comparative Fit Index = .98, chi-square ratio = 1.42, and Root Mean Square Error of Approximation (RMSEA [ε]) = .05, with a 90% confidence interval of .000 $\leq \varepsilon \leq$ .116. In addition, every indicator loaded on its assigned factor significantly ($p > .05$). The loadings were over .51. Recall that the electronics firm and the U.S. union samples were also used to generate the revised questionnaire. Thus, it was expected that these samples would demonstrate a better fit than the Canadian union and the temporary agency worker samples.

For the temporary agency sample, the Comparative Fit Index = .95, the Bentler-Bonett Non-Normed Fit Index = .90, and chi-square ratio = 2.32. Further, the RMSEA fit indicator indicated a moderate fit (RMSEA [ε] = .11). Also, every indicator loaded on its assigned factor significantly ($p < .05$). These loadings were .49 and above.

For the Canadian union sample, results indicated the Bentler-Bonett Non-Normed Fit Index = .92. The model was supported by most indices: Comparative Fit Index = .96, chi-square ratio = 1.50, and Root Mean Square Error of Approximation (RMSEA [ε]) = .07, with a 90% confidence interval of .000 $\leq \varepsilon \leq$ .136. In addition, every indicator loaded on its assigned factor significantly ($p > .05$). The loadings were .53 and above.

Multiple-Group Analysis. This approach was used to evaluate whether the questionnaire operated equivalently across different populations (Byrne, 1994). This analysis did not include the Canadian union sample. The results indicated the model was equivalent across the electronics firm, U.S. union, and temporary agency samples. Although the chi-square value of 75.02 with 34 degrees of freedom was significant ($p < .01$), the Bentler-Bonett Non-Normed Fit Index of .91, Comparative Fit Index of .93, and chi-square ratio of 2.21 all indicated that this multiple-group model represented an excellent fit to the data. Because the results indicated that the model was equivalent across all three samples, the samples were merged to test the model in order to have a higher statistical power.

Merged Sample Analysis. The results for all four samples indicated the model was supported by most indices (Bentler-Bonett Non-Normed Fit Index = .97, Comparative Fit Index = .98, Root Mean Square Error of Approximation, RMSEA [ε] = .050, with a 90% confidence interval of .021 $\leq \varepsilon \leq$ .080, chi-square ratio = 18.93 with 8 degrees of freedom). This was not unexpected because the chi-square value was biased against a large sample size. In addition, all indicators loaded significantly on their assigned factors. The loadings were .52 and above.

In summary, the revised questionnaire was supported by most fit indices of either single-group or multiple-group analysis. In other words, the revised teamwork skills questionnaire had acceptable reliability and promising validity. In addition, because the results indicated few differences between samples for the revised questionnaire, the four samples were aggregated for the following validity data analysis.

Additional Validity Information

The Relation Between High Performance Environments and the Revised Questionnaire. Using a construct validity approach, it was expected that there should be a relation between the revised teamwork questionnaire and responses to the set of items defining a perceived high performance environment. Teamwork scores should be higher in a self-reported high performance environment. In order to evaluate the relation between high performance environments and the revised questionnaire, the top one quarter and bottom one quarter were selected of all participants based on their total score for their responses to 11 items regarding high performance environments. This set of items was meant to measure whether the organization was a high performing one (see Appendix, Items 13–23). The maximum score for the high performance set of items was 44. The selected top one quarter of the participants, who had a score equal to or higher than 40, were perceived to work for a high performing environment, whereas the bottom quarter of participants, who had a score equal to or lower than 33, were perceived to work for a lower performing environment. The results indicated that there was the predicted relation between teamwork skills and type of performance environment (Table 12.9).

T tests were performed to measure the difference between high performance environment and low performance environment on the revised

TABLE 12.9
Relation Between Revised Scales and
High/Low Performance Environment

	High Performance Environment	Low Performance Environment
Cognitive teamwork scale*	25.02 (3.56) $n = 129$	22.17 (4.36) $n = 145$
Interpersonal teamwork scale*	14.84 (1.41) $n = 129$	13.97 (1.67) $n = 150$
Total questionnaire*	39.93 (4.01) $n = 127$	36.17 (4.36) $n = 145$

*$p < .05$

questionnaire dimensions. The results indicated that there were significant differences between high and low performance environments for all scales. In other words, as predicted, participants who work in high performance environments use more teamwork skills than participants who work in low performance environments.

The results indicated there were higher teamwork skills in the high performance environment group. It was assumed that such skills are valued in a high performance environment but not in a low performance environment. These results imply some construct validity for the scales. However, this criterion measure was used only for the first time in this study with four samples. Additional reliability/validity analyses need to be performed on the criterion measure.

Relation Between Working in Teams and the Revised Teamwork Questionnaire. Another analysis to provide some construct validity information was conducted by relating the revised questionnaire to how often participants worked in a team. It was expected that if they reported almost always working in a team, then they would exhibit higher teamwork skills. Item 26 of the questionnaire, "At work, how often do you work as a part of a team?" measured participants' perceptions of how frequently they worked as a team member at work. Responses ranged from (1) "almost never," to (2) "sometimes," (3) "often," and (4) "almost always." Participants who responded that they almost always work as a part of team were defined as high teamworkers; participants who responded that they sometimes or almost never work as a part of a team were defined as low teamworkers. It was expected that participants who almost always work as part of a team would exhibit higher levels of teamwork skills (measured by the teamwork skills questionnaire).

T tests were performed to measure the difference between high teamworkers and low teamworkers on the revised questionnaire dimensions. The analyses included all four samples. The results indicated there was a significant difference between high teamworkers and low teamworkers on their teamwork skills as measured by the cognitive teamwork skills scale and the total scale but not by the interpersonal teamwork skills scale (see Table 12.10).

TABLE 12.10
Item Means and Standard Deviations for
High/Low Teamworkers on Revised Scales

	High Teamworkers			Low Teamworkers		
	M	SD	N	M	SD	N
Cognitive teamwork scale	3.03*	.47	140	2.86*	.50	163
Interpersonal teamwork scale	3.62	.41	142	3.54	.42	165
Total questionnaire	3.23*	.35	138	3.09*	.37	162

*$p < .05$

In other words, high teamworkers were more likely than low teamworkers to use more of the teamwork skills from the cognitive dimension. In general, the revised questionnaire was able to distinguish high and low teamworkers, which indicated that the revised questionnaire has reasonable discriminant validity via this analysis.

CONCLUSIONS

This report summarizes the research regarding the reliability and validity of a teamwork skills questionnaire. A theoretical framework of teamwork skills and a rationale for measuring the construct via a self-report instrument were provided. Teamwork is a common, desired characteristic of many work and school environments that use collaborative problem-solving techniques. However, for many environments, there is no cost-effective way to measure teamwork/collaboration skills directly without having individuals participate in a team. A questionnaire technique was used as the means to accomplish an indirect measurement of an individual's potential contribution to a team.

The trait of teamwork skills was measured by a 12-item questionnaire. In general, this teamwork skills questionnaire has acceptable reliability. The results of the validity studies are also promising. These results have been replicated and extended using a Taiwanese sample of engineers and assembly line workers, who were given a Chinese version of the questionnaire (Weng, 1999). The revised teamwork skills questionnaire can be used as is in low stakes environments if a single teamwork skills score is desired. If scores for cognitive and affective teamwork skills are desired, then the interpersonal teamwork scale should be revised by adding more items. Current research in our lab has pursued this approach successfully (Kuehl, 2001). Obviously, additional reliability and validity studies would be needed if the questionnaire were to be used in a high school environment.

ACKNOWLEDGMENTS

The authors wish to thank Ms. Lynda Fownes and Mr. Eddy Ross for their assistance in the data collection for the Canadian union sample.

The work reported herein was supported by contract No. 85300-97-0065 from Statistics Canada, Government of Canada, and under the Educational Research and Development Centers Program, PR/Award No. R305B60002, as administered by the Office of Educational Research and Improvement, U.S. Department of Education. The findings and opinions expressed in this report do not reflect the positions or policies of the National Institute on

Student Achievement, Curriculum, and Assessment, the Office of Educational Research and Improvement, or the U.S. Department of Education; nor do they necessarily reflect the positions or policies of Statistics Canada, or the Government of Canada.

REFERENCES

Anderson, J. C., & Gerbing, D. W. (1988). Structural equation modeling in practice: A review and recommended two-step approach. *Psychological Bulletin, 103*, 411–423.

Baker, D. P., & Salas, E. (1992). Principles for measuring teamwork skills. *Human Factors, 34*, 469–475.

Bentler, P. M. (1997). *EQS: Structural equations program manual.* Encino, CA: Multivariate Software, Inc.

Byrne, B. M. (1994). *Structural equation modeling with EQS and EQS/Windows.* Thousand Oaks, CA: Sage.

Conference Board of Canada. (1993). *Employability skills profile.* Ottawa, Ontario, Canada: Author. (The Conference Board of Canada, 255 Smyth Road, Ottawa, Ontario, K1H 8M7, CANADA, 10/93)

Chung, G. K. W. K., O'Neil, H. F., Jr., & Herl, H. E. (1999). The use of computer-based collaborative knowledge mapping to measure team processes and team outcomes. *Computers in Human Behavior, 15*, 463–493.

Ericsson, K. A., & Simon, H. A. (1993). *Protocol analysis: Verbal reports as data* (rev. ed.). Cambridge, MA: MIT Press.

Kuehl, M. A. (2001). *Revision of teamwork questionnaire for the United States Marine Corps aviation community.* Unpublished doctoral dissertation, University of Southern California, Los Angeles.

Nash, B. E., & Korte, R. C. (1997). Validation of SCANS competencies by a national job analysis study. In H. F. O'Neil, Jr. (Ed.), *Workforce readiness: Competencies and assessment* (pp. 77–102). Mahwah, NJ: Lawrence Erlbaum Associates.

National Council of Teachers of Mathematics. (1989). *Curriculum and evaluation standards for school mathematics.* Reston, VA: Author.

National Council of Teachers of Mathematics. (1991). *Professional standards for teaching school mathematics.* Reston, VA: Author.

New York State Education Department. (1990, July). *Basic and expanded basic skills. Scales for validation study.* Albany, NY: Author.

O'Neil, H. F., Jr. (Ed.). (1997). *Workforce readiness: Competencies and assessment.* Mahwah, NJ: Lawrence Erlbaum Associates.

O'Neil, H. F., Jr., Chung, G. K. W. K., & Brown, R. (1997). Use of networked simulations as a context to measure team competencies. In H. F. O'Neil, Jr. (Ed.), *Workforce readiness: Competencies and assessment* (pp. 411–452). Mahwah, NJ: Lawrence Erlbaum Associates.

O'Neil, H. F., Jr., Lee, C.-Y., Wang, S.-L., & Mulkey, J. L. (1999, March). *Final report for analysis of teamwork skills questionnaire* (Deliverable to Statistics Canada). Sherman Oaks, CA: Advance Design Information.

O'Neil, H. F., Jr., Wang, S.-L., Chung, G. K. W. K., & Herl, H. E. (1998). *Final report for validation of teamwork skills questionnaire using computer-based teamwork simulations* (Deliverable to Statistics Canada). Los Angeles: University of California, National Center for Research on Evaluation, Standards, and Student Testing.

Salas, E., Dickinson, T. L., Converse, S. A., & Tannenbaum, S. I. (1992). Toward an understanding of team performance and training. In R. W. Swezey & E. Salas (Eds.), *Teams: Their training and performance* (pp. 3–30). Norwood, NJ: Ablex.

U.S. Department of Labor. (1991, June). *What work requires of schools: A SCANS report for America 2000*. Washington, DC: U.S. Department of Labor, Secretary's Commission on Achieving Necessary Skills.

U.S. Department of Labor. (1992a). *Learning a living: A Blueprint for high performance*. Washington, DC: The Secretary's Commission on Achieving Necessary Skills (SCANS).

U.S. Department of Labor. (1992b). *Skills and tasks for jobs: A SCANS report for America 2000*. Washington, DC: U.S. Department of Labor, Secretary's Commission on Achieving Necessary Skills.

Voss, J. F., & Post, T. A. (1988). On the solving of ill-structured problems. In M. T., Chi, R. Glaser, & M. J. Farr (Eds.), *The nature of expertise* (pp. 261–287). Hillsdale, NJ: Lawrence Erlbaum Associates.

Weng, A. L.-B. (1999). *A teamwork skills questionnaire: A reliability and validity study of the Chinese version*. Unpublished doctoral dissertation, Los Angeles, CA, University of Southern California.

APPENDIX:
REVISED TEAMWORK SKILLS QUESTIONNAIRE

SCORING KEY

Scales	Items
Coordination	2, 5
Decision Making	8, 11
Leadership	1, 4, 7, 10
Interpersonal	3, 6, 9, 12

COORDINATION

2. When I work as part of a team, I organize team activities to complete tasks on time.
5. When I work as part of a team, I keep track of time.

DECISION MAKING

8. When I work as part of a team, I identify possible alternatives.
11. When I work as part of a team, I understand and contribute to the organization's goals.

LEADERSHIP

1. When I work as part of a team, I exercise leadership.
4. When I work as part of a team, I teach other team members.
7. When I work as part of a team, I serve as a role model in formal and informal interactions.
10. When I work as part of a team, I lead when appropriate, mobilizing the group for high performance.

INTERPERSONAL

3. When I work as part of a team, I work well with men and women from diverse backgrounds.
6. When I work as part of a team, I interact cooperatively with other team members.
9. When I work as part of a team, I conduct myself with courtesy.
12. When I work as part of a team, I respect the thoughts and opinions of others in the team.

Revised Teamwork Skills Questionnaire

Please be assured that your answers regarding your teamwork skills will be kept confidential and not reported in an identifiable way to anyone in your company. We plan to share findings with your company at the end of the project. However, as this questionnaire is anonymous, there will be no individual feedback.

Background Questions:

Company: _____

Date: _____ Age in years _____ Gender (please circle): M   F

Teamwork Questions:

Directions: This set of questions is to help us understand the way you think and feel about working with others. We know that different parts of your life, such as your job, recreational activities, or service to your community, may involve working with others and have different requirements, and that you may react differently in each kind of activity. Nonetheless, read each statement below and indicate how you generally think or feel. There are no right or wrong answers. Do not spend too much time on any one statement. Remember, give the answer that seems to describe how you generally think or feel.

		Almost never	Sometimes	Often	Almost always
1.	When I work as part of a team, I exercise leadership.	1	2	3	4
2.	When I work as part of a team, I organize team activities to complete tasks on time.	1	2	3	4
3.	When I work as part of a team, I work well with men and women from diverse backgrounds.	1	2	3	4
4.	When I work as part of a team, I teach other team members.	1	2	3	4
5.	When I work as part of a team, I keep track of time.	1	2	3	4
6.	When I work as part of a team, I interact cooperatively with other team members.	1	2	3	4
7.	When I work as part of a team, I serve as a role model in formal and informal interactions.	1	2	3	4
8.	When I work as part of a team, I identify possible alternatives.	1	2	3	4
9.	When I work as part of a team, I conduct myself with courtesy.	1	2	3	4
10.	When I work as part of a team, I lead when appropriate, mobilizing the group for high performance.	1	2	3	4
11.	When I work as part of a team, I understand and contribute to the organization's goals.	1	2	3	4
12.	When I work as part of a team, I respect the thoughts and opinions of others in the team.	1	2	3	4

Background Questions About Your Company

What is the work environment like where you work?

	Almost never	Sometimes	Often	Almost always
13. a quality product/service is the main goal	1	2	3	4
14. customer satisfaction is a high priority	1	2	3	4
15. constructive criticism is encouraged	1	2	3	4
16. the work generally goes according to plan	1	2	3	4
17. everyone is encouraged to learn new things	1	2	3	4
18. people regularly share their ideas	1	2	3	4
19. the firm/company does well financially	1	2	3	4
20. people really put themselves into their work	1	2	3	4
21. our leaders have a clear vision of the company	1	2	3	4
22. team work is important	1	2	3	4
23. problem-solving skills are important	1	2	3	4

24. In total, about how many persons are employed by your company at all locations? (please circle)

Less than 20..1
20 to 99..2
100 to 500...3
501 to 999...4
1,000 to 2,499...5
2,500 to 9,999...6
10,000 or over 7
DON'T KNOW...9

25. At work, I sometimes work as part of a team. (please circle)   Yes   No

If you answered NO to the above question, skip the following question.

	Almost never	Sometimes	Often	Almost always
26. At work, how often do you work as part of a team?	1	2	3	4

Thank you.

Chapter 13

Using Technology to Assess Students' Web Expertise

Davina C. D. Klein
Louise Yarnall
Christina Glaubke
University of California, Los Angeles/CRESST

As the popularity of the Internet increases, almost everyone can find something on the World Wide Web (WWW) of interest to them. Web surfers can find an out-of-print book; look up government statistics on hundreds, if not thousands, of topics; even put a bid in on that perfect, hard-to-find item. It was estimated that almost one fifth of Americans (57 million people) had Internet access from home, work, or school in 1997 (U.S. Census Bureau, 1999) and that number certainly continues to rise. But, as popular and as populated as the Web is with facts, opportunities, and purchasing possibilities, searching the Web is often compared to looking for a needle in a haystack. With over 1.5 billion web pages thought to be available and with that number increasing at the incredible rate of 1.9 million web pages each day (Lawrence & Giles, 1999; The Web: Growing by 2 million pages a day, 2000), the real trick to using the World Wide Web is not learning how to surf as much as it is learning how to search. Such skills are important today and will be more important in the future.

Technology coordinators, media specialists, and classroom teachers alike have been tackling this issue in schools. With 9 million children using the Internet at school (U.S. Census Bureau, 1999), estimates of at least from 40% to 45% of American classrooms linked to the Internet (Becker, 1999; Market Data Research, 1998), and nearly 90% of teachers reporting they perceive classroom web access as valuable or essential for their teaching (Becker, 1999), information literacy curricula are beginning to appear and teachers are beginning to assign projects to students that include research on the Web (Breivik, 1998; Duffield, 1997; Ercegovac, 1998; Roblyer, 1998). In fact, teachers report that research is the most common classroom use for the Web, with web searching having surpassed skills practice to become the third most common use of computers by students at school (Becker, 1999). Recent studies into how children and adults use the World Wide Web show this environment holds both tremendous promise and thorny challenges for educators. As a research environment, the WWW has been compared to a universe (Berners-Lee, Cailliau, Groff, & Pollermann, 1992), containing a vast number of information sites on countless subjects. But this expansive environment also presents a problem for educators because much of this information is not designed for children's use (Kafai & Bates, 1997). Research focusing on the ways children can best use the web environment has underscored the importance of developing their web-searching skills or web fluency.

The terms *web fluency* and *web expertise* are used interchangeably in this chapter. These terms mean students' proficiency with the World Wide Web, generally developed through training or experience. What characterizes web fluency? What kind of navigational styles, cognitive characteristics, and search behaviors are beneficial when looking for information buried somewhere in the web of information? Recent empirical research has focused on describing how adults and children use the WWW environment. Novices to the WWW's open-ended environment face the challenge of defining a proper starting point and procedures to complete the information search (Hill, 1997). Empirical research regarding the navigational strategies adults use to maintain orientation in the WWW environment shows they do so by using the back button and returning to previously viewed pages (Catledge & Pitkow, 1995; Tauscher & Greenberg, 1997). Hill found that the more familiarity adults had with the structure of the WWW environment, the more they employed problem-solving strategies, such as integrating new information, taking varied viewpoints on the information they found, and extracting the relevant details. Hill also found that unfamiliarity with the WWW environment corresponded with prolonged attempts to form queries, define search options, and find one's place in the system. Finally, as expected, research on expert searchers suggests that search efficiency is also important (see, e.g., Salterio, 1996).

Although this research was predominately with adults, it also provides the rough outline of children's developing expertise as web searchers. Like adults, in order to prevent disorientation, children use the back button and frequently return to "landmark" pages that provide several links to other locations (Fidel et al., 1999). Even the youngest children can scroll through Web sites and use hyperlinks to surf the Web, whereas older children can distinguish among different search engines and use Boolean operators (Kafai & Bates, 1997). However, research has demonstrated that—compared to adults—children have particular difficulty forming effective queries and scanning search results (Bilal, 1998; Fidel et al., 1999; Kafai & Bates, 1997; Schacter, Chung, & Dorr, 1998). These difficulties appear to be related directly to children's lowered level of literacy, as most problems stem from off-topic queries, misspelled queries, natural language queries, and reluctance to spend time scanning search results. Studies of children and adolescents using the WWW show that these users have the same difficulties they have in other information database environments; examples of these difficulties include constructing effective queries, scanning search results pages critically, monitoring the progress of a search, and developing broad assessment strategies to determine the relevance of Web sites (Bilal, 1998; Borgman, Hirsch, Walter, & Gallagher, 1995; Fidel et al., 1999; Kafai & Bates, 1997; Kuhlthau, 1996; Marchionini, 1989).

Although teaching students how to search for information is surfacing as an important goal and recent research has begun characterizing children's searching abilities, little has yet to be said about the assessment of these newfound capabilities (see Schacter et al., 1998; Schacter, Herl, Chung, Dennis, & O'Neil, 1999, for notable exceptions). For guidance in developing an evaluative rubric for WWW fluency, consult research conducted with other open-ended search systems, such as library and hypertext databases.

Researchers in these areas have described the ideal sequential structure of search behavior. Good searching occurs as the searcher learns more about the information environment and repeatedly revises a query to adapt to that environment. Bates (1989) coined the phrase "berrypicking" to describe how adults adjust their search goals and queries as they review new information in a database, selecting relevant information as they proceed through a search. Rosenberg (1996) described the orientation phase in a hypertext environment as a process of exhausting various paths, which ultimately leads the searcher to establishing the structure of the information environment. Guthrie and Dreher (1990) outlined five phases of a search, including goal formation, category selection, information extraction, integration, and recycling. Some have described how a searcher's initial understanding of a question will influence navigational patterns. Depending on how open or focused the initial question is, searchers may employ such approaches as browsing, focused searching, and random discovery (Carmel, Crawford, & Chen, 1992; Cove & Walsh, 1988; Marchionini, 1989).

These descriptions suggest that the best searchers tailor their queries to the information environment. Previous research has then tended to measure how quickly and precisely searchers accomplish this feat. Expert database searchers find information more quickly, use more precise queries (such as Boolean operators), and cover more information overall (Salterio, 1996). Thus, the literature suggests two different types of outcome measures: information selection and search efficiency. Better searchers can be identified by their ability to find more relevant information for their query and by less time being devoted to finding good information. Interestingly, the literature does not equate good searching with few steps, but with many steps, because good searchers tend to review and revisit more information than poorer searchers.

When investigating how best to assess students' web fluency, measures were included that illustrated the outcomes of students' searches (e.g., precisely what they find and how efficiently they find it), the process involved in achieving those goals (e.g., the kinds of navigational techniques they use, their searching sophistication), as well as the prior attitudes students possess regarding the World Wide Web itself. Thus, a prototype assessment tool was created to begin to explore important factors in students' World Wide Web searches. This tool assesses students' fluency with the World Wide Web by using measures collected during an authentic, performance-based assessment task.

This research addresses two critical issues. First, it attempts to model the creation of a quality assessment instrument to be used in measuring important web skills. Although researchers agree as to the importance of these web skills, measurement instrumentation is sorely lacking. Second, this research approach involves operationally defining these technology skills. Using principal component analysis, various specific factors are outlined that make up the construct we called web fluency.

In order to investigate the validity and reliability of this assessment tool, a study was conducted with middle and high school students. The research approach was to study these experienced web users to identify a set of student measures that would allow for a better understanding and evaluation of students' facility with the Web. Multiple measures, captured both during student searches and as the results of these searches, were employed by the use of an online assessment system and its associated automated data-logging and scoring capability. These measures were then analyzed in order to gain a better understanding of the important constructs underlying students' web expertise.

METHODS

Participants

One hundred and twenty middle and high school students from three schools participated in this study. Schools were part of the Department of Defense school system and were participants in a large-scale program geared toward innovative uses of technology in the classroom (see Perez & Bridgewater, chap. 5, in this vol.). Due in part to this participation, students had strong technology background, had access to computers and the Internet in the classroom, and were familiar with navigating the World Wide Web. Students' grade level ranged from 7th through 12th grade. The sample was 57% female, with an ethnic breakdown as follows: 61% White, 18% African American, 3% Latino, 2% Native American, 1% Asian American, 13% of mixed ethnicity, and 3% other.

Instrumentation

In order to investigate students' web expertise, or fluency with the World Wide Web, the Web Expertise Assessment (WEA) was created. This online assessment automatically captures both process and outcome data that is subsequently coded and scored (by raters and by computer) in order to characterize students' WWW fluency.

The Web Expertise Assessment features four important functions: an on-line search engine, a web-based information space, a navigation toolbar, and an automatic logging capability. As may be seen in Fig. 13.1, in appearance, WEA pages resemble the World Wide Web, and the WEA interface (including the WEA navigation toolbar at the top of each page) looks like Netscape. The closed, content-controlled WEA information space created for this study features approximately 500 pages of information. The toolbar includes buttons for navigating back, forward, and home, and also includes buttons to initiate a search, to add a bookmark, to view bookmarks, and to conduct a find word in page search. Using this toolbar to navigate, students can use WEA's search engine to search through the information space. WEA automatically logs all keystrokes and mouse clicks, creating a permanent and extensive database record of all student performance. WEA assesses students' expertise with the WWW by presenting students with authentic search tasks (e.g., preparing for a school research report) and asking them to find relevant information in a closed web-based environment. Students are then asked to "bookmark" pages they judge relevant to the task.

Two kinds of measures were collected using the online tool. Some measures were directly quantifiable from the log data gathered during students' use of the WEA system. For example, the number of searches used to find information, some usage of navigational techniques to move through the information space (such as the number of times the back button was used), the number of bookmarks created throughout the search, and the number of steps taken to complete the search were automatically extracted from the data log. Other measures were coded by human raters following data collection. Examples of these kinds of measures included the quality of students' search terms, certain navigational techniques (e.g., the number of

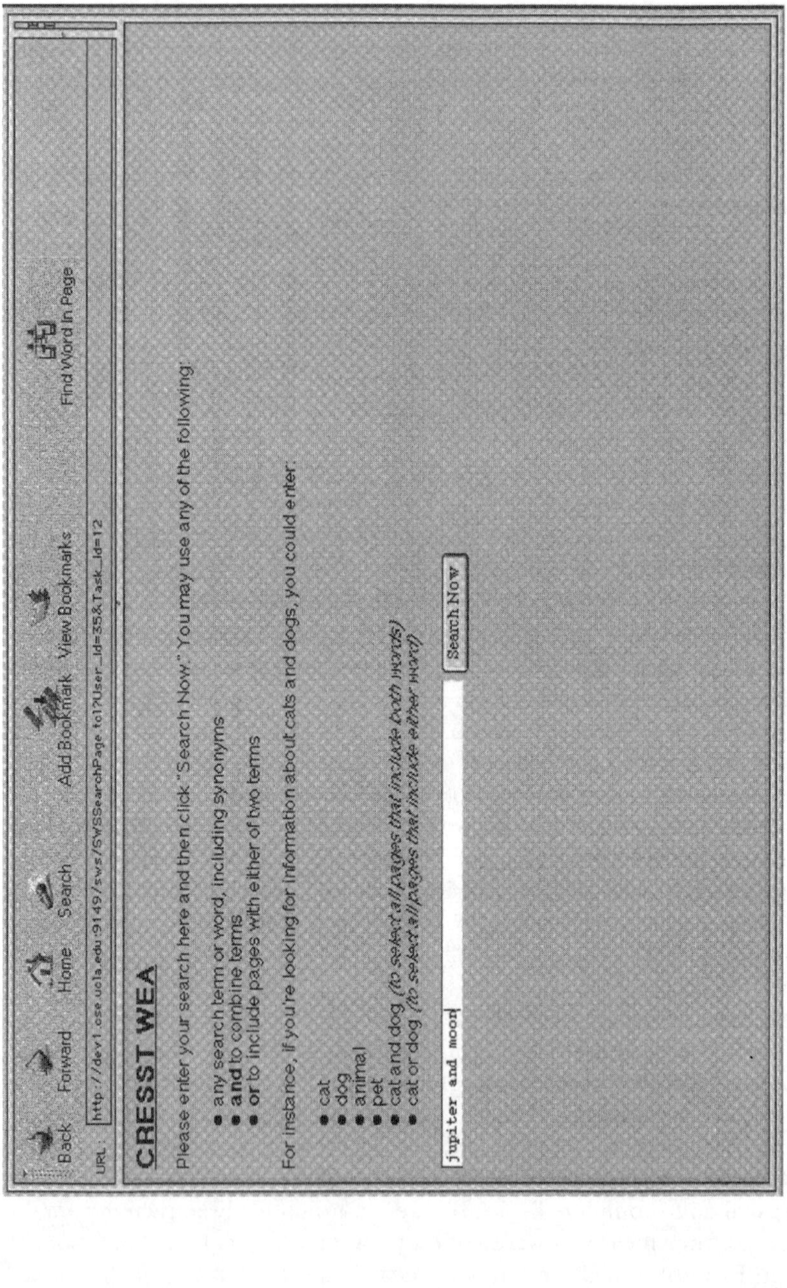

FIG. 13.1. Sample WEA page.

redirected searches), the quality of students' individual bookmarks, and the overall quality of students' bookmark sets.

Seventeen individual measures of performance were selected from WEA. Although data are presented on student performance on these various measures in the following section, for clarity these measures are defined in this section. The total number of searches a student completed included each search attempted. Each individual student search was rated as a good search if it was on topic and included keywords, Boolean operators, or synonyms. The number of keyword searches included all searches involving the use of a keyword. Searches were categorized as redirected if a student attempted a new search before visiting any page identified by the initial search's hit list. The quality of a student's searches was also judged as a set, with a score of 0 indicating no keyword searches or completely off-topic searches, a score of 1 indicating at least one on-topic keyword search, a score of 2 indicating more than one half the searches were on-topic keyword searches, and a score of 3 indicating at least one Boolean keyword search. The number of information pages visited was measured, including all pages visited by a student except for the search and home pages. The number of pages revisited by a student was also calculated, as was the number of times he or she used the back button. The amount and quality of in-page searches was also recorded. The number of steps a student completed was measured, with each mouse click counting as one step (e.g., selecting a page to visit from a hit list, conducting a keyword search, returning to the home page). Each page a student bookmarked (termed a bookmark) was assigned an individual score, with a score of 0 indicating an off-topic bookmark, a score of 1 indicating a bookmark on topic but not relevant to the student's task, a score of 2 indicating a bookmark peripherally relevant to the task, and a score of 3 indicating an on-topic and directly relevant bookmark. The total number of bookmarks created, the number of bookmarks scoring a 3, the highest single bookmark score, and the total summed bookmark score were recorded for each student. A student's average bookmark score was calculated as the mean of all his or her bookmark scores. Also assessed was the quality of the bookmarks a student made when examined together as a set to answer the student's prompt; this was measured on a scale of 0 (irrelevant response set), 1 (fair response set), 2 (good response set), and 3 (excellent response set). Finally, a ratio was used of the number of good bookmarks made by a student to the total number of pages visited to measure a student's searching efficiency.

In addition to searching for particular information using WEA, a WWW questionnaire addressed students' attitudes regarding the World Wide Web. On a scale of 1 ("I really don't agree"), 2 ("I don't agree"), 3 ("I'm neutral"), 4 ("I really agree"), and 5 ("I really agree"), students were asked to indicate how much they agreed or disagreed with statements such as,

"The information on the World Wide Web is not very useful." Although students were considered to be experienced web users (due to their teachers' involvement in a school-wide technology program), it was hoped that this questionnaire would further explore individual differences in students' web attitudes.

Procedure

During each testing session, researchers followed a basic test administration procedure. First, students filled out the WWW questionnaire, which was intended to measure students' attitudes about the World Wide Web. This form was read aloud while students completed it. Researchers then introduced the Web Expertise Assessment to students. Students were seated individually before computer screens while a research team member walked them through a practice search procedure. There was one research team member per class. During this initial presentation, students were taught to use WEA's navigation toolbar—using each of its buttons at least once during the practice search—and were reminded how to conduct searches using keywords and Boolean operators. After reviewing WEA's operation, researchers gave students their search task assignments. Students were told they had 20 minutes to bookmark relevant pages and to complete their searches. During the WEA administration, researchers reminded students to bookmark relevant pages. At the end of the 20-minute period, researchers asked students to conclude their searches by returning to the WEA home page. All data were logged online and subsequently coded.

RESULTS

Preliminary Analyses

Web Expertise Assessment.   Interrater reliability on items rated by humans using detailed scoring rubrics was computed by double-coding 25% of responses; reliability was found to be acceptably high on all measures (see Table 13.1). In addition, interrater reliability for coding of bookmark relevance (used to then score bookmark measures) was calculated at .97. A complete list of WEA measures, including interrater reliabilities (when applicable), means, and standard deviations are shown in Table 13.1.

As may be seen in Table 13.1, students performed a mean of about 4.83 searches in the 20-minute testing period. Students performed a mean of 1.97 good searches, with about one third of these searches (0.69 searches) being keyword searches. In addition, students redirected 2.33 other searches—deciding to retry a new search rather than visiting any page iden-

TABLE 13.1
Descriptive Statistics for Web Expertise
Assessment Measures ($N = 120$)

Measure	Interrater Reliability	M	SD
Total number of searches	—	4.83	3.13
Number of good searches	.98	1.97	2.05
Number of unique keyword searches	—	0.69	0.89
Number of redirected searches	.99	2.33	2.40
Quality of keyword searching set[a]	.99	1.69	0.81
Number of information pages visited	—	11.4	8.83
Number of revisited information pages	—	4.04	8.26
Number of times back button used	—	17.2	12.4
Quality of in-page searches[a]	.75	0.92	1.07
Number of steps in search	—	93.0	54.7
Total number of bookmarks made	—	5.96	6.47
Number of good bookmarks made	.97[b]	1.94	1.69
Average bookmark score[a]	.97[b]	1.82	0.82
Highest single bookmark score[a]	.97[b]	2.48	1.00
Total bookmark score	.97[b]	11.2	10.4
Quality of bookmark set[a]	.97	1.84	1.00
Efficiency of search	.97[b]	0.21	0.19

Note: Dash indicates computer coding of data.
[a]Coded on a scale of 0 to 3.
[b]Reported alpha is for coding of bookmark relevance only; following this human rating, calculation of each of these measures was automated.

tified by the search's hit list. These redirected searches demonstrated that students were able to browse a search output list and determine whether or not a more refined search was necessary. The quality of students' searches was also judged as a set; students' mean overall quality searching score was 1.69 (on a 0 to 3 scale, with a score of 2 indicating more than one half the searches were on-topic keyword searches). These searches led students to visit on average about 11 unique pages, with about 4 of those pages being revisited over the course of the session. Revisiting pages is an orienting technique used by experienced searchers to navigate through an information space. Use of the back button is another orienting technique used by experts; students used this technique often—clicking the back button on average 17.2 times during the course of their search. Having arrived at an information page, only about one third of students (37%) used the in-page search feature appropriately. In sum, students completed an average of 93.0 steps (excluding use of back button and revisited pages).

Because students were told to bookmark as many pages as were relevant and useful for answering the prompt, there were many ways to characterize their finding ability. Like their searches, the pages students bookmarked were rated "good" if they were on topic and directly relevant to the search prompt. Of the total number of bookmarks made per student ($M = 5.96$), about one third of these pages were considered good by raters ($M = 1.94$). Students' average bookmark scores ranged from 0 to 3 (a score of 2 signified a bookmark peripherally relevant to the search prompt), with the mean bookmark score of 1.82. However, when examining each student's highest bookmark score, the mean was found to be 2.48. In addition, 75% of students made at least one good bookmark. This indicates that most students were able to find at least one good page and identify it as such. Also, when overall scores were calculated by summing across all bookmark scores, the mean student overall bookmark score was 11.2. On a scale of 0 to 3, students' mean quality bookmark score (the quality of the bookmarks a student made when assessed as a set) was 1.84, with a score of 2 denoting a good, but not excellent, response set. Finally, on a scale of 0 to 1, students' mean searching efficiency rating was .21 indicating that, of all the pages students chose to visit, about one fifth were bookmarked appropriately.

WWW Attitudes Questionnaire. Results from the WWW attitudes questionnaire, including specific items, means, and standard deviations, are shown in Table 13.2. In general, students' responses were as might be expected from experienced Internet users. Only 6% of students agreed or strongly agreed that the information on the WWW is not very useful, and 61% of students reported disagreeing or strongly disagreeing with the statement, "There is not a lot of detailed and in-depth information on the World Wide Web." Given the erratic nature of information out on the WWW, it is not surprising that one half the students chose a neutral response, neither agreeing nor disagreeing with the statement, "The information out on the World Wide Web is accurate or correct." An additional 20% of students disagreed or strongly disagreed with this statement. This is an indication that

TABLE 13.2
Descriptive Statistics for WWW Attitudes
Questionnaire Items ($N = 120$)

Item	I really don't agree	I don't agree	I'm neutral	I agree	I really agree
The information on the World Wide Web is not very useful.	23%	53%	18%	3%	3%
There is not a lot of detailed and in-depth information on the World Wide Web.	20%	41%	31%	5%	3%
The information out on the World Wide Web is accurate or correct.	3%	17%	50%	28%	3%
The World Wide Web is helpful in finding information.	2%	1%	14%	46%	37%

Note: Scale: 1 = "I really don't agree" to 5 = "I really agree."

these students were critical consumers of web information. Regarding the helpfulness of the WWW, students were positive in their beliefs, with 83% of students agreeing or strongly agreeing that the WWW is helpful in finding information.

Principal Component Analyses

A set of 13 nonoverlapping items, whose statistical distributions were appropriate for further analyses (see Table 13.3), was selected from various WEA and WWW questionnaire measures. Scores for negatively worded questionnaire items (Items 2 and 5 on the WWW attitudes questionnaire) were reversed, and all variables were standardized. A principal components factor analysis using varimax rotation was then used to examine further the relations between the various variables. Table 13.3 shows the four significant factors that emerged from the principal components analysis (confirmed by Scree plot examination), accounting for a total of 71.2% of the variance.

TABLE 13.3
Rotated Factor Matrix for Web Expertise Assessment Items ($N = 120$)

	Factor Loadings			
Item	Factor 1: Navigational Strategies	Factor 2: Finding Ability	Factor 3: Web Attitudes	Factor 4: Searching Expertise
Number of times back button used	.97			
Number of steps in search	.92			
Number of revisited information pages	.76			
Average bookmark score		.92		
Quality of bookmark set		.87		
Efficiency of search		.85		
The World Wide Web is helpful in finding information.			.81	
The information on the World Wide Web is not very useful.[a]			.80	
The information out on the World Wide Web is accurate or correct.			.73	
There is not a lot of detailed and in-depth information on the World Wide Web.[a]			.69	
Number of good searches				.91
Quality of keyword searching set				.77
Number of redirected searches				.66
Eigenvalues	2.54	2.37	2.34	2.00
% of variance explained	19.5%	18.2%	18.0%	15.4%

Note. Factor loadings < .30 are not shown.
[a]Scores for negatively worded questionnaire items were reversed.

TABLE 13.4
Scale Descriptions, Related Items, and Alpha Reliability
Coefficients for Web Expertise Assessment

Scale Description	WEA Items	Scale α
Navigational strategies	Number of times back button used	
	Number of steps in search	
	Total number of revisited information pages	.88
Finding ability	Average bookmark score	
	Quality of bookmark set	
	Efficiency of search	.86
Web attitudes	The World Wide Web is helpful in finding information.	
	The information on the World Wide Web is not very useful. (reversed)	
	The information out on the World Wide Web is accurate or correct.	
	There is not a lot of detailed and in-depth information on the World Wide Web. (reversed)	.76
Searching expertise	Number of good searches	
	Quality of keyword searching set	
	Number of redirected searches	.71

Three variables loaded highly on Factor 1: Use of the back button, the number of steps in the search (the number of backs and number of revisits were not included in this calculation), and the number of revisited information pages were all included in this navigational strategies factor. Factor 2, students' finding ability, included three high loading variables: students' average bookmark score, the quality of their bookmark set, and the efficiency with which they searched. All four of the WWW attitudes questions loaded highly on Factor 3, the web attitudes factor. Finally, Factor 4, termed students' searching expertise, included high loadings for variables measuring the number of good searches, the quality of the search term set, and the number of redirected searches.

Based on the results of the factor analysis, four scales were created. Scale alphas were high, ranging from .71 to .88. Each scale, its associated items, and its reliability coefficient are shown in Table 13.4.

DISCUSSION

The goal for this research was to explore the constructs underlying students' web fluency—their ability to search for and find relevant information as they navigate through a large information web space—using as participants students experienced with the World Wide Web. Using the online

Web Expertise Assessment and accompanying WWW attitudes question-naire, students were able to demonstrate their WWW attitudes and their searching, navigating, and finding expertise. Important individual meas-ures were then identified, which were reliably coded. Results from the fac-tor analysis suggest four broad indicators of web expertise: navigational strategies, prior web attitudes, searching expertise, and finding ability. In general, these composite indicators make sense theoretically and results support the construct validity of each. These indicators appear to be reli-able—with alphas ranging from .88 to .71—with the searching composite measure clearly the least stable. In addition, these measures match the the-oretical conceptions grounded in the literature.

Results indicate that students experienced with the WWW tended to agree that information found on the WWW was useful and detailed. Fur-ther, although they reported finding the Web helpful in finding in-depth information, they were also aware of the presence of inaccurate informa-tion. Effective web users thus begin their tasks with strong familiarity with the WWW environment.

Turning next to searching expertise, students conducted searches, using quality keyword sets, Boolean operators, and synonyms. However, as dem-onstrated in previous research, students had difficulty searching: On aver-age, less than one half of students' searches were rated "good" and, al-though most students conducted at least one on-topic keyword search, the majority of their searches when reviewed as a set were not. This difficulty in searching may be part of the reason for this indicators' relatively lower reli-ability coefficient ($\alpha = .71$). Students were able to redirect their searches, critically reviewing their search output prior to continuing their searches. Good searchers, then, use on-topic keywords and Boolean operators in their queries as needed, scan their search results, and frequently adjust their queries after reviewing incoming information.

Regarding navigational strategies, students used two techniques showing expertise: Students used the back button often and revisited pages to orient themselves in the information space. The number of steps in the students' searches also helped define their navigational expertise.

Finally, although students' bookmark scores were not as high as might have been expected and performance on the finding measures were the least impressive of the set, WEA results showed that experienced students could identify (via bookmarking) relevant pages, create quality bookmark sets to answer their search prompts, and search with reasonable efficiency. So students may have been bookmarking excessively (and thus including less than ideal bookmarks) due to the continued urges to do so (as pilot testing had shown the need to remind students to bookmark frequently). Regardless, the data certainly suggest that web fluency includes the ability to find and identify necessary information efficiently.

Clearly, this study has some limitations. The participants in this study were considered experienced web users (due to computer and Internet access available at school); however, formal data on students' web experience were unavailable. Further, more data using additional search tasks would be helpful. However, given these limitations, research findings suggest four indicators of web fluency as a basis for future research. Hopefully, future studies will focus on these four areas.

CONCLUSIONS

This chapter has presented a set of indices to measure and characterize students' web expertise. An online authentic assessment in which students are asked to search for information in a content-controlled web space can indeed capture information toward this end. The assessment system incorporates a variety of measures to reliably evaluate students' WWW background experience, searching expertise, navigational strategies, and finding ability. It will contribute to the literature that seeks to identify the characteristics of web expertise among children and to provide educators with some guidelines on how to support students' web learning. Future work will focus on addressing two questions related to the validity of this assessment: Is it possible to distinguish between expert and novice web users using WEA? And, is WEA performance sensitive to instruction?

When these questions begin to be answered positively, then this automated online assessment may be used to evaluate students' web fluency. In its first years of existence, the World Wide Web has become one of the most frequently used computer technologies in school, with teachers accepting the Internet as an incredibly useful classroom tool. Assessing students' expertise in this area is important because the Internet is now pervasive; at a minimum, classroom computers equipped with connectivity to the "information superhighway" are being used for this purpose. Thus, it is imperative for educational researchers to set out guidelines for teaching the Web effectively, as well as examine the effects of Internet usage on students. If teachers are given authentic, performance-based ways of assessing these skills early on, then they will also use these techniques to help teach their students how to become better searchers, navigators, and finders within this latest information space.

ACKNOWLEDGMENTS

The work reported herein was also supported by the Educational Research and Development Centers Program, PR/Award No. R305B60002, as administered by the Office of Educational Research and Improvement, U.S. Department of Education. The findings and opinions expressed in this report do not reflect the positions or policies of the National Institute on Student Achievement, Curriculum, and Assessment, the Office of Educational Research and Improvement, or the U.S. Department of Education.

REFERENCES

Bates, M. J. (1989). The design of browsing and berrypicking techniques for the online search interface. *Online Review, 13*, 407–424.

Becker, H. J. (1999). Internet use by teachers: Conditions of professional use and teacher-directed student use. *Teaching, Learning, and Computing: 1998 National Survey* [Online]. Center for Research on Information Technology and Organizations, the University of California, Irvine, and the University of Minnesota. Available: http://www.crito.uci.edu/TLC/FINDINGS/internet-use/startpage.htm

Berners-Lee, C. L., Cailliau, R., Groff, J. F., & Pollermann, B. (1992). World Wide Web: The information universe. *Electronic Networking, 2*, 52–58.

Bilal, D. (1998, October). *Children's search processes in using World Wide Web search engines: An exploratory study.* Paper presented at the meeting of the American Society of Information Science Annual Conference, Pittsburgh.

Borgman, C. L., Hirsch, S. G., Walter, V. A., & Gallagher, A. L. (1995). Children's searching behavior on browsing and keyword searching online catalogs: The Science Library Catalog project. *Journal of the American Society for Information Science, 46*, 663–684.

Breivik, P. S. (1998). *Student learning in the information age.* Phoenix, AZ: Oryx Press.

Carmel, E., Crawford, S., & Chen, H. (1992). Browsing in hypertext: A cognitive study. *Transactions on Systems, Man, and Cybernetics, 22*, 865–883.

Catledge, L. D., & Pitkow, J. E. (1995). *Characterizing browsing strategies in the World-Wide Web* [Online]. Available: http://www.igd.fhg.de/archive/1995_www95/proceedings/papers/80/userpatterns/UserPatterns.Paper4.fotmatted.html

Cove, J. F., & Walsh, B. C. (1988). Online text retrieval via browsing. *Information Processing and Management, 24*, 31–37.

Duffield, J. A. (1997). Conducting research: A student-centered model. *Childhood Education, 74*, 66–72.

Ercegovac, Z. (1998). *Information literacy: Search strategies, tools & resources.* Los Angeles: InfoEn Associates.

Fidel, R., Davies, R. K., Douglass, M. H., Holder, J. K., Hopkins, C. J., Kushner, E. J., Miyagishima, B. K., & Toney, C. D. (1999). A visit to the information mall: Web searching behavior of high school students. *Journal of the American Society for Information Science, 50*, 24–37.

Guthrie, J. T., & Dreher, M. J. (1990). Literacy as search: Explorations via computer. In D. Nix & R. J. Spiro (Eds.), *Cognition, education, and multimedia: Exploring ideas in high technology* (pp. 65–113). Hillsdale, NJ: Lawrence Erlbaum Associates.

Hill, J. R. (1997). The World Wide Web as a tool for information retrieval: An exploratory study of users' strategies in an open-ended system. *School Library Media Quarterly, 25*, 229–236.

Kafai, Y., & Bates, M. J. (1997). Internet web-searching instruction in the elementary classroom: Building a foundation for information literacy. *School Library Media Quarterly, 25*, 103–111.

Kuhlthau, C. C. (1996). *The virtual school library: Gateway to the information superhighway.* Englewood, CO: Libraries Unlimited.

Lawrence, S., & Giles, C. L. (1999, July 8). Accessibility of information on the web. *Nature, 400,* 107–109.

Marchionini, G. (1989). Information-seeking strategies of novices using a full-text electronic encyclopedia. *Journal of the American Society for Information Science, 40,* 54–66.

Market Data Research. (1998). *Technology in Education 1998.* Shelton, CT: Author.

Roblyer, M. D. (1998). The other half of knowledge. *Learning and Leading with Technology, 25*(6), 54–55.

Rosenberg, J. (1996). The structure of hypertext activity. *Proceedings of Seventh ACM Conference on Hypertext, 7,* 22–30.

Salterio, S. (1996). Decision support and information search in a complex environment: Evidence from archival data in auditing. *Human Factors, 38,* 495–505.

Schacter, J., Chung, G. K. W. K., & Dorr, A. (1998). Children's Internet searching on complex problems: Performance and process analyses. *Journal of the American Society for Information Science, 49,* 840–849.

Schacter, J., Herl, H. E., Chung, G. K. W. K., Dennis, R. A., & O'Neil, H. F., Jr. (1999). Computer-based performance assessments: A solution to the narrow measurement and reporting of problem-solving. *Computers in Human Behavior, 15,* 403–418.

Tauscher, L., & Greenberg, S. (1997). How people revisit web pages: Empirical findings and implications for the design of history systems. *International Journal of Human-Computer Studies, 47,* 97–137.

U.S. Census Bureau. (1999). *Computer use in the United States: Population characteristics.* Washington, DC: U.S. Department of Commerce.

The Web: Growing by 2 million pages a day. (2000, March 6). *Industry Standard, 3*(8), 174–176.

Part IV

POLICY IMPLEMENTATION ISSUES

Chapter 14

Management Issues in Implementing Education and Training Technology

Robert J. Seidel
Kathleen E. Cox
U.S. Army Research Institute

There have been numerous predictions about the widespread use of technology in education and training (Doyle & Goodwill, 1971; Fletcher, 1988; Luskin, 1970; Seidel, 1980; Wilcox, 1972; Glick, 1965). For example, Doyle and Goodwill (1971) and Luskin (1970) reported that technology in the form of computer-assisted instruction (CAI) would be fully implemented and used on a regular basis in colleges and higher institutions on the average (median) by 1985. Similarly, researchers predicted that full computer adoption would be completed by 1985 in high schools and by 1990 in elementary schools.

As editor of the *New York World's Fair School of Tomorrow,* Glick (1965) predicted 10 significant changes that would occur as a result of technology use. Some of the characteristics of education as predicted for the year 2000 included: the schoolhouse being a connected unit in a national and international network of communication, and education being organized for self-educating individuals. A chart of these predictions is presented as Table 14.1. The predictions of technology *availability* (such as networking) have held up; but the *organizational adaptation* to exploit the technology has not really occurred.

Clearly, the use of computers in academic institutions has been increasing at all levels over the past decade (Becker, 1991; C. C. Kulik & J. A. Kulik, 1991; U.S. Dept. of Education, 1993, 1996; National Center for Education Statistics, 1997a, 1997b, 1998; Ryan, 1991; Thompson, Simonson, & Hargrave, 1996; Wenglinsky, 1998). Although there is national interest in the potential value of computers in education, the degree of change attributed

TABLE 14.1
Year 2000 Predictions From the World's Fair

School of Today (1964)	*School of Tomorrow (2000)*
1. Organized for groups of children	Organized for self-educating individuals
2. The self-contained classroom	The self-contained school
3. Teaching to transmit facts	Teaching to inculcate values
4. The teacher as general practitioner	The teacher as specialist and educational counselor
5. Education as a separate community service	Education as a subsystem of total community services
6. The schoolhouse as an isolated unit	The schoolhouse as connected unit in a national and international network of communication
7. School systems organized as elementary, junior high, and senior high schools	Schools organized as ungraded by primary, middle, high school, and community college
8. Schools operating 1,000 hours per year	Schools operating at least 4,000 hours per year
9. Financial support mostly from local real estate	Financial support mostly state and federal
10. Buildings designed for indestructibility and antisepsis	Buildings designed for performance and beauty

to computer implementation is significantly lower than anticipated. The question becomes, why have these changes not taken place? Recognize that ambiguities exist in the way technology is being implemented. Whereas industry and policymakers focus on hardware and software issues, the problem for implementation is much broader than the technology per se. Rather, the focus must be on the human aspects of educational reform processes in order to facilitate the implementation of technology in education (Loveless, 1996; Merrill, 1995; Seidel & Weddle, 1987). As Bandura (2000) recently noted,

> The [research] findings are quite consistent in what makes schools academically effective. There is a vast difference between knowing and being able to create them. The field of education does not lack good educational models, but it lacks effective models for implementing them. Because of the paucity of research on implementation models, there are a few guidelines on how to replicate and diffuse efficacious systems. Therefore, we gained little from educational success. (p. 4)

COMPUTER TECHNOLOGY USE IN EDUCATION TODAY: THE LATEST CONTROVERSY

It is true that the number of personal computers (PCs) in schools and in homes has been increasing over the past decade (Wenglinsky, 1998). In

1984, only 40% of high schools had five or more computers; that is approximately one computer to 200 or more students. By 1997, the ratio dramatically improved to one computer for every 10 students. In the same study, it is noted that over 40% of homes own computers today and 70% of high school and college students have access to home computers. Unfortunately, however, racial and income gaps exist. Access for Blacks is only 32% as compared to 73% for Whites. And, as compared to two thirds of Whites, one third of Blacks, with incomes over $40,000 have access to home computers. Therefore, research indicates that access is restricted to a narrow range of Black households (based on Nielsen media research telephone survey, December 1996 through January 1997).

Oppenheimer (1997) questioned public investment in computers in schools. He reported that computers are not effective for improving teaching and learning and yet their expense is forcing the curtailment of the arts, which some would claim are at least as equal a curricular component as mathematics for the foundation of civilization. Oppenheimer (1997) critiqued numerous studies, concluding that computers increase performance. He asserted that the statistical analyses for these studies were flawed and are not replicable. In addition, he cited Terry Crane, vice president of Apple, who sang the praises of student collaboration in the use of the computer. Crane reported that students are learning to explore information dynamically while communicating effectively about complex processes. However, Oppenheimer (1997) reported that although the Apple studies have invested quite a lot of money, they are doing no more than dumping computers in schools and classrooms that are not producing any exciting results about student collaboration. The discovery in this review was that ineffective teachers needed to change their approach in the classroom to move toward "project-oriented learning" where students learn by doing and teachers act as guides (e.g., Blumenfeld et al., 1991; Brown, 1997; Lambert & McCombs, 1998). The conclusion in this review was that the learning had less to do with the computer and more to do with the nature of teaching.

Oppenheimer (1997) cited many other potential disadvantages and dangers of the use or overuse of the computer, including personal isolation issues that arise from frequent Internet use (see also Turkle, 1995), and improper simulations that encourage students to learn irrelevant information. The heart of the computer implementation problem, as discussed by Oppenheimer (1997), is that the focus is on the manipulation of software rather than on student learning and teacher training.

With a similar argument, Papert (1997) concluded that the power must be given to students (Papert, 1993). In agreement with Oppenheimer (1997), Papert asserted that it is necessary to improve what is currently being done in schools with regard to technology implementation rather than radically changing the entire system. However, this improvement must go beyond the current short-term goals of improving what is currently being done in schools to implement three important reversals in thinking about education (Papert, 1997). First, children should become the driving forces, instead of the passive recipients, for educational change. This was first proposed by Dewey (1938; see, also, Lambert & McCombs, 1998). Second, the emergence of kid power as a force for change translates into effective digital technology being a learner's technology, not the teacher's technology. Unlike the teacher speaking out of a television set, the computer offers a fundamental reversal of relationship between participants in learning. His last assertion is that powerful advanced ideas can become elementary without losing their power. He noted one example from Canada, where making technology accessible to young children produced some very powerful ideas previously available only in specialized college courses (e.g., mathematical ideas, such as random variables, successive approximations, and negative feedback). In conclusion, Papert (1997) remarked "for those of us who want to change education the hard work is in our own minds, bringing ourselves to enter intellectual domains we never thought existed. The deepest problem for us is not technology, nor teaching, nor school bureaucracies. All of these are important, but what it is all really about is mobilizing powerful ideas" (p. 3).

Lemke (October, 1997) moderated an online discussion (involving Papert and others) concerning whether there is a computer dilution or media dilution. She noted that "the Atlantic monthly article [by Oppenheimer] is not about whether technology belongs in K through 12 schools. Rather it is about the complexity, challenges and choices involved in providing a quality educational experience for students living in today's digital age" (). Lemke (1997) also cited Oppenheimer's concerns about "a minimizing of the real, physical world in favor of an unreal 'virtual' world," suggesting it "may limit the development of children's imaginations" (Oppenheimer, 1997, p. 62).

Other data come from the latest Educational Testing Service (ETS) study on the influence of computers on student achievement (Wenglinsky, 1998). The ETS evaluation of the National Assessment of Educational Progress (NAEP) data on computer effectiveness showed that the principal influencing variable seems to be social economic status (SES). This finding also emphasizes a huge equity concern in the availability and use of new technologies.

Offering an administrative perspective, Alexander, Murphy, and Woods (1996) questioned the plethora of short-lived innovations in education. The authors concluded that the fading or ridiculing of highly touted saviors may be attributed to the tendency for educators to choose innovations (including technology) that seem familiar and manageable, rather than those oriented toward solving fundamental problems. Additionally, Alexander et al. (1996) proposed that the opponents of the innovations are often unaware of past experiences with the innovations and do not understand the principles underlying them, which of course are necessary for proper implementation.

As a counterpoint to the Alexander et al. (1996) argument, Morris (1997) asserted that educational decision-makers in school districts "undertake innovations under circumstances of unclear goals, unpredictable technology, and uncertainty in general" (p. 22). He went on to say that "because educational technology is one in which the cause/affect relationship between organizational structure and outcomes is poorly understood, districts conform to external criteria concerning the way that schools ought to look and function in order to establish legitimacy and so secure a reliable flow of resources" (p. 23). According to Morris (1997), the purposes and measures of effectiveness or achievement justifying technological innovation are rarely understood or agreed on by the parties involved in the implementation. His answer was to invoke a system concept and context for education (see also Morris, 1996).

Having examined the latest incarnation, the question remains concerning why this controversy over technology-push verses educational need-pull still persists. The answer is best summarized as the recurring implicit or explicit assumption by the technology innovators that: technology per se will force educators and school systems to change. What is not taking place yet is not confined specifically to technology. Rather, missing are the educational reform processes that are directly facilitated by the technology. These processes depend on massive reform in the way education does business. In order for computers to achieve long-term effectiveness, attention must be paid to the systemic educational change requirements.

MANAGEMENT PRINCIPLES

A list of some 14 issues significant for successful implementation of educational technologies has been compiled. It is important to recognize that the list has been accumulated from both training and educational research and development experiences and thus synthesizes a range of ideas from multiple stakeholders. For example, whereas Morris (1997) made the point that innovation and reform must be separated as a dichotomy, this discussion extends that point. Years of research and surveying academic computer use have recorded five purposes for which computers were being introduced. However, these purposes rarely were agreed on by the innovator and the educational adoption decision-maker. As such, the innovator might have been focusing on accelerating computer literacy, whereas the controller of the school district was making an adoption decision based on cost-effectiveness (Seidel, 1980).

It may be useful to consider the series of management issues listed here as applicable to one or more of the customary stages of a systematic education/training development process: analysis, design, development, implementation, or evaluation:

1. *Expectations:* For successful project management, the expectations of the sponsor must coincide with those of the researcher or developer, as well as with the hopes and goals of the user of any computer-based system.

2. *Appropriate Evaluation:* The evaluation models should be appropriate and consistent with the project purpose (e.g., value added, enrichment, reform, or cost/effectiveness). Formative evaluation is appropriate for testing and improving a prototype system; summative evaluation is appropriate when alternative systems are being compared following a thorough debugging and shakedown period.

3. *Prototype Needs:* In a prototype project, project management must be aware of, and resist if possible, the pressures by training system sponsors or users hungry for evidence on which to base decisions to continue, or to plan for implementation.

4. *Evaluator Role:* In any complex implementation project, the roles and needs of the independent evaluator, as well as the roles and needs of the developers, must be continually coordinated and clarified in order to prevent any ambiguities regarding the project responsibilities and outcomes.

5. *Staffing Mix:* Maintaining a careful and appropriate balance of staffing based on task requirements is an extremely important part of the manager's job.

6. *System Stability First:* There needs to be serial development of critical system components. There is the absolute necessity for establishing a stable hardware and software environment prior to developing course materials on the system.

7. *Training:* For successful implementation, from the highest level of institutional administration to the instructors and students, it is necessary to provide a multilevel, user training program (e.g., from general awareness of computers, discipline-related knowledge, to specific programing skills).

8. *Control:* A clear line of project control is necessary, along with a congruent allocation of authority and responsibility.

9. *Communication:* Frequent communication is necessary for monitoring expectations and understanding among the various specialists within the project. They speak different technical languages. Therefore, continuous communication mediated by the project manager must exist.

10. *Resource Allocation:* Adequate provision and control must be maintained over project staff and resources.

11. *Coordination:* Adequate coordination must be maintained among project staff, sponsors, and users.

12. *Common Understanding:* One should understand and communicate with appropriate personnel at the sponsoring and user agencies. This will help to place the project purpose and requirements in the proper context and, although not eliminating trouble, it can help minimize difficulties.

13. *Iterative Planning:* Implementers must be made aware of the need to plan for updates and change as requirements for using different materials change.

14. *Coordinated Planning:* There is a need to close the loop between research, development, and implementation. Coordinating plans from the outset for how technological research products will be used by the developer and be implemented by the user can lead to a common understanding of the needs of all parties.[1]

A PROPOSED MODEL

A model is needed for evaluating technological innovation in training or educational environments (see Seidel & Perez, 1994, for details). This model should consider purpose, process, outcome measures, and the maturity of the innovation and is presented as Fig. 14.1. The model represents three major stages, adoption, implementation, and institutionalization, and two major processes, assimilation and accommodation of the innovation. These stages and the processes occur within a context of multiple levels in order to achieve technology transfer.

The first stage is to adopt the use of the computer. Adoption occurs with the initial use of new technology within an administrative unit. Thus, the single use of the new technology, such as in a college course, is adoption. The second stage to be considered is implementation. In this stage, the innovation is used beyond the initial adoption, such as in a typical department; it is used across the board in an entire school system or within a local

---

[1]One way to accomplish closing the loop between research, development, and implementation would be to establish a national instructional technology evaluation center, to be a full partner in the controlled research, operational testing, development, and implementation of new technologies. Given the focus as an experimental educational institution, the necessary feedback from the user can be obtained in a timely manner. Clear lines of communication and control among partners can be articulated. This will enable collection of data, and permit testing and revision of system components as well as diffusion of findings and products. The result should be commitment by all stakeholders, including the instructors, the community, administrators, researchers, and the sponsoring agency. It should also enable a complete and comprehensive establishment of center missions, functions, and organization. Depending on available funding and modern, distributive technology, such an approach could be a national model.

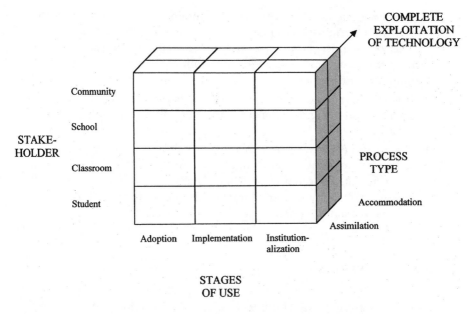

FIG. 14.1.   A model for technology evaluation.

organizational structure. The third stage and the goal is to institutionalize the innovation. In this stage, the innovation itself is an integral part of the entire educational training system.

In addition to stages of implementation, innovations also go through two processes: assimilation and accommodation. Assimilation is characterized by the incorporation or absorption of the innovation into the existing environment (e.g., user applying the computer in much the same way they used paper and pencils in the past). That is, the innovation (e.g., computer) helps individuals to do something they ordinarily do, but helps them to do it better or faster. Accommodation refers to the adaptation or adjustment of the environment to the technological innovation.

The real value of an innovation of advanced technologies occurs when things reach the point that it is possible to accommodate to the value added, to the uniqueness, to the flexibility that the technological innovation provides. Vary rarely does this occur. The potential, however, is enormous. For example, when students begin to perform tasks they would not otherwise be able to perform without computers, or when the computer offers degrees of flexibility that go well beyond actual equipment, then conditions are being created that people never conceived possible without the computer.

Current research and evaluation in the use of computers as tools should seek a deeper understanding of the context in which these tools are used rather than simply asking the question: Does the computer make a difference in learning a specific task or topic? Think of the context of evaluation as having multiple levels like a target with concentric circles. The bull's eye is student use. Each surrounding ring enlarges the area of concern to include another important level of influence. From curricular/instructor environment, through school system, and surrounding influential community, all levels comprise the necessary and sufficient conditions to permit appropriate computer use and assessment thereof. Moreover, things must proceed from the outside levels into the center of the circle to avoid the risk of attempting to measure a nonevent, that is, trying to measure student achievement when other levels prevent this.

The following, adapted from Kearsley (1983), is a checklist for the implementation of management issues to aid successful technology implementation:

	Yes	No
1. Does a high degree of user involvement exist?	[ ]	[ ]
2. Is there a high level of commitment towards CAI or CBT (computer-aided instruction, -based training) and the project?	[ ]	[ ]
3. Are the necessary resources available to carry out the project?	[ ]	[ ]
4. Is the technology (hardware/software/courseware) ready for operational use?	[ ]	[ ]
5. Is there a clear acknowledgment of a training need which CBT can address?	[ ]	[ ]
6. Can the project demonstrate meaningful results?	[ ]	[ ]
7. Has a clear cut understanding about the purpose and nature of the project been established?	[ ]	[ ]
8. Are all the individuals who will be affected by CBT actively involved?	[ ]	[ ]
9. Has adequate training and orientation been planned and conducted?	[ ]	[ ]
10. Are adequate controls over project resources and progress available and used?	[ ]	[ ]
11. Have explicit criteria been established to assess system and courseware acceptability?	[ ]	[ ]
12. Have project tasks been assigned according to skills needed?	[ ]	[ ]
13. Has an appropriate evaluation model and plan been developed and implemented?	[ ]	[ ]

14. Has a stable system been established before starting
    courseware development?   [ ]   [ ]
15. Does everyone understand the iterative nature of
    a CBT project?   [ ]   [ ]

If there are "No" answers to any of the previous questions, they point to potential stakeholder trouble spots requiring immediate attention in order to achieve successful implementation. This is merely one instrument to help the implementer. Others will need to be designed specifically for given implementations. The analysis ends with a few familiar examples of successful implementations.

SUCCESSFUL CASE STUDIES

The following are examples of successful stakeholder partnerships. Although each has a slightly different technological emphasis, each shares a common management focus. The Teacher Education Initiative (TEI) was developed as a 5-year program by the National Education Association Center for Innovation and has just finished its second year. Through a national application process, seven institutions were selected to participate in the program. The seven sites selected were George Mason University, the University of Memphis, Montclair State University, the University of South Carolina, University of Southern Maine, Texas A&M University, and the University of Wyoming. All institutions are involved in major technological reform predicated on nine key principles of the TEI process:

1. Partnerships with prekindergarten through grade 12 schools where all stakeholders are involved.
2. Expanded roles for university and prekindergarten through grade 12 educators.
3. Ongoing evaluation, dissemination, and contribution to the professional knowledge base by all stakeholders.
4. Extended clinical experiences, mentoring, and support for beginning teachers, and systemic professional development for experienced teachers.
5. Systemic change at the local, state, and national levels.
6. Systemic change at the internal level, which rewards simultaneous renewal efforts.
7. Infusion of technology at all levels.
8. Advancement of diversity/equity.
9. Teaching and learning linked to student outcomes.

Of principal import for the purposes of this chapter is that the technological innovations occur in a context as one component of reform and not as something thrust on existing, entrenched conditions. In particular, a key component of this initiative is the comprehensive evaluation of the success of the restructured teacher education programs. Each of the seven sites employed a common set of instruments and methodologies to address, over a 5-year period, the following four research questions: (a) How are the nine principles actually defined and interpreted to fit sites specific needs, interests, and partner views? (b) To what extent are the individual principles being implemented at the sites? (c) What are the effects of restructuring on the partner institutions (schools, college of education, and university) in terms of quality of instruction and field-based supervision, school culture /climate changes, role definitions and role changes, and other factors? (d) How does the ongoing restructuring effort influence the quality of teacher preparation as evidenced by efforts, career choices, and performance of candidates and graduates?

Reynolds (1999) reported multiple benefits to the schools and school systems participating in the TEI project. There have been positive changes in the quality of instruction, school climate, lower student–teacher ratios, increased parental involvement, and heightened professionalism among staff. With regard to their goal of infusing technology at all levels, the project has made some progress. One university mentor noted, "With technology as a high priority in our area, there has been great progress made" (p. 24). For example, two sites received large grants to aid with technology infusion.

A significant feature of the TEI initiative is that the partnership includes not just the schools in the institutions of higher education, but also involves the local stakeholders as well. It is important to note that technology plays a significant, yet contextual, role as one of the nine principles. The following quotation from the University of Memphis second year site progress report illustrates how technology is being integrated within this context (Reynolds, 1999):

> Professional development workshops, conducted by the project SMART teachers (leadership roles) and university faculty, enabled teachers to work with software and materials which served as sources of student productivity. Technology resource persons were identified in the classrooms and faculty served as trainers and information specialists daily. Parents actively volunteered their services to help Web page development, project development, and topic dissemination. Students emailed scientists in Antarctica, talked with favorite authors, researched dinosaur fossils with scientists at the University of Chicago, and became actively involved in their own learning. Students, preservice teachers, school and university faculty have benefited from action research projects that were planned and implemented by school—university collaborators. (p. 34)

The next phase of the TEI project (professional development schools) is to measure student achievement variables resulting from these enriched environments in which teachers are being trained.

Another example of successful stakeholder partnerships involves case studies from the Department of Defense Education Activity (DoDEA). The Vanguard for Learning program is a 3-year research project sponsored by the U.S. Department of Defense Education Activity (DoDEA) and funded by the National Science Foundation from 1995 to 1998. The Vanguard for Learning program is conducted by the teachers, administrators, students, parents, and military personnel serving the Aviano Air Base, Italy, the district superintendent of DoDDS Italy district, and educational researchers, technologists, and consultants from BBN Corporation in Cambridge, Massachusetts, Boston College, and other educational institutions. Dr. Candace Ransing, Italy district superintendent, is the primary point of contact for DoDEA. Beverly Hunter, currently in the Learning Communities Research Group, Boston College School of Education, is the principal investigator. The goals of Vanguard for Learning are to (a) learn how to build a school community's capacity to initiate, evaluate, and institutionalize new ways of learning and teaching that take advantage of electronic technologies; (b) use innovation efforts in that school community to investigate selected key components of reform that can inform DoDEA system-wide practices; and (c) use lessons learned from Aviano and DoDEA to advance understanding of systemic reform processes in education generally.

In such a circumstance of multiple agency involvement, multiple and sometimes conflicting expectations are inevitable and unavoidable because the separate agencies have different missions and there does not exist a superordinate management entity with the authority to resolve these differences. The Vanguard for Learning researchers employed several strategies aimed toward managing and mitigating the "multiple expectations" problem. These strategies have been at least partially successful because they focus on engaging a full range of local stakeholders in creating and taking ownership of their own common vision and initiating and testing their own innovations.

The Vanguard program also employed strategies in order to address local problems and needs within the framework of system-wide strategic priorities and the project's funded research purposes. First, the research team analyzed the strategic priorities of DoDEA, the sponsoring agency. Working with stakeholders in the local community in Aviano, the researchers translated systemic priorities into "themes" to guide the local innovation. Then researchers facilitated the formation of voluntary teams of teachers, administrators, parents, students, and military. Fifteen teams, called Team Action Plans (TAPS), were self-formed based on a shared vision for school improvement that would leverage the systemic themes at the local level. The externally funded project staff, as well as the school administration, supported the work of these teams and to some extent was able to shield and protect the teams from the negative effects of the multiple expectations problem.

For instance, one Vanguard theme is "Linking Across the Community," which corresponds to DoDEA Strategic Plan Benchmark 8.1. During a Vanguard summer workshop in 1996, a group of 25 military and civilian parents and school administrators from all four schools serving Aviano Air Base formed a team they called the school/home/community team. They wanted to solve some of the problems they had encountered in attempting to build closer linkages between parents and the schools. Because of the recent build-up of the air base and the frequent arrival of families new to the base, it was important for the parents to quickly establish ties with their children's schools. At the same time, the team wanted to take advantage of new computer and communications equipment and network infrastructure under construction in the schools. They decided first to create a physical "place" within or near each school that the parents would feel is their place in the school—a place where school volunteers could learn and work, and a place where parents and other community members could learn to use the technologies their children were learning, review the electronic products their children were producing on the World Wide Web, and take advantage of the networks to support their work with activities such as Scouts and science fairs. Providing space for parents on this physically crowded base also communicated to parents and teachers the high level of importance that was being placed on the school–family linkage.

The value of the SHC Resource Center model in Aviano schools is evidenced in several ways, including system-wide dissemination of the model. With the support of the DoDEA Italy district superintendent's office and DoDEA headquarters, the Aviano SHCRC experience is being shared with other school communities through workshops and through the design of new school buildings. The Department of Defense Dependent Schools Activity (DoDEA) specifications for all new school buildings now includes space for such a resource center. The new school building for "Aviano 2000" incorporates a SHCRC as a central feature of the school.

Another example that highlights the importance of the aforementioned management issues is the Global Learning and Observations to Benefit the Environment (GLOBE) program (Means, December 1998, personal communication). Some goals of GLOBE that aligned with our management issues included the alignment of expectations among stakeholders, evaluation of technology, and clarification of roles. With regard to the alignment of expectations, GLOBE is an interagency program with its own office of directors who are in charge of the agenda. However, there is a weaving together of expectations among the various developers from National

Aeronautics and Space Administration (NASA) and National Oceanic and Atmospheric Administration (NOAA), the researchers from SRI and TERC and the teachers involved in the program. One striking example was the alignment of expectations between the researchers, who were expecting to have access to databases for their analysis and have complete long-term data from sites where data was not collected previously, and the teachers, who involved the students in the data collection because they were interested in what the students could learn from the data collection. With regard to evaluation, after a blend of formative and summative evaluations took place, GLOBE shifted the teacher training strategy. Originally, to maximize impact per training dollar, the model was to train one teacher from each school. However, the continuous evaluation showed that the demands of implementing GLOBE were overwhelming for teachers working alone. Therefore, GLOBE's teacher training now uses multiple teachers within schools or across schools in one locality. Finally, with regard to clarification of roles, all stakeholders maintain a constant dialogue about the design, research activities, and program changes that occur.

The Hanau Model School Partnership is also a program sponsored by the Department of Defense Education Activity (DoDEA) and has project goals that incorporate some important management issues (Wasser & McNamara, 1998). The goal of the program is to employ technology to meet the most fundamental aims of systemic reform: to support the implementation of standards-based reform in core content areas, to ensure that all students have equitable access to resources and best practices, and to build capacity within schools to sustain reform objectives from within. Some goals of the Hanau School project that aligned with management issues included the alignment of expectations among stakeholders and the use of multilevel training. With regard to the alignment of expectations, one of the greatest success factors that has been seen in the program is the overall program adoption by the superintendent in the district. By making the program a district priority, strong direction was given to the principals in the professional development activities they provided to teachers and such encouragement lead significantly more teachers to be interested in the program goals. In addition, the Hanau Schools use multilevel training. Not only are teachers provided with multiple training activities, they also had on-site training coaches in the classroom to answer questions and model techniques to integrate technology. This on-site support provided a rich source of ideas and exchange between teachers, principals, and program staff.

A final example comes from the training context. The Training Technologies Field Activities (TTFA) program was established to link the dimensions of research, management of instruction and training, and the operational training itself in order to institutionalize technological innovations in the army (see also Seidel & Perez, 1994). TTFA required the Army Research Institute and the research and development arm of the army to work closely with the TTFA office, as well as with pilot schools that were the targeted training sites for the program. Seidel and Perez (1994) noted:

> Projects were chosen that focused on different psychological skills (perceptual motor, complex problem-solving, and procedural skills) along with varied requirements for types of trainees (commissioned officers, noncommissioned officers, and enlisted personnel). These occurred within a spectrum of different costs, which varied for active versus reserve components of the army. The products developed by this approach were unique to the schools, such as procurement for improving a particular targeted course at the school; and some technologies were to be generalizable across all schools, such as technique for doing training data management (broadly speaking computer managed instruction). Another was the development of the technology transfer model to apply to all army schools once these four pilots were underway. (p. 205)

Although broader based institutionalization was not achieved because of funding cutbacks, a pilot program did result in some important outcomes.

CONCLUSIONS

It has been the position herein that technology innovation will only be implemented successfully on a widespread basis if the needs and perceptions of all the stakeholders are taken into account. In order to achieve long-term technology innovation, management issues were included in this chapter to ensure all of the stakeholders' needs have been considered. As well, important case examples have been included to illustrate the benefits of using these management issues in order to achieve important technology implementation. As long as schools are the principal educational structure, and schooling is the process wherein students learn, it will be necessary to create partnerships with all the stakeholders so that reform will be a reality instead of a continual prediction.

REFERENCES

Alexander, P. A., Murphy, P. K., & Woods B. S. (1996). Of squalls and fathoms: Navigating the seas of educational innovation. *Educational Researcher, 25*(3), 31–36, 39.

Becker, H. J. (1991). How computers are used in United States schools: Basic data from the 1989 I.E.A. computers in education survey. *Journal of educational computing research, 7*(4), 385–406.

Bandura, A. (2000). A Sociocognitive Perspective on Intellectual Development and Functioning. NEP, v. 3 #2, p. 4.

Blumenfeld, P. C., Soloway, E., Marx, R. W., Krajcik, J. S., Guzdialm M., & Palincsar, A. S. (1991). Motivating project-based learning: Sustaining the doing, supporting the learning. *Educational Psychologist, 26*, 369–398.

Brown, A. (1997). Transforming schools into communities of thinking and learning about serious matters. *American Psychologist, 52*(3), 399–413.

Dewey, J. (1938). *Education and experience.* Boston: Riverside Press.

Doyle & Goodwill (1971).

Glick, W. J. (1965). Education in the year 2000 A.D: Teaching machines, teacher training, the small college, education's future, public and private education, and educational T.V. In *Hall of Education's The School of Tomorrow: New York World's Fair 1964–1965.* New York: Macfadden-Bartell Corporation.

Kearsley, G. (1983). *Computer-based training: A guide to selection and implementation.* Reading, MA: Addison-Wesley.

Kulik, C. C., & Kulik, J. A. (1991). Effectiveness of computer-based instruction: An updated analysis. *Computers in Human Behavior, 7,* 75–94.

Lambert, N. M., & McCombs, B. L. (1998). *How students learn: Reforming schools through learner-centered education.* Washington, DC: American Psychological Association.

Lemke, C. (October, 1997). *Milken Exchange on education technology.* [On-line discussion]. Available: http://www.milkenexchange.org

Loveless, T. (1996). Why aren't computers used more in schools? *Educational Policy, 10*(4), 448–467.

Luskin (1970).

Merrill, D. (1995). *Evaluation of educational technology: What do we know and what can we know.* Washington, DC: The RAND Corporation.

Morris, D. R. (1996). Institutionalization and the reform process: A system dynamics perspective. *Educational Policy, 10,* 427–447.

Morris, D. R. (1997). Adrift in the sea of innovations: A response to Alexander, Murphy, & Woods. *Educational Researcher, 26*(4), 22–26.

National Center for Education Statistics (1999). *Advanced telecommunications in U.S. private schools, K-12.* Fall 1995 (Policy report). Washington, DC: U.S. Government Printing Office.

National Center for Education Statistics (1997b). *Advanced telecommunications in U.S. public elementary and secondary schools, Fall 1996* (Policy report). Washington, DC: U.S. Government Printing Office.

National Center for Education Statistics (1998). *Internet access in public schools* (Policy report). Washington, DC: U.S. Government Printing Office.

Oppenheimer, T. (1997). The computer delusion. *The Atlantic Monthly, July,* pp. 1–25.

Papert, S. (1993). *Mindstorms: Children, computers, and powerful ideas* (2nd rev. ed.). New York: Basic Books.

Papert, S. (October, 1997). *Milken Exchange on Education Technology.* [Online discussion.] Available: http://www.milkenexchange.org

Reynolds, A. (1999, February). *Seven-site replication study of teacher preparation: Cross-site technical report.* Unpublished report submitted to the National Center for Innovation, National Education Association.

Ryan, A. (1991). Meta-analysis of achievement effects of microcomputer applications in elementary schools. *Educational Administration Quarterly, 27*(2), 161–184.

Seidel, R. J. (1980). It's 1980: Do you know where your computer is? *Phi Delta Kappan,* March, 481–485.

Seidel, R. J., & Perez, R. S. (1994). An evaluation model for investigating the impact of educational technology (pp. 177–212). In H. O'Neil & E. Baker (Eds.), *Technology assessment in software applications.* Hillsdale, NJ: Lawrence Erlbaum Associates.

Seidel, R. J., & Weddle, P. D. (1987). *Computer-based instruction in military environments.* New York: Plenum.

Thompson, A. D., Simonson, M. R., & Hargrave, C. P. (1996). *Educational technology: A review of the research* (2nd ed.). Washington, DC: Association for Educational Communications and Technology (AECT).

Turkle, S. (1995). *Life on the screen: Identity in the age of the internet.* New York: Simon & Schuster.

U.S. Department of Education (1993). *Using technology to support educational reform.* Washington, DC: U.S. Government Printing Office

U.S. Department of Education (1996). *Getting America's students ready for the 21st century: Meeting the technology literacy challenge.* Washington, DC: U.S. Government Printing Office.

Wenglinsky, H. (1998). *Does it compute? The relationship between educational technology and student achievement in mathematics* (Policy information report). Princeton, NJ: Educational Testing Service.

Wasser, J. D., & McNamara (1998, August). Professional development and full-school technology integration: A description of the professional development model of the Hanau Model Schools Partnership. *Research Report Series, No. 5.*

Wilcox, J. N. (1972). A survey forcast of new technology in universities and colleges. Unpublished thesis. Massachusetts Institute of Technology, Cambridge, MA.

Chapter 15

Learning Futures: An English Perspective on Information and Communication Technologies in Education

Tom Bentley
Demos

David H. Hargreaves
Wolfson College, Cambridge

When, at the end of the 20th century, the head of a national government announces that the top three political priorities are "education, education and education," it is evident that the information and communication technologies (ICT) will play a key role in education policy—so it has been since Tony Blair became prime minister in May 1997. The main thrust of policy so far has been to lay down the ICT infrastructure and to train the teachers in the applications of ICT.

In the United Kingdom (UK), the establishment of this infrastructure has proceeded rapidly, and its completion will place the English educational system in a leading position as far as both schools' access to computer technology and the availability of online resources for teaching and learning are concerned.

However, the longer term effects of such large-scale investment are as yet unclear. Moreover, the challenges faced by educational systems, prompted partly by the diffusion of ICT more broadly across societies, have not yet been fully articulated. This chapter provides an overview of progress so far, and sets out the most important challenges that teachers, learners, and policymakers will have to face.

THE NATIONAL GRID FOR LEARNING

At the heart of the infrastructure is the National Grid for Learning (NGfL), launched in January 1998 and designed to create a nation capable of using ICT as one of the building blocks of the knowledge economy, and to use the benefits of ICT to raise educational standards. The NGfL is a mosaic of interconnecting networks, including commercial providers, managed by the British Educational and Communications Technology Agency (BECTa),[1] which provide materials for teaching, learning, and administration. It is planned that, by 2002, the following will have been achieved:

• All schools, colleges, and universities, as well as public libraries and museums, will be connected to the NGfL.

• All school teachers (around 425,000 in England) will be computer literate and comfortable with ICT in the school and classroom, and a range of managed services to support institutions in the implementation of ICT developments will be organized. (At the time of writing (spring 2000) significant progress on each of these basic aims is being made.)

• Two thirds of primary (elementary) schools and 95% of secondary (high) schools are now linked to the Grid. The target should thus easily be reached before 2002.

• Helping teachers to acquire ICT skills is a more ambitious objective. Some two thirds of teachers say that they feel confident about using ICT. The chief inspector of schools for England and Wales reports that information technology is the least well taught element in the national curriculum. Much work in primary and secondary schools makes only trivial use of expensive equipment. This fault must be rectified if students are to develop in the schools the ICT skills they will need in later life. Better training for teachers is required if they are to use ICT to enhance the quality of their teaching. Another emerging issue is that of handling pupil-related data for assessment. Since the Education Reform Act of 1988 (Ref), the volume of quantitative data on student achievement that can be recorded and analyzed on school computers has grown rapidly. Sophisticated analysis and interpretation of such data, and their application to educational problems, is beyond the skills of most teachers. Supervised by the Teacher Training Agency, an extensive program of mainly on-site training has started, with some 50 providers, from which each school may choose, at a cost of around US $1,300 per teacher. However, the standards of competence and quality in this relatively new field of professional development are still remarkably vague.

These two core elements of ICT policy, pedagogical training and use of assessment data, can successfully be put in place because they are within government control. Achieving the purposes for which the material and human infrastructure is designed is, however, a very different matter, be-

---

[1]British Educational Communications and Technology Agency, Milburn Hill Road, Science Park, Coventry CV4 7JJ. http://www.becta.org.uk

cause this involves elements over which government has much less—or even no—direct control. It is here that the most important limitations and vulnerabilities of educational ICT policies are to be found.

This problem of control is compounded by a further difficulty. New technologies, historically, have been used in two principal ways. Initially, they are applied to familiar tasks and routines in an attempt to increase the speed or effectiveness with which the task is performed. The personal computer, for example, was (and still is) used by many as a kind of supercharged typewriter for the production of conventional documents. Over time, the diffusion and development of these technologies also produces new applications that were not foreseen by their inventors, or initially by their purchasers. The use of personal computers to enable internetworked communication, for example, between and within companies, is a good example. These new applications, however, tend to emerge over considerable periods of time, and their effectiveness must be tested through a repeated process of trial and error. It is this second form of technology application that has the most radical effect on what people do, and on the structure and role of core institutions such as schools and universities. The evolution of such applications is further shaped by the changing demands on such institutions, brought about by broader economic, social, and cultural change.

In order to illuminate the full potential of ICTs for education, there must be a better understanding of both dimensions: those areas in which the new technologies can improve the effectiveness of existing teaching and learning procedures, and those in which the technologies will combine with changing social and economic demands to produce entirely new ways of organizing teaching and learning. This distinction, between direct application to familiar tasks and the development of new tasks and standards of quality and performance, helps to clarify the immediate challenges facing the NGfL.

Despite progress in connecting schools to the NGfL, there remain significant problems of access, for example, when small schools do not have enough computers to achieve even modest educational applications. However, a major concern is the quality of content. In a system where schools have delegated budgets, the costs of the hardware and online access must be balanced against the costs of teachers and other school-based staff. If the quality of content available on the NGfL is poor, then school principals may, with parental support, prefer to invest in people. This is one reason why ensuring that school principals have a clear vision for the role of ICT in achieving excellence in pedagogy and learning is so important.

The content of the Grid is increasing rapidly. Currently, some 250,000 documents are being indexed, of which over 45,000 relate directly to schools, over 65,000 to museums and galleries, and over 80,000 to government agencies. In autumn 1999, the total weekly hits on the NGfL exceeded 1.5 million, plus 0.5 million on the Virtual Teachers' Centre, a dedicated network providing resources and information for teachers. But, unless quality continues to improve and is responsive to rapidly evolving user needs, teacher motivation and interest could wane. Discussion groups of various kinds are very popular, and greater interactivity will be a high priority in further development. The provision of information through the Grid may take second place to systems for supporting communications between schools and teachers. The NGfL's capacity to stimulate teacher creativity and on-site continuing professional development is as yet untested.

In the same way, a desirable balance between commercially produced or teacher-generated materials and software is still to be determined. Increasingly there is a conviction that what teachers can produce in terms of curriculum materials, for instance, will be strictly limited, because they have neither the time nor the financial resource to produce high quality resources. But the risks to the commercial sector of investing in costly ventures that might not be widely accepted by teachers are considerable. There is at present no expectation that the commercial sector will invest the money or ingenuity devoted to the creation of computer games. Moreover, what works for teachers may depend on what works for students. One of the challenges of ICT is that students-as-consumers may be a source of market test that cannot be predicted from expectations or evaluations of teachers-as-consumers.

In immediate terms, far too little is known about what works in terms of the capacity of ICT to enhance the effectiveness of teaching and learning. Research in the UK has been limited in size and scope and is of very variable quality. Wood's report on the evaluation of integrated learning systems (BECTa, 1998) is a notable exception, from which no simple picture emerges. Even for basic educational questions, such as discovering the nature of best practice using ICT for literacy and numeracy, the evidence is far thinner than is needed (University of Newcastle, 1999). The British government is moving toward an evidence-informed basis for educational policy and professional practice, so the commissioning of more and better research into ICT is becoming essential. Massive spending on hardware, and even on training teachers, is an unwarranted act of faith unless it is accompanied by substantial spending on a new research and development (R&D) strategy for ICT in education.

Rapid and effective feedback from R&D studies to the teaching force will be required, although so far there is little knowledge and experience about how this might be done (Hargreaves, 1999). The success of such a strategy will depend partly on the teaching profession and public authorities embracing a very different model of innovation and dissemination from those with which they currently work. In the short term, the current study by the Centre of Educational Research and Innovation at the Organization for Economic Cooperation and Development (OECD), which will examine the

criteria for judging the quality of education software, the market development of software and supplier–user partnerships, and the evaluation of the
impact on teaching and learning, should add considerably to knowledge as
well as stimulating more local investigations within country-specific contexts.

ICT developments are beginning to make important changes to the relations between home and school. The number of schools putting curriculum materials on their Web sites for students to access from home is increasing sharply. In the next few years, there will be many more help-lines
for students with homework. Increasingly, parents will search the Internet
with their children for resources relevant to solving educational problems
or enriching educational projects. At present, one in three homes in the
UK contains at least one PC. In a thriving market, it is estimated that over
two million home PCs will be sold over the next year. Such developments,
and the diffusion of new forms of Internet access, such as interactive television, are opportunities to strengthen the teacher–parent partnership, although it is not always clear how this should be done without excluding students from low technology homes. As part of its policy of Excellence in
Cities to help disadvantaged areas, the government is establishing 85 City
Learning Centres (CLCs), which will provide ICT-based learning opportunities for students and adults in low income families and for local teachers.

Most people involved in the education service in the United Kingdom
see the government's commitment to such a rapid advance in ICT as a vital
investment in creating a 21st century education system. Predicting the future is always hazardous, but nowhere is more caution to be exercised than
in the field of ICT. All the figures given here will be out of date by the time
they reach you, the reader. So everyone would be foolish to assume a simple
linear road to the future. Given the relatively short timetables to which politicians necessarily work in democratic societies, very soon there will be a demand for some kind of demonstration of the added value provided by ICT,
although in other fields (e.g., business) this has been difficult to quantify.
The rhetoric and the "hype" has tended to be well ahead of the realization
of the potential of ICT to raise standards of attainment.

The speed of technological development and change inevitably means
that national expenditures on educational ICT will have to be high enough
to include "mistakes," even very large ones, because neither the technology
nor user reaction can be accurately predicted. If so, the traditional concept
of national planning is called into question. Governments, more than ever
before, will lack the information and intelligence needed accurately to
forecast the rates of development of new technologies, and therefore to
plan the ways in which they should be procured and deployed. Even more
challenging for policymakers, the uses to which these new technologies can
be put will be unkown at the times they first become available. This possibil-

ity raises fundamental questions about the role of government in directing, controlling, and regulating the provision of formal education in the future.

No one can accurately claim that, by 2000, ICT developments in education have fundamentally changed the nature of teaching and learning in classrooms or the structure and culture of schools. ICT will inevitably have a profound impact on formal (and informal) education. The key question, however, is whether the impact will be relatively superficial, as was the case with the introduction of radio and television, or whether it will constitute a true revolution or transformation, by improving the quality of teaching and learning in significant ways.

LEARNING FUTURES

What, then, is the vision today of the potential of ICT to transform K–12 education? Discussion of new technologies is often slanted by the dispositions and instincts of those involved. As a result, the predictions range from the utopian to the apocalyptic. The reality, of course, is more complex and uncertain. The most important potential effects of ICT in education run along dimensions already identified:

- The role of teachers
- Access to unprecedented levels of information
- New connections between home, school, and wider learning opportunities
- The growth of peer communication and new networks of learners
- New links between underlying knowledge of human development (e.g., cognitive science) and strategies for teaching and assessment
- The potential for accredited learning to take place in a far wider range of settings

In the longer term, the most important potential lies in the effect of these technologies on core educational institutions. This change, however, is not a direct result of the technology itself, but of the capacity to reconfigure a wider set of resources. This wider reconfiguration is the product of a much larger set of variables—the interaction between the evolving capacity of institutions and the social, cultural, economic, and demographic demands placed on them by society at large. The final sections focus on this process of institutional transformation.

Within the space of the 20th century, the teacher's role as a principal gateway to knowledge for the learner has been in progressive decline. Far more information than school students need is now being rapidly made accessible through ICT, much of it in a form that is attractive and easily assimilated. Thus, the role of the teacher changes to helping students to find/access what they need, to evaluate its source, relevance, and quality. Beyond these skills and capacities, the challenge for teachers will be in enabling students to construct and apply knowledge in ways that are accurate and valuable. See Mayer, chapter ? in this book for an extended discussion of constructionism.

The early years of primary education will, more than ever, need to emphasize basic literacy and numeracy along with ICT skills. But, in the later years of schooling, there might be less formal instruction and more individual and group work. If ICT does enable many students to learn more in a shorter time—and that is still a big "if"—then it may release time to allow students to engage in much more off-site project work in authentic workplace and community settings (Bentley, 1998). This extension of learning oppportunities, however, does not need to be carved out exclusively from time gained by accelerated learning. A wider range of teaching styles, learning opportunities, and contexts for learning mean that the formal school timetable will become merely the foundation, rather than the sole focus of, organized learning activities. As the expectation grows that students will be involved in lifelong learning long after their school career is over, some pressure for coverage of basic curriculum content during school years may also diminish. The average "learning week" will increase in duration for most students, and be only loosely related to the length of the "teaching week." This extension also creates the potential for a far wider range of people—from parents to mentors, specialist teachers, volunteers, and higher education students—to be drawn into a variety of teaching and coaching roles. ICT also enables the development of accurate, continuously monitored learning timetables that can be monitored from a central school database but do not require all students to be on one or two sites during a standardized school day. The introduction of smart card systems for monitoring and recording attendance patterns would mean that individualized, multisite curricula are now a practical possibility that does not come at the expense of the school's current overseeing, or custodial role.

At the same time, there will be real challenges for the teacher when students begin regularly to unearth information that is unknown to the teacher, who is then put in the role of learner. Students will find new knowledge independently, and teachers must take on the very different task of judging its quality and trustworthiness, which may then be used to challenge the authority of textbooks, which now become out of date so rapidly. It seems likely that the young will always be more comfortable than their elders with the emerging technologies. Teachers may have to learn how to learn about ICT from their students.

A second direct effect is that, quite soon, this new world of readily accessible information will be available in most homes. Not only will teachers cease to be the sole gatekeepers of knowledge, but schools will no longer be the only site from which such knowledge can be accessed. This points to a new role for parents, who will more readily be able to help students with their work, often as co-learners. In principle, students from disadvantaged backgrounds should be better off than in the past, for they will have much the same access as their middle-class counterparts, and the advantage of having middle-class parents with their knowledge should decline (but not, of course, disappear). Because much information about students (e.g. homework assignments, assessments, progress reports) will be available to parents through ICT, it will be easier for parents to be informed about their offspring and to check on them.

A third direct effect is the rapid growth of peer communication. Oracle, the software corporation, is currently developing a powerful tool for students to produce and communicate their own work through peer networks (the tool is currently called Think.com), in the process supplying all 9 to 14 year olds in the UK with their own e-mail address. From home, students will be able to interact with their friends and share pieces of work through e-mail and its future development in a way that greatly exceeds peer interaction via telephones. Just as the young have become major users of mobiles, they will become major users of e-mail. Peer interaction between schools and countries, producing new sorts of virtual peer networks, could easily grow rapidly and be used for positive educational benefits. Student–student electronic exchanges between countries are rich in possibilities for enhancing student motivation and learning of other languages and cultures. But also note the potential negative effects. It will become increasingly difficult to know whether the work students produce is really their own work or is cribbed or even purchased from other sources. There are already indications that some institutions are returning to unseen examinations as the only obvious way of guaranteeing that the student's work is produced independently.

Other direct effects are impossible to predict at this stage. Integrated Learning Systems developed by a range of software companies seemed full of promise, but the Woods review (BECTa, 1998) suggested that there is a long way to go before there is really strong evidence that investment in these systems has a clear and cost-effective payoff. Rather than providing a series of enclosed, predesigned learning environments through which students can progress toward predefined learning outcomes, it may be that the most important teaching applications are those that allow students to piece together knowledge and information drawn from disparate sources, although specialist software designed to enhance cognitive development and to diagnose and deal with specific learning difficulties still holds promise. There will be many ICT "dead-ends" in education over the next decade— bright ideas that cannot be made to work in practice and, after some early enthusiasm and promising results, simply fade way, a repetition of what might be called "the teaching machine effect." For teachers, deciding what kind of ICT can be used when, in what way, and for what purpose will become an ongoing and integral part of their professional responsibility.

In the short to medium term, some of the most important educational applications will not come directly from novel things that the hardware or software can do, but from finding imaginative applications of ICT to aspects of teaching and learning that are known to have a substantial impact on the quality or speed of learning (Schacter & Fagnano 1999).

For example, ICT is changing the nature of school records, particularly of student work and its assessment. For the first time, the curriculum followed by a student, and the work undertaken in pursuit of that curriculum, can be easily and comprehensively recorded, with considerable value for the transfer of records between classes within the school and especially between schools. Eventually, this integrated record is likely to become a much more important feature of the individual's lifelong learning career—a tool for personal management of learning and development, and a record linked with financial entitlements (e.g., the Individual Learning Account currently being implemented in the UK, which provides holders with a direct government subsidy and employer's contributions toward specific forms of lifelong learning), tax records (Inland Revenue agencies in several countries are moving toward digitization of personal tax histories), and other personal details (digitized personal identity cards and health records, for example, are also on the horizon).

Assessments can be recorded and easily retrieved by students and their parents as well as by teachers, so this data can be used much more formatively than in the past. Now it is known from the work of Black and William (1998) that formative assessment can have an unusually powerful effect on student learning. The potential of ICT to support better formative feedback is recognized, but still far from being realized. Without ICT, formative feedback to the individual student is exceedingly costly in teacher time, either in direct teacher–student interaction or through comments on students' written work. Teachers would like to give more formative feedback, but the demands of a classroom of students severely restricts the time available for intensive interaction with the individual student.

Could ICT help here? Almost certainly. It is not difficult to see how ICT could be designed for use by an individual student to support the core elements of formative assessment, without direct attention from the teacher. Such an application would require online reporting and scoring of pupil achievement, as well as administration of such assessments, services that could use the National Grid for Learning as a platform. Discovering ways in which ICT can enhance what is already known to be effective practice by teachers may prove to be a more important value of ICT than some of the new things that ICT can do, at least in the immediate future. Such a strategy is also likely to be extremely important in encouraging teachers to internalize the potential of the new technologies, and to use them intensively.

CAN ICT IN K–12 REALLY DELIVER?

The problem with grand visions, however, is that they are notoriously difficult to realize, particularly in education. It is arguable that any direct impact of ICT on schools is likely to be limited for several reasons:

- There is much hype about the potential for ICT in classrooms, but the evidence so far indicates rather limited change in the patterns of classroom life. There is little hard evidence that ICT is having a major impact on student motivation and learning within the constraints of formal education.
- The school is well known to be highly resilient to change: The title of Cuban's (1993) famous review, "Computers Meet Classroom: Classroom Wins' Remains Worryingly Apposite Almost a Decade Later."
- The teaching profession is too conservative to allow ICT to create a revolution or transformation in any meaningful sense of such terms. Teachers naturally stick by the ways they have always worked. There are currently relatively few incentives for teachers to devise highly imaginative ways of using ICT. Neither government nor business have so far shown any interest in paying the most creative ICT people high salaries for making educational advances that might work in classrooms
- The biggest change is that ICT hardware is getting very much cheaper, but that does not necessarily mean that more imaginative and effective educational uses will follow—compare the history of TV in education, which has had a much smaller impact than its early advocates suggested.

Rather, ICT may make its greatest impact on schooling indirectly through other social changes on other institutions. Recall that the institution of the school, with its emphasis on punctuality and obedience, was essentially a creature of the industrial revolution, socializing a rural populace for the controlled life of the factory in an urban setting—as was so well captured by Dickens' *Hard Times* (1911). The school is surviving the demise of the manufacturing age, in part because of its custodial function of keeping young people off the streets and out of the homes from which, increasingly, both working parents are absent. Back in 1971, Illich (1971) expected the technological revolution to hasten the death of the traditional school, but

30 years later, it remains resilient, in part because it serves other functions than strictly educational ones. It is not merely that the technological developments came more slowly than Illich expected, it is that advances in technology can be applied in educational institutions only when there are wider changes in the society in which schools are located and the functions of the school in industrial society can be redistributed and performed elsewhere.

There are strong signs that some changes are now taking place. For example, the growing importance of continuous learning in organizations across every sector of society, especially within the knowledge economy, mean that many more organizations are capable of providing learning opportunities for a wider constituency, including school students. As the social structure, religious and ethnic makeup of industralized countries continues to diversify, the pressure for more diverse, customized forms of educational provision will also intensify. Over time, these changes are producing institutional shifts that impact on the structures, working methods, and aims of the core schooling system.

This, perhaps, is the most significant long-term impact of ICT on education: not just providing specific applications and supplements to the processes of teaching and learning that are shaped by the current infrastructure, but transforming the infrastructure itself. Such transformations have been predicted before, but K–12 schools as institutions have proven to be remarkably resilient. However, given the fundamental restructuring going on in other sectors, from business to the family, there is confidence that these technologies will, in time, stimulate radical restructuring. Although there is a growing number of innovative examples in the K–12 area, more can be learned from the other areas of education, notably the university sector. Following these lessons, some other sectors of society (employment and households) are examined, whose changing structure and demands, partly facilitated by new technologies, will increase demand for new patterns of provision in K–12 schooling.

FROM WORK TO UNIVERSITIES

There is a growing tension between the kinds of learning promoted by university education, and the kinds of learners sought by employers in the knowledge economy (Seltzer & Bentley, 1999). Take the following contrast, illustrated in Figs. 15.1 and 15.2, which has been adapted from Candy and Crebert (1991).

So, how must the structure and culture of universities change to produce "graduates as learners" rather than simply students who are "doing university successfully"? The emergence of the knowledge economy will draw attention to this challenge and stimulate action to create a transition from university to

STUDENT-AS-LEARNER

is curriculum-driven

works to pre-set educational objectives

experiences learning as explicit and self-conscious

solves problems in terms of their theoretical coherence

applies abstract intellectual processes to solve them

expresses ideas and thoughts in writing

depends on external evaluation

develops long-term study projects

is introverted and isolated study habits

is jealous and protective of personal research

fails to develop inter-personal skills

FIG. 15.1.   Student-as-learner.

GRADUATE-AS-LEARNER

is task-driven

works without pre-set learning objectives

experiences learning as implicit, informal, un-self-conscious

solves problems in a practical, cost- and time-efficient way

applies lateral or critical thinking processes to solve them

expresses thoughts, ideas and solutions orally

uses self-criticism and self-evaluation

works to short-term goals

is extroverted and gregarious in work habits

shares outcomes with colleagues

views collaborative skills as being of premium value

FIG. 15.2.   Graduate-as-learner.

work by which graduates will meet the expectations of employers much more closely. Indeed, the emergence of corporate and online "universities" is part of a general movement in this direction, which will strengthen the challenge to traditional universities. Such a demand on university teachers will be resisted, just as schoolteachers have until relatively recently tended to avoid responsibility for the transition from school to work.

Response from universities to the demand for graduates-as-learners could dramatically increase the use of ICT in higher education. Examples include more authentic, real-world tasks captured on ICT; use of ICT for networking among students and between students and people in the workplace; mentoring of students by full-time employees through ICT; coordinated work placements as part of the degree structure; and so on.

FROM UNIVERSITY TO SCHOOL

Much of what goes on in English secondary schools is directly influenced by universities, and as the proportion of young people going to university continues to increase, so does the influence of higher education on the conduct and content of secondary schooling. As universities adapt to the new demands and opportunities of lifelong learning, which is still largely a rhetorical phenomenon, their institutional characteristics will change radically.

Universities have traditionally operated on four basic assumptions: (a) Most of their clients are in the 18–22 age range; (b) they study for between 3 and 6 years on a full-time basis; (c) they are resident at the university, which is convenient for the university teachers; and (d) they choose from among courses whose content is predetermined by university teachers.

The Open University (OU), one of Britain's outstanding educational innovations, has questioned the first and second of these assumptions, but not the second and fourth. However, the OU may be an intermediate stage between the conventional university and new forms of provision.

In the future, universities may have to serve (a) clients of all ages; (b) those who study more frequently but for short periods of time; (c) those who are only occasionally resident at the university (the lecturers may do much more work on other sites, e.g., workplaces); as well as (d) to supply customized educational services to meet individual needs or those of particular groups at particular sites (e.g., a group of workers at a particular firm). In such a world, ICT would play a far more important role that at present.

In other words, the issue is conceived not in terms of how will ICTs affect universities, but rather in terms of how will universities need to change to respond to new demands on them and what role will ICTs play in the way universities respond to those changing demands? The difference is crucial.

In the first version of the question, the role of ICT is relatively marginal, because it simply complements existing structural and cultural arrangements (e.g., students work on word processors and use them for making notes on lectures and reading and for writing essays; students can examine library catalogues at a distance, etc.). It does relatively little to influence communication within the university itself (although it enhances communication between universities among academic and research staff). In the second version of the question, because the role and function of the university teachers change, so do the university's structures and cultures, and so ICT comes into play, especially in new forms of communication. For example, ICTs allow tutoring at a distance, including video conferencing. They allow students access to study materials at a time and place of their choosing. If the ICT resources are rich enough, then it allows a much more customized service to the individual student, in vivid contrast to what is currently provided in a course of lectures for undergraduates.

FROM WORKPLACE TO SCHOOL

The new demands emanating from employers and the new economy are not applied exclusively to universities. New forms of workplace organization, new ways of coordinating and managing projects, and new kinds of skill specification will also impact on the nature of the school curriculum and the role that schools play in their local communities. Perhaps the most important shift arising from the transition to a knowledge economy is the demand for students who are able to employ their knowledge and skills creatively, often in teams (Seltzer & Bentley, 1999). This priority leads to a shift away from the traditional, standardized school curriculum toward a much stronger focus on interpersonal skills, project-based learning, performance measures based increasingly on concrete outcomes beyond the formal educational environment, and the skills of self-reliance and self-assessment (O'Neill, 1997).

For employers, this change is in part a response to the rising pace of innovation and intensification of competitive pressure. New products and services and productivity improvements come increasingly from the collaborative activity of productive networks, including employees, associates, organizational partners, suppliers, consultants, and so on. The forms of learning and evaluation that emerge from such patterns of collaboration are often very different from those associated with formal school, college, or vocational training. These underlying changes in the structure of workplace organizations, the wider environment in which they operate, and the kinds of work undertaken all affect the demand placed on K–12 school education by the economy and employers.

These changing patterns of demand from the economy on K–12 schools, and the fact that many students will be learning such skills from part-time work, community involvement, and other out-of-school activities will increase the pressure for schools to adapt in similar ways. New forms of community-based learning network, such as Citizen Schools in Boston, the Harlem Educational Activities Fund, or Children's Express (for detailed information on all three see Seltzer & Bentley, 1999) are impacting slowly on the core infrastructure of schooling, but so far without wholesale reform of the institutions themselves. In part, such projects are growing because of changing social demand, including the need for dual-income families to secure safe, stimulating, out-of-school care options for children, and concern for the prospects and motivation of at-risk young people in disadvantaged urban areas.

These programs use ICTs to record more authentic, real-world performances by students, to coordinate timetables and activities, and to maintain networks of parents, supporters, and volunteers. They are not a direct result of the introduction of ICTs, but they are facilitated by them, and help to show how the core institutions might respond to changing demand by using the new technologies. They point to a future role for schools as "hubs" of overlapping learning networks, maintaining collaborative relationships with a broad range of employers, civic and community organizations, brokering individual learning opportunities and helping to develop and assess new forms of assessment and evaluation that apply, not just to formalized learning within the school system, but also to real-world tasks and learning activities.

FROM HOME TO SCHOOL

The growth of home schooling cannot be ignored (Meighan, 1995). The motives of parents are in part the protection of their children from the dangerous influence of schools—the demotivating effect of institutional life, and the exposure to unsavory peer groups, drugs, sex, bullying, and delinquency. They are sometimes pressured to home provision by children vocal about their unhappiness at school. In the United States, home schooling is estimated to have grown from 15,000 to 350,000 children in a decade and may involve a million children. There are recent estimates of 10,000 families opting for home-based education in the UK, 20,000 in Australia, and 30,000 in Canada. Its expansion increases in association with the twinned growth of the new technologies and the arrival of lifelong learning.

School teachers were once needed because they knew more than most parents and what they knew was not readily available from an alternative source. Neither condition now applies for many homes. ICTs give easy access to all the information that the home-based student needs; and parents are better educated so that they know both what their children need (including being informed in England by National Curriculum guides and the syllabuses of the bodies which conduct public examinations) and how to access it (through the Internet and its successors). A growing proportion of the UK workforce are home workers and teleworkers. Such parents, nurtured in their youth on the ideas of Handy (1989), understand that schools and colleges are among the last of organizations to change, but will eventually share the fate of factories and offices. They supervise and coach (rather than teach) their children at home, working and learning together. They are freed from having to live near a "good" school or from wasting valuable time and money driving them to and from school each day through peak hour traffic.

If home schooling grows, then it is possible that this will create a demand for learning materials that could be met by the commercial sector. These parents would be willing to pay for these materials, especially if they were to be given tax reductions for not sending their children to state schools; this might be an attractive policy to a government seeking to release a greater share of the education budget to target those in greatest educational need. But there could also be an impact on schools and a growth of part-time schooling because home schooling is weak on certain aspects of the curriculum (i.e., practical science, athletics, the performing arts), as well as opportunities for students to mix with their age group. So students might attend school on 1 or 2 days a week and for specific purposes. In an age of self-managing schools, principals will be perfectly ready to accept students on a part-time basis if this increases the school's income. Thus, how schools handle ICT could be influenced by students from families using an ICT-rich diet from the home as part of their education with which, if it creates high standards, the school will want to compete.

CHALLENGES FOR POLICY AND PRACTICE

These processes of institutional change, driven unpredictably by the combination of many different social, cultural, and economic forces, will continue to produce major challenges for policymakers and educational professionals. Although K–12 education is the main focus of this chapter, the challenges are generic; these challenges apply equally to other forms of public education provision, especially universities, although of course the specific contexts for implementation and professional cultures vary.

Perhaps the greatest challenge, touched on at various points in the previous argument, will be for teachers to find ways in which they can respond to the escalating pressures to be more effective. A necessary component of this response is a new approach to educational R&D, and to the dissemination of good practice (Hargreaves, 1998, 1999). The old center periphery model of creating and distributing knowledge and advice for teachers, either from governments (e.g., the national curriculum) or from educational researchers and teachers trainers (through research, initial training, and courses for serving teachers), is now obsolete. As both the content of schooling and the school as an institution come under pressure to change rapidly, a more deliberate, explicit, and collective process of professional knowledge creation at school level will be needed. Teachers will have to engage in their own professional R&D as coproducers with other agencies (academics, commercial providers) rather than as end-users. If clusters of schools can collaborate on the same topic of professional knowledge creation and validation, then national progress in advancing the quality of teaching and learning could be rapid and cumulative. ICTs can play a major role in these forms of networking, on a scale and at a rate that has hitherto been almost unimaginable. They can also help to end the professional isolation of subject specialist teachers operating almost alone in individual schools.

Networks are the key to this different model of dissemination. The business world provides a model: In industries where the knowledge is both complex and expanding and the sources of expertise are widely dispersed, the locus of innovation is to be found in networks of learning. Innovating companies

> are executing nearly every step in the production process, from discovery to distribution, through some form of external collaboration. These various forms of inter-firm alliance take on many forms. . . . The R&D intensity or level of technological sophistication of industries is positively correlated with the intensity and number of alliances. . . . Knowledge creation occurs in the context of a community. . . . To stay current in a rapidly moving field requires that an organization has a hand in the research process. Passive recipients of new knowledge are less likely to appreciate its value or to be able to respond rapidly. In industries in which know-how is critical, companies must be expert at both in-house research and co-operative research with such external partners as university scientists. . . . A firm's value and ability as a collaborator is related to its internal assets, but at the same time collaboration further develops and strengthens those internal competencies. . . . When the locus of innovation is found in an inter-organizational network, access to that network proves critical. R&D alliances are the admission ticket, the foundation for more diverse types of collaboration and the pivot around which firms become more centrally connected. . . . As a result of this reciprocal learning, both *firm-level* and *industry-level* practices are evolving. (Powell, Koput, & Smith-Doerr, 1996, p.)

Schools have traditionally operated in isolation from one another, and this tendency has been exacerbated by parental choice and competition between schools for students. However, the demand for knowledge creation and dissemination may push teachers to new interschool collaborations, helped by ICT. In the world of modern business may be an intimation of not only the knowledge-creating school, but a knowledge-creating school system (i.e., a web of interlinked schools engaged in educational R&D). For teachers, access to know-how depends heavily on their knowledge of "know-who." Networking through ICT is a breakthrough in terms of maximizing know-who on which professional knowledge creation and dissemination will depend in knowledge economies.

These kinds of organizational change raise new challenges for central administrative and policymaking bodies. The model of organization and administration in which the most valuable knowledge is held by large-scale, central information-processing bureaucracies—whether examination and assessment bodies, government agencies, or even university departments— is under growing pressure. Policymakers will find it increasingly difficult to make unilateral decisions that can be implemented uniformly across whole systems of schools, whether at the district or board level, or even at the national level, as has increasingly been the case in England over the last 15 years.

Management of knowledge and information will be just as important as before, but will take place in a more fluid policy environment, in which interorganizational boundaries, competing commercial interests, lack of strong evidence, and the speed of change will all hamper the formulation of rigorous, evidence-based policy. The stimulation and management of innovation will become a central part of the policymaker's responsibility, while managing the risk and failure inevitably associated with it will create a new set of liabilities that will have to be set against public expectations and political pressures.

The increasing volatility and unpredictability of educational politics will be enhanced and intensified by the continued diversification of educational provision, through the invention of an ever wider range of alternatives to the standard school model. This will increase the scope for radical structural change, because they will increase the willingness of politicians, policymakers, professionals, and parents to experiment more widely with existing patterns of provision.

Only when the long-term, indirect effects of ICTs, combined with a far broader set of driving forces, have made their impact on schools and the teaching profession, will schools innovate with enthusiasm on the restructuring of the school day and patterns of working for both teachers and students. In the 1980s, England tried some radical experiments in restructuring the school day at a few secondary schools. But, these innovations were not sustained over time, nor were the ideas widely disseminated and emulated. For whole systems to change, a critical level of pressure is needed, drawn from the unpredictable combination of economic imperatives, human inventiveness, rising public demand, changing values, and political bravery. These are a precondition for the full exploitation of ICT, rather than a consequence of the new technologies in themselves.

ACKNOWLEDGMENTS

Tom Bentley is director of Demos, an independent think tank based in London, former special adviser to David Blunkett MP, as UK Secretary of State for Education and Employment.

David H. Hargreaves is a fellow of Wolfson College, Cambridge. He is the former professor of Education in the University of Cambridge, a director of BECTa, and joint vice-chairman of the government's Standards Task Force.

Demos is an independent think tank which aims to generate radical solutions to long-term problems. It carries out research projects and publishes on a wide range of policy areas. Details can be found at www.demos.co.uk, or through mail@demos.co.uk

REFERENCES

BECTa (British Educational Communications and Technology Agency) (1998). *The UK ILS Evaluations: final report.* Coventry, England.

Bentley, T. (1998). *Learning beyond the classroom: Education for a changing world.* London: Routledge.

Black, P., & William, D. (1998). Assessment and classroom learning. *Assessment in Education, 5*(1), 7–74.

Candy, P. C., & Crebert, R. G. (1991). Ivory tower to concrete jungle: The difficult transition from the academy to the workplace as learning environments. *Journal of Higher Education, 62*(5), 570–592.

Cuban, L. (1993). Computers meet classroom: Classroom wins. *Teachers College Record, 95*(2), 185–209.

Handy, C. (1989). *The age of unreason.* London: Random House.

Hargreaves, D. H. (1998). *Creative professionalism: The role of teachers in the knowledge society.* London: Demos.

Hargreaves, D. H. (1999). Revitalising educational research: Lessons from the past and proposals for the future. *Cambridge Journal of Education, 29*(2), 239–250.

Illich, I. (1971). *Deschooling society.* London: Calder and Boyars.

Meighan, R. (1995). Home-based education effectiveness research and some its implications. *Educational Review, 77,* 275–287.

O'Neill, H. F. (1997). *Workforce readiness: Competencies and assessment.* Hillsdale, NJ: Lawrence Erblaum Associates.

Powell, W. W., Koput, K. W., & Smith-Doerr, L. (1996). Interorganizational collaboration and the locus of innovation: Networks of learning in biotechnology. *Administrative Science Quarterly, 41,* 116–145.

Schacter, J., & Fagnano, C. (1999). Does computer technology improve student learning and achievement? How, when and under what conditions? *Journal of Educational Computing Research, 20*(4), 329–343.

Seltzer, K., & Bentley, T. (1999). *The creative age: Knowledge and skills for the new economy.* London: Demos.

University of Newcastle. (1999). *Ways forward with ICT: Effective pedagogy using ICT for literacy and numeracy in classrooms.* Newcastle upon Tyne, England: Author.

Author Index

361

Subject Index

A

Adaptive expertise, 178
Aphasia
    therapy, 168–169
Assessment design, *see also* Test construction
    construction, 215
    evidence centered, 216–222
    management, 214–215
    scoring and reporting, 216
    tryout and delivery, 215–216
Automated essay scoring, 227–228, 231–232
Automatic item generation, 235–239

B

Box-score approach, 85

C

CISL, 10
Cognitive science, 159–161, 168–170
    analyses, 161–164
        CSILE, 163
        DIAGNOSER, 162
Cognitive skill requirements
    tree-based regression, 222–224, 227
Computer-aided Instruction (CAI), 9–11
Computer-based Instruction (CBI), 9, 267–270
Computers
    as instructional devices, 38–49
    external influences, 32–36
    internal changes, 36–46

simulations, 40
Connecting learning theory, 173–179
COTS, 107–109

D

Databases, 21
Digital content
    difficulties in, 18–19
Digital divide, 26–27, *see also* Digital gaps
Digital gaps, 4

E

Educational Testing Service (ETS), 26
Effect size, 85–87
E-rater, 228–231

G

GLOBE project, 11, 335
GOTS, 104–107

H

Hypertext, 165–167

I

Instructional effectiveness
    and technology, 84–96
    individualization vs. interactivity, 81–83
Internet, future of
    communication, 22
    policy implications, 24
    Web-based resources, 22–23